The Economic Valuation of Landscape Change

NEW HORIZONS IN ENVIRONMENTAL ECONOMICS

General Editors: Wallace E. Oates, *Professor of Economics, University of Maryland, USA* and Henk Folmer, *Professor of Economics, Wageningen Agricultural University, The Netherlands and Professor of Environmental Economics, Tilburg University, The Netherlands*

This important series is designed to make a significant contribution to the development of the principles and practices of environmental economics. It includes both theoretical and empirical work. International in scope, it addresses issues of current and future concern in both East and West and in developed and developing countries.

The main purpose of the series is to create a forum for the publication of high quality work and to show how economic analysis can make a contribution to understanding and resolving the environmental problems confronting the world in the late twentieth century.

Recent titles in the series include:

The Economic Valuation of Landscape Change

Theory and Policies for Land Use and Conservation

José Manuel L. Santos

Professor of Environmental Economics, High Institute of Agriculture, Technical University of Lisbon, Portugal

NEW HORIZONS IN ENVIRONMENTAL ECONOMICS

Edward Elgar
Cheltenham, UK • Northampton, MA, USA

Published by
Edward Elgar Publishing Limited
Glensanda House
Montpellier Parade
Cheltenham
Glos GL50 1UA
UK

Edward Elgar Publishing, Inc.
6 Market Street
Northampton
Massachusetts 01060
USA

A catalogue record for this book
is available from the British Library

Library of Congress Cataloguing in Publication Data

Santos, José Manuel L., 1963–
    The economic valuation of landscape change : theory and policies
for land use and conservation / José Manuel L. Santos.
        (New horizons in environmental economics)
    Includes bibliographical references and index.
        1. Landscape protection—Economic aspects—Great Britain.
2. Landscape protection—Economic aspects—Europe. 3. Regional
planning—Environmental aspects—Great Britain. 4. Regional
planning—Environmental aspects—Europe. 5. Land use—Great
Britain—Planning. 6. Land use—Europe—Planning. I. Title.
II. Series.
HD596.S17   1999
333.73'16—dc21   98–31057
                                                                            CIP

ISBN 1 85898 781 4

Printed and bound in Great Britain by
Biddles Ltd, Guildford and King's Lynn

Contents

PART FOUR: METHODOLOGICAL APPRAISAL AND
CONCLUSIONS

List of Figures

List of Tables

Acknowledgements

Most of this book is based on a research undertaken when I was preparing my PhD dissertation at Newcastle University between 1995 and 1997. During this period, Ken Willis read previous versions of the book. Ken made comments and suggestions that very much improved it and for which I am very grateful. Ken and his wife Pat also contributed to making my family and me feel definitely at home in Newcastle.

I am also indebted to Ian Bateman, who provided me with a list of detailed comments, which significantly improved this book. I am also thankful to Ian Dobbs.

A.V. Garcia made detailed suggestions about the English, for which I am very grateful. I am also thankful to João C. Caldas for an attentive reading and helpful suggestions.

I am indebted to Fernando O. Baptista for having persuaded me, ten years ago, to study the environment from a social-scientific perspective.

To my family, I owe so many weekends spent working on the book.

The Dales questionnaire benefited from the existence of a previous survey instrument initially designed for a stated-choice survey by Ken Willis, Guy Garrod and W. Adamowicz. Neil Powe provided me with precious information on problems with that previous questionnaire and helped in piloting the one used in the Dales study. Discussions with Caroline Saunders improved conservation cost estimates in the Dales study.

I acknowledge the good quality interviewing work of Justin Beaumont, Richard Hardy, João M. Pereira and João P. Veloso, which made it possible to complete with success the two surveys reported here.

My studies in Newcastle were supported by a scholarship granted by the Portuguese Junta Nacional de Investigação Científica e Tecnológica (PRAXIS XXI/BD/4519/94). Both surveys received financial support from the Centre for Research in Environmental Appraisal and Management (CREAM) at Newcastle University, which is here gratefully acknowledged.

PART ONE

Introduction

1. Landscape Change, Conservation Policy and Policy Evaluation

There is a growing public concern over the loss of countryside assets presenting an aesthetic, cultural, wildlife or recreational interest. Although traditionally associated with urban–industrial encroachments, this loss of valued landscape attributes has been increasingly related to processes of agricultural change such as intensification on more fertile land and the abandonment of marginal farmland. This meant a significant change in the way we socially perceive the causes of landscape degradation. Many policy schemes using financial incentives for landscape conservation emerged during the 1980s and 1990s to meet this new concern with the 'erosion' of valued attributes of rural landscapes.

This chapter describes processes of landscape change in post-war rural Europe and reviews the recent emergence of incentive schemes for landscape conservation. The need to evaluate such schemes is also pointed out. A second section discusses an economic interpretation for agricultural change processes leading to the loss of valued countryside attributes; in so doing, the economic rationale for landscape conservation policy is introduced and discussed. The methodological consequences of the multidimensional nature of landscape changes for valuing these changes are then discussed. The final section presents the main issues to be discussed in this book and a preview of the different parts and chapters.

1.1 LANDSCAPE CHANGE AND POLICY SCHEMES FOR LANDSCAPE CONSERVATION

Over the centuries, agriculture suffered many important technological and socio-institutional transformations, which progressively changed the appearance of the countryside. Think, for example, of the expansion of the open field system in the Middle Ages or the enclosures movement in the 18th and 19th centuries. However, the pace of agricultural change had never been so fast as in the period after World War 2. Such an unprecedented period of agricultural change modified the face of the European countryside – a fact that partly explains why agriculture has come to be seen, during this period,

3

as a major factor of landscape degradation. This clearly contrasted with previous perceptions of urban–industrial development as the almost exclusive threat to the beauty of the countryside. This shift in social perceptions pressed for change in conservation policy, so that the countryside could be given adequate protection against the negative effects of agricultural intensification. This need for policy change was underlined by two facts. First, in most countries, planning and development control policies represented, until quite recently, the only policy tools for landscape conservation. Second, farmers (often seen as countryside stewards) were largely exempt from planning permission even to undertake modifications with such effects on landscape as hedgerow removal, grassland ploughing up or moorland afforestation.

In addition to agricultural change, the post-war period witnessed the emergence of urban-based interests in the countryside other than cheap food. Rising income, expanded leisure time and generalisation of the motor car promoted the development of a variety of outdoor-recreation pursuits in the countryside. At the same time, in countries like the UK, large numbers of urban-based middle class people were moving into the countryside; these were commuters, retired people or the owners of a countryside secondary residence (Bowers and Cheshire 1983). These new recreational and residential functions of rural areas, as well as the growth of the environmental movement, expanded the social demand for aesthetic, wildlife, cultural and historical attributes of the countryside – precisely those attributes that vanished under the influence of agricultural intensification. Hence, it was inevitable that farmers' demand for land for intensified agricultural uses conflicted with urban-based demands for countryside attributes. Different policies evolved to conciliate these conflicting demands.

Bowers and Cheshire (1983) blamed agricultural policy for post-war agricultural intensification and the attendant landscape degradation. In fact, capital grants for farm modernisation and high levels of price support for agricultural output had a crucial influence on intensification because of the structure of financial incentives they created for farmers. Hence, policy-induced high and stable prices for cereals led many fertile regions in Central and Northern Europe to specialise in arable production and to raise yields by intensifying fertiliser and pesticide use. With arable specialisation came the need for large fields for more efficient use of heavy machinery; hence the removal of hedgerows, which were so characteristic of lowland England or the French *bocage* landscapes. Likewise, wildflowers, butterflies and many birds vanished from extensive countryside areas with the intensification of the use of agro-chemicals (a story so eloquently told in Rachel Carson's 'Silent Spring'). Besides, policy-induced high prices for agricultural output meant an increase in land values, which raised the opportunity cost of leaving small uncultivated patches aside for wildlife or landscape purposes. Thus, virtually every single small wetland, heath, downs or rough grazing located in flat and fertile areas were 'improved' for agricultural use. Moreover, generous grants were available to carry out hedgerow grubbing as well as all these agricultural 'improvements'.

Although agricultural intensification started in the plains and lowlands of Central and Northern Europe, which were particularly suited to the new technology in arable farming, the movement soon reached the strongholds of livestock farming systems located further west or in medium-altitude uplands. There, meadows and other improved grasslands underwent a process of intensified fertiliser use and hay was replaced by silage as the main process for harvesting the forage; with these changes came the simplification of the sward and the decline of colourful wildflowers and ground-nesting birds. Likewise, large expanses of botanically-rich grassland were 'improved' by drainage, ploughing, fertilisation and re-seeding.

The emergence of a specific support policy for upland and hill farming, namely the European Union Hill Livestock Compensatory Allowances (HLCA), pushed the intensification wave further up on the hills and induced high stocking rates in the hills and moors. For example, in the UK, this overstocking of the moors with sheep led to a decline in heather cover and thus to a decline in grouse, a game bird with an extreme economic importance and which depends on heather for food and shelter.

In their 1983 book, Bowers and Cheshire presented the first specifically environmentalist critique of the Common Agricultural Policy (CAP). This book promoted a new perception according to which 'there was nothing immutable or haphazard about post-war countryside change – rather, it was the product of policy decisions quite consciously pursued within a large and complex network of institutions created for just this purpose' (Newby 1993, quoted by Potter 1996: 165). This emerging perception created pressure for policy reform. The main idea of environmental critics of the CAP was that support to farmers should be totally decoupled from agricultural output and coupled to levels of environmental amenities received by society as a whole from particular farmers. This pressure for environmental reform of the CAP led to the inclusion of an article on Environmentally Sensitive Areas (ESAs) in the European Commission (EC) Structures Regulation of 1985. ESAs were to be designated by member states in areas presenting a particular conservation interest and where the maintenance of traditional management and the prevention of further intensification would help protect this interest. Governments could then negotiate management agreements with farmers operating in ESAs, with farmers receiving payments in exchange for compliance with specified environmentally friendly practices. This was the first step in decoupling agricultural policy subsidies from output levels.

ESAs were only enthusiastically implemented by a few Northern European countries – precisely those who pressed for the introduction of ESAs in the EC Structures Regulation of 1985. Indeed the ESA concept poorly matched the situation of agriculture in many Southern European countries where the main environmental problems had to do with the abandonment of marginal farmland rather than agricultural intensification. The Southern European view on agri-environmental policy is well illustrated by the French concern with *désertification* (Baldock and Lowe 1996), which refers to problems such as the decay of terraced fields and other traditional structures; the encroachment of meadows, sheep walks, olive groves and woods by scrub; and the risk of large forest fires.

The second step of environmental reform of the CAP was the approval, as part of the MacSharry reform package of 1992, of a new regulation requiring each member state to design and implement its own programme for the agri-environment. Differences with respect to the previous ESA policy are that the requirement for each member state to implement an agri-environmental programme is now statutory and that costs of this programme may be partly reimbursed from Brussels. This new step of reform incorporated the view of Southern European member states by including as a policy goal the need to counteract the abandonment of marginal farmland in areas where traditional farming systems are crucial for environmental reasons.

The ESA scheme and the subsequent agri-environment regulation are far from having completely decoupled policy payments to farmers from output levels and coupled these payments to levels of environmental amenities. In fact, it is estimated that only 3.6 per cent of the Guarantee section of the European Agricultural Guidance and Guarantee Fund (that is: approximately 1.8 per cent of the total European Union budget) was spent in agri-environmental programmes in 1997 (COM 1997).

Shoard's (1980) 'theft of the countryside' thesis provides a different interpretation for the causes of post-war landscape changes, which applies mainly to the UK case. For Shoard, the fact of agriculture and forestry being exempt from the development control system explains the inability of this system to protect our most valued rural landscapes. Thus, she claimed, we should extend the development control system to agriculture and forestry by making particular operations, such as hedgerow grubbing or downland ploughing, dependent on planning permission. Differently from Bowers and Cheshire, who focused on the environmental effects of agricultural policy, Shoard emphasised the crucial role of the current structure of property rights on landscape attributes in landscape degradation processes. Therefore, she proposed the realignment of this structure of property rights so as to make it more suited to meet new social demands for countryside public goods. This would imply transferring to the general public rights over landscape attributes that have been implicitly held by farmers and landowners.

Agri-environmental policy has followed a path implying a view on property rights totally opposed to Shoard's. An example from the historical beginnings of agri-environmental policy in the UK, i.e. the fights for moorland conservation in the Exmoor National Park, illustrates this point. In this case, a previous report recommended the use of Moorland Conservation Orders – a control policy identical to those used in urban areas under the Town and Country Planning legislation and consistent with Shoard's view on property rights. The National Park Authority decided, however, to sign a management agreement with landowners in 1979, which 'set a precedent in that compensation was an annual payment equal to the estimated profit forgone' (Whittaker et al. 1991: 200). Based on this and other precedents, the Wildlife and Countryside Act 1981 gave full legal status to the principle of compensation for profits foregone. This Act was mainly used by the Nature Conservation Council (today English Nature) to establish management agreements with farmers required not to go ahead with potentially damaging operations in Sites of Special Scientific Interest (SSSIs).

Later, in spite of the growing influence of urban-based interests over both local development planning and agricultural policy reform (Marsden et al. 1993), farmers and landowners were successful in imposing their view on property rights within the policy process. This view is well illustrated by the following quotation (A. Woods / Country Landowners Association):

> We cannot rely solely on stewardship (...) The public has got to say, we value wildlife, we value landscape, we want these things from landowners just as much as the other commodities which we have wanted from them in the past (...) you can create a market in environmental goods, but we cannot do it unless you have customers willing to pay. To have a market you need a buyer as well as a seller. (quoted by Lowe et al. 1993).

As a result of this prevalence of farmers' and landowners' views within the policy process, the current policy approach to landscape conservation in rural areas is based on the compensation principle. Besides, most conservation schemes are voluntary in that farmers are free to decide whether to enter into a management agreement and are given the opportunity of negotiating the terms of such an agreement (Marsden et al. 1993). Although these examples come from the UK, most European regulations are based on similar policy principles as regards property rights over landscape attributes.

Meanwhile, landscape conservation policy evolved from the initial approach (incorporated into the UK Wildlife and Countryside Act 1981) of compensating farmers for not undertaking potentially damaging operations to that of financially inducing farmers to enter into voluntary management agreements, as in ESA policy (cf. Whitby 1994a). More recently, a policy statement by the Countryside Commission for England and Wales indicates a new change in approach, which is already shaping some of the Commission's grant and payment schemes (Countryside Commission 1993) and some English National Park Authorities' schemes (cf. e.g. Yorkshire Dales National Park 1995). Within this new approach, payments to farmers are linked to well-defined landscape products rather than to the management process supposed to produce them. Another characteristic of this new approach is that the agency running a payment scheme for landscape conservation is seen as using public money to buy landscape products on behalf of the general public, and thus it should only pay for those landscape products we all desire. Besides, as public funds are scarce, they 'must be carefully used to achieve the best value for money.' (Countryside Commission 1993: 9–13). These two last policy principles would imply that public preferences for landscapes should be assessed as a way to ensure that only those schemes achieving good value for taxpayers' money go ahead. This requirement will be given particular relevance within the frame of an evolving CAP, with payments to farmers being progressively decoupled from output levels and coupled to countryside amenity levels. In fact, in this new policy context, knowing the actual value of these amenities is crucial for evaluating policy schemes and for pricing amenity payments.

Therefore, to evaluate these new policy schemes for landscape conservation we should know how to value landscape benefits and how to compare these benefits with our estimates of the policy costs. Building economic-analytical tools for conservation policy evaluation is the main aim of this book. However, before facing this task, we should briefly discuss the way economists conceptualise the landscape conservation problem and justify, on economic grounds, the need for public intervention in the supply of landscape public goods.

1.2 THE ECONOMICS OF LANDSCAPE CONSERVATION: MARKET FAILURE AND THE NEED FOR EFFICIENT POLICY

The economic behaviour of farmers and other land users is guided by the prices of those inputs and outputs they buy or sell in the market. Thus, for example, when a decision on milk output is to be made, market prices provide information enabling a farmer to compare the marginal value of milk output with its marginal cost and to select the optimal output level accordingly. However, other outputs of farming are not traded in the market and thus command no market price. A good example is given by landscape attributes that depend on particular styles of farming for their production and maintenance. Landscape attributes are typically non-excludable public goods. Thus, farmers are prevented from charging others for the enjoyment of these attributes. On the other hand, society as a whole has no well-defined and enforceable rights over landscape attributes, and thus farmers are not charged for degrading the landscape.

The fact of landscape attributes being unpriced does not mean they have no effect on other people's welfare. It means, however, that, more often than not, farmers will not take this external effect on others' welfare into account. Thus, in particular price, technology or policy contexts, farmers are led to change management in ways that cause significant negative effects on others' welfare with no regard at all for these effects. For example, high labour costs may put an end to the upkeep of traditional structures such as stone walls or terraced fields, with the attendant process of decay having a negative effect on visitors to the countryside. Along the same lines, prices and policy may lead farmers to intensify fertiliser use, which reduces socially-valued flower diversity in meadows.

The above examples show that levels of landscape attributes, and hence the welfare of those valuing these attributes, are an unintended side effect of management decisions taken by farmers and other land users. Economists call this type of unintended side effect on others' welfare an externality. Externalities can be positive or negative according to the sign of the external effect on welfare. Thus, the upkeep of traditional structures is an example of a positive externality of some farming systems; likewise, grassland ploughing for conversion into arable may represent a negative externality.

A well-known theorem of neoclassical welfare economics states that, within a competitive market and assuming perfect information, choices by rational individuals will lead to a particular type of social optimum: the Pareto optimum. The Pareto optimum is a situation where nobody can be made better off without making someone else worse off (this is seen as an optimal situation because there are no more opportunities left for unequivocal improvements in resource allocation: all possible improvements for someone will leave others worse off). However, in the presence of externalities this theorem does not hold. Therefore, landscape externalities are a source of market failure: too high levels of negatively valued attributes and too small levels of positively valued ones (with respect to socially optimal levels) will be produced by the market if this is left to act by itself. Sometimes, as is well illustrated by the negative environmental effects of agricultural policy, the problem is not only one of market failure but one of policy failure as well. Market and policy failures provide a rationale for government to intervene in the supply of landscape attributes.

Some economists, based especially on a classical paper by Coase (1960), have argued that, in general, people affected by externalities have an incentive to bribe the originators of the external effect so that more positive externalities (and fewer negative ones) are produced. Provided benefits of such moves cover the minimum compensation required by the originator of the externality, a bargain may occur, which eventually leads to a Pareto optimum. The fact that this bargain does not occur spontaneously can be explained by the high costs of bringing together all people affected by an externality and all originators of it, reaching an agreement and enforcing compliance of all parties with this agreement. (This is particularly true with countryside externalities, which often involve large numbers of countryside users and farmers.) These so-called transaction costs are real economic costs: resources are used up in reaching and operating countryside management agreements. Thus, the non-occurrence of a spontaneous agreement could be explained as a result of transaction costs offsetting all gains to be made from the transaction. In this case, the current allocation may be seen as socially optimal, and hence there would be no justification for public intervention in the supply of landscape attributes.

However, it is possible that, although spontaneous bargaining is too expensive, there can be forms of public intervention with lower transaction costs – such as policies in which an agency buys landscape improvements from farmers on behalf of the general public. In this case, the lower transaction costs can be offset by the net benefits to be made from landscape improvement, which justifies public intervention on efficiency grounds alone.

Public intervention is not directly regulated by mechanisms, such as market operation, ensuring that public preferences for landscapes and resources used up in conserving them are taken into account by public decision-makers. Hence, from an economic standpoint, the problem with public intervention is that it is quite easy for conservation policy either to fall short of the optimum or to exceed it. One way to mitigate this problem is to value all effects of a particular conservation policy on social welfare and to compare all these values in a full cost–benefit analysis (CBA). From this analysis we can then draw an overall judgement on the social desirability of such a conservation policy. With respect to landscape conservation policy, a full CBA is complicated by the fact that many landscape goods to be supplied by the policy do not have a market price. Hence, non-market valuation techniques should be used to put a money value on the welfare effects of conservation policy on all those affected by the implied landscape change. The contingent valuation method (CVM), because of its flexibility, is today the non-market valuation technique with the largest scope of possible applications in valuing landscape change. This book is aimed at building an integrated CVM/CBA approach to landscape conservation policy.

1.3 MULTIDIMENSIONAL CHANGE AND POLICY EVALUATION

What is at stake in some conservation policy decisions is simply whether a single conservation scheme supplying a particular landscape at a particular site is socially desirable. In this case, the only decision is whether to go ahead with the scheme. However, very often there is a complex set of questions to be answered in the evaluation process, such as 'which particular attributes to conserve'; 'at which sites'; 'how much of each attribute' and 'how much acreage at each site'. Thus, the evaluation problem raised by conservation policies is typically multidimensional, and hence the analytical frame used for valuation and cost–benefit analysis of these policies should account for this multidimensionality. Two typical examples are presented below to illustrate the type of methodological problems caused by this multidimensionality of conservation policies.

The first is a multi-site problem. Suppose that we want to value the conservation of traditional landscapes in two areas with the same landscape type, located close to each other and visited by the same population. In this case, it is possible that each individual visitor perceives the two areas as close substitutes. Thus, suppose that landscape quality is declining in both areas and that a conservation scheme for area A alone is considered (landscape degradation would occur anyway in B). Suppose an individual is asked how much is he prepared to pay to ensure that area A is conserved and that his answer is £10. Probably, because the areas are similar, he would also be willing to pay £10 for B (with no conservation at A). If the two areas are perfect substitutes, a programme jointly conserving A and B will also be valued at £10. Thus, if conserving a single area costs £8, then the conservation of either A or B in isolation is worthwhile but the joint programme for A and B is not. In cases where substitution is less severe, it may simply happen that the sum of benefits elicited for each area in isolation is larger than the joint benefit for the two areas elicited in one single step (which is the relevant benefit if we want to evaluate the joint programme). Note also that if the two areas are perfect substitutes for each other, the fact of one of them being conserved implies there is no benefit from conserving the other. However, in general, if there is less-than-perfect substitution, we only know that the benefit of conserving one area will depend on whether the other area is to be conserved.

The second example refers to a multi-attribute problem involving only one site. Suppose that we have a cherished landscape and are deciding which attributes (of those traditionally associated with that landscape) to conserve. In this case, it is possible that the previous conservation of an attribute (say for example stone walls) may enhance the value of also conserving other attributes (e.g. flower diversity in meadows). This is because these attributes are perceived as parts of the same traditional landscape set and are jointly perceived within a same view. In this case, attributes are complements rather than substitutes in valuation, and the benefit of a joint conservation programme for both attributes is higher than the sum of the benefits of conserving the two attributes valued independently.

Substitution and complementarity are two opposite forms of interaction in valuation between attributes or sites. Interaction in valuation raises two important methodological issues. The first is that separate valuation and cost–benefit analysis of policy components lead to biased benefit estimates and possibly to wrong conservation policy decisions as well. The second is that an optimal attribute (or site) mix can only be selected through sequential cost–benefit analysis, which requires the analyst to evaluate costs and benefits of adding each attribute (or site) at particular steps in particular valuation sequences.

1.4 PREVIEW OF MAIN ISSUES IN THE BOOK

One of the main aims of this book is to analyse methodological problems raised by the multidimensional nature of landscape changes when evaluating conservation policy.

Hoehn and colleagues were the first to study interactions between policy components in the valuation of multidimensional environmental policies (cf. e.g. Majid et al. 1983; Hoehn and Randall 1989; Hoehn 1991, and Hoehn and Loomis 1993) and suggested that these interactions may be interpreted and modelled as ordinary substitution effects. These studies by Hoehn and colleagues are particularly important for at least two reasons. The first is that other authors (e.g. Diamond et al. 1993) later interpreted similar interactions in valuation as an artefact of a particular valuation method, the CVM, which questioned the validity of this method. The second reason for the relevance of Hoehn's studies is that they question the validity of procedures that are extensively used in cost–benefit analyses for aggregating benefits over policy components.

Hoehn's results created room for further research on how to interpret interactions in valuation. One way of proceeding with such an investigation was through empirical tests aimed at checking whether interactions in valuation actually behave as substitution effects. Surprisingly, there have been few studies along these lines. Although there are some honourable exceptions (cf. e.g. Diamond et al. 1993; Magnussen 1996; Bateman et al. 1996; and Randall and Hoehn 1996), this area of research is still full of unanswered questions. Therefore, in addition to being concerned with building an integrated CVM/CBA approach to conservation policy evaluation, this book tests the validity of CVM applications to landscape changes and the ability of neoclassical economic theory for explaining interactions in valuation. It also investigates whether substitution between policy components prevails across all classes of policies and resources (namely landscape), as suggested by Hoehn and others, or if there are particular contexts where complementarity occurs.

With respect to benefit aggregation over individual policy components, Hoehn and colleagues showed that valid aggregation requires the analyst to control for substitution effects between these components. This pointed out the fallacy of independent valuation and summation (IVS), which is the procedure used in most cost–benefit analyses to aggregate benefits over policy components. This book also appraises the importance of controlling for substitution effects in evaluating multidimensional landscape conservation policies. As suggested by Randall (1991), it also asks whether the accumulation of empirical evidence on substitution relationships is leading to the emergence of patterns of substitution effects typical of particular classes of environmental resources. The possible emergence of such patterns would allow us to derive simple rules to correct for the IVS bias.

Two original case-studies are used in this book to suggest possible applications for the proposed methods and to illustrate theoretical and methodological issues: the Pennine Dales ESA scheme, in England, and the application of a national agri-environmental programme to the Peneda–Gerês National Park (NP) in Portugal. Both case-studies refer to upland agricultural landscapes that are among the most cherished and visited landscapes at a national level. Thus, it was expected that benefits of landscape conservation would be significant and market failure considerable in both cases. On the other hand, there is a fundamental difference between these case-studies: whereas in the English case there are some problems due to agricultural intensification as well as some dereliction problems, in the Portuguese case farmland dereliction is the overwhelming problem. This difference is important because it enables us to derive policy conclusions with respect to the two most important problems faced by landscape conservation policy: agricultural intensification and the abandonment of marginal farmland. In addition, there are differences between visitors to the Pennine Dales ESA and visitors to the Peneda–Gerês NP (as regards income levels, attitudes towards the environment and attachment to the particular area) that make the comparison of landscape valuations between the two case-studies worthwhile.

In addition to Part One (this introductory chapter alone) this book includes three other parts.

Part Two is concerned with setting the conceptual framework for the valuation and cost–benefit analysis of landscape change. This Part includes chapters 2 to 6. Chapter 2 discusses criteria for landscape conservation decision-making and assesses the compared merits of (1) expert judgement on landscape quality and (2) economic valuation of landscape change. Chapter 3 discusses a Hicksian theory of demand for attributes applied to the valuation of multi-attribute changes; it identifies (and comments on the results of) a variety of empirical tests of this theory; the multi-attribute valuation function used in the case-studies in this book is also derived. Chapter 4 addresses a number of issues raised by the use of the CVM to value landscape changes: definition of benefits; strategies available to value multi-attribute changes; how to build valid CVM scenarios for landscape changes, and how to estimate WTP from discrete-choice (DC) CVM data. Chapter 5 is about the costs of landscape conservation; in addition to a formal treatment of the conservation cost function, it defines several categories of costs and analyses the cost-effectiveness of different policy schemes for landscape conservation. Chapter 6 discusses the theoretical foundations of cost–benefit analysis of landscape conservation and presents the particular method used in the case-studies to identify optimal landscapes: sequential cost–benefit analysis.

Part Three presents and discusses the two case-studies; it is aimed at empirically addressing theoretical and methodological issues raised in Part Two and consists of chapters 7 to 13. Chapter 7 is an introduction to the two case-studies. Chapter 8 presents the results of a study of landscape perceptions and preferences of visitors to the Peneda–Gerês area, which was carried out as a way to improve the CVM scenarios for this case-study. Chapter 9 presents the main aspects of the CVM surveys carried out in the case-studies and summarily describes and compares the surveyed samples of visitors in the two cases. Chapter 10 deals with estimating valuation functions and WTP for landscape conservation; it assess the validity and reliability of the estimates; tests alternative specifications for the multi-attribute valuation function; undertakes a new theory test based on the relationship between the substitution and the income effect; and aggregates landscape benefits to the whole visitor population. Chapter 11 estimates the costs of landscape conservation in each case-study according to several cost concepts. Chapter 12 presents and discusses our cost–benefit analysis of landscape conservation; it evaluates the current agri-environmental scheme in each case and selects an optimal policy-mix through sequential cost–benefit analysis. Chapter 13 compares benefit and cost estimates between cases, for purposes of validating these estimates and deriving more general implications for conservation policy.

Part Four is aimed at methodologically assessing the use of the CVM to value landscape changes; this is done through a meta-analysis of the benefit estimates in the relevant literature, where we assess the validity, reliability and transferability of these estimates (chapter 14). In Part Four, we also discuss the main methodological conclusions from the case-studies as regards the valuation and cost–benefit analysis of multi-attribute changes (chapter 15).

PART TWO

Valuation and Cost–Benefit Analysis of
Landscape Change

2. Landscape Values for Landscape Conservation Decision-Making

Securing landscape benefits usually implies a cost. Payments to land users, either as compensation for prohibited landscape-degrading practice or as an incentive for adopting environmentally sensitive management, are visible costs for the agencies running landscape conservation schemes. Furthermore, these agencies incur in a variety of other costs related to the administration of conservation schemes. Moreover, other types of public choices involving landscape changes, such as decisions about investment projects applying for planning permission or for policy grants, may impose considerable cost on society as a whole. For an example, consider a case where planning permission for a large irrigation project is refused on landscape conservation grounds; alternatively, the project is given planning permission but large amendments are required for mitigating the negative impact on landscape. These decisions are possibly hindering more valued uses of the land (considering conventional market outputs and inputs alone) or leading to scarce resources being used up in mitigation activities.

Given the potential significance of all of these landscape conservation costs, we should always assess the conservation option with respect to at least three important criteria. The first is whether this option will actually deliver the landscape benefits it is supposed to deliver. The second is whether there is an alternative way of securing the same benefits at a lower cost. The third is whether landscape-conservation benefits offset the corresponding costs. These criteria for the evaluation of conservation policy are usually known as technical effectiveness, cost-effectiveness and economic efficiency, respectively. The technical-effectiveness and cost-effectiveness criteria are not discussed here – not because they are unimportant, which surely they are not, but because they have been systematically addressed by others[1] and are discussed in other chapters in this book (cf. e.g. chapters 5, 11 and 12).

The economic efficiency criterion reminds us that policy decisions involving landscape change imply a trade-off of scarce economic resources for landscape quality. To explicitly assess such a trade-off, one should put a money value on landscape benefits so that these benefits can be weighted against costs. This money value does not refer to any intrinsic value in the landscape but to a practical context where a decision has to be made.

This point is worth making here as it stresses that, although the total worth of landscape is possibly not reducible to the money-metric, as it is fairly claimed by philosophers and environmentalists, this reduction is necessarily implied by any decision involving a trade-off of scarce resources for landscape quality. A simple example illustrates this point. Consider a decision-maker facing two alternative designs for a same project: one cheaper and the other more expensive but providing additional landscape benefits. The decision of selecting the cheaper design implies that the additional landscape benefits are valued lower than the cost difference between designs. On the other hand, selecting the more expensive design implies that the additional landscape benefits are more highly valued than this cost difference. Therefore, the actual outcome of the decision will necessarily assign, at least implicitly, a money value to the additional landscape benefits.

Thus, the real question is not whether to assign money values to landscape change but to clarify which (and whose) values are to be taken into account in decisions shaping our future landscapes. There are at least three answers to this question, each one implying a different way of deciding about the future of our landscapes. The first is to leave the decision entirely to policy-makers. The second is to rely on expert opinion on landscape quality. The third is to rely on estimates of how much the general public is prepared to pay for the landscape benefits at stake and to enter the estimated amount as the relevant benefit concept to be directly compared with conservation cost.

The first option (leaving the decision to policy-makers) is not fully discussed in this chapter.[2] Policy-makers will take into account their subjective assessment of landscape 'worthiness' and cost 'reasonableness' (sometimes supported by expert opinion on ecological significance, cost and technical effectiveness), as well as their perception of the relative strengths of the farming and conservationist lobbies. Alternatively, landscape considerations may be completely ignored. Either way, the final decision will implicitly ascribe a money value to the landscape change. Indeed, there is a frequently proposed approach to landscape conservation decision-making based on the use of landscape values revealed by past policy decisions as an input to new decision-making processes. A quotation from Bilsborough (1994) describes the essence of this approach:

> If society acts sensibly, it can be argued that the benefits from the landscape feature in question must be worth at least the cost to society of protecting it via a management agreement (...). Therefore the offer of a management agreement by a rural conservation agency can implicitly establish the values placed by society on such features. Looking at management agreements could help quantify these values. [These values could then be used as a] suitable basis for establishing conservation priorities. (Bilsborough 1994: 5–6).

However, if society (in this case, the Countryside Council for Wales, which is supposed to act on behalf of it) is already acting sensibly, why are such values required? Are they aimed at removing inconsistency across decisions? (As the author himself admits inconsistency across decisions is created by the fact that policy schemes are run on 'a "fire-fighting" basis, in response to ongoing threats of further damage, as opposed to a pro-active strategy designed to allocate conservation resources to the most important features' Bilsborough 1994: 5). But if policy decisions are made on an *ad hoc* basis, how could it be possible to extract systematic and coherent values from past policy decisions?

The following sections review the other two criteria for landscape conservation decision-making: landscape quality, as assessed by landscape experts, and willingness-to-pay for landscape conservation by the general public, as assessed by the environmental economist.

2.1 EXPERT OPINION ON LANDSCAPE QUALITY

Members of the landscape planning and design professions developed scales of landscape quality, which made landscape quality judgements more explicit than they were before. Explicit rules for landscape evaluation could be criticised and improved upon by the landscape expert community, which was a clear advantage over previous, *ad hoc*, procedures. Becoming an explicit exercise, landscape evaluation could be more openly scrutinised and contested by those interested in the decision. However, although improving upon previous ways of deciding about our future landscapes by making these ways more explicit and systematic, the use of expert landscape quality assessments possibly gave too much weight to the aesthetic criteria of these experts. Besides, there is empirical evidence on the fact of landscape experts having (precisely because of their specific professional formation) aesthetic preferences that are rather different from those of the bulk of the general public (cf. e.g. Jacques 1980 and Penning-Rowsell 1982). On the other hand, there is no consensus on whether, and to what extent, society should control the expression of artistic idiosyncrasies of landscape designers in the shaping of our future landscapes. It is, nevertheless, clear that landscapes (as well as townscapes) are different from paintings in that they are inherently public and thus necessarily affect the degree of satisfaction of a multitude of countryside dwellers or visitors (cf. Bourassa 1991).

The history of landscape quality evaluation by landscape planners and designers was a short but turbulent one.[3] The seminal works by Linton and Fines appeared both in 1968, with a common practical purpose: to provide planners with landscape quality maps, so that future development could be oriented by landscape considerations. However, the methods proposed were quite different with respect to the way the landscape quality scale was to be developed and used to evaluate landscapes.

Linton (1968) started by analysing those elements of the scenery that determine our reactions. Two main elements were land form and land use. Then, several categories for each element were created, each category being rated according to visual interest. For example, as regards land form, 8 points were given to mountains, 6 to bold hills, 5 to hill country, 3 to plateau uplands, 2 to low uplands and 0 to lowlands. The scale for rating each element was designed so that ratings for both elements could be added to build a scale of overall landscape quality. For example, 'continuous forest on lowland or low upland extinguishes the scenic effects of relief completely, so [its] score must be at least –2. Hill country which scores 5 does not have its scenic effects wholly obliterated, so the negative points for continuous forest should not be so many as –5. Probably the right score is –3, but in fact, a more conservative view has been taken here and the points actually awarded are –2.' (Linton 1968: 231). Points for land form and land use were added up, and some bonus points were considered for the water element, as well as for some particular features of mountainous scenery. The resulting scale of landscape quality was then used to produce quality maps from measurable landscape elements, which are often already mapped (field work is only required for confirmation purposes). The judgement on overall validity of the evaluations is based on the author's own experience and on the consistency of the produced landscape quality maps with previous appraisals by others.

Fines's (1968) method was based on different grounds. The difficulty of building a quality scale by rating individual landscape components was first recognised – none the less because the composition rule for these ratings can be non-additive and is in general unknown. A more feasible task is to give ratings to our overall appreciation of a view. Thus, a quality scale was first developed for a set of pictures depicting a world-wide range of scenes, by asking a group of people, including landscape experts and others, to rate every single scene. Eventually, only ratings by experts were averaged to build the final scale of quality, as the author verified that expert ratings revealed a greater 'awareness of subtleties of landscape' (Fines 1968: 43). Field surveyors were trained in the use of this scale and then produced quality evaluations of views all over the area to be surveyed, from a variety of viewpoints. Eventually quality figures for the different views were transformed in quality figures for different tracts of land, by combining the quality judgements attracted by all views comprehending a particular tract of land.

In spite of its internal consistency, Fines's method implied a very time consuming field work and presented the inconvenience of not relating landscape quality to the particular elements of the scenery that can be subject to management. To circumvent these limitations, a number of statistical methods appeared during the first half of the 1970s (see, for example Coventry-Solihull-Warwickshire Sub-Regional Study Group 1971, Robinson et al. 1976, and Dearden 1980). These methods start by dividing the study area in grid squares. Landscape elements in these grid squares can be directly measured in existing maps and aerial photographs. A sample of these grid squares is then assessed with respect to landscape quality by a team of observers, who are people usually trained in landscape design. However, Dearden (1980) used a sample of participants who were previously selected as representing the preferences of the wider public. The next step is to compute the average of the quality ratings given to each surveyed grid square. These ratings are then modelled using landscape elements measured in maps for the corresponding squares as the independent variables. When a good regression model is established, it is used to predict quality ratings for non-surveyed grid squares based on the values taken by the independent variables in these grid squares.

Statistical methods spare a great deal of field work, although increasing the burden of computational and analytical tasks. They also have the advantage of relating landscape quality to manageable landscape elements (Coventry-Solihull-Warwickshire Sub-Regional Study Group 1971). As this relationship between overall quality and elements is established through modelling, statistical methods remain entirely based on overall evaluation of scenes rather than on the rating of each landscape element. Thus, the use of possibly invalid composition rules (which is a problem with Linton's additive method when landscape elements' ratings are non-additive in preferences) is avoided. The introduction of interaction terms between elements in the regression model enables the analyst to control for non-additivity and to test several hypotheses about the actual composition rule characterising preferences for landscapes.

Methods of expert landscape evaluation such as the ones reviewed here, plus other particularly popular ones such as Tandy's (1971) method, were extensively used during the 1970s by local authorities in the UK for the preparation of their structure and development plans. However, by the early 1980s, the validity of all of these methods was the object of strong objections raised by planners, designers and others. A heated professional debate followed, which was fed by a proliferation of new techniques. This proliferation was 'the result of a growing appreciation of the need for visual quality assessments as an input to land use planning decision-making, coupled with a lack of satisfaction amongst researchers with existing techniques' (Dearden 1980: 52). One central aspect of this debate was the difficulty in defining 'landscape quality' (Dearden 1980). Clamp (1981) discussed whether values based on familiarity and attachment to specific places should be included when evaluating landscapes and concluded that visual quality alone should be used for purposes of designating areas for landscape preservation. In fact, general public opinion on visual quality of different landscapes is likely to be more enduring (as based on relatively stable cultural norms) than attachment of particular people to particular places. This opinion was, however, far from attracting consensus, and without a unique concept of landscape quality it was impossible to unequivocally assess the validity of measurements of this concept.

A second issue in this debate had to do with the multidimensionality of landscapes and with our lack of understanding of the 'manner in which the several features of the landscape combine to give an impression of the whole' (Clamp 1981: 13). Clamp (1981) claimed that the modelling approach used by statistical methods would be an appropriate way to deal with this problem, because split-sample tests of predictability could be used to validate the model relating visual quality to measured landscape elements.

A third issue was whether there is a significant degree of culturally based consensus on the relative quality of different landscapes. Only this consensus would authorise taking average rates from a few evaluators as representative of the general public.

The consensus debate raised a fundamental issue about what, according to Powell (1981), had been 'both the guiding principle behind the development of landscape evaluation techniques and the reason for their downfall' (Powell 1981: 18): the quest for an objective assessment of landscape quality. In fact, as demonstrated by Jacques (1980), landscape appraisal is a fundamentally subjective activity, although there is some homogeneity of landscape tastes and preferences within social groups. This social differentiation of patterns of subjective preferences for landscapes could have been the starting point for a scientific inquiry about landscape evaluation. However, 'instead of investigating directly the question of how people perceive quality in landscapes, efforts were engaged in obtaining information which fitted in with pre-conceived ideas about the (...) planning process' (Powell 1981: 17). One of these ideas was that of public decision-making requiring only objective, i.e. unquestionable and numeric, information. Because it was assumed that there is 'only one valid assessment of the quality of a particular landscape' (Powell 1981: 17), individual variations were treated as deviations from a supposedly existing inter-subjective consensus. Hence the exclusion of local residents from quality assessments; for these people, non-visual factors (such as evocations of the past, particular feelings and familiarity) could play an undue effect on an appraisal of visual quality, which was supposed to be as objective as possible. According to Powell (1981), this 'quest for objectivity' was suppressing 'the very thing upon which the perception of landscape quality depends.' (Powell 1981: 17).

This was why Penning-Rowsell proposed to substitute the concept of landscape values for that of landscape quality. Unlike landscape quality, which was supposed to be context-independent, objective and consensus-based, landscape values stem not only from landscape's appearance but also from 'all its social interactions, uses and associations' (1981a: 37). Furthermore, empirical work had shown that preferences for landscapes were 'inseparable from perceived uses of sites' and that 'pure aesthetic judgements were rare' (1981a: 33). The innovative approach proposed by Penning-Rowsell (1981b) to study landscape values (rather than quality) operated by dividing the landscape-value concept into its main facets. Facets were grouped in three main dimensions of value: appearance values; historical values, including historical associations as well as perceptions of scarcity and vulnerability; and use values, including access, familiarity, and visitor numbers. Various indicators were selected to measure each facet or dimension. Because indicators could be theoretically associated with facets but not directly with value, the validity of an indicator could only be assessed with respect to the corresponding facet. However, future theoretical developments would possibly suggest how to combine indicators of different facets into a synthetic index of landscape value (cf. Penning-Rowsell 1981b).

Scales of landscape quality used in the methods discussed so far in this chapter have an ordinal meaning in that they only refer to a ranking of landscapes. This means it is impossible to say, for example, how much landscape A is better in quality than B. The fact of landscape quality judgements having no cardinal dimension means they do not support elementary algebraic operations such as sums or products. As noted by Price (1978), this fact strongly limits the legitimate uses of landscape quality figures for conservation decision-making purposes. Thus, the aggregation of quality judgements over individuals is not possible, and hence we cannot for example decide, based on quality judgements, whether to improve a 'superb (rating 23) landscape, which is fairly remote (visited by 5,000 per annum), or (...) an ordinary (10), but more visited (100,000) landscape.' (Price 1978: 34). Likewise, we cannot compare different degrees of impact on different landscapes. For example, we do not know whether it is preferable to increase water supply by the same amount by 'slightly raising the level of a supremely beautiful natural lake, such as Ullswater (reducing its rate from 25 to 24) or by making an obtrusive dam in a pleasant Pennine valley (13 to 9)' (Price 1978: 34). Moreover, when there are several alternative designs for the same project (e.g. a road project), it is also impossible to aggregate multiple landscape impacts for each alternative design. For example, we are not able to choose, based on quality judgements, between a route for a motorway that encroaches on several landscapes of average good quality and an alternative route that intrudes on generally low quality landscapes, except one which is of extremely high quality (cf. Price 1978: 34).

During the 1980s the focus of landscape research shifted from landscape evaluation to landscape classification (Landscape Research Group 1988). This shift in research interest was due to the internal difficulties in the field of landscape evaluation, which were so visible in the early 1980s debate and led to a too pessimistic appraisal of the whole evaluation endeavour. For example, Powell claimed in 1981 that the 'techniques are almost always greeted with a large degree of scepticism by people not involved in their construction, and they have rarely been used in the process of actually reaching planning decisions' (Powell 1981: 16). However, as documented by Penning-Rowsell (1975), local authorities made extensive use of landscape evaluation studies over the 1968–75 period.

The shift away from landscape evaluation and towards landscape classification was also driven by a move in the perspectives of agencies funding landscape research, with the Countryside Commission publishing its own guidelines for landscape classification (cf. e.g. Cobham Resource Consultants 1993). Many landscape classification studies, such as the Cambrian Mountains landscape study (Countryside Commission 1990), followed these guidelines. Landscape classification was viewed as a way of justifying, sometimes *a posteriori*, recent conservation designations (cf. the case of the North Pennines, Land Use Consultants 1991).

Landscape classification stems from a perceived need to define landscape character and character areas, rather than quality, as a base for conservation and planning policies. This is very clear in the joint effort of the Countryside Commission and English Nature to produce the recently published map of 'The character of England: landscape, wildlife and natural features' (Countryside Commission and English Nature 1996). This characterisation effort 'is linked to a now apparently widespread recognition that the elements of the countryside which make places especially important are character and distinctiveness' (Swanwick 1997: 55) rather than quality (we would say). According to Swanwick, 'the Joint Character Map (and all that flows from it) could become the cornerstone for national approaches to planning for landscape and wildlife into the next century' (1997: 60).

This move away from landscape evaluation and towards classification, however useful it may have been for other purposes, meant, in practice, the abandonment by the landscape evaluation community of a previous commitment to directly addressing trade-offs of development benefits for landscape quality. In this sense, this move left a void to be filled up by a further research programme aimed at directly addressing such trade-offs. The following section aims at showing that the application of environmental economics to landscape change provides a coherent way of filling up this void while providing acceptable answers for many concerns raised by the landscape evaluation debate of the 1980s. The environmental economist's approach implies substituting the economic concept of value of a landscape change for that of landscape quality.

2.2 THE ECONOMIC VALUE OF A LANDSCAPE CHANGE

The economic concept of value refers to willingness-to-pay (WTP) for a reduction in the price of a market commodity or WTP for an increase in the level of a public good. Willingness-to-accept (WTA) compensation for price rises or decreases in public good levels are also used by economists as value concepts. Landscape values can be interpreted in a quite straightforward way in terms of WTP for beneficial landscape changes (or to avoid undesirable ones) or, alternatively, in terms of WTA for landscape degradation (or to forego beneficial landscape changes).

There are some fundamental differences between landscape quality, as measured by landscape evaluation studies referred to in the previous section, and the economic value of a landscape change. The first is that landscape quality refers to an appraisal of the relative visual attractiveness of a landscape as compared to others – hence, it is, by definition, an ordinal concept. On the other hand, landscape value refers to an amount of market commodities or income that an individual is prepared to trade for a landscape change; hence it is a cardinal concept. The second difference is that landscape quality refers to judgements about states of landscape, whereas landscape values always refer to changes in landscapes.

As a consequence of these two first differences, landscape quality is not directly comparable with the value of the resources used up by conservation (i.e. with conservation costs) whilst landscape values are. Indeed, this provides the basis for using landscape values in cost–benefit analysis (CBA). CBA of landscape conservation policies is a method whereby welfare-gains for those who are made better off by these policies (including landscape benefits measured through WTP) are directly compared with welfare-losses suffered by those who are made worse off by policy (measured through WTA compensation for losses).

The third difference is that landscape quality is assumed to be largely visual, context-independent, consensual and stable, with only long-term changes in taste associated with cultural change being admitted. On the other hand, landscape values are context-dependent, as they may vary with differences in the frequency of visits, types of use (recreational, residential), landscape scarcity, access conditions and personal taste. This implies that there are many reasons for valuing landscapes (use, familiarity, attachment, pure aesthetics, historical associations and so on), which satisfies the requirement for defining multiple-facet landscape values put forward by Penning-Rowsell (1981a and b). However, the environmental economist does not need to engage in the analytical method proposed by Penning-Rowsell (1981b) to define landscape value by enumerating its facets. Validity of measurements of economic value is directly assessed against the overall value concept and not with respect to each facet separately as proposed by Penning-Rowsell. In fact, we may directly assess the predictive validity of measurements of economic value provided individuals are given the possibility of actually deciding with respect to the implied trade-offs of income for landscape quality. This is at least conceivable and sometimes observed as well, as in the case of referenda where individuals are asked to make self-taxation decisions for securing higher levels of public goods (Mitchell and Carson 1989).

This possibility of assessing the predictive validity of landscape value measurements has no counterpart for landscape quality measurements, as we have no external validity criterion for them. This is a fourth difference between the landscape value and quality concepts.

CBA methodology (cf. chapter 6) enables us to aggregate value over individuals without making any assumption about the degree of social consensus on landscape quality. This allows for varying tastes and general context-dependency of values. Avoiding the consensus assumption is possible because individual values (WTP) for a particular landscape change can be directly summed, so providing an aggregate measure of value. This has itself a clear conceptual meaning: it represents the value of all commodities that the individuals affected by a landscape change are prepared to trade for that change. Moreover, this aggregate value is directly comparable with conservation costs. This aggregation criterion also allows each particular individual's preferences to be weighted according to the intensity of these preferences – intensity which is measured in terms of the amount of other valued goods he is prepared to give up for the landscape change. Thus, if the landscape expert or the conservationist have more intense preferences for landscapes (in the sense they are prepared to give up more of other scarce commodities for landscape quality), then their preferences will be more strongly weighted. However, they would never be the only preferences to be taken into account, as when we base landscape assessments on expert opinion alone.

The fact of landscape values being cardinal measures of value allows us not only to compare and aggregate value across individuals but also to compare and aggregate value across different impacts on different landscapes. This enables us to solve many decision-making problems that, as seen in section 2.1, had no solution within the landscape quality (ordinal) frame.

Of course, WTP for a landscape change is proportional to individual income. Thus when aggregating value over individuals, individual preferences are weighted according to individual purchasing power, which extends to decisions on landscape public goods the (in)equity criterion currently underlying market operation. This is a clear limitation of using landscape values within a CBA frame, to which we will return in chapter 6.

NOTES

1. Whitby (1994a) assessed particular ESA schemes with respect to technical effectiveness and cost. Willis et al. (1988) estimated the costs of management agreements signed by English Nature under the Countryside and Wildlife Act 1981. Colman (1994), Whitby and Saunders (1994) and Whitby (1994) addressed the cost-effectiveness of a variety of policy tools for landscape conservation.
2. The way the policy process works in shaping our future landscapes represents an area of positive research in itself and has been addressed by sociologists and political scientists (cf. Winter 1996).
3. Most of the landscape quality studies referred to in this section were carried out before the 1980s, when a professional debate (referred to later on in this section) raised many doubts about the validity and usefulness of these studies as an input into planning decisions. However, some methods using expert opinion on the amenity and aesthetic value of the physical environment continued to be used after 1980. Helliwell's (1990) method for the valuation of amenity trees and woodland is a good example of a method based on expert opinion still in use. Price's method for landscape evaluation (discussed in section 4.2 of this book) is a good example of an economic valuation method heavily relying on expert opinion.

3. Valuing Landscape Change I: Theory and the Multi-Attribute Issue

Most policy-relevant cases of landscape change involve changes in different landscape attributes often at more than one site. This multidimensional nature of landscape change has crucial implications for valuation and benefit aggregation, which need to be addressed from a theoretical (that is, general) standpoint.

This chapter presents and discusses a theory of demand for landscape attributes applied to the valuation of multi-attribute landscape changes. Although developed with the multi-attribute problem in mind, this theory applies as well to multi-site problems.

Theoretical explanations discussed here remain within the neoclassical (Hicksian) paradigm, as the aim is to explore, from within, the full potential and limitations of this paradigm in accounting for interactions in valuation between attributes. Neoclassical explanations for interactions in valuation stem from the general economic concept of substitution between goods.

Some effort is also devoted to testing theoretical explanations; hence, the presentation of the theory is oriented towards identifying possible empirical tests in the context of contingent valuation studies. Four types of tests are identified, and relevant empirical evidence from the contingent valuation literature is discussed.

A theoretically consistent valuation function for multi-attribute landscape changes is also specified, and uses of this function for hypotheses testing and predictive purposes are illustrated.

3.1 DEMAND FOR ATTRIBUTES AND SUBSTITUTION RELATIONSHIPS

This section presents and discusses a theory of demand for landscape attributes with particular emphasis on substitution relationships between attributes. Three types of substitution relationship are defined – substitution in utility, uncompensated and compensated substitution in valuation – and connections between these types are explored.

Nature of the Goods

Consider there are n commodities available in the market at prices $\mathbf{p'} = (p_1, p_2, ..., p_n)$.[1] An individual consumer is free to choose how much of a commodity i to buy at the fixed price p_i and eventually selects a commodity bundle represented as $\mathbf{x'} = (x_1, x_2, ..., x_n)$.

The state of landscape is described as a vector $\mathbf{z'} = (z_1, z_2, ..., z_m)$, in which the generic ($j$th) element is a measure of a particular landscape attribute at a particular site. Different z_js may represent, for example, the same attribute at different sites or different attributes at the same site.

Contrasting with the amounts x_is, which are chosen by the individual at fixed prices, the z_js are exogenously determined by the actions of others (farmers, urban developers and public decision-makers) and are typically provided at a zero price.[2] Thus, for the individual the z_js are like zero-priced rationed goods.[3]

Individuals react to subjectively perceived landscape rather than objective landscape. Hence, it is the former that matters when modelling individual choice. For $\mathbf{z}$ to represent the perceived state of landscape, each z_j should correspond to an attribute that is actually perceived by the individual; and should be measured in a perception-consistent scale. If landscape perception by the individual is misrepresented when specifying $\mathbf{z}$, then the individual's choices will be misinterpreted by the model, and wrong values will be ascribed to the landscape attributes at issue.

All of these properties of landscape attributes as economic goods also apply, in general, to the individual attributes of most environmental resources, such as wildlife or water quality. Hence, for sake of generality, the z_js are often referred to in this chapter as simply 'attributes'. Likewise, the theory of demand for attributes to be discussed here is considered applicable not only to landscape but also to a variety of other multi-attribute environmental resources.

Preferences

The wellbeing of the individual is assumed to depend on market goods $\mathbf{x}$ and attributes $\mathbf{z}$, which is a rather weak and acceptable assumption. However, neoclassical models of demand are usually grounded on a stronger assumption; in our case, this would imply that the individual's preferences for bundles $(\mathbf{x}, \mathbf{z})$ can be described as a utility function $U = U(\mathbf{x}, \mathbf{z})$. Despite its spread use and analytical convenience, this assumption is a fairly strong one in this context and hence deserves some closer examination.

Function $U(.)$ is often interpreted as having just an ordinal meaning, that is: as a mapping of bundles $(\mathbf{x}, \mathbf{z})$ into a preference ordering. However, for such a mapping to exist, the individual's preferences must be complete, consistent and transitive in the $n+m$-dimension space $(\mathbf{x}, \mathbf{z})$.[4] For ordinary commodities, continued participation in the market – with its sanctions for wrong choices – is generally sufficient to generate such well-behaved preferences, even if individuals on their own have incomplete, inconsistent, or intransitive preferences (cf., e.g., Crocker et al. 1996). On the other hand, individuals do not take direct market decisions on landscape attributes, and thus preferences for the z_js are not disciplined by usual sanctions such as regret for wrong purchase decisions.[5] This may be a serious problem for all non-market valuation methods: preferences, as usually interpreted by economists, cannot be revealed if they simply do not exist.

To proceed, an assumption is made of reasonably behaved preferences, which authorises us to take a utility function for approximately describing the individual's preferences for bundles $(\mathbf{x}, \mathbf{z})$. This assumption is made with an eye on its heuristic benefits. As usual, the utility function is assumed continuous, twice continuously differentiable, strictly quasi-concave and strictly increasing in both $\mathbf{x}$ and $\mathbf{z}$.

Substitution in Utility

Some properties of preferences for landscape attributes derive from the way we experience the landscape. So, for example, each landscape tends to be perceived as a whole, rather than as a collection of separate attributes. The fact of the different attributes of the same landscape being jointly experienced creates room for interactions in utility between these attributes. An illustrative example is that of the characteristic attributes of a cherished landscape, such as the Pennine Dales in the UK. In this particular case, attributes such as stone walls seem to magnify the visual impact of other attributes, such as flower-rich meadows. Hence, the aesthetic impact of the whole is larger than the sum of the parts' impacts. In this case, different attributes of the same landscape interact in utility with each other.

Likewise, attributes of different landscapes crossed within a same journey tend to affect our preferences for each other. For example, a sequence of enclosed farmed landscapes, densely wooded scenes and large tracts of open moorland can enhance the aesthetic impact of each type due to a diversity effect. Also here the whole is larger than the sum of the parts. The effect can be the opposite if a same attribute (for example extensive arable fields) prevails in all scenes crossed within the journey, so creating an impression of monotony. In both of these two opposite cases, landscape attributes of different landscapes interact with each other.

These interactions in utility can be described and analysed as substitution relationships. We say that there is a substitution relationship in utility between attributes j and h when a change in one of them shifts the marginal utility of the other (marginal utility of an attribute j is the partial derivative $\partial U/\partial z_j$). Attributes j and h are said substitutes (complements, or independent) in utility if marginal utility of one is shifted downwards (upwards, or not shifted) by a marginal increase in the other; formally, this means: $\partial^2 U/\partial z_j \partial z_h$ < (> or =) 0. From the examples presented above, we would say that stone walls and meadows in the Dales are complements in utility, whereas arable fields that recur across all scenes experienced within a journey are substitutes in utility for each other.

Uncompensated Demand Theory

Suppose that an individual facing prices $\mathbf{p}$, income y and a given state of landscape $\mathbf{z}$ will choose the bundle $\mathbf{x}$ of market commodities that he prefers the most in this context. This choice corresponds to the following constrained maximisation problem:

$$\max_{\mathbf{x}} U(\mathbf{x}, \mathbf{z}) \qquad \text{s. t.:} \quad \mathbf{x'p} \le y \quad \text{and} \quad \mathbf{x} \ge \mathbf{0}. \qquad (3.1)$$

The solution for this problem yields:

$$\mathbf{x} = \mathbf{x}(\mathbf{p}, \mathbf{z}, y) \qquad (3.2a)$$
$$\lambda = \lambda(\mathbf{p}, \mathbf{z}, y) \qquad (3.2b)$$

where $\mathbf{x}$ represents a vector of uncompensated demand functions for the n market commodities and λ is the Lagrange multiplier associated with the budget constraint. Notice that demands for market goods depend not only on prices and income, but also on the vector $\mathbf{z}$ of attributes. So, the model allows for demand shifts determined by exogenous changes in attributes. For example, countryside visitors can increase their purchases of petrol and other commodities related to recreational trips to a particular site if some valued attribute(s) of the site is (are) enhanced. Revealed preference valuation methods, such as the varying parameter travel cost model (Vaughan and Russell 1982), explore these traces of attribute changes in people's behaviour to uncover people's values for such changes.

Replacing the uncompensated demand functions back into the utility function yields the indirect utility function:

$$V(\mathbf{p}, \mathbf{z}, y) = U(\mathbf{x}(\mathbf{p}, \mathbf{z}, y), \mathbf{z}) \qquad (3.3)$$

This function gives us the maximum utility achievable by an individual facing circumstances $(\mathbf{p}, \mathbf{z}, y)$. Differentiating $V(.)$ with respect to prices and income, and invoking the envelope theorem, yields:

$$\partial V / \partial \mathbf{p} = - \lambda \, \mathbf{x} \, (\mathbf{p}, \mathbf{z}, y) \qquad (3.4a)$$
$$\partial V / \partial y = \lambda \, (\mathbf{p}, \mathbf{z}, y) \qquad (3.4b)$$

(3.4b) shows that the Lagrange multiplier associated with the budget constraint is marginal utility of income. Roy's identity is established by dividing minus (3.4a) by (3.4b):

$$- V_{\mathbf{p}} / V_y = \mathbf{x} \, (\mathbf{p}, \mathbf{z}, y) \qquad (3.5)^6$$

which gives us again the uncompensated demands for market commodities. The dual counterpart of Roy's identity with respect to attributes $\mathbf{z}$ is (Kolstad and Braden 1991):

$$V_{\mathbf{z}} / V_y = \pi \, (\mathbf{p}, \mathbf{z}, y) \qquad (3.6)$$

with $V_{\mathbf{z}}$ being the vector of marginal utilities of the attributes $\mathbf{z}$. Dividing $V_{\mathbf{z}}$ by marginal utility of income, as in (3.6), corresponds to re-scaling from utility to money. Hence, π is a vector of uncompensated marginal valuations of the attributes $\mathbf{z}$, that is: uncompensated inverse demands for these attributes. These are uncompensated (income-constant) functions because income is not continuously adjusted to compensate for changes in the attributes. Thus, utility rises (declines) as attributes are increased (reduced).

Uncompensated Substitution in Valuation

Within uncompensated demand theory, it is possible to define a second type of substitution relationship between attributes. Thus, attributes j and h are said uncompensated substitutes (complements, or independent) in valuation if the uncompensated marginal valuation of one of them is shifted downwards (upwards, or not shifted) by a marginal increase in the other attribute; formally, this means: $\partial \pi_j / \partial z_h < (> \text{or} =) \, 0$.

Finding out a relationship between uncompensated substitution in valuation and substitution in utility requires us to derive the jth element of vector π in (3.6) with respect to a different attribute h. From (3.4b) we know that, in general, marginal utility of income V_y depends not only on prices and income but also on attributes. However, we can reasonably assume that, for many attribute changes affecting only a small share of the individual's total welfare, V_y remains approximately constant over the change, and hence:

$$\partial \pi_j / \partial z_h = \partial(V_{z_j}/V_y)/\partial z_h = 1/\lambda . (\partial^2 V / \partial z_j \partial z_h) \tag{3.7}$$

where λ is constant marginal utility of income. Because λ is always positive, equation (3.7) shows that the sign of the uncompensated substitution relationship is identical to the sign of substitution in utility, $\partial^2 V/\partial z_j \partial z_h$. Thus, if two attributes are substitutes (complements or independent) in utility, then they are also uncompensated substitutes (complements or independent) in valuation.[7]

Compensated Demand Theory

Suppose that an individual facing prices **p** and given state of landscape **z** will choose the bundle $\mathbf{x}^c$ of market commodities that enables him to reach utility level U at the lowest cost. This corresponds to the following problem:

$$\min_{\mathbf{x}} \mathbf{x'p} \quad \text{s. t.: } U(\mathbf{x}, \mathbf{z}) = U \quad \text{and} \quad \mathbf{x} \geq \mathbf{0}. \tag{3.8}$$

This is the dual of the maximisation problem in (3.1) and the solution yields:

$$\mathbf{x}^c = \mathbf{x}^c(\mathbf{p}, \mathbf{z}, U) \tag{3.9a}$$
$$\eta = \eta(\mathbf{p}, \mathbf{z}, U) \tag{3.9b}$$

where $\mathbf{x}^c$ represents a vector of compensated demand functions for the n market commodities and η is the Lagrange multiplier associated with the utility constraint (η can be interpreted as marginal cost of utility). Compensated demands give the amounts purchased by the individual when income is adjusted to compensate for changes in **p** or **z** so that utility is held constant at U.

Replacing compensated demand functions into the objective function $\mathbf{x'p}$ we secure the expenditure function:

$$e(\mathbf{p}, \mathbf{z}, U) = \mathbf{x}^c(\mathbf{p}, \mathbf{z}, U)'\mathbf{p} \tag{3.10}$$

which gives the minimum cost, for the individual, of achieving utility level U under the circumstances $(\mathbf{p}, \mathbf{z})$.

Suppose the individual is now allowed to purchase increases in attributes **z**, as in a contingent valuation survey. In this new choice problem, the individual is assumed to be facing a price vector π^c for attributes and to choose the attribute bundle **z** that minimises the expenditure associated with utility level U. (The expenditure concept is now expanded to include expenditure in attributes as well.) This choice problem corresponds to:

$$\min_{\mathbf{z}} \; [\pi^c \, \mathbf{z} + e \, (\mathbf{p}, \mathbf{z}, U)] \qquad\qquad (3.11)$$

in which the fact of $\mathbf{z}$ being an argument of $e(.)$ ensures that the utility constraint is met. The solution for this problem yields:

$$\pi^c \, (\mathbf{p}, \mathbf{z}, U) = - \, \partial e \, (\mathbf{p}, \mathbf{z}, U) \, / \, \partial \mathbf{z} \qquad\qquad (3.12)$$

Because $\mathbf{z}$ is actually fixed for the individual, π^c could be interpreted as a vector of virtual prices. These are the prices at which an individual – with income continuously adjusted to keep utility constant at U – would choose precisely the current (given) bundle $\mathbf{z}$. This virtual price interpretation is proposed by Neary and Roberts (1980) in their analysis of rationed goods.

However, from a valuation perspective, there is a more interesting interpretation for (3.12). In fact, each element of π^c represents the maximum price the individual would be prepared to pay for the marginal unit of the corresponding attribute. According to (3.12), this marginal valuation of an attribute is equal to the reduction in expenditure on market goods (required to reach U) that results from having the marginal unit of the attribute. Thus, this marginal valuation of an attribute: (1) is explicitly defined as a trade-off of market goods for the attribute; and (2) represents the amount to be removed from the individual's income so that utility is held constant at U after a marginal increase in this attribute. In this sense, π^c is a vector of compensated marginal valuations of the m attributes; or, which is the same, a vector of compensated inverse demands for these attributes. This is different from the vector π of uncompensated marginal valuations defined in (3.6) in that elements of π^c are compensated (utility-constant) functions. This means income is continuously adjusted to compensate for changes in attributes, so that utility is held constant at U. In other words, along compensated curves, 'the consumer pays the full marginal valuation of each unit before making his valuation of the next' (Hicks 1956: 86).

Compensated Substitution in Valuation

It is now possible to define a third type of substitution relationship. So, we say that attributes j and h are compensated substitutes (complements, or independent) in valuation when the compensated marginal valuation of one of them is shifted downwards (upwards, or not shifted) by a marginal increase in the other; which formally means: $\partial \pi_j^c \, / \partial z_h < (>$ or $=) \; 0$.

Relationship between the Substitution and the Income Effects

Because of the duality between the utility maximisation and the expenditure minimisation problems, uncompensated marginal valuations in (3.6) and compensated marginal valuations in (3.12) must be identical at a point where income y is just sufficient to achieve utility level U, that is where $y = e$ (**p, z,** U). Thus, for every single attribute j:

$$\pi_j^c (\mathbf{p}, \mathbf{z}, U) = \pi_j [\mathbf{p}, \mathbf{z}, e (\mathbf{p}, \mathbf{z}, U)] \tag{3.13}$$

Differentiating with respect to another attribute h, we obtain:

$$\partial \pi_j^c / \partial z_h = \partial \pi_j / \partial z_h + \partial \pi_j / \partial y . \partial e / \partial z_h \tag{3.14}$$

Taking into account (3.12) and rearranging yields:

$$\partial \pi_j / \partial z_h = \partial \pi_j^c / \partial z_h + \partial \pi_j / \partial y . \pi_h^c \tag{3.15}$$

(3.15) is the counterpart for multi-attribute changes of the ordinary Slutsky equation for multi-price changes. Equation (3.15) shows that the shift of the uncompensated marginal valuation of j due to a marginal increase in h (on the LHS) has two components: a substitution effect (first term on the RHS) and an income effect (second term on the RHS).

The substitution effect represents the shift of the compensated (or utility-constant) marginal valuation of j. This shift is the only one that would occur if income was reduced in an amount π_h^c to keep utility constant as h increases.

The income effect occurs when income is not adjusted for the increase in h – as it happens when h is zero-priced. It is as if the amount of money π_h^c was 'given back' to the individual, so causing a jump to a higher level of utility. This expansion of real income causes a shift (of size $\partial \pi_j / \partial y . \pi_h^c$) of the marginal valuation of j.

From an earlier result in this section, it is known that the sign of uncompensated substitution in valuation (sign of LHS of equation 3.15) is equal to the sign of substitution in utility. Therefore, some useful relationships between substitution in utility and compensated substitution in valuation can be established from (3.15). To derive these relationships, note that the income effect is always positive when j is a normal good.[8]

So, if attributes j and h are complements in utility, then the LHS of the equation will be positive. In this case, the attributes can be compensated complements, independent or substitutes in valuation (that is: first term on the RHS can be positive, null or negative, respectively). For the attributes to be compensated substitutes in valuation in this case, the income effect must be larger in modulus than the substitution effect.

On the other hand, it is easy to verify that, if the attributes are independent or substitutes in utility (LHS null or negative, respectively) then they can only be compensated substitutes in valuation.

Thus, two attributes need not be substitutes in utility to be compensated substitutes in valuation. This is an important result because it warns us about the limits of intuitive predictions of the sign of substitution relationships. So, landscape attributes that intuitively appear as complements – because they enhance the aesthetic impact of each other, or because together they provide diversity – may well be compensated substitutes in valuation provided the income effect is large enough. In fact, such intuitive predictions are only valid with respect to substitution in utility, not to compensated substitution in valuation.

3.2 VALUATION OF DISCRETE MULTI-ATTRIBUTE CHANGES

The theory of demand discussed in the previous section refers to marginal changes in the attributes. This marginal setting is required to introduce major demand concepts such as those related to substitution. However, most policy-relevant landscape changes involve discrete changes in the attributes; hence, in the present section, welfare measures for discrete multi-attribute changes are defined and discussed.

A discrete multi-attribute change $\Delta \mathbf{z}$ can be described by identifying an initial state of landscape $\mathbf{z}^0$ and a final state $\mathbf{z}^1$. The welfare change associated with $\Delta \mathbf{z}$ is defined as:

$$\Delta V = V(\mathbf{p}, \mathbf{z}^1, y) - V(\mathbf{p}, \mathbf{z}^0, y) \qquad (3.16)$$

There is a major problem with this definition: as utility is unobservable, we cannot directly measure ΔV.[9] Thus, indirect money measures for ΔV are defined and discussed in this section.

Uncompensated Valuation Theory

A straightforward money measure for ΔV can be developed from (3.16) by representing this utility difference in the integral form:

$$\Delta V = \int_w dV = \int_w V_\mathbf{z}' d\mathbf{z} \qquad (3.17)$$

where w is a continuous integration path in the attribute space between $\mathbf{z}^0$ and $\mathbf{z}^1$. From (3.6):

$$\Delta V = \int_w V_y(\mathbf{p}, \mathbf{z}, y) \cdot \pi (\mathbf{p}, \mathbf{z}, y)\, d\mathbf{z} \qquad (3.18)$$

Assuming constant marginal utility of income:

$$\Delta V = \lambda \int_w \pi (\mathbf{p}, \mathbf{z}, y)\, d\mathbf{z} = \lambda S \qquad (3.19)$$

where λ is constant marginal utility of income.

The integrand functions in this equation (the elements of vector π) are the uncompensated marginal valuations of attributes. Thus, the integral in (3.19), that is S, gives us the individual's full uncompensated valuation of the discrete multi-attribute change $\Delta \mathbf{z}$. This is why S is an uncompensated money measure for the welfare change ΔV. Indeed, S provides a rather direct money equivalent for ΔV: note that λ works here as a mere constant coefficient of conversion of money into utility units.

The uncompensated money measure S has two major limitations: (1) if money (obviously cardinal) can be re-scaled into utility, then utility must be interpreted as a cardinal number; and (2) S may be not unique, that is, it may depend on the path w chosen to evaluate the line integral in (3.19).

The issue of cardinal utility is raised by the fact of most post-Hicksian economists viewing utility functions only as ways of representing preference orderings. For them, the existence of utility as a cardinal concept is not required to found neoclassical choice theory. On the other hand, the use of S as a direct money measure for ΔV requires such an existence.

The issue of path-dependency of S is a more involved one. If S does not yield a unique value for a same landscape change irrespective of the particular integration path w, then it will be an ambiguous and not very useful welfare measure. For S to be path-independent, every single cross derivative $\partial \pi_j / \partial \pi_h$ of the integrand functions must be identical to its counterpart $\partial \pi_h / \partial \pi_j$ (for all attributes j and h).[10] Assuming constant marginal utility of income and using (3.7), these derivatives are easily transformed into $(\partial^2 V / \partial z_j \partial z_h)/\lambda$ and $(\partial^2 V / \partial z_h \partial z_j)/\lambda$ respectively, which are identical for any continuous twice-differentiable function V according to Young's theorem. Hence, constancy of marginal utility of income is a sufficient condition for S to be a unique money measure.

Both assumptions of cardinal utility and constant marginal utility of income, which are required to work with S as a unique money measure for ΔV, are typically Marshallian in flavour. Indeed, S is the counterpart for attribute changes of Marshall's consumer's surplus for price changes.

Compensated Valuation Theory

These problems of uncompensated (Marshallian) valuation theory are avoided within compensated (Hicksian) valuation theory.

There are two types of compensated welfare measures: compensating and equivalent measures. Compensating variation (*CV*) of income is the amount of money that should be removed from the individual's income after a particular change for him to remain at the initial (pre-change) level of utility. Equivalent variation (*EV*) of income is the amount of money to be given to the individual for him to be as well off without the change as he would be with it. Applied to the discrete multi-attribute change Δz, these two welfare measures can be formally defined as follows:

$$V(\mathbf{p}, \mathbf{z}^1, y - CV) = V(\mathbf{p}, \mathbf{z}^0, y) = V^0 \qquad (3.20)$$

$$V(\mathbf{p}, \mathbf{z}^0, y + EV) = V(\mathbf{p}, \mathbf{z}^1, y) = V^1 \qquad (3.21)$$

with V^0 and V^1 representing the initial and final utility levels.

When Δz represents an improvement, both *CV* and *EV* are positive; conversely, if Δz represents a degradation, *CV* and *EV* will be negative. Thus, both measures validly indicate the sign of the underlying utility change.

Compensated welfare measures can also be interpreted in terms of amounts of money the individual is prepared to pay, or accept as compensation, for the change. So, in the case of an improvement, *CV* is maximum willingness-to-pay (WTP) for the improvement and *EV* is minimum compensation required (that is willingness-to-accept, WTA) to go without it. When what is at stake is degradation, *CV* is minimum WTA to tolerate the degradation and *EV* is maximum WTP to avoid it.

As shown by (3.20) and (3.21), defining compensated welfare measures does not require us to assume cardinal utility. This is because these definitions are based on the notion of indifference, as represented by the equal signs in these equations, rather than on that of a utility difference, as in (3.16).

It is easy to notice that compensated welfare measures are the discrete counterparts of the compensated marginal valuations $\pi^c(\mathbf{p}, \mathbf{z}, U)$ defined in (3.12). Thus, to obtain discrete welfare measures one should integrate marginal valuations along a path w leading from $\mathbf{z}^0$ to $\mathbf{z}^1$. The difference between *CV* and *EV* is that: (1) to obtain *CV* utility is held constant at V^0 throughout the integration; whereas (2) to obtain *EV* the integration takes place with utility held constant at V^1. Therefore, the two compensated welfare measures can be evaluated as follows:

$$CV = \int_w \pi^c(\mathbf{p}, \mathbf{z}, V^0)\, d\mathbf{z} \qquad (3.22)$$

$$EV = \int_w \pi^c(\mathbf{p}, \mathbf{z}, V^1)\, d\mathbf{z} \qquad (3.23)$$

For these welfare measures to be useful they should be unique, that is: independent with respect to the particular path w that is chosen to evaluate the integral. Path-independency requires every single cross derivative $\partial \pi_j^c / \partial \pi_h^c$ of the integrand functions to be identical to its counterpart $\partial \pi_h^c / \partial \pi_j^c$ (for all j and h). Differentiating (3.12) we can transform these two derivatives into $-\partial^2 e / \partial z_j \partial z_h$ and $-\partial^2 e / \partial z_h \partial z_j$ respectively, which are identical for any continuous twice-differentiable expenditure function e (Young's theorem).[11] Hence, it is shown that compensated welfare measures are unique or path-independent; and to demonstrate this there is no need to assume constant marginal utility of income – this assumption was required above to demonstrate path-independency of the uncompensated money measure S.

Sequential Paths

Since compensated welfare measures are path-independent, any particular continuous path w may be validly chosen to evaluate the integrals in (3.22) and (3.23). So let us consider, for example, sequential paths. A sequential path is one in which individual attribute changes comprised in $\Delta \mathbf{z}$ are valued sequentially, or by steps. This means that, at each valuation step, attributes other than the one valued at this step are held constant at their final or initial levels, depending on whether or not (respectively) they have already been valued earlier in the sequence. Sequential paths can be exemplified by the path $\mathbf{z}^0 = (z_1^0, z_2^0, z_3^0, ..., z_m^0) \rightarrow (z_1^1, z_2^0, z_3^0, ..., z_m^0) \rightarrow (z_1^1, z_2^1, z_3^0, ..., z_m^0) \rightarrow$ ...... $\rightarrow (z_1^1, z_2^1, z_3^1, ..., z_m^1) = \mathbf{z}^1$. Evaluating CV along such a path yields:[12]

$$CV = \int_{z10}^{z11} \pi_1^c(\mathbf{p}, z_1, z_2^0, z_3^0, ..., z_m^0, V^0)\, dz_1 + \qquad (3.24a)$$

$$+ \int_{z20}^{z21} \pi_2^c(\mathbf{p}, z_1^1, z_2, z_3^0, ..., z_m^0, V^0)\, dz_2 + ... \qquad (3.24b)$$

$$... + \int_{zm0}^{zm1} \pi_m^c(\mathbf{p}, z_1^1, z_2^1, z_3^1, ..., z_m, V^0)\, dz_m \qquad (3.24c)$$

If we think of $\Delta \mathbf{z}$ as an improvement, each integral in (3.24) represents maximum WTP for a particular attribute change with previously valued attributes at their final levels and attributes still to be valued at their initial levels.

Specifying the valuation context for a particular attribute change within a compensated sequence such as this involves identifying the attributes that have been changed and paid for by the individual earlier in the sequence. This payment element is essential for the sequence to be a compensated one: income must be reduced at each step by the full amount of WTP for previous attribute changes, so that utility can be held constant at V^0 throughout the sequence.

Using (3.12), the integrals above are easily solved into:

$$CV = e(\mathbf{p}, z_1^0, z_2^0, z_3^0, ..., z_m^0, V^0) - e(\mathbf{p}, z_1^1, z_2^0, z_3^0, ..., z_m^0, V^0) \quad (3.25a)$$

$$+ \, e(\mathbf{p}, z_1^1, z_2^0, z_3^0, ..., z_m^0, V^0) - e(\mathbf{p}, z_1^1, z_2^1, z_3^0, ..., z_m^0, V^0) + _{...} \quad (3.25b)$$

$$..._+ \, e(\mathbf{p}, z_1^1, z_2^1, z_3^1, ..., z_m^0, V^0) - e(\mathbf{p}, z_1^1, z_2^1, z_3^1, ..., z_m^1, V^0) \quad (3.25c)$$

Note that the last term of each line and the first term of the following line cancel out. So, the long summation in (3.25) collapses into:

$$CV = e(\mathbf{p}, z_1^0, z_2^0, z_3^0, ..., z_m^0, V^0) - e(\mathbf{p}, z_1^1, z_2^1, z_3^1, ..., z_m^1, V^0) \quad (3.26)$$

$$= e(\mathbf{p}, \mathbf{z}^0, V^0) - e(\mathbf{p}, \mathbf{z}^1, V^0) = y - e(\mathbf{p}, \mathbf{z}^1, V^0)$$

From (3.26) it is possible to confirm that CV is positive for an improvement, as expenditure on market goods required to achieve utility level V^0 declines when there is a change (for better) from $\mathbf{z}^0$ to $\mathbf{z}^1$.

It is also possible to establish a parallel with the marginal case. Thus, in the discrete case, (3.26) shows that CV is the expenditure difference associated with the discrete multi-attribute change $\Delta \mathbf{z}$; likewise, as shown by (3.12), compensated marginal valuation is the variation in expenditure associated with a marginal attribute change.

Comparing (3.25) and (3.26) demonstrates that sequential valuation (in 3.25) and one-step overall valuation (in 3.26) of the same multi-attribute change $\Delta \mathbf{z}$ must yield exactly the same result.[13] This is actually a corollary of general path-independency of compensated welfare measures.

Although the value of the whole multi-attribute change $\Delta \mathbf{z}$ is unique, the sequential value of each attribute change is not unique: it depends on the particular step at which the attribute change is valued. This is easily grasped by looking at equation (3.24), where each integral represents the sequential value of a particular attribute change. Note that, to evaluate this integral, previously valued attributes are held constant at final (higher, for an improvement) levels. Thus, if these previous attributes are compensated substitutes for the attribute under valuation, then the later this attribute is valued in the sequence, the lower its sequential value is.[14]

Independent Valuation and Summation

Independent valuation of an attribute change assumes that all other attributes are held constant at their current (initial) levels. As shown by Hoehn (1991), this valuation procedure provides a biased value estimate for cases where the other attributes are changing as well. Namely, the summation of independent valuations of all attribute changes included in a multi-attribute change Δz leads to a biased value estimate for Δz as a whole. This can be easily shown. Consider the independent valuation (IV) of attribute j:

$$IV_j = \int_{zj0}^{zj1} \pi_j^c (\mathbf{p}, z_1^0, z_2^0, \dots z_j, \dots, z_m^0, V^0) \, dz_j \tag{3.27}$$

The independent valuation and summation (IVS) result is obtained by summing the independent valuations of all attribute changes included in the multi-attribute change Δz:

$$IVS = \int_{z10}^{z11} \pi_1^c (\mathbf{p}, z_1, z_2^0, z_3^0, \dots, z_m^0, V^0) \, dz_1 + \tag{3.28a}$$

$$+ \int_{z20}^{z21} \pi_2^c (\mathbf{p}, z_1^0, z_2, z_3^0, \dots, z_m^0, V^0) \, dz_2 + \dots \tag{3.28b}$$

$$\dots + \int_{zm0}^{zm1} \pi_m^c (\mathbf{p}, z_1^0, z_2^0, z_3^0, \dots, z_m, V^0) \, dz_m \tag{3.28c}$$

Note that only the first line in (3.28) is identical to the first line in (3.24). All other lines in (3.28) are different from the corresponding lines in (3.24). Therefore, the IVS result is a biased estimator for the correct CV associated with the complete multi-attribute change.

For every single line $j \neq 1$, if attributes valued previously to attribute j (that is: all $h < j$) are compensated substitutes for j, then the independent valuation of j in (3.28) will be higher than the corresponding sequential valuation in (3.24). Hence, IVS overestimates the true CV associated with the complete multi-attribute change when attributes are compensated substitutes for each other. Conversely, if attributes are compensated complements, IVS will underestimate the true CV associated with the complete multi-attribute change. The only case in which there is no IVS bias is the one where all attributes are (compensated) independent in valuation.

The IVS bias is due to the use of an integration path that is not continuous (hence not valid): notice that we value a change in z_j from z_j^0 to z_j^1 and then 'jump backwards' by considering this attribute is still at z_j^0 when valuing a change in the next attribute z_{j+1}.

Simultaneous Paths

Path-independency of compensated welfare measures enables us to explore other valid (that is continuous) integration paths other than sequential paths. Simultaneous paths are an example of such valid paths. Along simultaneous paths all attributes change simultaneously from initial to final levels. Integrating compensated marginal valuations along a simultaneous path s yields (cf. Hoehn 1991):

$$CV = \int_s \pi_1^c (\mathbf{p}, z_1, z_2, z_3, ..., z_m, V^0) \, dz_1 + \qquad (3.29a)$$

$$+ \int_s \pi_2^c (\mathbf{p}, z_1, z_2, z_3, ..., z_m, V^0) \, dz_2 + ... \qquad (3.29b)$$

$$... + \int_s \pi_m^c (\mathbf{p}, z_1, z_2, z_3, ..., z_m, V^0) \, dz_m \qquad (3.29c)$$

where the line integral in each jth line represents the value of the change in the corresponding attribute j with all other attributes ($h \neq j$) changing as well from their initial to final levels along the path s. Each one of these integrals yields the simultaneously disaggregated value of the corresponding attribute change.

3.3 THEORY TESTS BASED ON CONTINGENT VALUATION DATA

This section uses multi-attribute valuation theory developed in sections 3.1 and 3.2 to derive empirically testable predictions. Evidence from CVM studies is checked for consistency with these predictions. Theory tests like these are important at least for two reasons.

First, the validity of the CVM has been the focus of a recent debate, a significant part of which can be related to substitution effects.[15] Critics of the method[16] argue that CVM-elicited values do not behave according to the theoretical properties of economic values and therefore cannot be considered as such. On the other hand, CVM supporters[17] argue that many hypotheses refuted by critics are not implied by theory and that poor survey design explains the 'theoretical anomalies' actually found by critics.

Second, the CVM debate shows how important and difficult it is to convey to respondents the complex scenarios required by sequential or simultaneous valuation. Thus, results of particular tests can always be discarded based on possible implementation failure, which may lead to selective denial of empirical evidence aimed at preserving the theory or, alternatively, the CVM's validity claim.

Types of Theory Test

Valuation contexts such as sequential or simultaneous paths (or independent valuation and summation) are in principle reproducible in CVM scenarios. This authorises us to derive from theory predictions that can be subject to empirical test using CVM data. Different types of prediction originate different types of theory test. In this section, four types are considered: sequential additivity tests; income-effect tests; tests based on assumed substitution relationships; and tests of the relationship between the substitution effect and the income effect.

Sequential Additivity Tests

Compensated sequential paths can be specified in a CVM scenario by identifying the attribute change to be valued at each particular step as well as the other attribute changes provided at previous steps in the sequence. For the path to be compensated, it is crucial to make clear that payment for the attribute change at issue would be made on top of payments for previous attribute changes.

A result established earlier in this chapter for compensated sequential paths is that the sum of sequential values of individual attribute changes and the one-step valuation of the complete multi-attribute change should yield exactly the same figure. This prediction, which is strictly implied by theory for compensated sequences alone, provides the null hypothesis for a first type of theory test: sequential additivity tests. Using a simpler notation than that in equations (3.24) to (3.26) this hypothesis can be written as:

$$WTP\,(A) + WTP\,(B \mid A) + WTP\,(C \mid A{+}B) = WTP\,(A{+}B{+}C) \qquad (3.30)$$

where: A, B and C are the individual attribute changes; A+B+C is the complete multi-attribute change; and *WTP* $(Y \mid X)$ is maximum willingness-to-pay for Y conditional on previous delivery and payment for X.

Three valuation studies that tested the sequential additivity hypothesis are reviewed here: Diamond et al. (1993) and Magnussen (1996), both using CVM data on typical public goods, and Bateman et al. (1996), using an experiment with actual payments for a typical private good.

Diamond et al. (1993) undertook a CVM study of wilderness areas managed by the US Forest Service. These areas were described in the survey as having stricter regulations than national parks.[18] Respondents were told that there are 57 such areas in Colorado, Idaho, Montana and Wyoming, and that, although varying in size, all areas are similar with respect to *habitat* and remoteness. Nothing was said about the nature conservation interest of each particular area. It was then suggested that, to reduce the budget deficit, federal government is examining the possibility of leasing some of these areas for logging at a specified annual rate. About the impact of this decision on the landscape, respondents were only told that logging would require 'building roads and bringing in mechanical equipment'. A federal income tax surcharge was presented as an alternative way of reducing budget deficit, while keeping some areas in their pristine state.

Diamond et al. test three additivity hypotheses similar to (3.30), each one involving a sequence of two or three wilderness areas. Attributes A, B and C correspond here to three particular areas described with respect to location and size. The four CVM scenarios involved in a 3-areas sequence are described here as an illustration of the survey design.

To avoid a potential 'first area effect', preservation of area A (the first step in the sequence) was valued conditional on the fact that nine other areas would be, anyway, leased for logging. The second valuation step involves eliciting WTP for preserving area B conditional on the previous decision of leasing for logging eight other areas (the initial nine minus area A). In the third valuation step, respondents were asked to value the preservation of area C with seven other areas already earmarked for logging. The fourth scenario corresponds to the one-step valuation of the conservation of areas A, B and C altogether conditional on the previous decision of leasing for logging seven other areas. A split-sample approach was followed, with each one of the four scenarios administered to a different sub-sample.

The tests carried out by Diamond et al. using rough data show that the sum of sample means of sequentially valued areas is larger than the sample mean of the one-step valuation of the multi-area change. However, sequential additivity is only significantly rejected for the 3-areas sequence (2-tail t-test). The additivity hypothesis is rejected as well for 2-areas sequences when extreme WTP values are dropped, or when trimmed means or parametric estimators are used.

Based on these findings, Diamond et al. conclude that WTP questions do not elicit economic values, because sequentially elicited values should be additive according to theory. And if elicited WTP amounts are not economic values they cannot be used in cost–benefit analysis or in damage assessment.

These conclusions must be qualified in two ways. First, Diamond et al.'s scenarios do not exactly correspond to the four terms in (3.30), and hence the additivity hypotheses they reject are not strictly implied by theory. Second, Diamond et al.'s survey reveals sharp methodological shortcomings; thus, it is not valid to conclude that a state-of-the-art CVM survey would also get results at variance with theoretical expectations. The theoretical issue is discussed first and the survey issue next.

Diamond et al's scenario for the valuation of B (see equation 3.30) assumes that A is already preserved but not paid for by the respondent. This is because the valuation of A was carried out by a different sub-sample of respondents. (The same happens with the valuation of C, which is conditional on A and B being preserved but not necessarily paid for by the respondent.) Hence, Diamond et al.'s scenarios correspond to uncompensated sequences. As shown in section 3.2, sequential additivity depends on path-independency of welfare measures, which is a property of compensated paths alone. Thus, Diamond et al.'s hypotheses of additivity for uncompensated sequences are not strictly implied by theory. These hypotheses can only be approximately derived from theory assuming the income effect is negligible.[19]

Concerning the survey issue, Carson (1993) made it clear that 'nobody would call a telephone survey of a wilderness area state of the art' CVM practice. In a telephone survey, the time is too short and the information passed on to the respondents insufficient for them to make a clear idea of the impacts of logging on the areas. Besides, a telephone survey does not take advantage of visual aids, which would be crucial for a sample of non-users such as this.

Possibly more important for additivity testing is the way the sequence was transposed into scenarios depicting the several steps in the sequence. In the first step, respondents were asked to value A, described by location and acreage, conditional on nine other areas already earmarked for logging. As the second valuation step was to be administered to a different sub-sample, the fact of A being already preserved should be explicitly mentioned as part of the context for valuing B. However, the scenario only mentions that eight other areas (implicitly, nine minus area A) would be leased for logging. This scenario is only valid assuming that: (1) respondents perceive eight wilderness areas as different from nine in a context where 57 such areas exist; and that (2) saying 'one particular area, described by location and acreage, would be preserved' is equivalent to saying 'one less area would be leased for logging'. As shown by Hanemann (1994), using Diamond et al.'s data, this is not the case: for example, respondents are not indifferent to the size of wilderness areas.

Briefly, according to the supporters of the CVM, Diamond et al.'s survey is bad CVM practice, and therefore nothing can be inferred, in general, from it with respect to inconsistency between CVM-elicited values and theory.

All this is possibly true, but it raises an important methodological issue about sequential additivity tests. Extreme difficulties are always involved in communicating to respondents the complex scenarios implied by split-sample sequential valuation experiments. In fact, in this case, the valuation context must clearly specify the levels of goods other than the one valued by the particular sub-sample. (In usual surveys the researcher, and hopefully the respondents as well, assume other goods are at their status quo levels.) The need to describe other goods and their levels adds to the stringent requirements for a correct description of a transaction put forward by Fischhoff and Furby (1988). It also adds to the cognitive burden imposed on respondents. These added survey difficulties with split-sample sequential experiments make the results controversial, and thus may lead to selective denial of empirical evidence that is inconsistent with theory.

This methodological issue led us to look at alternative ways of testing the sequential additivity hypothesis. One such a way is to ask the same respondent to sequentially value all attribute changes in the LHS of (3.30); and then ask a separate sub-sample to value in one single step the whole multi-attribute change (as in the RHS of equation 3.30). This is the procedure followed by Magnussen (1996).

Magnussen (1996) reports on a CVM study of water quality in three rivers in Østfold, a Norwegian county. Respondents were informed about the current pollution situation in each river and were asked for maximum WTP in increased sewage taxes for a given improvement. Interviews were undertaken at the respondent's residence, so creating conditions for a complete explanation of the scenarios, as well as for the use of maps and other visual aids depicting the geographical extent, reference and target levels for the improvement.

A test of sequential additivity using a null hypothesis similar to that in (3.30) was carried out with A, B and C corresponding now to the three rivers. Respondents in one sub-sample valued sequentially the three rivers. Cleanup of river A was first valued. Respondents were then asked about WTP for B, given cleanup and full payment (at maximum WTP) for A. Eventually, they were asked to value cleanup of C, given cleanup and full payment for A and B. Summation of these sequential values yields the LHS of (3.30). Respondents in a second sub-sample gave the one-step valuation of A+B+C – the RHS of (3.30). Magnussen's scenario design is superior to Diamond et al.'s at least on two grounds. First, the previous valuation of some rivers by the same respondent implicitly (but clearly) establishes the context with respect to rivers already improved at each valuation step. Second, the fact of respondents paying on top of what they have bid for previous rivers establishes a compensated sequence, for which additivity is directly implied by theory with no need for further assumptions on the size of the income effect.

With respect to results, the sum of sequential valuations is larger than the one-step valuation of the three rivers. However, the difference is not statistically significant. Thus, sequential additivity cannot be ruled out. This conclusion should be qualified, as: (1) small sample size is limiting the statistical power of the test; (2) respondents were allowed to review previous bids after being informed about the sum implied by their bids for each river.

Bateman et al.'s (1996) paper is based on an experiment designed to test the sequential additivity hypothesis using ordinary market commodities (vouchers for parts of a restaurant meal) and actual payments. Valuations for vouchers were elicited using a Becker–DeGroot–Marschak mechanism. This works in the following way: suppose the case of WTP to buy a voucher; the participant submits a bid; a price is then randomly selected; the transaction takes place (at this price) only if the price is not above the submitted bid. This mechanism is incentive-compatible in that it is in the participant's self-interest to bid precisely with maximum WTP for the good.

Two goods were valued in the Bateman et al.'s experiments: a voucher for a main course meal (good A) and a voucher for a dessert plus cream and a coffee (good B). Both vouchers were usable in a particular restaurant, which was familiar to most participants, and hence both correspond to ordinary private goods for which past market experience was available.

In order to keep incentive-compatibility, the same individual was not asked to value successively A and B|A (for sequence A→B). Therefore, two sub-samples were established in connection with the sequence A→B: (1) participants who valued A and independently valued A+B; (2) participants who received A free and were then asked to value B|A. WTP (B|A) was directly elicited from the latter and implicitly obtained from the former as WTP (A+B) – WTP (A). Sequential additivity was then implicitly stated for the sequence A→B as a null hypothesis:

$$\text{WTP (A+B)} - \text{WTP (A)} = \text{directly elicited WTP (B|A)}.$$

The counterpart of this null hypothesis for the sequence B→A was also tested for. Both hypotheses were rejected. Theoretically inconsistent non-additivity was therefore demonstrated. Apparently, this conclusion should be qualified, as Bateman et al.'s sequences are uncompensated ones (first voucher given free to participants), for which additivity is not immediately implied by theory. However, experimental design and modelling procedures were used which ensure (or demonstrate) that the income effect is actually negligible, and thus that the sequences are approximately compensated.

Taken together, the evidence from the three studies discussed so far is mixed with respect to theoretical expectations. On the one hand, a weak conclusion in favour of theoretically inconsistent non-additivity is warranted, as both Diamond et al. and Bateman et al. rejected the additivity hypothesis, and Magnussen failed to do so probably due to the small size of samples she used. On the other hand, the moment of the Diamond et al.'s results is limited by poor survey practice. The fact that the less objectionable rejection of additivity (Bateman et al.'s) was secured precisely in a non-hypothetical situation, involving familiar market consumption goods, has important consequences for the CVM debate, which are further explored in section 3.5.

Evidence in favour of non-additivity of sequentially valued goods is important because additivity tests represent a crucial contest between Hicksian demand theory and alternative explanations for people's valuations in a CVM context. This is a crucial contest of theories for three reasons: (1) if violations of sequential adding-up are proven in a survey 'there is no way to reconcile that survey with consumer theory' (Diamond 1996: 66); (2) alternative explanations, such as 'warm glow giving', can be used to predict sequential non-additivity; and (3) no alternative explanation accounts for sequential additivity in a simpler way than Hicksian theory does.

This contest of theories requires both an alternative to Hicksian theory and empirical predictions from this alternative theory. For additivity tests, the alternative explanation has been related to 'warm glow giving', a concept referring to the work of Andreoni (1989 and 1990). Andreoni presents a theoretical model of individual donations for public goods, in which the motivation for giving has two components: (1) the overall level of the public good, resulting from the individual's as well as from others' donations; and (2) the amount of the individual's donation itself. The former is the altruistic component of giving, as it relates to the level of collective enjoyment of the public good; the latter reflects egoistic motivations for giving – like strategic moral conformity, or simply a desire for a 'warm glow'. Andreoni's individual is, in general, impurely altruistic.

Kahneman and Knetsch (1992a) suggested that the desire to acquire moral satisfaction by contributing to good causes (or 'warm glow giving') could explain their findings of insensitivity of WTP to the scope of the public good, because 'moral satisfaction could be expected to be about the same for an inclusive cause and for representative subsets of it' (pp. 64–5).

Diamond et al. (1993) show that a scope-insensitive warm-glow component implies sequential non-additivity in split-sample experiments; this result is used to explain the non-additivity found in their study of wilderness areas.

On the other hand, moral satisfaction of giving for public goods cannot be invoked to explain Bateman et al.'s (1996) results on ordinary private goods with actual payments. Here, a broader revision of economic theory would be warranted if results such as these were repeatedly replicated in the future. Although Bateman et al. do not propose an alternative theory, they quote parallel results by other authors. For instance, Weber at al. (1988) used multi-attribute utility techniques (applied to the evaluation of a future job for graduate students) to investigate the possibility of changing evaluations by manipulating the attribute structure framing the evaluative tasks. They found that the more an attribute is spelled out in detail – by splitting it into sub-attributes – the more weight is given to this attribute. This attribute-splitting effect could explain why sequential valuation of two attributes yields a higher figure than one-step valuation: the former makes attributes more salient for the respondent. This perception effect is quite plausible, even for usual market behaviour, where it provides the basis for a host of advertising techniques.[20] The problem is with ordinary consumer theory, which models choices as if perceptions of quantity and quality of the goods were immediate, i.e.: as if only preferences (not perceptions) were subjective.

Income-Effect Tests

Income-effect tests are based on comparisons between compensated and uncompensated valuation paths. Assuming attributes are not inferior goods, it is implied by theory that WTP for a particular attribute change elicited in an uncompensated path should not be smaller than WTP for the same change elicited in a compensated path.[21] The reason for this is easier to grasp with sequential paths, and hence income-effect tests are first explained in this context.

It was discussed above how to establish compensated sequences within a CVM survey. Conveying uncompensated sequences involves a slightly different scenario in which respondents are first informed about attribute changes that would be given free and are then asked to value another attribute change conditional on that previous delivery. What is distinctive about this scenario is that the respondent would not be required to pay his full WTP for the former attribute changes; hence, utility (real income) would rise along the sequence. This income effect defines the sequence as an uncompensated one.

Hicksian theory predicts that the uncompensated sequential value of an attribute change cannot be lower than the value of this change elicited at the same step of the corresponding compensated sequence. This prediction is implied by (3.15), assuming a non-negative income effect, and provides the null hypothesis for an income-effect test.

Notice that, differently from sequential additivity tests, which are strictly implied by theory, income-effect tests are based on the auxiliary assumption of attributes being not inferior goods (for which the income effect would be negative). This assumption is probably valid for most environmental and recreational goods.

The same type of income-effect test can be run with simultaneous paths. Simultaneously disaggregated values of individual attribute changes as in (3.29) have been obtained in studies where respondents were asked to allocate a share of the value previously elicited for the whole multi-attribute change to a component attribute change.[22]

According to Carson and Mitchell (1995), the valuation question for the component attribute change at stake is usually poorly framed. In fact, it is difficult to make clear whether the other components would be available, and whether (and how much) the respondent would be paying for them. Provided respondents interpret this valuation question as 'how much less the complete change is valued if the component attribute change at stake is not included' (Carson and Mitchell 1995), the value elicited for the component will correspond to a value disaggregated along a compensated simultaneous path.

In compensated simultaneous paths, all the other components of the package are being simultaneously provided and paid for by the respondent at their full reservation price. These payments completely offset the income effect (only substitution effects occur in general along compensated paths), which means that utility is held constant along the path.

The uncompensated simultaneous path corresponds to a CVM scenario in which the respondent is led to perceive the other elements of the multi-attribute change as gratuitously (and simultaneously) supplied. Provided the uncompensated simultaneous path is correctly perceived by respondents, and that attributes are not inferior goods, theory implies that the value of an attribute change disaggregated along an uncompensated simultaneous path is not lower than the value of the same change disaggregated along the corresponding compensated simultaneous path. This is the null hypothesis for income-effect tests using simultaneous paths.

A paper by Hoevenagel (1996) and another study quoted by Hoevenagel (Hoen and Winther 1991) seem to be the only studies providing results that can be used to comment on income-effect tests using simultaneous paths, though this possibility is not acknowledged by the authors themselves.[23] Hoevenagel used a mail survey of the general public to value a package of six environmental programmes, as well as one of the individual programmes in this package. The six programmes consist of specified improvements by 2015 in six environmental dimensions: greenhouse effect, depletion of the ozone layer, deforestation, acid rain, water pollution and the animal manure problem. Improvements were described with respect to a baseline corresponding to the continuation of current policies. Respondents were told that improvements would result from measures taken by polluting companies, which would lead to higher prices.

Only some results presented in Hoevenagel's study are relevant to comment on income-effect tests. These correspond to three separate samples, which received three different scenarios. Respondents in sample III were informed about the complete package of six programmes and valued this package; they were then asked to allocate a share of this value to the acid rain programme alone. Respondents in sample V were only informed about the acid rain programme and valued this programme. Respondents in sample VI were informed about the complete package (using exactly the same information conveyed to respondents in sample III) but were not asked to value it; they were then asked to value the acid rain programme alone.

These scenarios imply different paths for the valuation of the acid rain programme. Thus, all programmes would be simultaneously delivered and paid for by respondents in sample III, which establishes a compensated simultaneous path. On the other hand, all programmes appear to be simultaneously delivered but not paid for by respondents in sample VI, which creates an uncompensated simultaneous path. Therefore, we can easily re-interpret Hoevenagel's results by establishing the following correspondence: (1) sample III yielded the compensated simultaneously disaggregated valuation (*csv*); sample V, the independent valuation (*iv*); and sample VI, the uncompensated simultaneously disaggregated valuation (*usv*) of the acid rain programme.

According to our null hypothesis, *usv* ≥ *csv*. Hoevenagel actually shows that *usv* is significantly larger than *csv*.[24] In the absence of an adequate theory, this result surprised Hoevenagel; however, it somehow confirms Hicksian theory by not rejecting the null hypothesis in an experiment in which the alternative result (*usv* < *csv*) is inconsistent with this theory (always assuming a non-negative income effect).

Hoevenagel also fails to reject the null hypothesis *usv* = *iv*, which implies that the other programmes are not necessarily substitutes in utility for the acid rain programme, despite the fact they are compensated substitutes in valuation for this programme (because *csv* < *iv*). Although not acknowledged by the author, this is an interesting illustration for a result derived earlier in this chapter (section 3.1): attributes need not be substitutes in utility to be compensated substitutes in valuation. As shown by Santos (1997), Hoevenagel's results, taken together with evidence from eight other embedding studies, are supportive of income effects that are strong enough to produce compensated substitutes in valuation from non-substitutes in utility. This size of the income effect is at variance with the much smaller income effects that can be inferred from the estimates of income-flexibility of WTP arrived at in most CVM studies.

The evidence presented here is somewhat limited by practical survey difficulties with simultaneous valuation paths. One of these is that respondents are only given detailed information about the attribute at stake after they have already valued the whole multi-attribute change including it. The effects of this added information on the comparability between the values given for the whole and for the part are not well known.[25]

Tests Based on Assumed Substitution Relationships

Assuming attributes are compensated substitutes in valuation, at least three other predictions can also be deduced from Hicksian theory:

1   the later an attribute is valued in a WTP sequence, the lower it is valued;[26]
2   the one-step (or other valid) valuation of a multi-attribute change is exceeded by the independent valuation and summation (IVS) result;
3   the compensated simultaneously disaggregated valuation of an individual attribute change is exceeded by the corresponding independent valuation.

(1) and (2) have already been established in section 3.2, and (3) refers to the phenomenon Kahneman and Knetsch (1992b) call 'regular embedding'.

Evidence in support of (1) can be found in Majid et al. (1983), Magnussen (1996), Mitchell and Carson (1989), and Hoehn (1991). Magnussen's (1996) and Hoehn and Loomis's (1993) results are supportive of (2). Many embedding studies, such as Kahneman and Knetsch (1992a), Magnussen (1992), Kemp and Maxwell (1993), Loomis et al. (1993), and Hoevenagel (1996), present evidence in favour of (3).

CVM supporters, such as Hoevenagel and Loomis et al., are quite happy with these results because they are consistent with theory, and they are right. Regular embedding, for example, can be 'explained' by ordinary substitution effects. On the other hand, critics of the CVM, such as Kahneman and Knetsch, claim the method produces arbitrary results, as regular embedding would show that alternative measurements of the same object yield astonishingly different results. Randall and Hoehn (1996) reply saying that what is valued in regular embedding tests is the same good but in a different context with respect to substitutes; and nothing in economic theory says value (the object under measurement) should be context-independent. However, as Kahneman and Knetsch (1992b) pointed out, 'the critical task is not to show that substitution (...) effects could produce the result, but to provide a plausible account, preferably supported by evidence, of their role in particular cases.' (p. 93). This seems quite difficult for all of the above three predictions, as none is strictly implied by theory unless attributes are independently shown to be compensated substitutes for each other.[27] Thus, predictions of compensated substitution relationships between attributes must be independently produced if a test of a hypothesis such as those presented above is to be considered a strict theory test. Different ways to anticipate compensated substitutability are systematically reviewed in what follows.

Prevalence of compensated substitution is strictly implied by theory when there is a large number of projects under evaluation. Using a single-household general equilibrium model, Hoehn and Randall (1989) investigated whether substitution and complementarity would cancel out in these large-number situations, and showed that this is not the case. As the number of projects becomes large, the IVS approach overstates the one-step valuation of the entire project portfolio,[28] so showing that substitution prevails. However, substitution may not characterise all pair-wise relationships between projects. Therefore, Hoehn and Randall's method does not apply to predicting the sign of each pair-wise substitution relationship (which is required to interpret tests of the three predictions above as strict theory tests).

Lancaster's (1966) theory of demand for attributes can be used to anticipate the degree of substitutability between goods. Majid et al. (1983) used this strategy in their study of substitutability between parks within a park system in New South Wales (Australia). They were interested in the marginal value of particular new parks as increments to the existing park system. Parks were specified as bundles of features comprising natural attractions and man-made recreational facilities. A household production frame was used, in which individuals combine public-good parks' features with marketed commodities in their activities. Activities and parks' features generate characteristics, which enter as the direct arguments of the utility function. New parks with features already existing in current parks cannot supply new characteristics but may provide opportunity for substitution between activities, so that the same characteristics are yielded at lower travel cost. On the other hand, new parks with unique features yield the possibility of producing new characteristics in addition to providing opportunity for cost-saving shifts between activities. If we assume diminishing marginal utility of characteristics produced from non-unique features, then: 'as the number of parks already in the system increases, WTP for adding a park with only common features diminishes more rapidly than WTP for adding a park with common and unique features' (p.383). This hypothesis was empirically confirmed in Majid et al.'s (1983) study, by significantly rejecting its null version.

The application of the household production frame requires that the goods at stake can be conceived as attribute bundles. Hence, this frame is not applicable, for example, to the case-studies in Part Three of this book, where what is at issue is substitution between individual attributes rather than between bundles of attributes.[29]

Hoehn (1991) used a different approach to predict substitution in valuation between changes in air quality at two separate places: the Grand Canyon and Chicago metropolitan area. Hoehn implicitly used the theoretical relationship in (3.15), which, as noted in section 3.1, authorises some predictions on the observable but difficult-to-anticipate sign of the compensated substitution effect to be made, provided more intuitive predictions can be made about substitution in utility. Hoehn (1991) uses the concept of two recreational activities spatially separated in consumption. For this case, the household production frame suggests that the utility function is additively separable on the activities, and thus environmental attributes used by different activities are independent in utility.[30] Hence, according to (3.15), these attributes must be compensated substitutes in valuation. Hoehn's results strongly support this prediction: the value of a visibility improvement programme for the Grand Canyon significantly declines from \$83 to \$11 when this programme is valued after a visibility improvement in Chicago.

Although spatial separation in consumption may lead to independence in utility, and hence to compensated substitution in valuation, 'complementarity is possible if environmental services are tied together by a specific consumption activity' (Hoehn 1991: 298). Hoehn and Loomis (1993) investigated this possibility in a study of substitution effects between environmental programmes for the San Joaquin Valley in California. The fact of the several programmes affecting environmental resources located within the same region created prospects for complementarity in valuation, because of: (1) joint consumption of environmental services within the same region; and (2) perceived positive cross-programme productivity effects. However, Hoehn and Loomis found that all programmes were compensated substitutes for each other and concluded that substitution seems to prevail in the intra-regional case, as well as in the inter-regional case studied by Hoehn (1991).

This conclusion supports the prediction by Hoehn (1991) of a generalised prevalence of compensated substitution in valuation: 'substitution occurs consistently across all valuation contexts and arises because of the mathematical structure of constrained optimisation' (p.293). In fact compensated substitution is expected to be somewhat more probable than compensated independence or complementarity because many goods that are independent or complementary in utility can be compensated substitutes in valuation provided the income effect is strong enough. Equation (3.15) and comments following it provide the theoretical rationale for this expectation.

Hoehn's prediction does not provide the null hypothesis for a strict test of theory because of its non-prohibitive nature: prevalence of substitution does not rule out the occurrence of complementarity in some cases. However, showing that substitution actually prevails across valuation contexts is somehow supportive of the theory.

Tests of the Relationship Substitution Effect–Income Effect

The theoretic relationship presented in (3.15) and comments following this equation provide the null hypothesis for a different type of theory tests. Equation (3.15) enables us to establish a relationship between, on the one hand, the sign of substitution in utility and, on the other hand, the comparative size of the substitution and the income effects. Thus, it enables us to test whether the observable sizes of the substitution and the income effects are compatible with an intuitive prediction of the sign of substitution in utility. The spirit of this type of test is in keeping with Kahneman and Knetsch's (1992b) suggestion of proceeding by more thoroughly accounting (and testing) for the actual role of substitution effects, rather than stopping the research by merely acknowledging that the observed results could have been produced by substitution effects.

It is possible to illustrate how a test of the relationship between the substitution and the income effects operates using Hoehn's (1991) Grand Canyon–Chicago data. As seen above, Hoehn independently predicted that attributes are independent in utility, which implies they are uncompensated 'independents' in valuation. Hence, the LHS of (3.15) is equal to zero. This means the income effect must exactly offset the (compensated) substitution effect. Therefore, the $71.7 (87 per cent) decline in the value given for the Grand Canyon programme, when valued after the Chicago one, should be completely due to the fact of respondents having already implicitly paid $179 for the Chicago programme. A very strong income effect is implied by these results. Using the average annual income of Hoehn's sample (about $27,000), it is as if a 0.7 per cent reduction in income (the $179 payment for the Chicago programme) alone reduced WTP for the Grand Canyon by 87 per cent. Notice that Hoevenagel's results, as worked out by Santos (1997), imply a similarly large income effect. These large income effects seem inconsistent with the income-flexibility of WTP estimated in many CVM studies, which is usually smaller than 1.0 (cf. Kriström and Riera 1996).

To make these results consistent with theory, it is possible to claim that estimating the income-flexibility of WTP from cross-section data on WTP and income (as in CVM studies) is an invalid procedure to obtain the intra-individual income-flexibility parameter in (3.15). There are two ways to support this contention. One is to claim a marked divergence between the income parameter in (3.15), which is the income derivative of the uncompensated marginal valuation function, and the parameter estimated from CVM data, which is its compensated counterpart.[31] The other is to assume respondents' valuations refer to an incomplete multi-stage budgeting context in which long-term (and other) commitments considerably reduce discretionary income.[32] In this case, specifying income in CVM-WTP models as average annual income would lead to specification error and hence to biased estimates of the true income-flexibility parameter in (3.15).

3.4 A MULTI-ATTRIBUTE VALUATION FUNCTION

This section builds the multi-attribute valuation function to be estimated from CVM data in the case-studies in Part Three of this book. It discusses model specification as well as model-based predictions and theory tests.

Model Specification

Consider there are three possible landscape conservation programmes for a particular area. Each programme aims at reaching target levels with respect to some landscape attributes as opposed to the baseline levels that would occur without the programme. A conservation scheme is defined as a combination of the three basic programmes and can be represented as a vector (P_1, P_2, P_3) where each P_i is a dummy variable indicating whether programme i is to be included in the scheme.

WTP for any possible conservation scheme (P_1, P_2, P_3) is given by the *CV* measure for the implied discrete multi-attribute change as represented in (3.26). Thus, the multi-attribute valuation function is: $WTP (P_1, P_2, P_3) = y - e (P_1, P_2, P_3, V^0)$.[33] V^0 is maximum achievable utility with the baseline programme vector $(0, 0, 0)$, corresponding to no conservation at all, and with current income, y. Thus we have $V^0 = V (0, 0, 0, y)$, and the multi-attribute valuation function becomes:

$$WTP (P_1, P_2, P_3, y) = y - e [P_1, P_2, P_3, V(0, 0, 0, y)] \qquad (3.31)$$

All variables (WTP, P_1, P_2, P_3, y) can be observed (or set by design) in a CVM survey. To estimate (3.31) from cross-section data, it is convenient to introduce a vector **c** of preference variables as an additional argument of the valuation function, so that differences across individuals can be controlled for. Hoehn's (1991) method for specifying multi-attribute valuation functions to be estimated from CVM data was followed here. A second-order Taylor series expansion was used for locally approximating the actual valuation function around the point $(0, 0, 0, \bar{y}, \bar{c})$ where $\bar{y}$ is average income and $\bar{c}$ is the vector of sample averages for the preference variables.

The known theoretical properties of WTP for multi-attribute changes constrain the valuation function to be equal to zero for baseline levels of the attributes, which requires: (1) the intercept to be null, and (2) income and preference variables to enter the model only as interactions with (P_1, P_2, P_3).

This yields the simplified empirical model:

$$WTP(P_1, P_2, P_3, y, \mathbf{c}) = (P_1, P_2, P_3)\,\beta \qquad (3.32)$$
$$+ (1/2)\,(P_1, P_2, P_3)\,\mathbf{D}\,(P_1, P_2, P_3)' + (P_1, P_2, P_3)\,\mu\,(y - \bar{y})$$
$$+ (\mathbf{c} - \bar{\mathbf{c}})'\,\mathbf{X}\,(P_1, P_2, P_3)' + u$$
$$= \mathbf{x}'\rho + u$$

where: ρ is a column vector comprising all parameters to be estimated (that is, the set $\{\beta, \mathbf{D}, \mu, \mathbf{X}\}$); $\mathbf{x}$ is a vector comprising all explanatory variables plus the relevant interactions; and u is a random term with 0 mean and unknown dispersion. The compact representation, $\mathbf{x}'\rho + u$ means the model is linear in all parameters (but not in all variables).

The interpretation for the parameters is the following:

1   β is a 3x1 vector including the first-order components of the marginal valuations of each programme;
2   $\mathbf{D}$ is a 3x3 substitution matrix, in which off-diagonal elements are the compensated substitution effects between programmes and diagonal elements are the second-order components of the marginal valuations of each programme;
3   μ is a 3x1 vector of marginal effects of income on WTP for each programme;
4   $\mathbf{X}$ is a matrix including the marginal effects of preference variables on WTP for each programme.

Diagonal elements of $\mathbf{D}$ cannot be estimated in this context, as the dummy specification used for each element of (P_1, P_2, P_3) implies that the square of each P_i is collinear with P_i.[34] The zero-intercept constraint, as well as another specification hypothesis (that of a possible third-order interaction term) are empirically tested in the case-studies in Part Three of this book.

The model in (3.32) permits each off-diagonal element of $\mathbf{D}$ to take negative, zero or positive values, which allows for either compensated substitution, independence or complementarity in valuation between programmes to emerge from the analysis. According to Hoehn (1991), this is an advantage of the Taylor series approach over alternative functional forms such as the Cobb–Douglas or the constant elasticity of substitution models.

Model-Based Predictions: Sequential Values and Substitution Effects

Sequential values of each programme and compensated substitution effects between programmes can be predicted with the model (3.32) in a quite straightforward way.

Average sequential valuations of each programme are obtained by taking the differences between average WTP amounts for the appropriate schemes. For example, the average sequential value of P1 when this is valued after P2 is given by:

$$WTP[P1 \mid (0,1,0)] = WTP\,(1,1,0) - WTP\,(0,1,0) \qquad (3.33)$$

Differences between the appropriate sequential values of a particular programme secure the compensated substitution effects between this and other programmes. For example,

$$WTP[P1 \mid (0,1,0)] - WTP[P1 \mid (0,0,0)] \qquad (3.34)$$
$$= WTP\,(1,1,0) - WTP\,(0,1,0) - WTP\,(1,0,0)$$

gives us the effect of P2 on the valuation of P1.

As we are interested in average figures for sequential values and substitution effects, all predictions from the model are to be computed using sample averages for income and preference variables.

Note that all predictions of sequential values and substitution effects involve linear combinations of WTP, which is, in turn, linear in all parameters. Thus, the estimated variance of each individual prediction can be easily computed, using matrix algebra, from the variance–covariance matrix of the parameter estimates. This is very useful for interval prediction as well as for hypothesis testing.

Model-Based Theory Tests

The model in (3.32) provides us with all parameters that are required to test hypotheses about, for example, the sign of the substitution effects or the magnitude of the IVS bias. All of these tests are undertaken in the case-studies in Part Three of this book. So, let us focus now on a particular test of the theoretical relationship between the income and the substitution effects to be carried out as well in Part Three. For this purpose, consider a sequence in which P1 is valued after P2. In this case, the RHS of (3.15) is $\partial \pi_1^c / \partial P_2 + \partial \pi_1 / \partial y . \pi_2^c$.

All of these terms can be estimated from model (3.32):

1   the substitution effect in (3.34) gives us (the discrete counterpart of) $\partial \pi_1^c / \partial P_2$;
2   *WTP* (0,1,0), a simple prediction from the model, yields π_2^c;
3   μ_1, which is the marginal effect of income on WTP for P1, gives us an approximate[35] estimate for $\partial \pi_1 / \partial y$.

As seen in section 3.1, the sign of the LHS of (3.15) is equal to the sign of substitution in utility between P1 and P2, which, in some cases, can be independently predicted on an intuitive basis. For example, as suggested earlier, the characteristic attributes of a cherished landscape tend to be complements rather than substitutes in utility. This is precisely what happens with the case-studies in Part Three, and hence we would expect the LHS of (3.15) to be non-negative in these particular cases. Thus, we can compute the difference $\partial \pi_1^c / \partial P_2 + \partial \pi_1 / \partial y \, . \, \pi_2^c$, using the estimated WTP model, and then test the null hypothesis of this difference being non-negative in accordance with theoretical (plus intuitive) expectations.

3.5   TESTING THEORY OR THE VALIDITY OF THE CVM?

In CVM validity tests, it should always be checked whether the results that happen to be inconsistent with theory are mere artefacts of the method or legitimate empirical evidence. This is an essential prerequisite for any verdict on the validity of the method or its particular application.

Therefore, empirical evidence such as that presented by Bateman et al. (1996), who found non-additivity of sequentially valued goods, is crucial in that this evidence is drawn from a context characterised by actual payments, familiar private goods and individuals' past purchase experience (cf. section 3.3). This throws new light on the CVM validity debate. Critics of this method have used some particular characteristics of the CVM to explain 'theoretical anomalies' that have been found in particular CVM studies. The hypothetical character of the payments (Navrud 1992), lack of familiarity with the goods, and scarce past experience with purchasing environmental improvements have all been invoked to explain these 'anomalies' and to qualify the applicability of the method.[36] More recently, the validity of CVM applications to goods in which non-use values prevail was strongly disputed in several Exxon-sponsored studies (Hausman 1993). On the other hand, Kahneman and Knetsch (1992a) argued that the dividing line seems not to be between goods having use values and goods with only non-use values, but 'between public goods for which private purchase is conceivable and other goods for which it is not...' (p.69). All these distinctions are questioned by results like Bateman et al.'s: it is as if 'theoretical anomalies' were expanding themselves from hypothetical CVM data on public goods to the field of actual payments for ordinary consumption goods. As long as similar results can be replicated in future research, the validity of economic theory to explain ordinary consumption and valuation behaviour is brought into question. Besides, it is not clear why a debatable theory should be used, as it currently is, as the standard for so called tests of theoretical validity of the CVM.

So far, the generality of results such as Bateman et al.'s is not well established, although similar results have been quoted. Hence, what has been argued here can be no more than speculation. However, it points to the typical attitude of economists of trying to ensure themselves that the world is behaving according to the theory, instead of actively searching for empirically refuting theories in a healthier Popperian mood (Blaug 1980).

As acknowledged by Hanemann (1996), economists 'are people who spend their time pondering whether things that are observed to happen in practice could possibly happen in theory' (p.38) This sceptical attitude towards empirical evidence expresses itself in terms like the 'Grand Canyon anomaly' (Diamond et al. 1993) and explains why so much effort is put in testing the theoretical validity of the CVM. This focus on theoretical validity tests alone implied that too little effort has been devoted to using the CVM as a method for testing economic theory.

Note that both validity and theory tests are carried out through formally identical hypothesis tests. In CVM validity tests, the hypothesis is assumed true because it is implied by theory, and hence rejecting the hypothesis is interpreted as a failure of the method in producing behaviours that conform with theory. On the other hand, if the test is interpreted as a theory test, the hypothesis must be subject to empirical test precisely because it is only based on theory; hence, if the method is assumed valid, rejecting the hypothesis is interpreted as evidence against the theory. For an example in which hypothesis tests are interpreted as tests of the theory see Majid et al. (1983). This is a good example of how a CVM-based study can be advantageously conducted to choose between two alternative theories of valuation behaviour, in a context involving substitution effects.

In this book, empirical tests are sometimes interpreted as validity tests. Validity tests are relevant because the CVM debate is practically important (in that it influences future prospects for the method) and because the validity of a method does not automatically ensure the validity of all of its particular applications. On other occasions in this book, empirical tests are explicitly interpreted as tests of economic theory.

Concerning tests of theory, it is still important to make clear whether we are testing the formal assumption of utility maximisation or substantive assumptions about preferences and constraints faced by the individuals. A good example of this problem is to be found in the interpretation of tests of sensitivity of WTP to the scope of valued goods. Scope-sensitivity tests are generally interpreted as tests of consistency with theory, because theory supposedly predicts that 'more of a good will always be better'. However, scope-sensitivity is a maintained assumption of theory rather than a proper theoretical prediction. Maintained assumptions can generally be identified with some common-sense expectations:

> Like many arguments in economics, the central feature of [this] debate concerns a common-sense empirical relationship economists expect to find in choice behaviour. In particular, if an individual is confronted with two quantities of the same good, say A and B where A > B, and the good has strictly positive marginal utility, then the individual should be willing to pay more for A than for B. (Carson and Mitchell 1995: 156).

Of course manipulating the maintained assumptions will change theoretical predictions, and so it can be argued, as Carson and Mitchell (1995) do, that 'more of a good' should imply something that is actually perceived by respondents as a significant improvement they care about. Likewise, nothing in the theory implies that utility functions should always be continuous[37] or that local satiation is not possible (Carson and Mitchell 1995). Using these new maintained assumptions, the theory does not even prohibit the occurrence of complete scope-insensitivity under some circumstances.

All this reveals a serious problem: if economic theory does not prohibit some states of the world to occur, then it is not empirically testable; what we are testing in these cases are the very assumptions on which predictions are based. As the previous example makes clear, maintained assumptions often concern the characteristics of the utility function; they may also concern the constraints faced by individuals. For tests of the maintained assumptions to be valid, the way testable predictions are derived from assumptions must be an acceptable procedure. Here economic theory (utility maximisation) is only used as an accepted logical way to derive empirically testable predictions from maintained assumptions about the utility function and the constraints. If we accept this new approach, empirical research will be more about exploring the properties of individuals' preferences and the particular constraints they face, than about testing theory. This would perhaps deny the scientific status to utility theory: this theory would be only a methodological device to explore people's preferences. Although more modest by scientific patterns, this new approach probably provides a clearer and more honest description of much of the empirical research in the valuation literature. This approach may also constitute a promising one in exploring issues concerning people's preferences for landscapes or the constraints people face when valuing landscapes. Examples of such issues are: whether attributes of the same landscape tend to be complements in utility; or whether incomplete multi-stage budgeting is a good description for the income constraint in choices involving landscapes.

NOTES

1. The sign ' is used for transposed vectors and matrices.
2. Individuals may incur implicit costs, such as travel cost, to use a landscape. However, this is different from purchasing landscape attribute changes, as the individual is only buying access to a given landscape.
3. Differently from typical rationed goods, landscape attributes are usually non-excludable and non-rival in consumption, that is: they are public goods. Most large-scale landscapes are among the finest textbook examples of pure public goods. As this has no practical implications for modelling choice at the individual level, the analogy with zero-priced rationed goods is retained here.
4. These properties of preferences have been explained by many authors since Hicks (1956); for a textbook presentation, see Varian (1978).
5. Some sanctions for wrong behaviour are indirectly provided when individuals participate in markets for commodities x_i (such as travel cost components) that are related to some of the z_js. Consider, for example, the case of an individual who regrets having travelled too far for a disappointingly vulgar landscape.
6. As usual, the notation $V_\mathbf{p}$ represents the vector comprising the partial derivatives of V with respect to all prices.
7. Note, however, that this result depends on assuming constant marginal utility of income. Moreover, the definition of substitution in utility is only meaningful in a world of cardinal utility. Both of these assumptions are clearly Marshallian in flavour.
8. $\partial \pi / \partial y$ is positive for normal goods; and from the properties of the utility function (namely, strictly increasing in $\mathbf{z}$) it is possible to show that π_h^c is strictly positive as well (Santos 1997).
9. Besides, a cardinal interpretation of utility is required for the difference on the RHS of (3.16) to make sense.
10. For a fuller explanation of the path-independency conditions cf. Johansson (1987).
11. These properties of the expenditure function are ensured by the properties initially specified for the utility function (cf. Santos 1997).
12. Adopting the particular order $(1, 2, ..., m)$ for the attributes, we are still considering sequential paths in general because attributes' indices are purely arbitrary.
13. Hoehn (1991) used this method to establish this identity between sequential and one-step overall valuation of the complete multi-attribute change.
14. This is due to the fact of more substitute attributes at higher levels shifting downwards the integrand (marginal valuation) functions in (3.24). The opposite happens when previously valued attributes are complements for the attribute at issue: the later this attribute is valued in the sequence, the higher it is valued. If previously valued attributes are substitutes but the change represents a degradation, then the later an attribute change is valued in the sequence, the higher (in modulus) it is valued. This is because attributes are now being reduced; and the (negative) welfare effect of a decline in the level of an attribute grows with scarcity of substitutes.
15. The purpose of this section is not to present a comprehensive review of the CVM debate but to draw pieces of empirical evidence from this debate, which are relevant for testing the

theory presented in sections 3.1 and 3.2. Hence, issues that occupy a significant part of the literature on the CVM debate, such as perfect embedding or scope-insensitivity (Kahneman and Knetsch 1992b; Desvousges et al. 1993; Fisher 1996; Carson and Mitchell 1993 and 1995; and Carson et al. 1996), are not discussed here.

16. See e.g. Kahneman (1986), Kahneman and Knetsch (1992a and b), Diamond et al. (1993), and Desvousges et al. (1993).

17. See e.g. Smith (1992), Hanemann (1994), and Carson and Mitchell (1995).

18. Access is limited to hiking, camping, fishing and hunting; roads, commercial development, mechanical equipment and other improvements are prohibited

19. A negligible income effect ensures the uncompensated sequence is approximately compensated (proof can be obtained from equation 3.15). This leads Diamond et al. to try showing that the income effect is actually small enough, by quoting the fact of most CVM studies producing estimates of the income-flexibility of WTP in the range 0.2–0.6. However, as we shall see below, the correspondence between income effect and income-flexibility of WTP estimated across respondents is open to question. This seems to be the point Duckworth (1993) was trying to make in his comment to Diamond et al.'s paper; this point somewhat weakens Diamond et al.'s conclusions.

20. For an example of divergent perceptions of an environmental public good, water quality, see Hanemann (1984a).

21. Note that, with WTA measures, the income effect runs precisely the other way round, and hence the inverse prediction is implied by theory in this case.

22. See e.g. Kahneman and Knetsch (1992a), Magnussen (1992), Kemp and Maxwell (1993), Willis et al. (1993), and Loomis et al. (1993).

23. No references seem to exist in the literature which provide relevant results for income-effect tests using sequential paths. Some studies, such as Diamond et al. (1993), report results on uncompensated sequential paths but not on the corresponding compensated paths, which would be required to undertake the comparison.

24. At the 0.0005 level of probability, two-tail t test.

25. Cf. Smith (1992), and Hanemann (1994).

26. The opposite is true for WTA sequences (see e.g. Randall and Hoehn 1996).

27. Hence, empirical tests of the three predictions above cannot be taken as strict tests of Hicksian theory. The opposite predictions would have been warranted by theory had the attributes been assumed compensated complements.

28. This is because the one-step approach is bounded above by the productive capacity of the economy, whereas IVS is not. Hoehn and Randall's result stresses the potential for 'too many proposals passing the benefit cost test' when each of many individual agencies independently evaluates its own projects as if they were the next change to the status quo.

29. In Majid et al. (1983), bundles of attributes (parks) were added to a pre-existing set of bundles (the park system) to identify the optimal set. In the case-studies in this book, landscape attributes are added to a pre-existing landscape (the relevant bundle) to identify the optimal bundle.

30. Hoehn assumes that air quality at each location enters the utility function as the input of a spatially separable recreational activity. However, if people hold significant non-use values for air visibility, separability in utility is much more difficult, if not impossible, to justify.

31. According to Mitchell and Carson (1989): these two parameters are in general different; the relationships between them are complex; and to estimate one from the other requires the functional form of the utility function to be known. Notwithstanding, can these analytical complexities explain the difference between estimated income-flexibilities, usually smaller than 1.0, and the two-orders-of-magnitude-larger values implied by results such as Hoehn's or Hoevenhagel's?

32. Kahneman and Knetsch's (1992a) elicitation of the categories of spending which would be reduced by respondents to fund their WTP contributions confirms this assumption: 'added spending on environmental (...) services would be drawn from discretionary spending, and especially from entertainment. Respondents would not expect to alter their eating habits.' (p. 67). Moreover, Randall and Hoehn (1996) showed that incomplete multi-stage

budgeting strongly increases substitution effects in demand systems estimated from market data.

33. Prices of market goods are dropped because they are taken as parametric.
34. Thus, the estimated parameters β should be interpreted as describing the combination of first and second-order effects of attributes on WTP (cf. Hoehn and Loomis 1993).
35. This is an approximate estimate because $\partial \pi_l / \partial y$ refers to the uncompensated marginal valuation function, whereas μ_l is its compensated counterpart.
36. See, for example, the operational conditions proposed by Cummings et al. (1986).
37. Smith (1993) and Fisher (1996) have stressed the non-continuous implications of perceived minimum safety levels for a resource.

4. Valuing Landscape Change II: Survey and Estimation Issues

This chapter discusses a number of survey and estimation issues raised by the application of a particular valuation technique – the contingent valuation method (CVM) – to landscape change. Comparisons with other valuation techniques are presented with respect to some specific issues, but most of the discussion takes place within a CVM context.

The benefit concept to be measured is first defined and different empirical strategies for valuing this concept are reviewed with respect to their ability for disaggregating benefits over individual attribute changes. Disaggregation over attributes is often required to evaluate alternative management options.

Problems associated with the use of a survey approach to landscape change (as the CVM) are discussed as well. In addition to general problems with describing complex landscape changes and staging hypothetical transactions involving such changes, a new method is proposed for studying respondents' perceptions and preferences for landscapes, which is intended as a tool for the improvement and evaluation of CVM scenarios for landscape changes.

The final section discusses how to estimate multi-attribute valuation functions from discrete-choice CVM data.

4.1 DEFINING THE BENEFITS TO BE VALUED

The non-market valuation literature distinguishes two main categories of value people hold for environmental resources: use and non-use values. To define these two categories, consider a modified version of (3.26), the equation defining the compensating variation (CV) associated with a discrete multi-attribute change:

$$CV = e(p, \mathbf{z}^0, V^o) - e(p, \mathbf{z}^1, V^o) \tag{4.1}$$

with p representing now the implicit price to gain access to the landscape.

Suppose that $p^c(\mathbf{z})$ is the 'choke price' for access (that is: the price level above which the individual decides not to visit the area) and that the landscape change is perceived as an improvement, with $\mathbf{z}^0$ and $\mathbf{z}^1$ representing the policy-off and policy-on states of landscape. Adding and subtracting $e(p^c(\mathbf{z}^1), \mathbf{z}^1, V^0) + e(p^c(\mathbf{z}^0), \mathbf{z}^0, V^0)$ and rearranging yields:

$$CV = [e(p^c(\mathbf{z}^1), \mathbf{z}^1, V^0) - e(p, \mathbf{z}^1, V^0)] - [e(p^c(\mathbf{z}^0), \mathbf{z}^0, V^0) - e(p, \mathbf{z}^0, V^0)] \quad (4.2)$$

$$+ [e(p^c(\mathbf{z}^0), \mathbf{z}^0, V^0) - e(p^c(\mathbf{z}^1), \mathbf{z}^1, V^0)]$$

The first difference in brackets in (4.2) represents the value of access with the policy-on landscape and the second brackets the value of access with the policy-off landscape. Therefore, the first line in this equation represents the change in access value that results from the landscape improvement. This is often called the use value of the change, since the realisation of this value requires *in situ* use of the landscape.

If the implicit price of access is held at choke-price level, the individual will not visit the area, neither before nor after the improvement. Nevertheless, he may still care about the landscape, and, in this case, the improvement raises utility. Hence, there possibly is a value component that is independent of *in situ* use; this is represented by the second line in (4.2) and is usually known as the non-use value of the change. Thus, (4.2) shows that the total effect of a landscape change on utility, that is its total economic value (TEV), is given by the sum of use and non-use values.[1]

Many plausible justifications have been given in the literature for the existence of non-use values. Existence in itself and bequest motives are referred to by Krutilla (1967) and Walsh et al. (1984) within a deterministic setting. Weisbrod (1964) and Fisher and Hanemann (1990) move to a setting with risk and uncertainty (thus, different from that of equation 4.2), where they define option and quasi-option values. The basic idea underlying non-use values is '... a concern that even after all of the various benefits associated with using an environmental amenity have been estimated and entered into the benefit calculation, something important might be missed' (Randall 1991: 303).

There is, however, no compelling motive for disaggregating TEV over value categories for purposes of policy evaluation. Benefit disaggregation over individual landscape attributes may be useful, provided these are separable in production. In this case, disaggregated values for individual attribute changes can inform the choice among available management options. However, disaggregation over the use/non-use dimension is often irrelevant, as use and non-use components of the TEV of a particular attribute change are usually not separable in production.

The same happens with other, more or less artificial, value disaggregations over benefit classes. For example, many benefits of landscape conservation schemes are aesthetic in nature, in that they are realised by people through sensory experience. This led Graves (1991) to distinguish a category of aesthetic benefits as separable from recreation, health or non-use benefits: differently from aesthetic values, which would refer solely to sensory experience, recreation and health benefits would imply 'material effect on the body', and non-use values would refer to 'knowledge rather than experience' (p.213).[2] However, aesthetics may be thought of as a particular (not necessarily separable) dimension of the recreational, residential, travelling or almost every single human experience. Aesthetic changes may even generate health improvement benefits, as suggested by Kaplan and Kaplan (1989). Non-use values of users may, as well, stem from direct aesthetic experience. Likewise, imagined aesthetic experience, re-constructed from literary references, may explain part of non-users' values. Besides, other motives, such as the association of landscape with wildlife *habitat*, may give a non-aesthetic content to landscape values.

Therefore, asking respondents to apportion TEV over recreation, health, wildlife or other dimensions of value, as proposed by Graves (1991), seems to represent quite a cumbersome task. Moreover, the resulting allocation of value to different dimensions has no clear behaviour-predictive implications: what does the fact of a respondent stating wildlife makes two thirds of his enjoyment of a site actually mean in terms of behavioural implications? (On the other hand, the fact of respondents accepting to pay £X for the conservation of a landscape has clear behavioural implications in that it is, at least in theory, testable against some relevant behaviour, such as, for example, voting on a referendum implying exactly the same trade-off.)

In addition, disaggregating value over motivational components is often useless in informing practical decisions. In fact, it is immaterial to know how much of the TEV of a management option is ascribed to 'aesthetic', 'recreational', or 'wildlife' motives when all of these value dimensions will be jointly produced as a result of choosing that option.

Despite its irrelevance for policy evaluation, the distinction between use and non-use values has a clear-cut implication for selecting the valuation techniques that are appropriate to estimate TEVs of landscape changes. This is because the so called revealed preference techniques (such as travel cost or hedonic price models) assume weak complementarity (Mäler 1974) between the environmental attribute to be valued – landscape quality at a site, for example – and some commodity for which actual transactions are observable – visits to that site, for example. In this case, weak complementarity means changes in landscape quality only affect utility as long as the individual is visiting the site. Hence, if the implicit price of access is held at choke-price level, then there will be no visits and thus landscape changes will not affect utility. This means the second line in (4.2), that is non-use value, vanishes. Therefore, by definition, revealed preference techniques yield use values alone, and hence the CVM and stated preference techniques in general remain the only options for estimating TEV.

Very often, landscape conservation schemes only deliver their full effects in the medium-long term. For improvements, the targeted landscape may be delayed by lags in the reaction of vegetation to changed farming practices, or by non-immediate uptake of voluntary schemes by farmers. For policy schemes aimed at preventing landscape degradation, current trends in farming practice may only work out their full detrimental effect on the landscape within a 10–20 year period (the policy-off scenario). In these cases, the scheme's full effect is only visible after a long period of time. The CVM has a clear advantage for valuing these future prospects: descriptions of future changes can be conveyed to and valued by respondents. On the other hand, revealed preference techniques, such as hedonic price models, can only be used to value these prospects if future benefits are perceived in advance by the agents in the market and hence have an effect on current prices (of housing, for example). Willis et al. (1993a) argue that this is very unlikely.

These delays in time also create uncertainty, namely with respect to the precise landscape states that will actually occur in the future, with and without the policy. Values elicited before this uncertainty has been removed are *ex ante* values; after uncertainty is removed, values become *ex post* values. Revealed preference techniques are based on observed past behaviour and hence usually secure *ex post* values. Projecting these *ex post* values for the future, in *ex ante* evaluation of new policies may lead to biased benefit estimates, especially when individuals are prepared to pay a significant premium for increased probability of delivery of the landscape change, over and above expected consumer surplus. In this case, the CVM makes possible to frame valuation questions so that *ex ante* values are directly elicited.

4.2 VALUATION STRATEGIES FOR MULTI-ATTRIBUTE LANDSCAPE CHANGES

There are many possible survey and modelling strategies for valuing multi-attribute landscape changes. This section reviews these alternative empirical strategies with a special focus on their suitability to the task of disaggregating landscape benefits over individual attribute changes that are separable in production. As seen in the previous section, this is the only benefit disaggregation that matters for practical management decisions. Eventually, the strategy proposed and applied in this book is presented and discussed.

Valuing a Particular Multi-Attribute Change as a Whole

This approach uses the CVM to value, as a whole, a particular multi-attribute landscape change that is completely fixed with respect to its component attribute changes and that exactly matches the policy scheme to be evaluated. Bateman et al. (1992), Willis et al. (1993), and Hanley et al. (1996a), among others, applied this strategy. The estimated benefit is only usable for the evaluation of a particular policy scheme, which makes the approach more suitable for *ex post* global evaluation of existing schemes. It is of no use for evaluating changes in scheme design, either at early phases of a new scheme or at the review of an existing scheme to select policy components to keep for the future and new components to be added to the scheme.

Willis and Garrod (1991 and 1992) applied a variant of this approach, which involves the valuation of as many landscape changes as the number of alternative management options, or schemes, available for a particular area. Pictures by an artist of the future states of landscape that correspond to each alternative scheme were presented to and valued by respondents. Thus, a holistic picture of each alternative landscape was valued, rather than asking respondents to engage in artificial tasks such as valuing single attribute changes or allocating total value over attributes. In fact, landscape perception is holistic, and it is certainly not easy for respondents to realise how single attribute changes will combine to produce a new overall landscape picture. (This survey problem is referred to here as the 'composition problem'.) Hence, there are definitive advantages in valuing each alternative state of landscape as a whole. There is, however, a problem with Willis and Garrod's approach, which stems from the fact of respondents having been asked to select their preferred landscape and to value this landscape. Thus, it is not clear what is the policy-off state of landscape in each case and it is not ensured that this baseline state is constant across respondents. Hence, it is impossible to define precisely the change that was valued by each respondent, which hinders a consistent aggregation of benefits.

Independent Valuation of Individual Attribute Changes

A second strategy is the independent valuation of individual attribute changes. One possible example is Hanley and Ruffell's (1993) use of the CVM to value pairs of photographs representing forest scenes only differing with respect to one single attribute. After choosing the preferred scene, respondents were asked how much extra they would pay to visit the preferred forest rather than the other. There are two problems with this approach, which are acknowledged by the authors themselves. First, it is difficult to ensure that photos in a pair only differ with respect to one single attribute.

Second, it is not possible to measure from photos the levels of attributes in terms of management-relevant units, and thus we cannot estimate per-unit values of each attribute, which is precisely the result that would be more useful to inform forest management decisions. There are further problems with the approach. One is that each attribute change is valued as it was the next change to the status quo; hence, benefit aggregation over attributes to build benefit estimates for multi-attribute policies is prone to IVS bias (cf. section 3.2). Another is that changes are poorly framed: we do not know where the attribute change depicted in each pair of photos would take place or which policy would deliver that change. It seems that the search for general values for forest attributes led the authors to design CVM scenarios that are too abstract to convey meaningful choice occasions.

Valuation as a Whole Followed by Apportionment to Individual Attributes

This approach starts by valuing the whole multi-attribute change. This 'total' is then subdivided over individual attributes, according to survey information about participants' apportionment of an amount of points, or 'tokens', corresponding to this 'total' over individual attributes. Drake (1992) allocates in this way CVM-elicited WTP for the conservation of all Swedish agricultural landscapes to different crops and land uses over the country. Benson (1992), and Willis and Benson (1989) subdivide, also in this way, travel cost estimates of access value of UK forests by attributes of the forest experience (landscape, wildlife and so on). The lack of behaviour-predictive implications of apportionment tasks of this kind was already criticised in section 4.1. Note, as well, that this approach yields simultaneously disaggregated rather than sequential values of attribute changes.

Direct Sequential Valuation of Individual Attribute Changes

This fourth approach involves the sequential valuation of the diverse attribute changes included in the multi-attribute change under consideration. The approach is theoretically appealing, although the difficulties in designing understandable CVM scenarios for sequential valuation (see section 3.3) made it much less so in practice. No example of direct sequential valuation is found in the landscape literature; Magnussen (1996) provides an interesting parallel example for water quality.

Multi-Site Models for Valuing Attribute Changes

Hedonic price and multi-site travel cost models explore differences in attribute levels across sites so that value can be ascribed to attribute changes. Garrod and Willis (1991a and b) and Powe et al. (1997) modelled houses' market prices to reveal implicit prices for diverse landscape attributes in the neighbourhood of houses, such as woodland views, access to woodland and woodland type. The varying parameter travel-cost model (Vaughan and Russell 1982) could be used with a similar purpose where landscape is the support for recreation rather than residential uses.

Using inter-site attribute variability, this approach is affected by multicollinearity among landscape attributes in the data. Multicollinearity causes a known statistical difficulty in identifying attributes that significantly affect landscape values but that are strongly correlated with other attributes.

Besides, the fact of the same attribute being possibly related to landscape value in ways that vary across landscape types may lead to specification bias in multi-site models. For example, tree cover generally increases, up to a certain limit, the value of most landscapes. However, trees can be seen as an eyesore in open marshland scenes (Appleton 1994). Thus, coefficients for attributes such as trees are not necessarily stable across all sites, which leads to specification problems.[3]

Multi-site revealed preference models should exactly specify all attributes that are perceived by people and that actually affect people's choices of a particular house or recreation site. Failure to include all these attributes may lead to omission (specification) biases; for example, the identification of spurious correlation leading to ascribe value to wrong attributes. As many revealed preference applications rely exclusively on observed behaviour plus objectively measured data on sites' attributes, they have no access to subjective insights into people's perceptions and decisions. On the other hand, such subjective insights may be gained by using a survey approach to valuation. This is a possible advantage of the CVM in this context.

Hanley and Ruffell (1993) present a multi-site model of CVM-elicited WTP for access (plus option value) to forest sites. Measurement of forest attributes used as WTP predictors resulted from respondents' rating of the sites with respect to each attribute, which enabled the authors to take into account respondents' perceptions rather than some objectively measured physical attributes. Likewise, Bostedt and Mattsson (1995) used visitors' ratings of attributes in their model of WTP for access to Swedish forests. Of course, these multi-site CVM applications are prone to multicollinearity and other general problems of multi-site models.

Converting a Technical Index of Landscape Quality into a WTP Value

The sixth valuation strategy consists of establishing a one-to-one relationship between landscape economic value and a technical index of landscape quality. In this case, the first step is a technical evaluation of landscape quality at several sites by a landscape expert using a scalar index of quality. Then, a valuation technique is used to put money values on these sites' landscapes. Finally, a relationship is established between the technical scale of landscape quality and the monetary scale of value. Once this relationship has been established, further landscape valuations are reduced to the task of expert evaluation of landscape quality, plus an adjustment of the landscape quality figure to convert it into a monetary value.

This general valuation strategy was first proposed by Price (1978) and received further amendments in Price (1991); it was applied, for example, by Bergin (1993) in association with a travel cost model, used to generate the relevant scale of monetary values. This approach to landscape valuation is particularly suited for valuing the impacts of changes that differently affect multiple views. Consider, for example, all possible views impacted by a new motorway along all of its length. In this case, it is virtually impracticable to ask respondents to value the impacts of the change in every single view.

On the other hand, as all the multi-attribute information is previously compressed into a scalar quality index, the approach is not fitted to the task of disaggregating landscape values over attributes.

Modelling CVM-Elicited WTP for Multi-Programme Policy Schemes

This is the approach proposed and applied in this book, which combines those aspects of reviewed valuation strategies that were judged more fitted to the tasks of valuing multi-attribute landscape changes and sequentially disaggregating the resulting benefits over individual attribute changes.[4]

The first step consists of identifying all attribute changes that are relevant for actual management decisions. Secondly, each set of jointly produced attribute changes is identified as a programme. Different combinations of programmes are then specified as possible alternative schemes. The 'nil scheme', that is the one comprising no conservation programme at all, is set as the baseline. Thirdly, respondents are presented the future states of landscape resulting from each alternative scheme, and are asked to independently value these target states of landscape as opposed to policy-off state corresponding to the 'nil scheme'. When several attribute changes affect the same scene, they are presented in a same picture, which allows the composition effect to be accounted for. When several attribute changes affect different scenes, corresponding to different sub-areas, these changes are presented in separate pictures, and the corresponding sub-areas are precisely located in a map. Finally, CVM-elicited answers for all alternative schemes are pooled and modelled, using the programme-mix vector associated with each scheme plus all relevant interaction terms included in the model presented in (3.32) as the predictors. The estimated multi-attribute valuation function enables us to sequentially disaggregate benefits over individual programmes, taking into account substitution effects between programmes.

This valuation strategy appropriately deals with the 'composition problem' by making respondents value bundles of programmes rather than individual programmes; likewise, it avoids asking respondents to engage in the demanding task of sequential valuation by securing sequential values indirectly through the modelling of WTP for programme bundles.

As CVM is used, attribute changes included in each scheme can be explicitly spelled out to respondents, so avoiding reliance on (not always correct) analyst interpretation of the relationship between observed choices and observed attributes that characterises revealed preference techniques. Besides, the multicollinearity problem can be avoided here through adequate scenario design, which is not possible with revealed preference techniques, where data are observed as produced by real life.

Potential problems with the proposed valuation strategy refer to designing CVM scenarios so as to convey detailed and understandable descriptions of the landscape changes to be valued. This is dealt with in section 4.3. Other problems with the proposed approach have to do with achieving the large number of observations that are required to efficiently estimate the multi-attribute valuation function in (3.32) while maintaining sample sizes in keeping with available budgets. In the case-studies in this book this was solved by asking each respondent to value several schemes. This, in turn, led to adopt the discrete-choice (DC) CVM format, as discrete take-it-or-leave-it choices were the only valuation task that could realistically be asked from on-site surveyed respondents asked to value several schemes. In each DC question, the choice is between a particular scheme at a specified price and the 'nil-scheme' at zero price. Thus, respondents had to be instructed to value each scheme independently from previously valued schemes and from bid amounts proposed for these schemes. A potential problem is, therefore, the possibility of the bid proposed for the first DC question acting as a value clue framing the answers to the following questions. This first-bid effect is tested for in one of the case-studies presented in Part Three of this book.

4.3 CONTINGENT VALUATION SCENARIOS FOR LANDSCAPE CHANGES

Contingent valuation surveys propose to respondents staged transactions, which are supposed to be value-revealing. According to Fischhoff and Furby (1988), for a transaction to be value-revealing, participants should: (1) be given and understand in the intended way an appropriate amount of information about the good, the payment and the social frame of the transaction; (2) be able to make a non-coerced choice; and (3) be able to identify the choice best serving their self-interest.

Tversky and Kahneman (1973) pointed out that people often decide as if 'what is out of sight is out of mind'. Along the same lines, Fischhoff and Furby (1988) stressed the need for spelling out, in detail, every single aspect of the good, payment and social frame, unless we can assume participants already understand some of these details. For example, aspects of the good such as location, attributes affecting the recreational experience and current state of landscape are implicitly defined in on-site visitor surveys. Likewise, using an existing policy that is known by respondents as the model for the staged transaction may implicitly define elements of the scenario such as the method for delivery of the good or the payment vehicle. For example, existing landscape conservation schemes are generally funded through general taxation and operate through financial incentives for voluntary participation by farmers. This may spare a lot of explanations in the questionnaire, but may also cause trouble if we want respondents to value certain delivery of the improved landscape and respondents distrust the ability (or interest) of government or farmers to make sure the good is delivered. It is also of major importance that respondents perceive the payment as absolutely necessary for securing the good. This perception can be promoted by making respondents realise the actual connections between payment and the policy (that is: all the chain of events) that will deliver the good (Carson et al. 1996).

Carson (1991) stresses the importance of describing the good, payment and context (that is: the CVM scenario) in a way that is understandable, plausible and significant for the respondent. If the scenario is not understandable, respondents are led to value the wrong thing. If it is not plausible, respondents will substitute a plausible scenario for the proposed one, and hence will value the wrong thing as well; alternatively, they may not take the valuation exercise seriously and give non-considerate answers or refuse to answer. This may also happen if the object of choice is an insignificant problem for the respondent. According to Mitchell and Carson (1989), respondents' misperceptions of the scenario are '...among the most important and most problematic sources of error in CV surveys' (p. 247).

Let us now discuss some implications of these general methodological principles for the design of valid scenarios for landscape changes, focusing on descriptions of the landscape changes to be valued.[5]

Garrod and Willis (1990), Bergstrom et al. (1985), and Hanley and Spash (1993), among others, report results showing that different descriptions of the change can yield different WTP amounts. Many of these description effects are legitimate, as different descriptions often lead respondents to value different goods. An unsolved problem is that of the adequate amount of information required for valid CVM valuation.

Willis et al. (1993) faced the problem of conveying slight landscape changes that are typically associated with many conservation schemes. They devised a presentation procedure aimed at avoiding that respondents consider much larger changes than the ones intended by the researcher. This procedure consists in presenting some photographs that are common to both the policy-on and the policy-off scenarios, so that it is pointed out that, for some attributes, the policy will make no difference.

The use of photographs to depict policy-on and policy-off states of landscape in CVM studies can be traced back to the visibility studies carried out by Randall et al. (1974) and Brookshire et al. (1976). More recently, Hanley et al. (1996a) used computer-based image manipulation to convey to respondents the effects of slight attribute changes on the overall landscape. Johnson et al. (1994) developed similar presentation media to suggest how different forestry practices would impact on the particular view from a respondent's home. These more sophisticated presentation media are particularly useful for unfamiliar changes (for example, in non-user surveys) or for exact depiction of specific changes affecting a particular view.

Another issue in describing landscape changes is the identification of the causes of the landscape conservation problem. According to Fischhoff and Furby (1988), it is not immaterial for respondents whether it is air pollution or a natural phenomenon that causes a haze impairing visibility. Respondents do not care about sensory states of the world alone, but also about meaning (here a categorisation of perceptions along the natural/artificial dimension). Therefore, it is important to describe the actual causes of the change to avoid that respondents wrongly guess causes and that different respondents guess differently. A related issue is the perception by respondents of non-sensory implications of landscape change, for example impact on wildlife *habitat*. Concern for wildlife is constantly high across several CVM studies. Again, it is important to describe all these reasons for people to care about the landscape change; otherwise valuations will be based on wrong and heterogeneous perceptions of these reasons.

Misperception of CVM scenarios is more likely when respondents are unfamiliar with the good to be values (Mitchell and Carson 1989, and Graves

1991). Landscapes on a particular area can be familiar for visitors to that area. Visitors may have already experienced even expected future change, in a small scale, at particular places where processes of farm dereliction, for example, are more advanced. Thus, surveying only visitors can be a way of ensuring familiarity of respondents with the changes to be valued.

On the other hand, people may be familiar with a particular landscape, but unfamiliar with verbal descriptions of it, or with particular photos poorly matching their usual way of seeing this landscape. Graves (1991) stresses the possibility that the '... survey instrument may inject features of the good that the respondent would not normally consider nor think important while missing features that the respondent cares about'. Going even further, he recognises that the '...very effort to capture an aesthetic good in words or pictures may cause a respondent to value it differently than he or she would based solely on his or her prior experience' (p. 215).

Thus, landscape descriptions should focus on those attributes that are more readily perceived by respondents or that somehow match their previous perceptions of the landscape. Yet, new attributes and new information in general may be introduced in CVM scenarios. Indeed, additional information on such aspects as wildlife significance is more often than not required and should obviously have a legitimate effect on valuation. However, it is necessary to make sure that respondents' preferences are not simply constructed from, or biased by, the CVM scenario. Hence, for adequately designing CVM scenarios for landscape changes, researchers need some previous information on the respondents' perceptions and preferences for landscapes. This information may be secured through a systematic study of such perceptions and preferences. Section 4.4 proposes a method to carry out such a study. This method is applied with an illustrative aim in chapter 8.

4.4. STUDYING LANDSCAPE PERCEPTIONS AND PREFERENCES TO IMPROVE AND EVALUATE CVM SCENARIOS FOR LANDSCAPE CHANGES

Two main questions should guide any study of perceptions and preferences aimed at improving CVM scenarios for landscape changes. First, it is important to know whether respondents distinguish the effects on the landscape of different management options. Second, we should investigate whether they have clear preferences for these alternative states of landscape. Detailed evidence on these issues is particularly important when the valuation study aims at disaggregating the benefits of a multi-attribute change over management-relevant attribute changes.

This section proposes a method for studying perceptions and preferences, which is based on the immediate reactions of respondents to particular scenes presented through the use of photographs. Scenes are sampled so as to cover a wide range of landscape types, which is revealing of the effects of alternative management options on the scenery. Respondents are only asked to rate each scene in a 5-point preference scale.

Studying Perceptions of the Landscape

Environmental perception is not only a matter of reception of sensory stimuli, as it implies, as well, people's ability to constitute and recognise particular distinctions and similarities among the objects in the external world. Recognising each experienced situation as an instance of a general type and reacting accordingly '...is quite obviously important to survival' (Kaplan and Kaplan 1989). This is why most individuals are able to react to particular scenes (even when these are only partly depicted in photographs) as particular instances of general types or categories, as suggested by Clamp (1981) and others. Identifying these categories of perception enables us to list the distinctions and similarities that individuals establish in their visual and physical involvement with the scenery.

One way of investigating these categories is to rely on verbal landscape descriptions. For example, Shuttleworth (1979 and 1983) and Barrios et al. (1985) analysed ratings of scenes by participants according to checklists of attributes and adjective pairs provided in a questionnaire. Shuttleworth ran a cluster analysis of these ratings and arrived at a variety of perceptual categories he called 'landscape images'. One of the weaknesses of these studies is they assume perceptual distinctions are easily verbalised, which is not the case for every single group of people.

There is another way of investigating perceptual categories of people, which is not based on verbal statements but on immediate reaction to visual input, usually photographs or slides. Cognitive psychologists, such as Herzog (1984) and Kaplan and Kaplan (1989), have proposed and applied this method. This is also the method proposed here to study landscape perceptions as a way to improve CVM scenario design. Based on immediate reaction to visual input, the cognitive-psychological method avoids verbal descriptions. Indeed, cognitive psychologists distrust verbal material as a starting point for studying perception: if perception is to accomplish its adaptive role in increasing survival chances, categorisation should be an almost automatic reaction to a scene and hence should not be mediated by verbalisation.

The cognitive-psychological method identifies perceptual categories by using preference ratings given by participants to each one of n scenes. Preference ratings are not used in their absolute magnitudes; instead, the correlation of preference ratings for each pair of scenes across all participants is first calculated. The fact of two scenes being highly correlated means that individuals who strongly prefer (dislike) one of them will also have a strong (weak) preference for the other. This reveals the two scenes are perceived as similar. Pair-wise correlation of preference ratings is, therefore, used as a measurement of perceived similarity. Thus, a perceptual category can be identified as a group of scenes internally highly correlated and weakly correlated with other scenes. This identification is done in a systematic way by establishing, first, the n x n matrix of correlation coefficients for every single pair of the n scenes; scenes with similar vectors of correlation coefficients are then grouped by cluster analysis.

Having once obtained the perceptual categories, it should be investigated whether (and how) these categories relate to the different management options to be valued in the CVM survey. It may also be important to investigate whether respondents perceive finer variations in particular management-relevant attributes. For this, it is convenient that the researcher establishes a typology of scenes based on land-use and management variables previously to the survey of perceptions, that is: independently from the results of the cluster analysis. Once established by cluster analysis, the perceptual categories can then be compared with these *a priori* management-relevant types, which may be done through simple cross-tabulation of both results. This cross-tabulation indicates which landscape changes will be less clearly understood by respondents to the CVM survey; more intensive pre-testing of the CVM scenario with respect to these changes is advisable.

To establish whether respondents perceive a variation in a particular management-relevant attribute is more difficult a task. This implies a more intuitive *a posteriori* procedure based on the study of the dendrogram resulting from the cluster analysis and aimed at giving the analyst a feeling of the attributes that explain the categorisation of the scenes.

Studying Preferences for Landscapes

The method for studying preferences proposed in this section is based on the absolute values of preference ratings given by participants to the different scenes. These ratings are, first, averaged across respondents to estimate the mean preference rating for each scene. Average ratings are then compared across categories and across scenes within the same category. Inter-category comparisons enable us to check whether there are well-defined preferences for the states of landscape associated with different management options. Inter-scene comparisons, within each landscape category, lead to the selection of the particular landscape attributes that are supposed to affect preference judgements. Using the attributes so selected as the explanatory variables in a multiple-regression model of the scenes' average preference ratings enables us to test whether the selected attributes significantly affect preference judgements.

Two very different kinds of landscape attributes have been used as explanatory variables in preference models. The first is the one adopted by Kaplan (1975), Herzog (1984), Woodcock (1984), Kaplan and Kaplan (1989) and other cognitive psychologists. These authors aim to explain environmental preferences 'in a relatively generic sense – in terms of attributes that are likely to be pertinent across the diversity of humankind' (Kaplan and Kaplan 1989). These attributes are concepts like 'coherence', 'complexity', 'legibility' and 'mystery', which are intended to describe human needs and motivations that underlay our preference judgements. Ruddell et al. (1989) call this the psychological approach to landscape preference and argue this approach 'although strong from a theoretical standpoint (...) fails to provide results that are useful in predicting the aesthetic impact of landscape management'. This inability '...is due to the abstract nature of many of the variables used' (Ruddell et al. 1989).

The second kind of preference predictors in the landscape literature is the one characterising what Ruddell et al. (1989) call the psychophysical approach, which is the one adopted by planners, landscape architects and foresters. Here, predictors are biophysical attributes of the scenes that are objectively measured. The strength of this approach, with respect to the psychological one, is '... its ability to relate changes in manageable site characteristics to resulting impacts on aesthetic quality' (Ruddell et al. 1989). Thus, although not generating results with general validity (as they are not based on a general theory of landscape preferences), psychophysical models are more effective in dealing with individual management problems. Hence, this is the approach best suiting our present aim of checking for preference-relevance of management-relevant attributes to be included in a CVM scenario.

The findings of a study of preferences along these lines show whether respondents have preferences for broad management-related landscape changes, as well as for more detailed management-related attribute changes. This may help CVM scenario designers to focus on those attributes for which people have well-defined preferences; hence avoiding the imposition of 'artificial' choices that may occur when people have no well-defined preferences for the states of landscape associated with alternative management options.

Ex Post Facto Evaluating CVM Scenarios for Multi-Attribute Changes

The results of a study of preferences for landscape attributes can also be used, *ex post facto*, for systematically evaluating the performance of CVM scenarios in accurately conveying the attribute changes intended by the researcher. One simple way to carry out this evaluation is to compare the disaggregated valuations for individual attribute changes (resulting from the CVM survey) with the preference ratings given to the corresponding attributes in the previous preference study. These latter are absolutely independent from the particular wording used in the CVM scenario. Thus, the fact of the ranking of the attributes being the same in both cases is a clear demonstration that the particular wording of the scenario did not distort respondents' previous preferences for these attributes. If the rankings do not coincide, the burden of proof rests with the researcher, who should either plausibly explain why this happened or reject the validity of the CVM results. A possibly valid reason for this inconsistency is that new valuation-relevant information (for example, about wildlife significance of an attribute) was introduced by the CVM scenario, which may have legitimately increased preferences for this particular attribute with respect to the situation where the participants were only reacting to visual input.

Note that the proposed comparison of attribute rankings is not a test of the validity of the absolute magnitudes of elicited WTP amounts, but solely a test of the validity of relative amounts attracted by each attribute.

4.5 THE ESTIMATION PROBLEM: MULTI-ATTRIBUTE VALUATION FUNCTIONS FROM DISCRETE-CHOICE CONTINGENT VALUATION DATA

This section discusses the estimation of multi-attribute valuation functions from discrete-choice (DC) contingent valuation data. The DC way of questioning is particularly suited to surveys asking each respondent to value several schemes, because the cognitive burden of answering each question is much reduced with this format. Thus, although there are unsolved problems with the DC format,[6] this was adopted in the case-studies in this book.

DC valuation questions for a landscape conservation scheme take the following form: 'If this particular scheme cost you a £t increase in income tax, would you pay this amount if this was the only way for the scheme to go ahead?' The answer is a 'yes' or 'no' (or a 'don't know'), which only reveals whether respondent i's maximum WTP for scheme j (WTP_{ij}) is above the proposed tax increase (£t_{ij}). This represents an observation on a binary variable I_{ij} that is either:

$$I_{ij} = 1 \ (\text{'yes'}) \quad \text{if} \quad WTP_{ij} \geq t_{ij} \qquad (4.3)$$

$$I_{ij} = 0 \ (\text{'no'}) \quad \text{if} \quad WTP_{ij} < t_{ij}$$

The problem discussed in this section is how to estimate a multi-attribute valuation function $WTP_{ij} = \mathbf{x}_{ij}'\rho + u_{ij}$, such as that specified in (3.32), from observations of this binary variable across respondents i and multi-attribute schemes j. Methods proposed in the literature for estimating WTP from DC CVM data are reviewed here with respect to their applicability to this particular estimation problem.

Bishop and Heberlein's Approach

The DC way of questioning people about their valuations for non-market goods was first applied by Bishop and Heberlein (1979), who analysed hunters' reactions to hypothetical as well as actual money offers to induce them to give up their hunting permits. Different respondents were allocated different offers t_k ($k=1,...,K$) and the number of acceptances and refusals to each bid t_k was registered. The probability of 'yes' answers was then modelled through a logit binary-response model. Bishop and Heberlein modelled minimum compensation required (WTA) to give up a permit. However, the WTP measure is used here for exposition purposes, as this is the more frequent welfare measure in CVM studies.

A logit binary-response model can be used to model the probability P_k of a randomly selected respondent being prepared to pay the offered amount t_k. In its log-odds form, this logit model is:

$$Z_k = \ln\left(\frac{Pk}{1-Pk}\right) = f(t_k|\beta) \qquad (4.4)$$

where: Z_k is the natural logarithm of the odds ratio in favour of a 'yes' answer; $f(.)$ is a function of t_k, called the logit index, and β is a vector of parameters to be estimated. Bishop and Heberlein (1979) used a logit index linear in parameters and comprising a logarithmic transformation of t_k:

$$f(t_k|\beta) = \beta_1 + \beta_2 \log(t_k) \qquad (4.5)$$

From (4.4) we derive the formula for the probability of a 'yes' answer:

$$P_k = 1/[1 + e^{-f(t_i|\beta)}] = \Theta[f(t_k|\beta)] \qquad (4.6)$$

where $\Theta(.)$ is the standard logistic cumulative distribution function (cdf). Replacing (4.5) in (4.4) and adding a zero-mean random term to $f(t_k|\beta)$ yields the log-logistic model. This can be estimated through weighted least squares (or the minimum chi-squared method according to Aldrich and Nelson 1984), as Bishop and Heberlein (1979) did.

Alternatively, the logit model can be estimated through the maximum-likelihood (ML) method. From (4.6), we derive the log-likelihood function for the logit model:

$$\log L = \Sigma_i -I_i \log[1 + e^{-f(t_i \mid \beta)}] + (1-I_i)\log\{ e^{-f(t_i \mid \beta)}/[1+e^{-f(t_i \mid \beta)}]\} \qquad (4.7)$$

where I_i is the binary response variable defined in equations (4.3) and the index i represents now a particular individual allocated to a particular bid amount t_i. Note that available computer-based ML algorithms require the logit index function to be linear in parameters, which is obviously the case with Bishop and Heberlein's log-logistic specification in (4.5).

After estimating the binary-response model, it is necessary to compute the sample mean of WTP for the good. For this, notice that P_i (the probability of a ''yes' answer) corresponds to the probability of the true *WTP* of a randomly selected respondent i being larger than t_i, that is: $P_i = \Pr(WTP \geq t_i)$. Thus, $\Pr(WTP < t_i) = (1 - P_i)$ gives us the *WTP* cdf. Taking (4.6) into account, this cdf becomes:

$$\Pr(WTP < t_i) = 1 - 1/[1 + e^{-f(t_i \mid \beta)}] = 1 - \Theta[f(t_i \mid \beta)] \qquad (4.8)$$

As we know from statistics (cf. Johansson et al. 1989), the expression for the sample mean of *WTP*, when this variable can take negative values, is:

$$\overline{WTP} = \int_0^\infty 1/[1 + e^{-f(t \mid \beta)}]dt - \int_{-\infty}^0 1 - 1/[1 + e^{-f(t \mid \beta)}]dt \qquad (4.9)$$

If *WTP* does not take negative values, which is ensured in the particular case of Bishop and Heberlein's log-logistic model by the log transformation of the bid amount, then the expression for the *WTP* mean is simplified to:

$$\overline{WTP} = \int_0^\infty 1/[1 + e^{-f(t \mid \beta)}]dt \qquad (4.10)$$

Note that this *WTP* estimator yields the marginal sample mean of WTP, as it results from the integration of the marginal (that is: non-conditional) cdf of *WTP* across the sample. Thus, to secure sample means of *WTP* conditional on particular values of some explanatory variables we must: (1) include these variables in the logit function, beside the bid variable; (2) estimate the corresponding coefficients; and then (3) integrate the resulting conditional cdf of WTP with explanatory variables other than the bid variable held constant at the desired levels. Thus, estimating a conditional mean of *WTP* for different levels of the explanatory variables would require us to evaluate once again the integral of the conditional cdf of *WTP* for these new levels of the explanatory variables. This is quite a cumbersome procedure when compared to the much simpler use of a valuation function such as that specified in (3.32) to predict conditional means of WTP, by simply substituting into this function the desired values of the explanatory variables.

Another problem with this integral approach is that only point estimates of *WTP* means are produced. For interval estimation, one should resort to sampling from the multivariate probability distribution of the logit parameter estimates and then integrating the *WTP* cdf resulting from each sampled set of parameter estimates. This must be repeated many times (say 1,000) so that the resulting set of *WTP* means can be taken as accurately characterising the sampling distribution of these means. The $\alpha/2$ per cent extreme values are then dropped to yield a $(1-\alpha)$ per cent confidence interval for the population mean of *WTP*. It is probably because of this method's heavy computational burden that the first DC CVM studies (which used the integral approach) omitted confidence intervals for their benefit estimates.

Hanemann's Approach

Hanemann (1984b) proposed an analytical frame for deriving the logit index from a specified utility function. Hanemann's approach gave, for the first time, an economic-theoretic foundation to binary-response models of DC CVM data and hence helped to make the DC approach to questioning – and, indeed, the CVM as a whole – more appealing to the theoretically oriented economist (cf. McConnell 1990).

Hanemann's original models are here expanded to develop estimators for multi-attribute valuation functions that are absolutely in keeping with the basic spirit underlying the approach. The need for this expansion is related to the particular estimation problem that motivates our review. So, suppose that the respondent's indirect utility function is $V(\mathbf{z}, y, \mathbf{c})$, where: $\mathbf{z}$ is a vector of landscape attributes; y is income; and $\mathbf{c}$ a vector of socio-economic or preference variables. Assume there is an additive component in utility that is randomly generated from the point of view of the researcher. Randomness of utility is attributed by Hanemann (1987) to variation of tastes across individuals that is not controlled for by variables $\mathbf{c}$. Thus, the indirect utility function is:

$$V(\mathbf{z}, y, \mathbf{c}) = v(\mathbf{z}, y, \mathbf{c}) + \varepsilon \qquad (4.11)$$

where ε is a random variable with zero mean. The introduction of the random term in the indirect utility function brought home models of DC CVM data to applied economists, who have extensively used random utility models (RUM) to study discrete choices such as mode of transport, and shopping destination (cf. McFadden 1974). Within the RUM frame, it is possible to interpret the choice of an individual i on whether to accept having $\mathbf{z}^j$ (the policy-on state of landscape) as opposed to $\mathbf{z}^0$ (the baseline) in exchange for t_{ij} as a comparison between two levels of utility: one, yielded by more of $\mathbf{z}$ but less income; the other, with baseline $\mathbf{z}$ but keeping current income. The respondent will accept the staged transaction if:

$$v(\mathbf{z}^j, y - t_{ij}, \mathbf{c}^i) + \varepsilon_{ji} \geq v(\mathbf{z}^0, y, \mathbf{c}^i) + \varepsilon_{0i} \qquad (4.12)$$

Otherwise, the transaction is not accepted. Hence, the probability of a 'yes' answer is:

$$P = \Pr\{v(\mathbf{z}^j, y - t_{ij}, \mathbf{c}^i) - v(\mathbf{z}^0, y, \mathbf{c}^i) \geq \varepsilon_{0i} - \varepsilon_{ji}\} \qquad (4.13)$$

$$= \Pr\{\Delta v \geq \varepsilon_{0i} - \varepsilon_{ji}\} = \Pr\{\Delta v \geq \eta\}$$

If ε_{0i} and ε_{ji} are iid extreme-value random variables, then η is standard-logistically distributed. The cdf of the standard logistic is $P = 1/[1 + e^{-\Delta v}]$, and thus, according to (4.6), we have $f(.) = \Delta v$. This means that the logit index can be interpreted as an utility difference, which gives us a theoretical basis for specifying the logit index as well as to check whether a particular logit index is consistent with an analytically definable utility function.

Hence, consider the following multi-attribute utility function:

$$v(z_1, z_2, y, c_1, c_2) = \alpha + \beta_1 z_1 + \beta_2 z_2 + \delta z_1 z_2 + \mu y + \xi_1 c_1 z_1 + \xi_2 c_2 z_2 \qquad (4.14)$$

The utility difference associated with landscape change $(z_1^0, z_2^0) \rightarrow (z_1^j, z_2^j)$ is:

$$\Delta v = \beta_1(z_1^j - z_1^0) + \beta_2(z_2^j - z_2^0) + \delta(z_1^j z_2^j - z_1^0 z_2^0) \qquad (4.15)$$

$$- \mu\, t_{ij} + \xi_1 c_1^i (z_1^j - z_1^0) + \xi_2 c_2^i (z_2^j - z_2^0)$$

All parameters of the indirect utility function, except α, can be recovered, using either the minimum chi-squared or the maximum-likelihood method for estimating the logit index equation in (4.15) from DC CVM data. The fact of α not being recovered is immaterial: $[V(.) - \alpha]$ is a monotonic transformation of $V(.)$ and hence represents exactly the same preference ordering as $V(.)$.

A second step consists of securing the WTP function from the estimated parameters of the utility function. For this, we first invert the indirect utility function $[V(.) - \alpha]$ with respect to income to secure the expenditure function:

$$e(.) = v(z_1, z_2, y, c_1, c_2)/\mu - (\beta_1/\mu)z_1 - (\beta_2/\mu)z_2 \qquad (4.16)$$

$$- (\delta/\mu)z_1 z_2 - (\xi_1/\mu)c_1 z_1 - (\xi_2/\mu)c_2 z_2 + \varepsilon/\mu$$

As in (3.26), the WTP (or valuation) function is then recovered as a difference between two appropriate levels of expenditure:

$$WTP(\mathbf{z}^j, \mathbf{z}^0, y, \mathbf{c}) = y - e[\mathbf{z}^j, V(\mathbf{z}^0, y, \mathbf{c}), \mathbf{c}] = \qquad (4.17)$$

$$= (\beta_1/\mu)(z_1^j - z_1^0) + (\beta_2/\mu)(z_2^j - z_2^0) + (\delta/\mu)(z_1^j z_2^j - z_1^0 z_2^0)$$

$$+ (\xi_1/\mu)c_1(z_1^j - z_1^0) + (\xi_2/\mu)c_2(z_2^j - z_2^0) - \varepsilon/\mu$$

Note that the parameters of this multi-attribute valuation function are secured through a simple re-scaling of the estimated parameters of the multi-attribute utility function, using estimated marginal utility of income, $E(\partial V/\partial y)=\mu$, as the re-scaling factor.

The multi-attribute valuation function in (4.17) can be used in directly estimating *WTP* means that are conditional on particular values of the variables characterising the scheme *j* (z_1^j, z_2^j) and the respondent *i* (c_1^i, c_2^i) by simply substituting the appropriate values for these variables in (4.17) and taking expectations. In this way, the complications of the integral approach to computing estimated *WTP* means are avoided.

The multi-attribute valuation function in (4.17) can be directly used to predict means for sequential values of attribute changes using the method illustrated in (3.33). However, the parameter estimate for the interaction in valuation between attributes (that is: δ/μ) does not correspond, in general, to the pair-wise compensated substitution effect represented by any non-diagonal element of the parameter matrix **D** in (3.32). Moreover, income does not enter the valuation function in (4.17), which prevents us from estimating the effect of income on WTP, as well as the income-related parameters required by tests of demand theory introduced in section 3.4. On the other hand, the valuation function in (3.32) provides all parameters that are required by the valuation problem and hypotheses tests in this book. Yet, deriving such a valuation function within a utility-difference frame would require us to work hard in trying to find out which (possibly very awkward, if existent at all) utility function generates this particular valuation function.

Cameron's Approach

Given this difficulty with the Hanemann's approach in generating valuation functions matching the estimation needs of particular studies, one may rather follow the alternative approach of starting by specifying directly the valuation function and ignoring, for the time being, whether this could be derived from a defined utility function.[7] Indeed, whether there is a utility function generating our valuation function is immaterial, provided this latter: (1) satisfies some broad theoretical requirements; (2) fits well the data; and

(3) enables the analyst to undertake the intended model-based predictions and hypotheses tests (cf. section 3.4).

The idea of starting by specifying a valuation function and then estimating this function from DC CVM data was first proposed ten years ago by Cameron and James (1987). These authors stressed the similarity between the analytical frame they were proposing and ordinary multiple regression. The new problem was how to estimate a regression equation when there is no information on the (continuous) dependent variable *WTP* other than observations on the binary response variable I_{ij} defined in (4.3). Because the information on the dependent variable is censored, Cameron calls censored regression to the proposed method. The first model proposed by Cameron and James had a normal random term. However, in a later paper, Cameron (1988) expanded the approach to consider the case of a logistically distributed random term as well. The present discussion considers this case of censored logistic regression alone.

Cameron's approach to censored regression is quite straightforward and based on the three following assumptions: (1) we have observations on a binary response variable I_{ij} that is related to the independent variable WTP_{ij} in the way defined in (4.3); (2) WTP_{ij} is generated by a model of the type $WTP_{ij} = \mathbf{x}_{ij}'\rho + u_{ij}$, such as that specified in (3.32), where the u_{ij} are iid logistic random variables with zero mean and κ dispersion parameter; and (3) we have observations on offered bids t_{ij}, plus all explanatory variables $\mathbf{x}_{ij}$. If these assumptions are satisfied, then the probability of a 'yes' answer is:

$$\Pr(I_{ij}=1) = \Pr(WTP_{ij} \geq t_{ij}) = \Pr(\mathbf{x}_{ij}'\rho + u_{ij} \geq t_{ij}) = \Pr(u_{ij} \geq t_{ij} \qquad (4.18)$$
$$- \mathbf{x}_{ij}'\rho) = \Pr\{ u_{ij}/\kappa \geq (t_{ij} - \mathbf{x}_{ij}'\rho)/\kappa\} = \Pr(\psi \geq (t_{ij} - \mathbf{x}_{ij}'\rho)/\kappa\}$$

where ψ is a standard logistic random variable (mean 0; dispersion parameter 1), which has the cdf defined in (4.6). Hence, the log-likelihood function for the observed data is:

$$\log L = \Sigma_i\Sigma_j \{- I_{ij} \log \{1 + \exp[(t_{ij} - \mathbf{x}_{ij}'\rho)/\kappa]\} \qquad (4.19)$$
$$+ (1 - I_{ij})\log\{\exp[(t_{ij} - \mathbf{x}_{ij}'\rho)/\kappa] / (1 + \exp[(t_{ij} - \mathbf{x}_{ij}'\rho)/\kappa])\}\}$$

The maximisation of this function yields the ML estimates for all parameters ρ plus asymptotic standard errors for all these parameter estimates. This maximisation, within a general optimisation computer programme, requires some amount of programming effort. However, Cameron (1988) identified a second possibility for estimating parameters ρ, which relies on the correspondence between the log-likelihood function of the censored logistic regression model in (4.19) and the log-likelihood function of the ordinary logit model in (4.7). In fact, taking:

$$\eta = (- 1/\kappa, \rho'/\kappa)' \text{ as the new parameter vector, and} \qquad (4.20)$$

$$\omega_{ij} = (t_{ij}, \mathbf{x}_{ij}')' \text{ as an augmented vector of predictors}$$

the log-likelihood function becomes:

$$\log L^r = \Sigma_i \Sigma_j \{- I_{ij} \log \{1 + \exp[- \omega_{ij}'\eta]\} \qquad (4.21)$$
$$+ (1 - I_{ij}) \log \{\exp[- \omega_{ij}'\eta]/ (1 + \exp[- \omega_{ij}'\eta])\}\}$$

which is exactly the log-likelihood function of the ordinary logit represented in (4.7). Thus, it is possible to reparameterize the valuation function according to (4.20) and estimate the logit model corresponding to (4.21); then, the parameters of the censored logistic model (the valuation function) are easily recovered from the estimated logit parameters by inverting the reparameterization in (4.20).

Due to the invariance property of ML estimators, identical point estimates for the censored regression parameters are obtained by either direct ML estimation of the censored model or indirect estimation of the censored model through ML estimation of a logit model plus reparameterization (cf. Cameron 1988). There are, however, two problems with the indirect use of ordinary logit algorithms to estimate censored WTP models. The first is that most available logit algorithms require the logit index to be linear in the parameters, which implies the censored regression equation (that is: the valuation function) to be linear in parameters as well. The second is that asymptotic standard errors for the parameters of the censored model are not immediately available among the outcomes of the ordinary logit algorithm. These asymptotic standard errors are required to test hypotheses about the effects of explanatory variables on *WTP*, to build confidence intervals (CI) for conditional means of *WTP*[8] and to carry out model-based tests of demand theory referred to in section 3.4.

A method proposed by Cameron (1991) is used here to compute approximate asymptotic standard errors (se) from the logit's parameter variance–covariance matrix, which provides an approximate variance–covariance matrix for the censored model. This whole matrix is required by interval estimation of the censored variable (*WTP*) and hence for all hypotheses tests involving the *WTP* variable. Cameron's (1991) method comprises four steps: (1) the parameter variance–covariance matrix of the logit is inverted, so yielding the logit's information matrix, **I**; (2) a transformation matrix **J** is generated from the derivatives of the logit parameters with respect to the censored model parameters; (3) the matrix product $\mathbf{JIJ'}$ yields the information matrix of the censored model; (4) inverting this matrix one gets the desired variance–covariance matrix of the censored model $(\mathbf{JIJ'})^{-1}$.

As referred to earlier in this section, the first DC CVM applications did not present CIs for *WTP* estimates because of the computational burden required by interval estimation with the integral approach. Having defined analytical expressions for *WTP* means based exactly on the estimated parameters of the logit model, Hanemann (1984b) opened up the way to an easier computation of confidence intervals. This consists of sampling from the multivariate distribution of the logit parameter estimates and fitting the analytical formula for *WTP* to each sampled set of parameters, in order to generate a complete empirical distribution for *WTP* sample means. Dropping the extreme $\alpha/2$ per cent observations at each tail of this distribution yields the $(1 - \alpha)$ percent CI for the population mean of WTP. This Monte Carlo Hanemann-based approach to interval estimation[9] was followed in some studies completed since 1990 (cf., e.g., Hanemann et al. 1991 and Langford et al. 1996).

Cameron (1991) proposed an analytical (as opposed to numerical) approach to interval estimation of *WTP*, which produces CIs identical to those resulting from the Monte Carlo Hanemann-based approach, with considerable savings of computational work. Interval estimation with Cameron's censored regression model is completely analogous to interval estimation in OLS (Cameron 1991). We only need to substitute the $(k \times k)^{10}$ upper left sub-matrix of the variance–covariance matrix $(\mathbf{JIJ'})^{-1}$ for the OLS variance–covariance matrix $\sigma^2(\mathbf{X'X})^{-1}$ in the usual formulas of CIs for the mean. This technique can be used to build CIs for the *WTP* variable, as well as for the sequential values of individual programmes defined in (3.33); this is because all of these variables are linear combinations of the censored model parameters. Resort has to be made to Monte Carlo interval estimation when test variables are non-linear functions of these parameters, as it is the case with the variable for the test described in section 3.4. However, even in this case, a linear approximation to the non-linear function may be sufficiently accurate (cf. Santos 1997).

Let us now return to the actual differences between Hanemann's and Cameron's methods for analysing DC CVM. Cameron (1988) argued that the RUM-logit approach to DC CVM data is too restrictive because these data convey more information than the conventional DC data that are taken as the paradigm of Hanemann's RUM approach. Information that DC CVM data present in excess of conventional choice data is the variation of the bid amount across respondents. This variation, associated with the corresponding discrete answers, yields censored observations on the underlying continuous variable of interest (*WTP*), which enable us to identify the location and the scale of the underlying continuous *WTP* variable. This is why censored regression techniques are able to recover all the parameters of the valuation function – all of these parameters are identifiable in (4.19) precisely because we have observations on the bid variable t_{ij}. Hence, Cameron (1988) argues that censored regression is the only approach taking full advantage of all the information that can be extracted from DC CVM data.

These critical comments by Cameron are entirely applicable to the numerical integration approach proposed by Bishop and Heberlein (1979) but are unfair with respect to Hanemann's method. In fact, as shown earlier in this section, it is possible to derive and estimate valuation functions within Hanemann's approach, with all parameters of the valuation function being recovered as transformations of the estimated parameters of the utility function. Thus, model-based tests of hypotheses and interval prediction within both approaches are perfectly analogous.

Indeed, the deterministic components of Hanemann's and Cameron's models (that is: a utility difference and an expenditure difference, respectively) are the exact dual of each other, as shown by McConnell (1990), who recognises that, to a certain extent, 'the choice between the (...) approaches is a matter of style' (p. 34). In fact, the only important difference between these models lies on the way the random term enters each model. As rightly pointed out by Cameron (1988), '... the "true" error structure is entirely moot, so either assumption is equally plausible' (p. 372).

The only significant difference that matters when choosing one or the other approach for empirical purposes is the fact they have opposite starting points for specifying the econometric model. Hanemann starts from utility, whereas Cameron starts from the valuation function itself without any concern at all for whether this valuation function is consistent with an existent utility function. Thus, some Cameron-based econometric models are not Hanemann-compatible, and hence choosing a particular approach may have practical implications with respect to the parameters that can be estimated from the data (McConnell 1990).

The Cameron approach is the preferred one in estimating valuation functions from DC CVM data because it permits directly specifying a valuation function: (1) including all parameters to be estimated; (2) yielding all benefit estimates to be predicted; and (3) sufficiently flexible to investigate, for example, the actual structure of substitution relationships between attributes in the data.

On the other hand, the existence of a definable utility function (ensured by Hanemann's approach) is only absolutely required by welfare estimation when one is working with revealed preference data on prices and quantities. In this case, non-compensated demand functions are estimated, which must be integrated back to the utility function if the aim is to estimate compensated welfare measures.[11] However, as noted by Cameron (1988), nothing of this is required with CVM, which is supposed to elicit directly Hicksian compensated welfare measures, rather than non-compensated ones. Thus, it is preferable to specify and estimate directly valuation functions, to keep enough flexibility for choosing among candidate functional forms (satisfying some theoretical requirements but not necessarily being Hanemann-compatible) on grounds of goodness-of-fit.

NOTES

1. Additivity of the two categories of value is ensured by the fact they are sequentially defined in (4.2). First, price is increased to choke-price level, while keeping landscape at its policy-off state; then, the landscape improvement takes place with price at choke level; eventually, price returns to current level, while keeping the policy-on state of landscape.
2. This is why Graves fails to acknowledge the possibility of using revealed preference techniques such as the varying parameter model (Vaughan and Russell 1982) to uncover people's values for aesthetic changes. These changes would affect only the senses and hence would not leave visible traces in behaviours such as the choice of a recreation site.
3. As noted by Hanley and Ruffell (1993), this problem can be partly avoided by introducing interaction variables. For example, in their model, the interaction between conifer diversity and proportion of broad-leaved trees yielded a negative coefficient, according to previous expectations that conifer diversity should have a stronger effect in predominantly coniferous forests.
4. Though new in the field of landscape economics, parts of the approach proposed here derive from a general survey and modelling strategy proposed by Hoehn (1991) and Hoehn and Loomis (1993) for the valuation of multidimensional environmental programmes.
5. Payment vehicle, social context, coerced choice, information-processing capacity and self-interest identification issues are not specific to landscape valuation but general to all CVM applications. Hence, the reader is referred to the general methodological literature: for example, Fischhoff and Furby (1988); Mitchell and Carson (1989); Carson (1991); Cummings et al. (1986); Harris et al. (1989), and Bjornstad and Kahn (1996).
6. A brief discussion of the comparative advantages and weaknesses of the discrete-choice as compared to the open-ended format can be found in chapter 14.
7. A related problem with Hanemann's approach is that utility-theoretic models derived by Hanemann (1984b) from some simple utility specifications have been subsequently tested by other authors (Boyle and Bishop 1988; Bowker and Stoll 1988; and Sellar et al. 1986), who concluded that these models performed worse, in terms of goodness-of-fit, than the original log-logistic specification proposed by Bishop and Heberlein (1979).
8. CIs for benefit estimates are required for these estimates to be used in cost–benefit policy evaluation. Only these CIs can inform a policy-maker about the probability of the cost–benefit analysis selecting the wrong policy decision.
9. Another numeric approach is the parametric bootstrap used by Langford et al. (1996).
10. k is the number of parameters of the censored model, but the size of the variance–covariance matrix is $(k+1).(k+1)$, as it also includes the κ dispersion parameter of the logistic random term.
11. This is usually known as the 'exact' method for welfare estimation (Hausman 1981), as opposed to the 'approximate' method, which uses uncompensated welfare measures as approximate estimates for the valid compensated measures (cf. Willig, 1976).

5. Costs of Landscape Conservation

Landscape change is usually caused by a modification in the way the land is managed. Hence, whether the aim is improving the landscape or preventing degradation, what is at stake is some adjustments in land management allowing us to secure (or keep) a desired state of landscape. Very often, these adjustments use up scarce resources, and hence there is an opportunity cost associated with landscape conservation.

This chapter is about the cost of conserving the landscape. Agricultural land uses are the basic application here, because of (1) the role of farming in creating, maintaining and destroying some of our most valued landscapes, and (2) the current importance of policy schemes for farming and conservation.

The farming–landscape relationship is analysed to identify the set of all technologically feasible solutions: the farming–landscape possibility set. Landscape constraints are then incorporated into a landscape-restricted profit-maximisation problem. Eventually, subtracting landscape-restricted profit from unrestricted profit originates the conservation cost function.

Later sections in this chapter distinguish the financial and the social cost concepts, introduce the issue of transaction costs and discuss the cost-effectiveness of different policy arrangements for landscape conservation.

5.1 THE FARMING–LANDSCAPE TECHNOLOGY

The technical relationship between farming and the landscape differs in some respects from other types of society–environment interactions, such as natural resource use, pollution or land development. In this section, particular features of the farming–landscape relationship are described and incorporated into a model of the underlying technology.

Some inter-temporal linkages, such as lagged effects of changing farming practice on the vegetation, characterise the farming–landscape relationship. These lagged effects can be represented in recursive mathematical programming models (Moxey et al. 1995). However, inter-temporal linkages are not as central to the farming–landscape technology as they are, for example, in natural resource economics, where the central issue is precisely the inter-temporal allocation of stock resources. Therefore, a comparative-static approach is adopted in this chapter to compare the non-restricted profit-maximising equilibrium with the landscape-restricted equilibrium that will occur subsequently to all (ecological and economic) adjustments to a set of landscape constraints.

Farming-related landscape change is a direct consequence of shifts in farming practice at the particular site where the landscape is changing. Therefore, landscape is produced *in situ* as a technical consequence of local farming practice, and there are usually no important spatial linkages between sites in the technology of producing landscape attributes. This is in marked contrast with pollution models, where complex spatial linkages are very often implied by the environmental process of transport and assimilation of the pollutant (cf. Baumol and Oates 1988; and Mäler 1974 and 1985).

Farming-related landscape change usually proceeds by quasi-continuous variations in some previously existing attributes. These variations can be illustrated with the following examples: declining heather cover with raising stocking levels; increasing extent of poorly repaired stone walls or terraces; or progressive intensification of meadow use with the attendant decline in flower diversity. These quasi-continuous changes can be described with respect to the same set of attributes – that is: with respect to the generic m-dimensional attribute vector z, which, in this case, remains a valid indicator of the state of landscape throughout the change. For quasi-continuous multi-attribute changes, the problem of selecting an optimal landscape in the m-dimensional attribute space is meaningful and, at least in theory, analytically tractable.[1]

The properties of the farming–landscape technology just referred to allow us to describe this technology as a well-defined functional relationship between current farm inputs and outputs at a particular site, on the one hand, and, on the other, the state of landscape at this site.

Farm inputs may be either flow or state variables. Market inputs (labour, livestock, seeds, fertiliser and so on) used up at the particular site per time period are represented by a vector r of flow variables. Land in a Ricardian sense plus all past investments on this land with a permanent character (given adequate maintenance) are described by a vector k of state variables characterising the site's fertility and farm structure at a particular instant. Ordinary commercial outputs of the site per time period are represented by a vector q of flow variables. An m-dimensional z attribute vector denotes the state of landscape at the site.

All elements of r, q, k and z are assumed to be non-negative and real-valued. The composite vector (r, q, k, z) at the particular site is called an allocation. The crucial task of defining the farming–landscape technology is that of identifying the set T of all technically feasible allocations within the (r, q, k, z) space. This set is called the farming–landscape possibility set of the site. The properties of set T are explored in what follows.

It is possible to sub-divide the attribute vector z in three classes of landscape attributes according to the way these attributes are related to elements of r, q or k.

Some landscape attributes result from past investment on the land. Think, for example, of dry-stone walls, field terraces, hedgerows, ponds and shrub-free pasture. All of these have a permanent character, provided maintenance is kept at adequate levels. Maintenance requires the use of inputs r such as labour, building materials and mechanical equipment. Some of these attributes still have a positive productivity effect on the farm but, for many, proper maintenance is no more justified for the farmer. In this case, the typical landscape problem is one of dereliction. Note that these attributes are like typical outputs of farming, q, in that they require for their production (or maintenance) the use of inputs r and are non-decreasing in the amounts of these inputs. Hence, attributes of this type shall be called input-requiring (or output-like) landscape attributes and make up an attribute sub-vector z^q.

Other landscape attributes are negatively related at the margin with some farm inputs: for current levels of input use, further land-use intensification leads to a decline in these attributes. For an example, think of flower diversity in meadows, which is threatened by increases in fertiliser use. These attributes are designated input-restricting landscape attributes and make up the attribute sub-vector z^r. The inputs that are inversely related to these attributes are called landscape-restricted inputs and are included in the input sub-vector r^z.

Attributes included in a third attribute class act, under particular market circumstances, as structural constraints to farm profitability. Think, for example, of dense hedgerow country, dry-farmland in Mediterranean countries, wetlands and the unimproved grasslands of hill country. When some point is reached in market conditions (or agricultural support policies), costly investments in removing these constraints become profitable. Thus, we assist to landscape changes such as those associated with hedgerow grubbing, large-scale irrigation, drainage and grassland improvement. Landscape attributes of this type shall be called investment-restricting landscape attributes and make up a third attribute sub-vector: z^k. On the other hand, landscape-degrading investments on the land are designated landscape-restricted investments and are included in the sub-vector k^z (k^{nz} is its complement with respect to k).

To define these three classes of landscape attributes, one should focus on the particular technical relationships underlying the management problem at hand (that is, within some neighbourhood of the current allocation). These relationships do not need to hold all over the (r, q, k, z) space. Hence, the assignment of a particular attribute to a particular class may change for a different management problem implying a different underlying region of the $(\mathbf{r}, \mathbf{q}, \mathbf{k}, \mathbf{z})$ space. A good example is that of many semi-natural ecosystems, such as hay meadows and heather moorland. The creation and maintenance of semi-natural ecosystems require input use to clear the climax vegetation (for example, woodland) and to interrupt the ecological succession leading back to the climax. In this sense, semi-natural ecosystems would be classified as input-requiring attributes. However, when a particular intensification margin is reached, flower-diversity in meadows and heather cover in moorland become threatened by further intensification of fertiliser use or stocking rates respectively. Thus, previous input-requiring attributes become input-restricting attributes as that input-use threshold is crossed. In other words: landscape and commercial farm output are joint productions as well as competitive at some intensive margins (cf. Meyer 1989 or Cheshire 1989).

From the previous discussion of the relationships between particular types of landscape attributes and elements of $\mathbf{r}$, $\mathbf{q}$ and $\mathbf{k}$, it is possible to derive a simplified formal model of the farming–landscape technology.[2]

So, we can first define a production possibility set T^q including all feasible sub-allocations $(\mathbf{r}, \mathbf{q}, \mathbf{k}, \mathbf{z}^q)$. T^q defines the technical relationships between inputs $\mathbf{r}$ and investments $\mathbf{k}$, on the one hand, and, on the other hand, commercial outputs $\mathbf{q}$ and output-like landscape attributes $\mathbf{z}^q$. This sub-set expands the classical notion of production function to a multiple-output case where some landscape attributes (shrub-free pasture or well-kept hedgerows, for example) are jointly produced with farm outputs (sheep, wool and milk, for example). Hence, T^q is defined so that both outputs and output-like attributes are non-decreasing in inputs and investment on the land.

On the other hand, input-restricting landscape attributes $\mathbf{z}^r$ are non-increasing in landscape-restricted inputs $\mathbf{r}^z$. Hence, if we define a set T^r including all feasible sub-allocations $(\mathbf{r}^z, \mathbf{z}^r)$, then we can derive a landscape-restricted input set $R^z(\mathbf{z}^r)$ including all vectors $\mathbf{r}^z$ of landscape-restricted inputs that are consistent with a particular vector of input-restricting attributes, that is:

$$R^z(\mathbf{z}^r) = \{\mathbf{r}^z : (\mathbf{r}^z, \mathbf{z}^r) \in T^r\} \tag{5.1}$$

Likewise, investment-restricting attributes $\mathbf{z}^k$ are non-increasing in landscape-restricted investments $\mathbf{k}^z$. Therefore, if set T^k includes all feasible sub-allocations $(\mathbf{k}^z, \mathbf{z}^k)$, then we can derive a landscape-restricted investment set $K^z(\mathbf{z}^k)$:

$$K^z(\mathbf{z}^k) = \{\mathbf{k}^z : (\mathbf{k}^z, \mathbf{z}^k) \in T^k\} \tag{5.2}$$

which includes all vectors $\mathbf{k}^z$ of landscape-restricted investments that are consistent with a particular vector of investment-restricting attributes.

The complete farming–landscape possibility set T, including all technically feasible allocations within the $(\mathbf{r}, \mathbf{q}, \mathbf{k}, \mathbf{z})$ space, is defined by combining sets T^q, $R^z(\mathbf{z}^r)$ and $K^z(\mathbf{z}^k)$ in the following way:

$$T = \{(\mathbf{r}, \mathbf{q}, \mathbf{k}, \mathbf{z}) : (\mathbf{r}, \mathbf{q}, \mathbf{k}, \mathbf{z}^q) \in T^q \wedge \mathbf{r}^z \in R^z(\mathbf{z}^r) \wedge \mathbf{k}^z \in K^z(\mathbf{z}^k)\} \quad (5.3)$$

The landscape-restricted farmer's possibility set F(z), including all possible options for farmers (with respect to input-use $\mathbf{r}$, output-mix $\mathbf{q}$ and investments $\mathbf{k}$) that are technically consistent with the state of landscape $\mathbf{z}$, is defined as:

$$F(\mathbf{z}) = \{(\mathbf{r}, \mathbf{q}, \mathbf{k}) : (\mathbf{r}, \mathbf{q}, \mathbf{k}, \mathbf{z}) \in T\} \quad (5.4)$$

It is also possible to derive from T the producible-landscape set $Z(\mathbf{r}, \mathbf{q}, \mathbf{k})$:

$$Z(\mathbf{r}, \mathbf{q}, \mathbf{k}) = \{(\mathbf{z}) : (\mathbf{r}, \mathbf{q}, \mathbf{k}, \mathbf{z}) \in T\} \quad (5.5)$$

which includes all possible states of landscape $\mathbf{z}$ that are technically producible when farmers' decisions on input-use, output-mix, and investment on the land result in the allocation $(\mathbf{r}, \mathbf{q}, \mathbf{k})$.

5.2 LANDSCAPE-RESTRICTED PROFIT MAXIMISATION

Suppose farmers are effectively bound by landscape constraints $\mathbf{z} \geq \mathbf{z}^C$ either through regulation or financial incentives like management agreements. According to (5.4), the landscape-restricted farmer's possibility set for $\mathbf{z}^C$ is $F^C = \{(\mathbf{r}, \mathbf{q}, \mathbf{k}) : (\mathbf{r}, \mathbf{q}, \mathbf{k}, \mathbf{z}^C) \in T\}$. For simplicity, let us also assume that non-landscape-restricted investments are to be held constant at current levels $\mathbf{k}^{nz}$ over the planning period (on the other hand, landscape-restricted investments $\mathbf{k}^z$ are allowed to vary). Under these circumstances, farmers are assumed to choose the particular bundle $(\mathbf{r}, \mathbf{q}, \mathbf{k}^z)$ that, satisfying $(\mathbf{r}, \mathbf{q}, \mathbf{k}^z, \mathbf{k}^{nz}) \in F^C$, maximises the quasi-rent resulting from the adding of variable inputs $(\mathbf{r}, \mathbf{k}^z)$ to the fixed investments $\mathbf{k}^{nz}$. If $\mathbf{p}$, $\mathbf{w}$, and $\mathbf{v}$ are vectors of strictly positive given prices for market outputs, inputs and landscape-restricted investments, then we have the following landscape-restricted profit maximisation problem:

$$\max_{\mathbf{q}, \mathbf{r}, \mathbf{k}^z} \quad \mathbf{pq} - \mathbf{wr} - \mathbf{vk}^z \quad \text{s.t.:} \ (\mathbf{r}, \mathbf{q}, \mathbf{k}^z, \mathbf{k}^{nz}) \in F^C \quad (5.6)$$

Assuming the solution for this problem exists and is unique[3], this solution yields the landscape-restricted profit-maximising bundle $(\mathbf{r}^C, \mathbf{q}^C, \mathbf{k}^{zC})$, where: $\mathbf{r}^C(\mathbf{p}, \mathbf{w}, \mathbf{v}, \mathbf{z}^C, \mathbf{k}^{nz} \,|\, T)$ represents landscape-restricted demands for market inputs; $\mathbf{q}^C(\mathbf{p}, \mathbf{w}, \mathbf{v}, \mathbf{z}^C, \mathbf{k}^{nz} \,|\, T)$ represents landscape-restricted supplies of market outputs; and $\mathbf{k}^{zC}(\mathbf{p}, \mathbf{w}, \mathbf{v}, \mathbf{z}^C, \mathbf{k}^{nz} \,|\, T)$ represents landscape-restricted demands for investments on the land. Introducing these supply and demand functions back into the objective function originates the landscape-restricted profit function:

$$\Pi^C(\mathbf{p}, \mathbf{w}, \mathbf{v}, \mathbf{z}^C, \mathbf{k}^{nz} \,|\, T) = \mathbf{pq}^C(.) - \mathbf{wr}^C(.) - \mathbf{vk}^z(.) \qquad (5.7)$$

yielding the maximum achievable quasi-rent when farmers' decisions are bound by the landscape constraints $\mathbf{z} \geq \mathbf{z}^C$, fixed investments on the land $\mathbf{k}^{nz}$ and technology T. Assuming variable factors are not perfect substitutes for fixed investments on the land, this quasi-rent accrues to the owner of the fixed factors – the farmer-owner or a landowner.

5.3 PRODUCIBLE LANDSCAPE UNDER UNRESTRICTED PROFIT MAXIMISATION

Usually, farming practice is not bound by landscape constraints. Moreover, the fact of the state of landscape $\mathbf{z}$ being a non-excludable pure public good prevents farmers from charging a price for it. Thus, landscape attributes $\mathbf{z}$ do not enter the landscape-unrestricted profit-maximising problem that supposedly underlies farmers' decisions.

This landscape-unrestricted problem can be solved either: (1) by maximising the objective function in (5.6) while ignoring the landscape constraints $\mathbf{z} \geq \mathbf{z}^C$; or (2) by allowing these constraints to vary so that we may select a vector of landscape constraints $\mathbf{z}^C = \mathbf{z}^*(\mathbf{p}, \mathbf{w}, \mathbf{v}, \mathbf{k}^{nz} \,|\, T)$ yielding the maximum possible value of the landscape-restricted profit function in (5.7). Introducing this $\mathbf{z}^*$ back into this restricted profit function originates the landscape-unrestricted profit function $\Pi(.)$, that is:

$$\Pi(\mathbf{p}, \mathbf{w}, \mathbf{v}, \mathbf{k}^{nz} \,|\, T) = \max_{\mathbf{z}^C} \Pi^C(\mathbf{p}, \mathbf{w}, \mathbf{v}, \mathbf{z}^C, \mathbf{k}^{nz} \,|\, T) \qquad (5.8)$$

Assuming $(\mathbf{r}^*, \mathbf{q}^*, \mathbf{k}^{z*})$ is a bundle of input demands, output supplies and demands for investment solving for the landscape-unrestricted problem, the producible-landscape set under unrestricted profit maximisation will be: $Z^* = \{(\mathbf{z}): (\mathbf{r}^*, \mathbf{q}^*, \mathbf{k}^{z*}, \mathbf{k}^{nz}, \mathbf{z}) \in T\}$. Any $\mathbf{z} \in Z^*$ is consistent (and any $\mathbf{z} \notin Z^*$ inconsistent) with unrestricted profit maximisation. In this sense, possible states of landscape are determined as a by-product of farmers' decisions on input-use, output-mix and investment. This side-effect nature with respect to the central economic decisions of the agent is precisely what typifies farming-related landscape change as an externality.[4]

Note, however, that, in general, the state of landscape is only incompletely determined by unrestricted profit maximisation. In fact, whilst the solution for the maximisation problem must be located on the boundary of the feasibility set with respect to priced items $\mathbf{r}$, $\mathbf{q}$ and $\mathbf{k}^z$ (a strict requirement of technical efficiency), the non-priced post-maximisation $\mathbf{z}$ is not necessarily on the boundary of Z^*. This means that an opportunity may exist for small landscape improvements to take place while keeping, at the same time, the maximum possible profit. It is strictly required by rationality that such opportunities for free landscape improvement should be the first improvements to be considered. Along these lines, the Countryside Commission for England and Wales proposes using payment schemes for countryside management only in those situations where landscape benefits 'would not be produced or maintained without payments because they cost more than land managers can afford to spend' and 'could not reasonably be expected as part of good husbandry' (Countryside Commission 1993: 8–9). Despite this opportunity for free improvements, the externality problem and other considerations (Santos 1997) imply that socially optimal states of landscape $\mathbf{z}^0$ will often lie outside Z^*. Reaching such an optimum, or undertaking other major improvements across the boundary of Z^*, requires trade-offs to be made between farmers' quasi-rents and landscape quality.

5.4 TRADING-OFF QUASI-RENTS FOR LANDSCAPE QUALITY

Let us start with a landscape-unrestricted profit-maximising allocation ($\mathbf{r}^*$, $\mathbf{q}^*$, $\mathbf{k}^{z*}$, $\mathbf{k}^{nz}$, $\mathbf{z}$) where $\mathbf{z} \in Z^*$. If the aim is improving the landscape, a set of landscape constraints $\mathbf{z}^C$ can be imposed on farmers. Suppose these constraints are gradually tightened so that additional landscape improvements are successively achieved. For the first improvements, $\mathbf{z}^C$ may still be inside Z^*; landscape constraints remain non-binding and hence the unrestricted maximum profit is still achievable. Thus, for these first cost-free improvements, the landscape-restricted profit function $\Pi^C(.)$ is constant in $\mathbf{z}^C$ and coincides with the unrestricted profit level Π (see Figure 5.1).

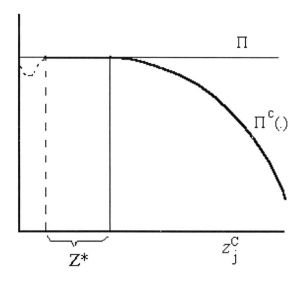

Figure 5.1 Landscape-restricted profit function

Once the increasing landscape constraints cross the right boundary of Z^*, a profit-maximising allocation (r^*, q^*, k^{z*}) is no more feasible, and hence:

$$\Pi^C(p, w, v, z^C, k^{nz} \,|\, T) < \Pi(p, w, v, k^{nz} \,|\, T) \qquad (5.9)$$

This implies $\Pi^C(.)$ is strictly decreasing in the constraints in some neighbourhood at the right of Z^*. Moreover, as suggested by Santos (1997), properties of the farming–landscape possibility set T, which seem fairly general (though admitting exceptions), imply Π^C is strictly decreasing and concave ($\partial\Pi^C/\partial z^C < 0$ and $\partial^2\Pi^C/\partial z^{C^2} \leq 0$) over significant regions of the (r, q, k, z) space at the right of Z^*, as represented in Figure 5.1 with respect to attribute j.

All profit functions used in this chapter actually yield quasi-rents accruing to the owner of the fixed factors. Thus, assuming outputs (and inputs) are sold (bought) at infinite price-elasticity, the quasi-rent variation:

$$\Delta y = \Pi^C(p, w, v, z^C, k^{nz} \,|\, T) - \Pi(p, w, v, k^{nz} \,|\, T) \qquad (5.10)$$

yields the entire variation in the owner's personal income resulting from the imposition of landscape constraints z^C. For simplicity, this owner of the fixed factors is thereafter identified with the farmer.

Compensating variation (CV) is adopted here to assess the welfare effects on farmers of landscape constraints z^C. CV^F represents now (the negative of) the minimum compensation (or WTA) farmers would require for voluntarily complying with these constraints. Denoting the indirect utility function of farmers as $V(z, y)$, CV^F is implicitly defined by: $V(z, y) = V(z^C, y + \Delta y - CV^F)$. Hence, if farmers are assumed indifferent (in aesthetic or other related terms) to the state of landscape,[5] then:

$$CV^F(\mathbf{p}, \mathbf{w}, \mathbf{v}, \mathbf{z}^C, \mathbf{k}^{nz} \mid T) = \Delta y = \Pi^C(.) - \Pi(.) \qquad (5.11)$$

Equations (5.11) and (5.9) imply CV^F is negative outside Z^*, as we would expect for any change reducing farmers' income. Thus, it is possible to conclude that minimum compensation required by farmers for voluntarily complying with constraints z^C is the modulus of the difference between the landscape-restricted profit function at z^C and the unrestricted profit function. The function giving this modulus of $CV^F(.)$ is the conservation cost function:

$$CC(\mathbf{p}, \mathbf{w}, \mathbf{v}, \mathbf{z}^C, \mathbf{k}^{nz} \mid T) = - CV^F(.) = \Pi(.) - \Pi^C(.) \qquad (5.12)$$

which depicts the trade-offs to be made between farmers' quasi-rent and a landscape improvement from a profit-maximising state of landscape $z \in Z^*$ to the particular state z^C. The conservation cost function is implicitly represented in Figure 5.1 as the vertical difference between Π and $\Pi^C(.)$ for any level of the constraint z_j^C. The properties of the conservation cost function are directly implied by properties of the landscape-restricted profit function presented earlier in this section. Thus, the cost function should always be non-negative; nil and constant within Z^*; and positive, strictly increasing and convex at the right of Z^*.

Note that $\partial CC(.)/\partial \mathbf{z}^C = - \partial \Pi^C(.)/\partial \mathbf{z}^C$ generates a vector of marginal cost functions for all landscape attributes, which are non-decreasing in the corresponding attributes if the conservation cost function is convex. Marginal cost functions depend in general on all variables $\mathbf{p}$, $\mathbf{w}$, $\mathbf{v}$, $\mathbf{z}^C$, $\mathbf{k}^{nz}$ and T. Inverting these functions with respect to the corresponding z_j^Cs generates a vector of supply functions for all landscape attributes, that is the vector:

$$\mathbf{z}^S = \mathbf{z}^S(\mathbf{p}^z, \mathbf{p}, \mathbf{w}, \mathbf{v}, \mathbf{k}^{nz} \mid T) \qquad (5.13)$$

yielding the levels of landscape attributes that would be supplied by farmers under market, structural and technological conditions $(\mathbf{p}, \mathbf{w}, \mathbf{v}, \mathbf{k}^{nz} \mid T)$ if attributes were priced according to the m-dimensional price vector $\mathbf{p}^z$.

5.5 FINANCIAL *VS* SOCIAL COSTS

So far, input, output and investment prices have been assumed parametric and given by ruling market prices. This partial equilibrium setting is valid as long as the adjustments in land management required by landscape conservation are small enough with respect to the economy as a whole.[6]

Let us now identify, within this partial equilibrium frame, the particular prices that should be used in estimating conservation costs. Ruling market prices, agricultural subsidies (such as per head livestock premiums) and capital grants received in connection with landscape-restricted investments should enter the calculation of quasi-rent variation when the aim is estimating the minimum compensation farmers would require for voluntarily complying with the landscape constraints. This is in keeping with the voluntary nature of the post-World War 2 approach to farming and conservation. Indeed, the central concept in this approach is that of full compensation of farmers for any profit forgone as a consequence of environmentally sensitive practice.[7]

If market prices, subsidies and capital grants enter the calculation of quasi-rent variation, this calculation yields the compensation-payment cost incurred by the agency operating the conservation scheme. At the level of government, as a whole, adjustments in land management implied by conservation may also originate some financial economies. For example, part of the agricultural policy subsidies and grants are no more payable to farmers who reduced land-use intensity because of the scheme. At this more global level in government, these financial economies should be deducted from the financial cost incurred by the conservation agency. All of the above costs are referred to as financial conservation costs, as they represent expenditure for the particular agency operating the scheme, or for government as a whole.

Suppose now that all effects of agricultural policy and other market imperfections are deducted from market prices and that no direct subsidies or grants enter the estimation of the quasi-rent variation. In this case, a different cost concept is estimated – social conservation cost – in which resources are valued at prices that only reflect agents' marginal WTP and existing resource scarcity. According to the individualistic foundations of neoclassical economics, this is the cost concept reflecting the effect on social welfare of adjustments in land management implied by the conservation scheme.

Existing high levels of agricultural support mean that a large divergence probably exists between financial and social conservation costs. This divergence was clearly demonstrated by Willis et al. (1988) with respect to management agreements under the 1981 Wildlife and Countryside Act. In this case, landscape constraints were mainly imposed on landscape-restricted inputs and investments (for example: fertiliser constraints to keep botanical diversity, and constraints on drainage to keep habitat-enhancing winter flooding), and hence caused a decline in farm output. When this output decline is valued at policy-inflated market prices and includes all sorts of subsidies, the estimated financial conservation cost exceeds social conservation cost. Therefore, high levels of agricultural support add to the financial costs of compensating farmers for not intensifying land use. Willis et al. demonstrated that, although social conservation costs were quite small in most cases, the policy-inflated value of agricultural output always magnified these costs by significant amounts.

As shown by Willis et al. (1988), agricultural and conservation policies conflict with each other in cases where input- and investment-restricting attributes are at the core of the conservation problem. However, we can expect quite the opposite relationship between these policies in cases where input-requiring attributes are the main policy concern. In these cases, the problem is how to maintain or increase unprofitable land uses so that landscape attributes that go hand in hand with human use (think of well-kept stone walls or scrub-free pastures) can be conserved.[8] High levels of agricultural support may help in achieving this goal. Likewise, high levels of support increase farm income and thus reduce the payments that would be required to induce farmers to stay in those economically marginal areas where farmers' presence is essential for the upkeep of traditional landscapes. Hence, for input-requiring attributes, high levels of agricultural support reduce financial conservation costs.

5.6 TRANSACTION COSTS

There is a different type of costs of conservation schemes which should be added to quasi-rent variation if we want to estimate the full cost of conservation. As an illustration, pick the case of voluntary schemes for farming and conservation. These schemes must first be designed, areas must be chosen, landscape goals targeted and management prescriptions specified. Then, farmers ought to be informed about available agreement conditions. Possibly, legal costs are incurred in writing and sealing management agreements. Eventually, farmers' compliance with agreed management prescriptions must be monitored and the whole scheme assessed. All these tasks use up resources, which remain no longer available for other uses.

These social opportunity costs, which should be assessed as part of the scheme's full effect on social welfare, are usually called transaction costs.

Coase introduced the idea of transaction costs to environmental economists in an influential paper published in 1960. There, he establishes a result thereafter known as the Coase theorem: in a world without transaction costs (that is, where all transactions operate without friction), voluntary negotiation between parties involved in an externality leads to a Pareto-optimal level of this externality (that is: to an allocation where nobody can be made better off without making someone else worse off).

The implications of the transaction cost concept for landscape conservation policy may seem straightforward: (1) there are very large numbers of both farmers and landscape users; thus, (2) transaction costs are prohibitively high for a private negotiation to take place; (3) transaction costs are real economic costs; hence, (4) the current state of affairs, including the state of landscape, is socially optimal. However, as Baumol and Oates (1988) pointed out, the Coase theorem is, by definition, non-applicable to large-number cases such as the landscape externality. This is because, even if transaction costs are prohibitively high for a voluntary negotiation to take place, an alternative policy arrangement may exist, which can be, for example, management agreements with farmers negotiated by a conservation agency on behalf of the public. If transaction costs of this alternative policy arrangement are sufficiently low, nothing hinders net social welfare gains to be made from this policy (in this case, the current state of landscape is obviously non-optimal in the Pareto sense). To check whether this is the case, a cost–benefit analysis taking into account the transaction costs associated with the proposed policy is the proper analytical tool.

5.7 COST-MINIMISING CONSERVATION POLICY

The restricted profit function in (5.7) gives us the maximum possible profit given the landscape constraints z^C, and hence the conservation cost function in (5.12) yields the minimum cost of complying with these constraints. This is only so because all profit-enhancing adjustments (in input-use, output-mix and investment) to the landscape constraints are possible in the landscape-restricted maximisation problem. If this was not the case, and further rigidity was introduced in this problem, the resulting conservation cost would exceed the minimum cost of complying with the landscape constraints.

For an example, think of a conservation scheme where the target is maintaining current flower diversity in meadows, which is threatened by intensification of fertiliser use. In this case, the relationship between fertiliser use and flower diversity is mediated by other choice variables such as dates of application of the fertiliser, stocking rates and hay cutting dates. Thus, imposing a single constraint on a particular input (fertiliser) may introduce more rigidity than that which is required by compliance with the landscape constraints. This is because this input constraint hinders substitution between inputs in the production of landscape and hence prevents farmers from taking advantage of all profit-enhancing adjustments that are consistent with the landscape constraints. Therefore, the final allocation is not cost-minimising.

This point is worth making because many policy schemes for landscape conservation, such as Environmentally Sensitive Area (ESA) schemes, operate through management agreements with farmers based on input and other management constraints. As shown above, management constraints are generally not cost-effective.

There is, however, a recent trend in conservation schemes in the UK for more directly linking payments to valued 'countryside products, rather than [to] the management process or practice that is supposed to produce them' (Countryside Commission 1993: 9). The cost-effectiveness property of this new approach is explicitly mentioned when the Commission says that paying 'land managers for (...) countryside benefits will give them an incentive to experiment to produce these benefits at lowest cost to themselves' (Countryside Commission 1993: 9). This means signing product agreements rather than management agreements.[9] The Commission already assayed this product-oriented approach to farming and conservation issues within the Countryside Stewardship scheme.

A different issue for any conservation agency is whether to offer standard management agreements across entire regions or to sign case-specific agreements with particular farmers. Whitby and Saunders (1994) compared conservation costs in two cases: standard management agreements in ESAs and individually tailored agreements in Sites of Special Scientific Interest (SSSI).

Heterogeneity in farming–landscape conditions within a region implies that some farmers can supply the same levels of landscape attributes z^C at lower cost than others. Thus, an agency acting as a price-discriminating monopolist (as with individually-tailored agreements) can reduce to a minimum the compensation payments required to achieve the same state of landscape z^C across the whole region. It may possibly happen that for many farmers there are no compliance costs at all, and these farmers need not be compensated.

On the other hand, with standard management agreements and standard payments (as in ESAs), any eligible farmer in the region may apply for, and eventually get, an agreement. Thus, many farmers facing no conservation costs at all (that is, those who will adopt environmentally sensitive practice anyway) are particularly motivated to enter into such standard agreements.

This adds to the financial (payment) costs but not to the landscape benefits of the scheme.

In addition, if all farmers are to be offered standard payment rates, then the level of such payment rates should be sufficiently high to induce those farmers facing the highest compliance costs within the region to enter into an agreement. Only this would make sure that all land within the region is given convenient protection. Under these circumstances, all farmers must be offered a vector of payment rates $\mathbf{p}^z$ covering the marginal costs of complying with constraints $\mathbf{z}^C$ under the most unfavourable conditions within the region (cf. equation 5.13). Hence, region-standard agreements create a differential rent for those farmers with marginal compliance costs lower than $\mathbf{p}^z$. Again, this rent adds to the financial (payment) cost but not to the landscape benefits of the scheme, which would lead to prefer individually tailored agreements – where such a rent need not be paid to farmers – on cost-effectiveness grounds. However, individually tailored agreements imply higher transaction costs than standard agreements. This is why we can conclude (cf. also Whitby and Saunders 1994) that, provided transaction costs are not sufficiently different between agreement types, individually tailored agreements are more cost-effective than standard agreements.[10]

NOTES

1. This is not the case for large-scale afforestation, land development or dam construction projects, for which final and initial states of landscape are not comparable with respect to the same set of landscape attributes. Thus, for these projects, what is at stake is a discrete decision on whether to go ahead with the project rather than the selection of an optimal state of landscape in a continuous multi-attribute space.
2. This model is more fully explored and specified in Santos (1997).
3. Assuming Γ^C is non-empty, closed and bounded from above on the $\mathbf{q}$ for each finite $(\mathbf{r}, \mathbf{k}^z)$, the fact of the objective function being continuous ensures, by the Weierstrass theorem, that a solution exists. Assuming F^C is strictly convex, the fact of the objective function being non-constant and quasi-concave ensures the solution is unique (Gravelle and Rees 1992).
4. Baumol and Oates (1988) discuss how the externality concept should be formally defined.
5. Assuming farmers are completely landscape-indifferent is certainly a strong assumption; however, Santos (1997) shows that this raises no major problem for applied cost–benefit analysis provided landscape change valuation by farmers as landscape 'users' is added to the other values. The need of assuming producers derive no non-pecuniary benefits from the change, in order to ensure that quasi-rent variation includes all welfare effects on producers, is understood by Mishan (1968).
6. If this is not true, the welfare effects of output and input price changes on consumers and producers must be evaluated. In this case, the change in quasi-rent illustrated in Figure 5.1 is no longer the true measure of producers' welfare change, since both the landscape-unrestricted and the landscape-restricted profit functions are shifted by price changes.
7. Cf. Willis et al. (1988); Whittaker et al. (1991); Whitby and Saunders (1994); Colman (1994) and Countryside Commission (1993).
8. Cf., for example, Santos and Aguiar (1994); and Campos (1993).

9. Of course, for this new approach to work, it is essential that farmers have access to high quality advice on farming–landscape technology and that payments are (as for any commercial relationship) conditional on the delivery by farmers of landscape products conforming to initial specifications that were agreed upon (Countryside Commission 1993).
10. Cf. also Colman (1994) and Hanley et al. (1996).

6. Cost–Benefit Analysis of Landscape Change

This chapter brings together concepts presented in chapters 3 and 5 with the aim of developing cost–benefit rules for the selection of (1) socially desirable landscape changes and (2) socially optimal states of landscape. First, we review the social-welfare criteria underlying such decision rules. Cost–benefit rules are then derived for cases where benefit and cost functions are continuous in attributes, that is: where each landscape attribute can take any position in a continuous scale. However, for many practical conservation decisions, the choice set is restricted to a number of possible conservation programmes, each one involving a discrete change in some landscape attributes. In this discrete case, the problem is how to select the best possible programme-mix. A sequential cost–benefit procedure aimed at solving this problem is proposed and discussed in the final section.

6.1 SOCIAL-WELFARE CRITERIA AND THE COST–BENEFIT RULES

For landscape conservation policy to enhance the level of social welfare, decision-makers should be able to identify those landscape changes that are welfare-improving or even those states of landscape that maximise social welfare. This identification task can be based on three conceptual approaches to social welfare, which have been developed by economists: the social-welfare function, Pareto optimality and compensation tests.

Social-Welfare Function

The idea of a social-welfare function originated from the work of Bergson in the late 1930s. A social-welfare function, $W=W(U_1, U_2,..., U_I)$, should be understood as a complete and consistent ordering of all possible vectors ($U_1, U_2,..., U_I$) representing the utility levels of individual members of society. It is usually assumed that W: (1) depends only on the U_is, that is on the utility of individuals; (2) increases with a *ceteris paribus* increase in any U_i; and (3) can be held constant if one individual is made worse off by making another individual better off (Johansson 1993). Substituting in $W(.)$ indirect utility functions $V_i(\mathbf{p}, \mathbf{z}, y_i)$ for the utility levels of individuals i shows us that $W(.)$ depends only on market prices, landscape attributes and individuals' incomes, that is: $W = W[V_1(\mathbf{p}, \mathbf{z}, y_1), V_2(\mathbf{p}, \mathbf{z}, y_2), …, V_I(\mathbf{p}, \mathbf{z}, y_I)] = w(\mathbf{p}, \mathbf{z}, y_1, y_2, …, y_I)$. Thus, function $w(.)$ gives us a consistent ranking of all bundles of prices, landscape attributes and individuals' incomes with respect to the 'preferences of society'. If we knew this function, it would be very easy to investigate whether a landscape change is an improvement from the 'society's point of view' or to select socially optimal states of landscape. If weighting landscapes is weighting people's opinions about landscapes (Howard 1992), the social-welfare function would provide an adequate basis for weighting these opinions: society's opinion itself. This would end all debates about who should decide what a desirable landscape is.

However, there are at least two fundamental problems with the use of a social-welfare function for the assessment of landscape changes. The first is an analytical problem, known as the Arrow impossibility theorem: it is impossible to secure a unique social ranking of vectors $(\mathbf{p}, \mathbf{z}, y_1, y_2, …, y_I)$ from the indirect utility functions of the individuals when these functions have only an ordinal sense.[1] The second flaw is that – contrarily to the economists', somewhat naïve, concept of society's preferences as something personified in the democratically elected institutions – there is no such thing as a consistent set of societal preferences. Institutions have in-built contradictions and conflicts, which are the quintessence of the political process. Agents in the policy arena fight to impose their different views and often change and negotiate these views as a part of the policy-making process itself. Hence, it is very unlikely that a complete and coherent ranking of states of the world can be secured from an analysis of past policy outcomes.

Pareto Optimality

By the end of the last century, Pareto defined his concept of a social optimum – the so-called 'Pareto optimum' – as a situation where it is impossible to make anyone better off without making someone else worse off. This situation would be optimal because there would be no more potential improvements left to be made. Pareto only considered as unambiguous improvements those changes in resource allocation making nobody worse off and at least one individual better off. These changes are known today as 'Pareto improvements'. It is hard to think of social-welfare functions for which such changes do not raise the level of social welfare, and hence the Pareto criterion is often thought of as a sufficient condition for social-welfare improvements.

There are, however, many possible changes that seem to enhance social welfare but do not pass the Pareto criterion. For example, think of a case where the conservation of the surroundings of a popular waterfall requires the maintenance as old woodland of 5 hectares included in a huge estate. Even if the landowner only suffered a marginal loss by not converting this small area to commercial forestry, the conservation option would not be a Pareto improvement. When someone is made worse off – no matter how much worse and how much others are made better off – the initial and final states are said to be Pareto-noncomparable (Just et al. 1982). Assessing a movement between two Pareto-noncomparable states of landscape means that the losses incurred by some individuals must be weighted against the gains to others. This assessment is impossible within the Pareto frame, where the well-being of an individual cannot be traded off for the well-being of others. Only with a social-welfare function can these trade-offs be assessed. Thus, although all landscape changes passing the Pareto criterion are welfare-improving, we cannot rule out the possibility that many landscape changes not passing the Pareto criterion may also be welfare-improving. Therefore, the Pareto criterion provides a sufficient, but not necessary, condition for social-welfare improvements.

Most landscape conservation policies imply trading off land users' quasi-rents for landscape quality; hence, the policy-off and policy-on states of landscape are often Pareto-noncomparable. In these cases, the Pareto frame, as it is, is useless.

Compensation Tests

In the late 1930s, Kaldor and Hicks created criteria for comparing Pareto-noncomparable states. These criteria are grounded on the idea of compensation. According to the Kaldor criterion, a change is socially desirable if there is a hypothetical post-change redistribution of income making everybody better off than before the change (Johansson 1993). In the case of a landscape improvement, this means gainers with the improvement can fully compensate losers and still remain better off than before the change. Thus, for a landscape change to be socially desirable, it would be required that aggregate WTP of gainers exceeds aggregate compensation demanded by losers. Therefore, the algebraic sum of Hicksian compensating variations across all parts affected by the landscape change should be positive for a socially desirable change, that is:

$$\Sigma_i \, CV^U_{\,i} + \Sigma_j \, CV^F_{\,j} > 0 \qquad\qquad (6.1)$$

where the CV^U_is represent the (positive) compensating variation of landscape users (the gainers with a landscape improvement) and the CV^F_js represent the (negative) compensating variation of land users (the losers).

A conservation policy that passes the Kaldor criterion and is followed by actual compensation corresponds to a Pareto improvement, as, in this case, losers are fully compensated and gainers are better off after the change (even after compensating losers) than before. As full compensation is often neither ensured nor possible, conservation policies passing the Kaldor criterion are only potential Pareto improvements. Therefore, the Kaldor criterion is a necessary, but not sufficient, condition for a landscape change to be welfare-improving in the Pareto sense.[2]

Hicks proposed a different criterion for potential welfare-improvements: if there is any hypothetical pre-change redistribution of income making everybody better off than after the change, then this change should be seen as socially undesirable (Johansson 1993). This represents the case where losers can fully compensate (bribe) gainers for the change not to go ahead. Hence, the Hicks criterion implies that, for a landscape change to be socially desirable, aggregate WTP of losers to prevent the change should not exceed aggregate compensation demanded by gainers to go without it. The Hicks criterion operates by algebraically summing the Hicksian equivalent variations (EV) across all parts affected by the change and by proceeding with the change if this sum is positive, that is if: $\Sigma_i EV^U_i + \Sigma_j EV^F_j > 0$.

Kaldor's criterion (rather than Hicks's) is used in what follows to derive cost–benefit rules for landscape conservation schemes because of the particular structure of property rights that is embodied in these schemes. In fact, this structure implicitly entitles farmers with rights to change landscape attributes according to their individual needs. Thus, the agency managing the conservation scheme is supposed to buy these rights from farmers on behalf of the general public. This structure of property rights dictates the use of the Kaldor criterion to assess improvements with respect to the status quo.[3]

Welfare-Improving Landscape Changes

Using (3.26) and (5.11), the Kaldor compensation test in (6.1) originates a cost–benefit rule to assess multi-attribute landscape changes. Thus, we call the change $\mathbf{z} \to \mathbf{z}^C$ a (potentially) welfare-improving landscape change if:[4]

$$N . CV^U(\mathbf{z}, \mathbf{z}^C, \bar{y} \mid U(.)) + S . CV^F (\mathbf{p}, \mathbf{w}, \mathbf{v}, \mathbf{z}^C, \mathbf{k}^{nz} \mid T) > 0 \qquad (6.2)$$

where: N is the number of landscape users; CV^U is the compensating variation (i.e.: WTP) function of users; S is the acreage of the conservation area (in hectares); and CV^F is the per-hectare (negative) compensating variation function (i.e.: *WTA*) of farmers. Note that, according to (6.2), the social desirability of a particular landscape change $z \to z^C$ depends on: (1) average income of landscape users; (2) users' preferences as defined by $U(.)$; (3) prices of farm outputs, inputs and investments **p**, **w**, and **v**; (4) past investment on the land and soil fertility, k^{nz}; and (5) the farming–landscape technology T.

Socially Optimal State of Landscape

The LHS of (6.2) is the net benefit of the landscape change $z \to z^C$. This net benefit represents the difference between gainers' WTP for the change and the minimum compensation losers would require for accepting that change. Thus, any marginal change in z^C yielding a positive net benefit is a potential Pareto improvement. The possibilities for such marginal improvements cease when the net benefit function in the LHS of (6.2) reaches a global maximum, i.e.: when marginal net benefits become nil. Hence, ignoring boundary solutions, this maximum can be identified through the following first-order conditions:

$$N . \partial CV^U(.)/\partial z_j^C + S . \partial CV^F(.)/\partial z_j^C = 0 \tag{6.3}$$

$$(\text{for all } j = 1, 2, ..., m)$$

or, according to (3.12), (3.26) and (5.12):

$$N . \pi_j^c(.) + S . \partial CC(.)/\partial z_j^C = 0 \tag{6.4}$$

$$(\text{for all } j = 1, 2, ..., m)$$

where: $\pi_j^c(.)$ represents the compensated marginal valuation of attribute j by an average user and $\partial CC(.)/\partial z_j^C$ is the marginal cost of attribute j.

Note that the cost–benefit rule in (6.4) corresponds to the static efficiency rule for multi-attribute changes. It can be read as: proceed with landscape improvements up to a point where marginal benefits are identical to marginal conservation costs for all landscape attributes – that is, where marginal benefit and marginal cost curves cross in every single attribute plane.

It should also be noted that the expression $N . \pi_j^c(.)$ for marginal benefits reveals that individual marginal valuations are aggregated vertically, as it is required by the non-rival character of landscape attributes – each additional unit of an attribute can be 'used' by all landscape users.

The state of landscape z^o solving for (6.4) should be interpreted as a Pareto-optimal state of landscape. In fact, z^o represents a state of landscape where all possible improvements for any individual cannot be made without making someone else worse off, even if compensation is possible. This means that gainers cannot compensate losers for any departure from z^o.

The Pareto-optimality of a particular state of landscape depends on given preferences, technology, income distribution, prices and all other factors listed in (6.2). Hence, for example, there is a different optimal landscape for each alternative distribution of income. This reminds us that compensation tests (and Pareto optimality) suppose a choice on whose preferences should count in landscape conservation decision-making and how to weight these preferences. Within the Pareto–Kaldor–Hicks frame, preferences that count are those of all individuals affected by a landscape change; the intensity and sign of these preferences count; and this intensity is weighted according to each individual's purchasing power.

Second-Order Conditions and Multiple Optima

Non-convexity of the farming–landscape possibility set and non-concavity of the valuation function may cause problems in identifying optimal landscapes, as second-order conditions for z^o (selected according to first-order conditions) to be a global maximum of the net benefit function may not hold. The case of a non-concave valuation function is discussed here. This is an important case because it has been shown to occur in practice in valuation studies. For example, Johansson (1989) reports on a CVM study where respondents were told about 300 endangered species living in Swedish forests. Then, they were asked to independently value different levels of conservation, corresponding to 50 per cent, 75 per cent and 100 per cent of the 300 species. The resulting valuation function is first strictly concave with respect to the number of species (diminishing returns); then, an inflection point occurs and the valuation function becomes convex, being indeed very steep at the close neighbourhood of the point where all the 300 species are preserved. Johansson (1993) explains this inflection point in terms of changes in risk-related behaviour, that is: after people had a minimum number of species conserved, they started to behave as risk-loving gamblers. There is, however, a much simpler and more appealing explanation for this convex part of the valuation function, which applies even to a deterministic world. This explanation is based on the idea that people strongly prefer complete conservation schemes to partial ones, because the former somehow preserve the integrity of nature or a cherished landscape. Hence, they are prepared to pay an increasing premium over and above the valuation of the individual species (or individual landscape attributes) when the scope of the conservation scheme approaches completeness. This completeness-premium may explain the increasing-returns (that is convex) part of the valuation function. This can be expressed in terms of the theory of demand for attributes presented in chapter 3 by saying that the attributes become compensated complements of each other as the scheme scope approaches completeness. This occurs in the Portuguese case-study presented in Part Three of this book.

A valuation function that is first concave and becomes convex beyond a certain level of the attributes generates a marginal valuation function that is first decreasing and then increasing. This is illustrated in Figure 6.1.

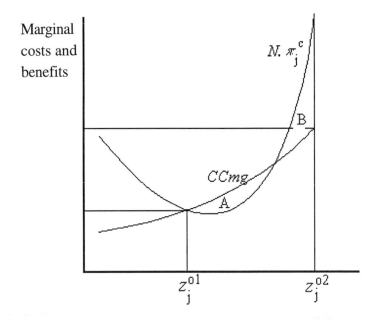

Figure 6.1 Non-concavity of benefit function and multiple local optima

In such a situation, first-order conditions in (6.4) lead us to identify z_j^{o1} as the Pareto-optimal level of attribute j. However, when area B is larger than A, the Pareto optimum is at z_j^{o2}. Thus, if second-order conditions do not hold, the use of first-order conditions may lead to misidentify the optimal state of landscape. In this case, only the knowledge of the complete cost and benefit functions would enable us to select among the several candidates to a global optimum by undertaking the relevant cost–benefit comparisons between candidate points. Yet, it is important to stress that, in practice, we usually know only some stretches of these functions. Therefore, the Pareto-optimal landscape is not always achievable in practice.

6.2 COST–BENEFIT ANALYSIS OF LANDSCAPE CONSERVATION IN PRACTICE

There are, in principle, no insoluble problems in econometrically estimating continuous valuation and cost functions such as those in (3.32) and (5.12) provided we have the appropriate data. This is an important point because it stresses that the analytical approach presented so far in this chapter for selecting an optimal state of landscape within a continuous setting is, in principle, entirely applicable. However, in this section we discuss a simpler, discrete, choice problem that is more in keeping with typical decisions to be made by landscape conservation agencies.

Practical Conservation Decision-Making Problems

For most practical choice problems in landscape management, the choice of precise levels of attributes in continuous scales is not a possibility and hence the choice set is restricted to discrete changes in some particular attributes. In this context, the proposed assessment approach starts by identifying the most complete conservation scheme that is possible and by dividing this scheme into a number of conservation programmes.[5] Each programme comprises a particular subset of landscape attributes for which policy-off and policy-on levels are well defined. Landscape attributes included in different programmes should be independent in production, so that the agency may choose to implement any possible combination of programmes. A combination of programmes is called a programme-mix or scheme. The problem for the conservation agency is how to select the best possible programme-mix.

This choice problem can be described as the selection of an optimum at the qualitative margin, since what is at stake is the targeted state of landscape assuming that the size of the conservation area is fixed. Another choice problem is the selection of an optimal size for a conservation area, that is, the selection of an optimum at the extensive margin. Note that 'programmes' can be interpreted as corresponding to areas (sites) rather than attributes, and thus the whole approach is applicable to multi-site problems as well as multi-attribute problems. More complex choice problems are the joint optimisation at both the qualitative and the extensive margins or the joint optimisation of several schemes at different sites.

Sequential Cost–Benefit Analysis for Selecting an Optimal Programme-Mix

The solution for multi-site and multi-attribute problems corresponds to the selection of a programme-mix that is somehow optimal. A sequential cost–benefit procedure is proposed here to solve this problem. This procedure consists of sequentially evaluating the welfare effects of adding a particular programme to a previously constituted programme-mix. If the evaluation is considered positive, then the programme at issue is added to the previous mix; another candidate programme is considered next, and so on. The cost–benefit rule to be used in the discrete choice at each step of this sequential procedure is the one in (6.2).[6] The procedure continues incorporating more programmes in the mix until there are no more remaining programmes with sequential benefits offsetting the corresponding costs.

To take into account all substitution effects between programmes (and thus to avoid the IVS bias), the evaluation sequence must correspond to a valid (that is, continuous) sequential integration path (section 3.2). Sequential (rather than independent or simultaneously disaggregated) valuations of programmes are required by a sequential cost–benefit procedure.

A sequential cost–benefit algorithm is now defined, which can be applied to select the best possible approach to a Pareto-optimal state of landscape when the available choices are restricted to a set of particular discrete choices with respect to some particular attributes.

Multiple Optima in Practice: Solved and Unsolved Questions

Multiple-optima problems that were described above for the continuous case appear as well in the discrete case. The solution for these problems in the latter case is exactly the same as in the former. There is, however, a multiple-optima problem specific of sequential cost–benefit analysis, which is due to the discrete nature of the choice set: path-dependency of the optimum. The possibility for such a problem is quite easy to grasp. Think of a case where there are two possible programmes: P1 and P2. $WTP[\text{P1} \mid (0,0,0)]$ is the valuation of P1 when this is the first to be evaluated; $WTP[\text{P1} \mid (0,1,0)]$ is the valuation of P1 when P2 has already been included in the programme-mix. If both programmes are compensated substitutes then $WTP[\text{P1} \mid (0,0,0)] > WTP[\text{P1} \mid (0,1,0)]$. Suppose the cost of P1 is C. Since attributes included in different programmes have no joint costs, as they are independent in production, the cost of P1 will always be C irrespective of whether P2 has been previously selected. Thus, a possibility exists for $N.WTP[\text{P1} \mid (0,0,0)] > C > N.WTP[\text{P1} \mid (0,1,0)]$, in which case P1 should be included in the optimal programme-mix if this is the first programme to be assessed but should not be included if evaluated after P2. Hence, at least two mixes are selected as optimal: one with and the other without P1. The choice between these is a choice between sequential paths, and, in general, there are no paths better than others. Therefore, there is no general way to solve the path-dependency problem.

An important caveat is here due: provided that $WTP[P1 \,|\, (0,0,0)] > WTP[P1 \,|\, (0,1,0)]$ reflects genuine compensated substitution relationships between P1 and P2 and is not a mere artefact of a particular valuation method, path dependency cannot be imputed to this method. It would be, indeed, a very general problem of cost–benefit analysis whatever the valuation method (Hoehn and Randall 1989 and Randall and Hoehn 1996).

NOTES

1. For a simple illustration, see Johansson (1993). Gravelle and Rees (1992) provide a comprehensive but simple treatment of the Arrow impossibility theorem.
2. Actual compensation is not required for a landscape change to pass the Kaldor criterion. Hence, cost–benefit rules such as that in (6.1) can lead to some changes being misidentified as welfare-improving. With no compensation, there are gainers and losers, and hence a social-welfare function is required to weight gainers' gains against losers' losses. It is easy to establish that the change in social welfare, ΔW, is given by: $\Delta W = \Sigma_k W y_k . C V_k$, where CV_k is the compensating variation of individual k and $W y_k$ is the partial derivative of the social-welfare function with respect to the income of this individual. For the Kaldor criterion ($\Sigma_k CV_k > 0$) not to lead to misidentifications of welfare-improving landscape changes ($\Delta W > 0$), the signs of ΔW and $\Sigma_k CV_k$ should coincide in general, which implies $W y_k$ (that is always positive) must be constant across individuals so that it can pass outside the Σ operator. Constancy of $W y_k$ across all individuals means there are no possible income re-distributions that would raise social welfare, that is: the current distribution of income is already optimal. Besides, we obtain by differentiation: $W y_k = W_k . V^k_y$; where W_k is the marginal effect on social welfare of increasing the utility of individual k (that is: how much society cares about k's welfare) and V^k_y is the marginal utility of income for this individual. Thus, constancy of $W y_k$ across all individuals also means that society should care less about poorer individuals (for which marginal utility of income is presumably higher). This is an awkward result when one thinks, for example, of the general occurrence of progressive income taxation schedules in many countries. Hence, the conditions for the signs of ΔW and $\Sigma_k CV_k$ to coincide in general (ensuring the Kaldor criterion is not misleading) are somewhat difficult to satisfy. Notwithstanding, however imperfect, the compensation principle is probably the best cost–benefit rule one can ever expect to have for welfare appraisal of landscape change.
3. Hanley et al. (1996) compared three types of policy principles for the provision of public goods from farming: the Provider Gets, Beneficiaries Pay and Polluter Pays principles. Each principle assumes a different structure of property rights. The relevant one for landscape conservation payment schemes is the Provider Gets principle. For both the Provider Gets and the Beneficiaries Pay principles, the adequate welfare criterion for improvements to the status quo is the Kaldor test, as it implies the general public or specific landscape users (the gainers with landscape policy) should pay farmers for them to accept landscape constraints. Bromley and Hodge (1990) discuss the more general issue of the distribution of property rights between farmers and other countryside users and analyse predicted future changes on such property rights.

4. z is here used for the policy-off (profit-maximising) state of landscape; and z^C for the policy-on state of landscape occurring after farmers' compliance with the landscape constraints.
5. The notions of 'conservation scheme' and 'conservation programme' in this sense have already been defined in section 3.4 and used in section 4.2.
6. The benefit/cost-ratio analogue of (6.2) was used in the case-studies in Part Three of this book.

PART THREE

The Case-Studies

7. Landscape Conservation in the Pennine Dales and Peneda–Gerês Areas: Presenting the Case-Studies

Previous chapters in this book have discussed methods to estimate costs and benefits of landscape conservation and to assess conservation schemes on a cost–benefit basis. In Part Three, two case-studies are used to illustrate particular applications for these methods and to discuss problems raised at the application level as well as general theoretical and methodological issues. These case-studies are the Pennine Dales Environmentally Sensitive Area (ESA) scheme, in England, and the Peneda–Gerês National Park (NP), in Portugal. This chapter presents both case-studies by describing the areas and the conservation policy schemes at work. In so doing, we establish the local setting for all analyses and discussions to be presented in the next chapters.

7.1 PENNINE DALES

Running north–south from the Tyne valley, in Northumberland, to the Trent valley, in the Midlands, the Pennine hills constitute the 'backbone of England' (Raistrick 1968) and comprise some of the most spectacular upland scenery in this country. Geology created there spacious dale (valley) bottoms, steep dale sides and flat hill tops, as well as magnificent waterfalls, gorges and caves (Waltham 1987). However, it was man who clothed the landscape. Hence, although in-bye land (i.e.: enclosed meadow, pasture and arable) only represents 26 per cent of the whole Pennine area,[1] traditional agriculture definitely makes the character of dale landscapes. Most rich patterns of colour and texture in the landscape were actually shaped by past farming practices and still depend on traditional management for their conservation.

Many of these cherished landscape features are currently threatened by changes in farming practice. Derelict walls and field barns are already visible in the landscape and spread as labour for repair work becomes increasingly scarce, farms are amalgamated and cattle are centralised in conveniently located modern sheds. Flower-rich hay meadows are losing their landscape and wildlife interest due to increased fertiliser use or ploughing, drainage and re-seeding of old meadows. In addition, overstocking and poor management of grazing negatively affect small broad-leaved woods and extensive heather moors.

A number of policies are today in operation to manage landscape change so as to preserve the most cherished attributes of the Pennine Dales landscape. These policies include those based on general planning and development control laws,[2] as well as, more recently, a variety of payment schemes aimed at financially inducing land users to engage in landscape-friendly practices. The Pennine Dales Environmentally Sensitive Area (ESA) scheme is the most influential of these schemes, at least with respect to the conservation of such typical attributes of dale landscapes as dry-stone walls, field barns and hay meadows.[3]

The Agricultural Act 1986 (article 18) established the terms for the English Ministry of Agriculture Fisheries and Food (MAFF) to designate ESAs and establish management agreements with land users within these areas. ESAs were to be designated wherever it appeared to the Minister that the maintenance or adoption of particular agricultural methods in a particular area would promote the conservation or enhancement of landscape, wildlife, geological, or archaeological features. The Pennine Dales ESA scheme came into operation in 1987, as part of a first round of ESAs (Statutory Instruments 1986). This scheme targets conservation effort at enclosed grassland in the valley floor and lower slopes. It initially covered an area of 16,000 hectares in 8 separate areas. Farmers could voluntarily enter into a management agreement with MAFF, in which case they received, under the initial ESA scheme, £100 a year per hectare of grassland for complying with ESA management prescriptions over a 5-year term. One year after the inception of the scheme, there were already 221 agreements, covering 61 per cent of eligible area. By 1991, these figures had risen to 303 agreements and 74 per cent of eligible area (Whitby et al. 1992).

The Pennine Dales ESA scheme was reviewed in 1992. Significant changes were introduced (Statutory Instruments 1992a). First, the ESA itself was enlarged and the term of management agreements was increased from 5 to 10 years. Second, a number of new management prescriptions were added and others were modified so as to make them stricter and more effective from a conservation standpoint. Third, different payment rates were adopted for different land uses and different tiers of management constraint. Fourth, capital grants were made available for conservation plans aimed at restoring or creating new valued landscape features. The reviewed ESA covers today 39,900 hectares of eligible land (MAFF 1995) in 21 separate areas. The reviewed management prescriptions for management tiers 1 and 2 are presented in Table 7.1. Per-hectare payment rates in the reviewed ESA are,

Table 7.1 Pennine Dales ESA management prescriptions

TIER 1

A. GENERAL LAND USE: (1) maintain grassland and do not plough, level or re-seed the land; (2) do not install any new drainage system or substantially modify any existing one; (3) meadow land must be identified on the agreement map and continue to be managed as such for the length of the agreement.

B. GRAZING / CUTTING MANAGEMENT: (4) exclude stock from meadows at least seven weeks before the first cut for hay or silage and by 1st June at the latest; (5) do not cut grass for hay or silage in any year before 8th July; (6) all meadows must have their first cut in August at least once every five years (proposed programme for August cutting must be indicated on agreement map and agreed upon with MAFF); have regard to the welfare of fledglings of ground nesting birds when planning cuts; (7) the aftermath of any cut shall be grazed; (8) when cutting grass for silage, wilt and turn it before removal; (9) do not graze any land so as to cause poaching, over-grazing or under-grazing.

C. FERTILISER USE: (10) do not exceed the existing level of inorganic fertiliser; (11) in any case, do not exceed 25 Kg of nitrogen, 12.5 Kg of phosphate and 12.5 Kg of potash per hectare per year or the equivalent in artificial organic fertiliser; (12) fertiliser must be applied in one application per year; (13) do not apply slurry or poultry manure; (14) apply only farmyard manure produced on the farm, and do not exceed the existing level of application on any field; (15) in any case, do not use more than 12.5 tonnes of farmyard manure per hectare per year; (16) apply farmyard manure in a single dressing; (17) do not apply lime, slag or any other substance to reduce soil acidity.

D. OTHER CULTIVATION PRACTICES: (18) cultivate meadows only with a chain harrow or roller, as soon as possible in the spring once stock have been removed; (19) pastures must not be harrowed or rolled; (20) do not use fungicides and insecticides; (21) do not apply herbicides except to control bracken, nettles, spear thistle, creeping or field thistle, curled dock, broad-leaved dock or ragworth; (22) when applying herbicides always use a weed wiper or spot treatment; (23) where bracken cannot be controlled by mechanical means, asulam should be used; (24) do not cut or spray existing areas of rushes in pastures.

E. BARNS AND WALLS CONSERVATION: (25) maintain stockproof walls and hedges in a stockproof condition using traditional materials; (26) maintain weatherproof field barns which the farmer owns or is responsible for in a weatherproof condition, using traditional materials.

F. WOODLAND MANAGEMENT: (27) obtain written advice within two years on the management of existing woodland or on proposals to plant any new woodland.

G. OTHER: (28) sheep dip must be disposed of safely and not spread where it may affect areas of nature conservation value; (29) do not damage or destroy any feature of historic interest; (30) obtain written advice on siting and materials from MAFF before constructing buildings, roads or before any other engineering operations which do not require planning permission or prior notification determination by the local planning authority.

TIER 2 (meadows alone)

All tier 1 constraints plus the following: (1) stock excluded from meadows by 15th May; (2) no application of inorganic or artificial organic fertiliser; (3) all area cut every year, with the crop removed; (4) cut for hay not before 15th July, and for silage not before 1st August.

Source: adapted from Statutory Instruments (1992a) and MAFF (1992).

as amended by Statutory Instrument (1992b): £125 for meadows under tier 1 management; £210 for meadows under tier 2 management; £90 for other land under agreement (mostly pasture and rough grazing); £25 for managed woodland qualifying for supplementary payment for loss of grazing and shelter.[4] Conservation plans may benefit from capital grants covering 50–80 per cent of costs associated with: repair works in stone walls; wall building; renovating field barns; planting and laying hedges; re-creating herb-rich meadows; tree planting, and protecting historic features.

By November 1995, ESA management agreements covered 25,702 hectares, which represented 64 per cent of eligible area, distributed as follows: 5,340 hectares of tier-1 meadows; 1,217 hectares of tier-2 meadows; 19,132 hectares of pasture and rough grazing; and 13 hectares of managed woodland. A total of £2,671,489 were paid to farmers with respect to both ESA tiers during the financial year 1994/95 (MAFF 1995).

ESA management agreements seem to ensure adequate protection to the most representative attributes of dale landscapes (stone walls, field barns and hay meadows). However, broad-leaved woods are not satisfactorily protected by the ESA scheme, because agreement farmers are only required to seek written advice on woodland management. Moreover, ESA policy does not cover at all an important Pennine habitat: heather moorland. Likewise, almost 8,000 hectares of limestone grassland, representing 50 per cent of the national resource, are completely outside ESA boundaries (Yorkshire Dales National Park 1994). Nevertheless, a variety of other payment schemes for landscape conservation in the Pennines (Countryside Stewardship Scheme, Wildlife Enhancement Scheme and other schemes; cf. Santos 1997) contribute to fill up these gaps left by the ESA scheme.

7.2 PENEDA–GERÊS NATIONAL PARK

Located in the North of Portugal, alongside the Portuguese–Spanish border, the Peneda–Gerês area is included in the only Portuguese national park (NP), which gives it an exceptional conservation status at the national level. The NP comprises blunt mountains, high plateaux cut by deep valleys, rocky steep slopes and large granite peaks. A high rainfall gives birth to a profusion of streams, waterfalls and large reservoirs. The NP was endowed with precious nature-conservation assets such as the only significant remains of Atlantic oak woodland in the whole country, a relevant share of the wolf population and a number of scarce rocky, upland and meadow habitats.

Although the NP is often depicted as a natural and wild place, most landscapes in the park were profoundly shaped by man. Hence, for example, terraced landscapes in the main valleys are the product of the historical expansion of irrigated farming and maize fields, up to the slopes, since the 17th century. The high plateaux in the park retain an older agricultural landscape, reminiscent of the medieval farming system, which comprises rye fields, hay meadows and small oak and birch woods; here, village flocks are still grazed in common on large expanses of open moorland. Farmland in the strictest sense (meadow, arable and plantations) accounts for only 8 per cent of the NP land. However, traditional agricultural landscapes are a crucial factor of landscape diversity in the park.

Farming in the NP is operated by small family units, which became economically marginal. With the abandonment of farms came significant landscape changes. These are well illustrated by the decay of terraced landscapes and the encroachment by scrub of meadows, rough grazing and small broad-leaved woods. Farm abandonment is perhaps the main problem to be faced by any conservation strategy for the NP, as the conservation of typical landscapes and scarce semi-natural habitats, like hay meadows and oak woods, heavily depends on the continuation of traditional management.

NP policy is based on planning and development control tools, which, although relatively fitted to manage the built environment within the park, are helpless in stopping more diffuse processes such as farmland dereliction. Other policy tools, namely payment schemes for landscape conservation, would be more appropriate to this task. The transposition of the European regulation 2078/92 (the so-called agri-environment regulation) to Portuguese law, in 1994, created legal provision for the implementation of such payment schemes in Portugal (IEADR 1994). Portuguese agri-environmental policy is currently based on a nationwide scheme comprising 24 policy measures, some applicable all over the Portuguese territory and others to rather extensive areas (IEADR 1994). Each agri-environmental measure is a standard management agreement with a standard payment rate on a per-hectare or per-head basis. Being conceived at the national level, these standard agreements cannot precisely target payments at the most valued landscape attributes in each area. Zone-specific plans for areas with special conservation interest, such as the Peneda–Gerês NP, were initially previewed. Nevertheless, only one of these zone-specific plans has already been implemented, and this is not for the Peneda–Gerês NP.

The uptake of seven agri-environmental measures by NP farmers during 1994 and 1995 is presented in Table 7.2. There were 1,784 applications for these measures – a figure that is not comparable with that of 2,505 farms in the NP (INE 1989), as many farmers applied for different measures.

The most extensively applied measure was measure 6, which is aimed at maintaining 'traditional mixed farming systems of the North and Centre'. This measure covered 43 per cent of agricultural area and accounted for 39 per cent of all agri-environmental payments in the NP during 1994 and 1995.

In the NP, traditional mixed farming systems occur at low altitudes and are responsible for the upkeep of the terraced landscapes so typical of the main valleys. A significant problem with this measure in the NP is that agreement conditions do not require farmers to keep terraces in good condition. This problem is due to the nationwide character of the current programme and would be solved with a zone-specific plan for the NP.

Table 7.2 Uptake of the agri-environmental measures in the Peneda–Gerês NP (1994 and 1995)

Agri-environmental measure	number of applications	hectares or heads	annual payments	
			,000 esc.	%
6. Traditional mixed farming	733	2,438	60,105	39.1
8. Traditional irrigated meadows	85	589	7,363	4.8
9. Extensively used pastures	148	505	8,094	5.3
18. Local livestock breeds	475	1,345	31,867	20.7
20. Upkeep of abandoned forests	14	832	26,301	17.1
21. Upkeep of farm forests	264	552	13,689	8.9
22. Management of woods with a special conservation interest	65	451	6,422	4.2
Total hectares	1,784	5,368	153,842	100.0
heads		1,345		

Source: estimated from data provided by IEADR (1996); last update in April 1996.

Measure 8 is aimed at conserving 'traditional irrigated hay meadows'. This measure was supposed to apply to the meadow landscapes of the high plateaux in the NP. However, many farmers in these plateaux entered their meadows in measure-6 agreements, because the corresponding payment rate is higher than that for measure-8 agreements. As a consequence, only 28 per cent of the 2,116 hectares of NP meadows are covered by measure-8 agreements. Eligibility conditions for measure 6 were not sufficiently selective to avoid this, and hence a significant area of meadows was left under the wrong type of management agreement (Santos 1997).

Measure 9 ('extensively used pastures') would provide an excellent opportunity to improve the management of extensive tracts of rough grazing on NP common land, but the small areas covered by measure-9 agreements show that this opportunity was not effectively used.

A particularly successful agri-environmental measure in the NP was measure 18. This is a per-head payment to keep local livestock breeds, which, in the NP, applies mainly to 'barrosão' cattle, currently threatened with extinction. This measure covers most of the cows of this breed in the park, so contributing to its conservation. Payments to 475 farmers for 1,345 heads absorb 1/5 of all agri-environmental payments in the NP.

Measures 20, 21 and 22 apply to forests. In the NP, measure 20 pays for the management of scrub in extensive pine forests, in order to reduce the risk of forest fires. Applicants for measure 20 were generally institutions managing these forests rather than individual farmers. This measure applied to an area of more than 800 hectares and absorbed 17 per cent of all agri-environmental payments in the park. Measure 21 has the same general aim, but applies to forests managed by small-scale farmers; only farmers applying for measure 6 were eligible for measure 21. In the NP, measure 22 applies to oak woods mainly controlled by farmers. Uptake is still low and has been delayed by the fact that applications can only be accepted after the completion of a conservation plan, to be made by the Forest Institute, for each individual case.

The evaluation of the application of Portuguese agri-environmental policy to the Peneda–Gerês area undertaken in this book focused on those measures with the strongest potential impact on the area's landscape. Thus, only benefits and costs associated with measures 6, 8 and 22 (traditional mixed farming systems, traditional hay meadows and oak woods with special conservation interest) were estimated and considered for policy evaluation purposes.

NOTES

1. This figure was worked out from data presented by Silsoe College (1991) and Laxton (1986).
2. The southern half of the Pennine Dales is covered by the Yorkshire Dales National Park (NP) and the northern half by the North Pennines Area of Outstanding Natural Beauty (AONB).
3. Santos (1997) reviewed other payment schemes operating in the Pennine Dales area.
4. According to MAFF (1995) payments for tier-1 meadows and other land have been updated to £135 and £95 respectively.

8. A Study of the Landscape Perceptions and Preferences of Visitors to the Peneda–Gerês National Park

Descriptions of landscape changes in CVM scenarios should focus on those attribute changes that are not only relevant to policy evaluation but also readily perceived by respondents. Chapter 7 identified the main landscape attributes at issue in the evaluation of the agri-environmental measures applied in the Peneda–Gerês NP: traditional farming systems associated with terraced landscapes, irrigated hay meadows and small oak woods managed by farmers. Thus, the CVM scenarios used in this case-study were to be focused on these landscape attributes. It was, therefore, important to make sure that respondents correctly understood descriptions of these attributes, so that they were able to make preference-revealing choices about changes in such attributes. Hence, these CVM scenarios should be built so as to match previous landscape perceptions and preferences of respondents. (Otherwise, answers could be completely constructed during the interview, and thus would only reveal unstable preferences.) This required having some knowledge of the landscape perceptions and preferences of visitors to the Peneda–Gerês NP prior to designing the CVM questionnaire to be used in the main visitor survey.[1] To satisfy this requirement, we used methods proposed in section 4.4 to carry out a study of these perceptions and preferences. This chapter reports on this study.

8.1 SURVEYING AND ANALYSING LANDSCAPE PERCEPTIONS AND PREFERENCES

The study of perceptions and preferences reported in this chapter is based on the immediate reactions of respondents to visual stimuli comprising a set of photographs depicting NP landscapes. As mentioned in section 4.4, this study is intended to investigate whether respondents perceive the effects on the landscape of different management options and whether they have well-defined preferences for these effects. Thus, the scenes presented to respondents had to be sampled so as to represent the actual diversity of management-induced types of scenery in the NP. For this purpose, 10 management-related types of landscape were defined according to prior knowledge of the area. These types are represented in the first column of Table 8.1.

A total of 158 photographs were taken in the NP between the 12th and 14th of April 1995, which were aimed at depicting the previously defined 10 types of landscape. The photographs were taken along the main roads crossing the NP, which allowed both the coverage of most farmland inside the NP and the capture of those scenes that are more familiar to many visitors who only engage in car driving and sightseeing around the park.

Photographs were standardised in four respects. First, panoramic and large-scale vistas were excluded, by focusing on small to medium-scale scenes directing the viewer's eyes towards land cover. Second, only scenes presenting a single class of land use, or where such a class was dominant, were selected. Third, scenes dominated by impressive natural features, such as rocky peaks or waterfalls, were excluded. Fourth, scenes dominated by built features, such as houses or other large buildings, were excluded as well. The two first criteria were aimed at allowing us to associate perceptions and preferences with well-defined management options. The third aimed at avoiding the inclusion in the analysis of factors that do not depend on management but nature. The fourth was justified by the need to avoid that a 'built' category of perception (which was not of interest here) emerged from the analysis, cutting across finer perceptual dimensions and concealing more interesting distinctions as regards alternative management options for farming within the NP. Notwithstanding, one must bear in mind, throughout the analysis, the great simplification this standardisation implied with respect to the actual diversity of scenery in the NP. This can only be justified by the purposes of this particular study.

The need to undertake short interviews led to establishing the maximum number of photographs presented to each respondent as 35. This allowed us to present at least three photographs to illustrate each type, which is suggested as an absolute minimum by Kaplan and Kaplan (1989). If this minimum was not respected, it would become impossible to control for those reactions to each scene that are based on specific features of that scene rather than on the commonalties shared within a type of scenes.

With respect to results presented in this chapter, respondents were only asked to spread the 35 photographs (previously arranged in a random order) over five piles, according to their preference ordering for these scenes. Respondents were allowed to change the position of photographs, as the task progressed, and were asked to place at least three photographs on each pile. After the interview, the position of each photograph was registered as a preference rating given to that scene in a 5-point scale. This technique was used by Dearden (1984) and described by Kaplan and Kaplan (1989).

Visitors to the NP were interviewed on a 'first come, first served' basis in the streets of the Caldas do Gerês village and at a nearby camp site, between the 25th and 27th of April 1995. Only five visitors refused to participate and 32 visitors ranked the 35 photographs.

The identification of categories of perception followed the cognitive-psychological approach, as described in section 4.4. A 35x35 symmetrical matrix of pair-wise correlation coefficients among preference ratings given to the 35 scenes by the 32 participants was first established. Closeness between scenes was measured by comparing the way each scene is correlated with all the other scenes. Scenes with similar patterns of correlation were grouped using a hierarchical cluster analysis. The cluster algorithm used was of the agglomerative type, and the criterion to establish the degree of closeness was the average distance from scenes in one cluster to scenes in another. At each stage, the agglomerative procedure combined the 2 clusters with the smallest average distance (Hair et al. 1995).[2]

The study of preferences for landscapes followed the psychophysical approach, as described in section 4.4.

8.2 RESULTS AND CONCLUSIONS ON LANDSCAPE PERCEPTIONS

The cluster procedure was stopped at the 31st step, which produced four clusters or perceptual categories, whose content is clearly described as 'farmland', 'moorland', 'woodland' and 'scrubland'. Table 8.1 presents a cross-tabulation showing the close correspondence between these four categories of perception and the previously defined 10 management-relevant types. The high degree of correspondence between perceptual categories and management types shows that the main distinctions made by visitors are based on a single domain of content: land use. The only exceptions to this correspondence were management types 2, 4 and 10 (cf. Table 8.1), which spread across perceptual categories. The small numbers of scenes in each type and a high internal diversity probably explain the exceptional behaviour within these types. This explanation matches particularly well what happened with type 10 (parkland): two scenes with carefully mown lawns in the foreground and surrounding park trees merged with 'farmland' scenes, whereas a third scene representing a view from the inside of an open birch park merged with 'woodland' scenes.

Steps of the cluster procedure previous to the 31st one were considered so that more detailed perceptual distinctions inside each one of the four main categories of perception could be identified. This exercise led to the selection of landscape attributes that are actually perceived by visitors and allowed us to check whether these attributes are management-relevant.

Table 8.1 Correspondence between management-relevant types of landscape and categories of perception

Management-relevant types	Main categories of perception			
	'farmland'	'moorland'	'woodland'	'scrubland'
1. hay meadows	7			
2. abandoned meadows	1	1	1	
3. terraced farming	3			
4. vine hedgerows	2		1	
5. dense deciduous woods			3	
6. open deciduous woods			3	
7. pine forests			3	
8. high and dense scrub				3
9. moorland		4		
10. parkland	2		1	

'Farmland'

'Farmland' is the last category to be constituted in the agglomerative procedure, which shows that it is a quite heterogeneous category. However, two clusters inside this category were already formed in the first steps of the procedure and only merged together in the final step when the main category emerges. Hence, each of these clusters is internally highly homogeneous and rather distinct from other 'farmland' scenes. These two clusters can, therefore, be considered as perceptual subcategories. The first comprises a nucleus of four meadow scenes with a strong presence of stone walls. The second perceptual subcategory comprises all three scenes of the previously defined management type 'terraced farming'; terraces are the major common theme of this subcategory and the lack of grapevine-hedgerows distinguishes it from other 'farmland' scenes.

'Moorland'

'Moorland' is a category internally highly homogeneous and quite distinct from other categories of perception: it agglomerates at an early stage and remains separated until the 33rd step of the cluster procedure.[3]

'Woodland'

Like 'farmland', 'woodland' is also a strongly heterogeneous category formed at a late stage of the clustering procedure. Also like 'farmland', two clusters inside the category emerge early in the process and can, therefore, be considered as two separate subcategories. The first includes three scenes of pine plantations, which exactly correspond to the previously defined management type 'pine forest'; all of these scenes present, as well, a significant degree of openness and smooth ground texture, suggesting the possibility of access for recreation. The second subcategory includes three scenes of open deciduous woodland and one of more dense deciduous woodland; content (deciduous trees) is an important common theme but other commonalties are a high degree of openness and a relatively smooth ground texture. These two woodland subcategories merge early, a fact that is probably explained by a similarly high degree of openness and a smooth ground texture, which oppose these subcategories to other 'woodland' scenes, which join the cluster later on and present higher density of trees and coarser ground texture.

'Scrubland'

This category includes three quite similar scenes of high and dense scrub, which, in the season the pictures were taken, was partially covered with flowers (completely impossible to avoid in this season).

Implications of the Study of Landscape Perceptions for CVM Scenario Design

From the cluster analysis summarily presented above, it can be concluded that the landscape attributes underlying the perceptual distinctions made by visitors to the NP are the following ones: (1) main types of land use (i.e.: farmland, moorland, woodland and scrubland); (2) meadows with stone walls (probably walls, rather than meadows, are the perceived attribute, as meadows seem not to be clearly perceived as such e.g. as opposed to arable land); (3) terraces; (4) trees in meadows (weakly perceived as distinctive); (5) open structure and smooth ground in woodlands; (6) pine versus deciduous trees in woodlands.

Let us now consider the implications of these conclusions for the design of CVM scenarios to be used in the main visitor survey.

Terraced fields are a clear perceptual subcategory. With respect to terraces, the major impact of the agri-environmental programme would be visual in nature. Hence, the CVM scenario used two pictures (already used in this study of perception) to evoke an image of currently existing terraced landscapes, which clearly pre-exists in the mind of respondents. To depict a degraded terraced area, which would characterise the park in the future in the absence of an appropriate conservation policy, a photograph of a derelict terrace with some scrub encroachment was shown.

Hay meadows seem to be poorly perceived as such by most respondents. Thus, particular care had to be exercised in describing meadows and pre-testing parts of the CVM scenario related to changes in meadows. In order to adequately describe changes in meadows and reasons that may lead respondents to care about them, it was decided to focus this part of the CVM scenario on five main aspects: (1) meadows' location within the NP (this was important, as this location corresponds to the less visited areas of the park); (2) the particular farming practices responsible for the production and maintenance of meadows; (3) the contrast introduced in the landscape by meadows' green colour; (4) the presence of trees and walls in meadows' boundaries (which seem to be perceived attributes); (5) the wildlife significance of meadows; (6) the consequences of not conserving meadows, which were presented using a picture of a degraded meadow, where irrigation already ceased and which became invaded by broom.

Visitors distinguish deciduous woods from other land use categories. In addition, the degree of openness of woods seems to constitute a major perceptual distinction. This is important, as openness is the most important visual impact of the agri-environmental programme with respect to deciduous woods in the NP. As a complement to this visual impact, which is already perceived by visitors, it was decided to include in descriptions of woods in the CVM scenario other, sometimes less visible, aspects of woodland conservation. These were: (1) the wildlife significance of oak woods; (2) the scarcity of these woods in Portugal and the extreme importance of those particular woods still remaining in the NP; (3) the recreational attributes of deciduous woods; and (4) the closed and wildlife-poorer aspect of dense woodland, which would develop in the absence of policy-induced proper management.

8.3 RESULTS AND CONCLUSIONS ON PREFERENCES FOR LANDSCAPES

Average preference ratings for the different categories of perception and for several groups of scenes inside each category are presented in Table 8.2.[4] 'Woodland' is undoubtedly the most preferred category. If pine plantations are excluded, the remaining seven 'woodland' scenes attracted preference ratings higher than those for 'scrubland', 'moorland' and most 'farmland' scenes. Inside the 'farmland' category, only terraces, meadows with many trees and parkland scenes attracted preference ratings as high as those for deciduous woodland scenes. The most preferred scene of the entire set is, indeed, a scene of parkland with a mown lawn surrounded by an open mixed wood. Thus, in addition to woods being a preferred landscape attribute, the presence of trees in non-woodland scenes significantly increases the preference for these scenes. Herzog (1984) and the numerous studies summarised by Kaplan and Kaplan (1989) reported this preference of people for woods and trees.

Within the 'woodland' category, deciduous trees are clearly preferred to pines. Open deciduous woodland with smooth ground is also clearly preferred to dense deciduous woodland with coarse-textured ground. This last preference relationship probably reflects different perceived access conditions for recreation. The three woodland scenes showing pathways are amongst the most valued 'woodland' scenes. This preference for pathways inside woods is also reported by Herzog (1984) and Kaplan and Kaplan (1989). It is related by the Kaplans to 'mystery': a generally very strong positive psychological predictor for preference, which is associated with scenes where it is clearly suggested that more would be learnt if one could enter the scene and changed the vantage point.

It was, therefore, decided to include three explanatory variables in our multiple-regression model of preferences for 'woodland' scenes. These were the following dummy variables: DECIDUOUS, which takes the value 1 when are many deciduous trees in the scene; OPENNESS, which takes the value 1 if the wood presents an open structure; PATHWAYS, which takes the value 1 if there is a clearly identifiable pathway in the scene. The estimated model is presented in Table 8.3. This model has a good R squared (even when adjusted for degrees of freedom), with almost 80 per cent of the variation in the preference ratings being explained by the explanatory variables listed above.[5] Globally, the model is significant at a 2 per cent level of probability. The signs of the estimated coefficients for all explanatory variables agree with previous expectations, and thus our null hypotheses on causal relationships between the three attributes of forest scenes and preferences for these scenes are at least not denied by the data. The first two coefficients are significant at a 5 per cent level of probability, even if the third is not. Lower levels of significance of the estimated coefficients for OPENNESS and PATHWAYS are due to collinearity between these two variables. As a conclusion, deciduous trees and openness can be retained as the attributes that most clearly affect preferences for 'woodland' scenes. Note that both of these attributes were already shown to have a structuring role in the perception of woodland scenes.

*Table 8.2 Average preference ratings for each category of perception and
each subgroup of scenes*

Categories and subgroups	number of scenes	average rating	minimum rating	maximum rating
'Farmland'	17	3.2	2.4	4.3
parks and meadows with trees	5	3.6	3.2	4.3
hay meadows with stone walls	4	3.1	2.9	3.3
meadows with tufts of herbs	2	2.4	2.4	2.4
fields with vine hedgerows	3	2.9	2.7	3.1
terraced fields	3	3.6	3.4	3.8
'Moorland'	5	2.4	2.1	2.6
'Woodland'	10	3.6	3.1	4.1
open deciduous woods	3	4.0	3.9	4.1
open birch plantation	1	3.6	3.6	3.6
dense deciduous woods	3	3.5	3.4	3.7
pine forests	3	3.3	3.1	3.5
'Scrubland'	3	3.0	2.6	3.2

The 'farmland' category as a whole has not a high average preference rating (Table 8.2), but this is an internally very heterogeneous category with respect to preferences. Thus, the difference between the ratings of the most preferred and least preferred 'farmland' scenes is almost 2.0 points (Table 8.2), whereas the corresponding difference for 'woodland' scenes is only 1.0 point. This is hardly surprising given the fact of 'farmland' being the most heterogeneous category of perception.

From the average preference ratings given to each 'farmland' scene, we can identify the attributes that seem to affect preferences for 'farmland' landscapes. Hence, strong presence of trees and terraces seem to be highly preferred; stone walls are less preferred; fields with grapevine-hedgerows are even less preferred, and tufts in meadows are clearly detractors. Some respondents' comments about fields with grapevine-hedgerows suggested that these hedgerows are perceived as having too tame a character for what people expect from the NP, but that these attributes are not displeasing in other places. Photographs of meadows showing small irrigation ditches gently following the contours have been rated higher in preference, and so the visibility of traditional irrigation structures was also to be tested as a positive predictor for preference ratings. The comparison of mean preference ratings also suggested that fence posts reduced preference for 'farmland' scenes with this attribute.

Table 8.3   Multiple-regression preference model for 'woodland' scenes

Variable	estimated coefficient	t-ratio	level of signif.
Intercept	2.909	16.06	0.000
DECIDUOUS	0.528	3.29	0.017
OPENNESS	0.361	2.49	0.047
PATHWAYS	0.229	1.58	0.166
number of observations = 10	F variable = 7.84		
$R^2 = 0.797$	(level of significance = 0.017)		
adjusted $R^2 = 0.695$			

Thus, our model of preference ratings for 'farmland' scenes included the following dummy variables: (1) TREES, indicating the presence of deciduous trees in farmland or lawns; (2) TUFTS, indicating evident tufts, giving an irregular aspect to the ground; (3) WALLS, indicating the presence of stone walls when terraces are not dominant; (4) POSTS, indicating clearly visible fence posts; (5) TERRACES, indicating a succession of terraces, which is dominant in the scene; (6) IRRIGATION, indicating visibility of small irrigation canals in meadow scenes; and (7) VINEHEDG, indicating the presence of vine hedgerows in field boundaries.

The estimated model is presented in Table 8.4.[6] This model has an extremely high R squared (and adjusted R squared as well), with 93 per cent of the variation on preference ratings being explained by the explanatory variables. Globally, the model is also highly significant (probability level of 0.1 per cent). All the estimated coefficients of the explanatory variables have the expected signs, and hence our null hypotheses about preference predictors for 'farmland' scenes are, at least, not denied. Coefficient estimates for TREES, TUFTS and TERRACES are significant at a probability level of 5 per cent. Those for WALLS, POSTS and VINEHEDG are still significant, but now only at the 10 per cent level, whereas that for IRRIGATION is not significant. Hence, trees, terraces, tufts, stone walls and posts can be retained as the attributes most clearly affecting preferences for 'farmland' scenes. Note that trees, terraces and stone walls were already identified as attributes underlying the perception of farmland scenes.

'Moorland' is clearly the least preferred category of perception, with all moorland scenes rated below all 'woodland' scenes, all 'farmland' scenes (except the two scenes of tufted meadows) and all but one 'scrubland' scenes (cf. Table 8.2).

'Scrubland' is slightly preferred to 'moorland' (Table 8.2). With a difference of 0.6 points between the scrub scenes with more and less flowers, it is likely that scrub scenes received a seasonal premium due to the presence of flowers in all 'scrubland' scenes.

Table 8.4 Multiple-regression preference model for 'farmland' scenes

Variable	estimated coefficient	t-ratio	level of signif.
Intercept	2.951	18.09	0.000
TREES	0.348	2.38	0.045
TUFTS	− 0.734	− 5.08	0.000
WALLS	0.315	2.09	0.070
POSTS	− 0.214	− 2.14	0.064
TERRACES	0.773	4.76	0.000
IRRIGATION	0.099	0.88	0.404
VINEHEDG	− 0.284	− 1.88	0.097

number of observations = 16	F variable = 14.71
R^2 = 0.928	(level of significance = 0.001)
adjusted R^2 = 0.865	

Implications of the Study of Landscape Preferences for CVM Scenario Design

All landscape attribute changes to be valued in the main CVM survey were related with impacts of farm abandonment on NP landscapes, such as scrub encroachment on fields, terraces, meadows and non-managed oak woods. In the study of preferences, respondents have shown a strong distaste for all unmanaged scenes – comprising vegetation tufts in meadows, broom encroachment of fields and dense undergrowth in deciduous woods – with respect to their managed counterparts. This is an important result, as it ensures that, in the main survey, respondents would only be asked about their WTP for policies securing states of landscape that are preferred to policy-off states.

Terraced fields and open deciduous woodland, which were the targets of two of the agri-environmental measures to be valued in the CVM survey, were the most preferred landscape attributes. This probably ensured that benefits of conserving these attributes would be significant enough for respondents to take sufficient time in giving considered valuation answers in the CVM survey. The situation with respect to meadows is more ambiguous. Respondents tend to prefer scenes of meadows with a strong presence of trees, but have less intense preferences for meadows where walls, rather than trees, make the field boundaries. Meadows have already been identified as a poorly perceived land-use category. To avoid these problems, some verbal information about meadows and their significance was added to the description of changes in meadows in the CVM scenarios (as discussed above). In addition, pictures of both meadows with trees and meadows with walls were presented as part of the CVM booklet, so as to avoid presenting meadows with trees alone.

NOTES

1. Landscape perceptions and preferences of visitors to the Pennine Dales were already approximately known from a large number of guide books to the area, which referred to the sites and landscape features more appreciated by visitors. These references provided very consistent indications about those landscape attributes that are clearly perceived and strongly preferred by visitors to the Pennine Dales, which permitted avoiding undertaking an original study of landscape perceptions and preferences in the Pennine Dales case-study.
2. Diverse other agglomerative algorithms were used with almost identical results, thus showing the robustness of the solution.
3. The perceptual category 'moorland' includes four actual scenes of moorland plus one scene of abandoned meadow invaded by broom (cf. Table 8.1).
4. Two farmland scenes were included by the cluster analysis in the 'woodland' category. Indeed, these two scenes attracted preference ratings closer to similar farmland scenes than to actual woodland ones. Thus, in studying preferences, these scenes were included in the 'farmland' category. The fact of such scenes only merging with true 'woodland' scenes at a late stage in the clustering procedure may justify this decision.
5. It is, however, important to interpret carefully the results from all models presented in this section, as the number of observations per explanatory variable is rather small. This means the model may be over-fitted to the particular sample of scenes, which implies it could be non-generalizable to alternative samples depicting the same attribute differences (Hair et al. 1995). This comment is also valid with respect to the interpretation of the t-ratios for individual explanatory variables.
6. Notice that one scene (the most preferred one), which presented a standard residual higher than 2.0, was excluded from the model estimation. This scene presented a particularly pleasant composition of grassland, trees and woodland, which is probably responsible for its outlier character with respect to the model.

9. CVM Surveys and Summary Statistics of Visitors to the Pennine Dales and Peneda–Gerês Areas

Benefits of landscape conservation in the Pennine Dales and Peneda–Gerês areas were estimated from the results of two visitor surveys carried out in these areas. This chapter discusses the design and implementation of these surveys; it also describes the two visitor samples with an eye on those variables that might explain differences in WTP for landscape conservation between areas as well as across individual visitors to each area.

9.1 CVM SURVEYS OF VISITORS TO THE PENNINE DALES AND PENEDA–GERÊS AREAS

This section discusses those aspects of the CVM visitor surveys undertaken in the Pennine Dales and Peneda–Gerês areas that may have had an effect on the quality of data used to estimate benefits of landscape conservation in both areas. The following factors are considered here: questionnaire and scenario design; mode of questionnaire administration; pilot surveys; and aspects such as the definition of the population, sampling procedures and non-response, which should be considered to ensure that valid benefit estimates at the population level can be inferred from sample-based WTP averages.

Questionnaire and CVM Scenario Design

The questionnaires used in the two case-studies had the same general structure and used identical wordings for many questions. However, the way CVM scenarios were presented to respondents differed slightly between studies. We describe, first, the Pennine Dales questionnaire and then comment on aspects that differed in the Peneda–Gerês case.

Questionnaires were divided into six parts. Part A was aimed at characterising the visitor and the visit; it comprised questions such as whether the visit was the first ever made to the area and whether it was part of a holiday or just a day trip. Part B was about the perceptions and

139

preferences of respondents for the area's landscape. It asked respondents to compare this landscape with that of other areas they were familiar with, by rating the former in a 4-point scale from 'worse' to 'the best'. This gave an indication of the perceived uniqueness of the area for each respondent. A second question in this part asked respondents to choose from a checklist the attributes of the area's landscape they most preferred. Part C presented the CVM scenario and is described in detail below. Part D was about the respondent's general attitudes and behaviours towards the environment and the countryside. Part E collected information on socio-economic variables characterising the respondent and his household. Part F asked the interviewer to rate each interview with respect to factors affecting the quality of the data.

In the Dales study, the CVM scenario started with the idea that Dales landscape was subject to pressures to change associated with modifications in farming practice. Respondents were informed about the goals and operation of the Pennine Dales ESA scheme and asked to read a booklet named 'Pennine Dales – Alternative Landscapes'.[1] It described the typical Dales landscape, to be maintained under the ESA scheme, and the alternative landscape that would evolve in the future without the ESA scheme. The booklet included: (1) a map of the area covered by the Pennine Dales ESA scheme; (2) a brief summary of the goals and operation of this scheme; and (3) text and visual material depicting the main differences between the policy-on and the policy-off states of landscape.

After the reading of the booklet, the Pennine Dales ESA scheme was sub-divided in three separate programmes, which were then presented to respondents: programme 1, which comprised the conservation of stone walls and field barns; programme 2, which comprised the conservation of flower-rich hay meadows; and programme 3, which comprised the conservation of small broad-leaved woods. A show-card was handed to respondents, which summarised, for each programme, the policy-on and policy-off states of landscape and the way programmes would operate. Respondents were asked to read this card carefully and then to rank the three programmes by order of preference. This ranking exercise provided direct information about relative preferences for the three programmes (used later, when modelling WTP for different combinations of programmes) and ensured, as well, that respondents gave a second look at the content of each programme before answering the valuation questions.

The payment vehicle for the CVM exercise was presented as an increase in the respondent's income tax to make sure that funds were available to carry on with management agreements in the Dales. Hence, landscape benefits would be conditional on the specified payments to be made by the respondent through the tax system.

Each respondent was asked to consider, separately, different landscape conservation schemes for the Dales and their costs for him (as a taxpayer). Schemes were presented as combinations of one or more of the three basic programmes above. Seven such combinations are possible, all of which were presented to respondents. Since a maximum of six schemes was to be presented to each respondent, three versions of the questionnaire were designed and randomly assigned to respondents.

The discrete-choice (DC) format was adopted for the valuation questions, for reasons discussed in section 4.2. In each valuation question, respondents were asked whether they would be prepared to pay a given annual tax-cost – the offered bid amount – for a particular conservation scheme. As usual, bid amounts for the same scheme differed across respondents, so that mean WTP for this scheme could be estimated from the yes/no answers. For each scheme, seven bid amounts were randomly assigned to respondents. A 7-bid set was initially defined for the most complete conservation scheme (that combining the three programmes altogether). Reducing these initial bids by 20 and 50 per cent, we derived bid sets for schemes with one or two programmes respectively.[2]

The first valuation question in all versions of the questionnaire was about the most complete conservation scheme. This fact was supposed to lead respondents to take their WTP for this scheme (supposedly the highest) as a 'ceiling' when valuing the partial conservation schemes that followed. Previous to the second valuation question, a small introduction stressed the partial nature of conservation schemes to be valued in the 2nd to 6th valuation questions. Respondents were asked to take the partial scheme in each question as the only alternative to the policy-off (no-conservation) scenario. So, the choice in each question was between having the proposed partial conservation scheme at the proposed cost or no conservation at all. Respondents were also asked to consider the scheme and bid amount offered in each question independently from schemes and bids offered in previous questions. Partial conservation schemes were presented in different orders in the three versions of the questionnaire so as to avoid possible question-order biases. Each respondent was allowed to change (in either sense) his answers to previous questions as he progressed through the valuation questions.

The precise wording of the valuation questions can be illustrated with the case of a particular partial conservation scheme:

Consider now a conservation scheme comprising two programmes: the conservation of currently existing stone walls and barns, and the conservation of hay meadows at current levels of flower diversity. So, programmes 1 and 2. Suppose your share of the costs now resulted in an increase of £ X per year in your household income tax. Would you be willing to pay £ X per year, every year, to ensure that this scheme can be carried out? When answering please do it as if you actually had to pay.

A question asking respondents to choose in checklists the category best describing the reason for a 'yes' or 'no' answer followed the first valuation question. The corresponding answers were used in the diagnosis of protest 'nos', non-considerate 'yea saying' and other problematic answers.

Before the valuation questions, respondents were instructed to take into account their actual budget constraint as well as the possible existence of other areas of the countryside also in need of conservation.

The Peneda–Gerês scenario somewhat differed from that of the Pennine Dales in that the former was slightly simpler and the conservation programmes were obviously different. The idea that many of the Peneda–Gerês landscapes are due to traditional farming was first introduced by presenting two photos of terraced and meadow landscapes. The economic difficulties of traditional farming in the NP were explained and related to a trend for generalised abandonment of farmland; the corresponding landscape changes were also described. Respondents were then informed about a Ministry of Agriculture's agri-environmental programme in application in this area. For this purpose, they were asked to read a booklet named 'Conservation of traditionally farmed landscapes of Peneda–Gerês'. This booklet included a map of the Peneda–Gerês NP, showing the area covered by the agri-environmental programme within the park, as well as three pages describing the three conservation programmes. These programmes were aimed at conserving traditional farming in terraces (programme 1), irrigated hay meadows (programme 2) and oak woods currently managed by farmers (programme 3). Each programme was described using two photos depicting the current landscape, which would be maintained with the programme, and another photo representing the expected landscape without the programme. This way of presenting the landscape changes to be valued was conceived as a simplification with respect to the Pennine Dales scenario in that the previous booklet and programmes card were merged into a single booklet.

Questionnaire Administration

In both case-studies, the survey used on-site in-person interviews. Although costly, this option was easily justified given (1) the large number of schemes to be valued by each respondent, (2) the need to show the landscape booklet and (3) the requirement to make sure that respondents understood the choice to be made in each valuation question. Furthermore, this option presented all the other advantages generally recognised to in-person interviews as opposed to self-administered questionnaires (mailed or distributed on-site). One of these advantages is the possibility of reducing sample selection bias by avoiding that respondents auto-select themselves according to factors (e.g. interest in conservation issues) that are related to WTP for conservation. With self-administered questionnaires, respondents can read the whole questionnaire before deciding whether to participate and thus it is impossible to avoid this bias (cf. Mitchell and Carson 1989). On-site interviews were also the only practical way of randomly sampling visitors to each area.

Pilot Surveys

In both studies, field pilot surveys were carried out previous to the main survey to check whether CVM scenarios were understandable and plausible for the respondents and whether bid sets performed acceptably.

In the Pennine Dales study, the pilot survey took place in July 1995 and produced 58 completed questionnaires. In the Peneda–Gerês case, the pilot was in July 1996 and produced 124 completed questionnaires.

In both pilots, the CVM scenarios were revealed to be generally understandable and plausible for the respondents. Yet, different respondents perceived the actual delivery of the landscape benefits promised by each scheme at different levels of probability. Some were not sure that the money they would pay would be allocated to this scheme rather than other government programmes; others suspected that farmers would not comply with all prescriptions included in management agreements. This suggested that different valuations could be based on different levels of certainty of actual delivery of the landscape benefits. Likewise, many 'no' answers could mean a refusal of the scenario (protest answers) rather than a true valuation. To standardise respondents' perceptions of certainty levels, interviewers were instructed to reply to respondents' doubts, during the main surveys, by asking them to take all policy outcomes described in the scenarios as certain. Benefit estimates resulting from these surveys should, therefore, be interpreted as corresponding to policies with certain outcomes.

Regarding previously defined bid sets, pilot surveys revealed an increase in the proportion of 'no' answers with the bid amount; besides, the highest bid amounts received only a few 'yes' answers. Both results confirmed that bid sets were performing acceptably. Moreover, bid sets allowed the estimation, from pilot data, of logit models explaining the 'yes/no' binary answers with much higher levels of statistical significance than what was expected for such small samples. Hence, previously defined bid sets were maintained for the main surveys.

In the Dales case, extensive parts of the questionnaire were reworded after the pilot. Hence, pilot questionnaires were not comparable with main-survey questionnaires and thus only main-survey data were used in the analysis. Yet, in the Peneda–Gerês study, the pilot suggested only small changes to the questionnaire and pilot interviews were carried out in a rather standardised way. Thus, in the analysis, pilot data were merged with main-survey data.

Population, Sampling Frame and Non-Response

Two of the most important steps in a CVM survey whose results are to be aggregated for policy evaluation purposes are the definition of the population and the sampling from this population. Important benefit-aggregation biases can be originated at both of these steps. High non-response rates can also have a biasing effect on aggregated benefit estimates.

If the aim of the CVM exercise is to assess a policy scheme for landscape conservation, the survey population should include all individuals affected by the policy-induced landscape change. This population includes three sub-populations, i.e.: those who lived in the relevant area(s) during a particular time period of reference, those who visited this area and those who did not use it at all. Very often, nonusers' WTP for landscape conservation represents a very significant share of the aggregate benefits of policy schemes such as ESAs (Willis et al. 1993). Measuring these non-use values requires surveying nonusers. However, in the Pennine Dales and Peneda–Gerês studies, nonusers were not interviewed, as only visitors or residents would have a degree of familiarity with the landscape required for undertaking the intended valuation tasks. (Note, for example, that each respondent was asked to value several alternative states of landscape, some only differing in rather subtle aspects.)

Residents were also not surveyed in both studies, as residents' share of the aggregated benefit of policy schemes was expected to be insignificant, given the small number of residents when compared to visitors (cf. also Willis et al. 1993; and Willis and Garrod 1991). Having sampled only visitors, our CVM results could only be aggregated to the visitor population, and thus aggregated benefit estimates presented in this book should be interpreted as lower-bound estimates.

In both studies, the survey population was defined as the set of all households visiting the particular area (Pennine Dales or Peneda–Gerês) over the 12 months previous to the last day of the main survey. The household rather than the individual visitor was considered as the relevant population element because of the used payment vehicle (household income tax increase) and the non-excludable public-good nature of landscape changes to be valued.

For valid aggregation of sample statistics (e.g. average WTP) to the whole population, the sampling frame (the method used to list the elements of the population who can potentially be sampled) should ensure that any visiting household had a known, positive, probability of being selected. However, in both surveys, because of time and budget constraints, only some households who visited the area within a short period during the summer and who passed by one of a few interviewing sites have been selected.[3] This introduced two possible sources of sampling frame bias: one seasonal and the other related to the possibility of the particular interviewing sites not yielding a representative sample of all types of visitors. Both of these sources of bias were investigated and shown to be not too severe in the two case-studies (cf. Santos 1997). The seasonal component of bias was investigated by comparing the proportions of different types of visitor (day-trippers *vs* holidaymakers; weekend *vs* midweek visits) in our samples with those in a past study of visitors to the Pennine Dales (PA Cambridge Economic Consultants 1992) and in a past traffic count in the Peneda–Gerês area (cf. Santos 1997). These previous studies also revealed that 48 and 67 per cent of the annual number of visits (respectively in the Dales and Peneda–Gerês areas) occurred in the peak holiday period of July–September, which reduced the potential for severe seasonal bias. The site-component of sampling frame bias was somewhat mitigated by choosing interviewing sites so as to catch a sample of visitors as diverse as possible with respect to aspects like the type of outdoor-recreation activities carried out in the area. For example, in the Dales case, visitors interviewed at Muker were mainly holidaymakers engaged in specialised activities such as long walks, while many of those interviewed at Grassington were day trippers engaged in non-specialised activities like car driving, general sightseeing and visiting village shops and pubs. Furthermore, the use of WTP models to correct possible sampling frame biases revealed that the potential for bias was always rather small (cf. Santos 1997).

At each site, interviewees were selected on a 'next person to walk past' basis, with only one person per household being interviewed. In the Pennine Dales, 514 interviewees were selected in this way, from which 87 refused to participate, 5 produced incomplete or unusable questionnaires and 422 produced usable questionnaires. Hence, unit non-response rate was kept at less than 18 per cent. In the Peneda–Gerês survey (pilot plus main survey) 917 visitors were selected, with 211 refusing to participate, 2 leaving before the end of the interview and 704 producing usable questionnaires. Thus, this survey had a unit non-response rate of 23 per cent. As those refusing to participate were only read a short statement, vaguely related to the theme of the survey, it is unlikely that they decided not to participate according to factors related to WTP (Mitchell and Carson 1989). Thus (if existent at all) sample selection bias was kept at a minimum level in both case-studies.

Only 29 and 42 respondents (respectively in the Dales and Peneda–Gerês surveys) gave 'no' answers to all valuation questions and invoked a 'protest' reason for these answers.[4] The answers from these respondents were considered protest 'nos' and were, thus, deleted when estimating mean WTP. In addition, 22 and 33 valuation questions (respectively in the Dales and Peneda–Gerês cases) received 'don't know' answers from other respondents. Adding up protest-no and don't-know answers, we estimated item non-response rate for the two surveys as 8 and 7 per cent respectively. The corresponding non-response bias should, therefore, be small. It was, nevertheless, corrected for in benefit estimation. For this purpose, we followed the usual procedure of considering all usable questionnaires (rather than only those with valid answers to the valuation questions) to compute the means of the independent variables to be entered in WTP models when producing WTP estimates (cf. Mitchell and Carson 1989).

9.2 VISITORS' SUMMARY STATISTICS[5]

In this section, we describe visitors to the Pennine Dales and Peneda–Gerês areas and their diversity. This is done with the purpose of selecting those variables that, according to theory and previous empirical knowledge, should account for differences in WTP for landscape conservation across individuals. Testing the explanatory power of such variables and checking for consistency between the sign (and size) of these variables' effect on WTP and previous expectations allow us to assess the theoretical validity of our CVM-based WTP estimates (Mitchell and Carson 1989). These types of test are carried out with WTP models to be presented in chapter 10. Another form of theoretically validating WTP estimates is to check whether the difference between benefit estimates from the two case-studies is consistent with previous expectations based on known differences between visitors to the two areas (an exercise undertaken in chapter 13).

This section presents figures describing visitors and their diversity with respect to: frequency of visits, recreational activities, socio-economic variables, environmental commitments and landscape perceptions and preferences. Unless stated otherwise, the figures presented here result from the Dales (D) and Peneda–Gerês (PG) CVM surveys.

The Visits: Distance Travelled, Frequency and Recreation Purposes

In both case-studies, there is a clear-cut difference between two types of visitors, at least as regards frequency of visits and familiarity with the area: day trippers and holidaymakers. Many day trippers (68 per cent in the D; 47 per cent in the PG) travelled for less than 80 Km (50 miles) to arrive in the area whereas about 60 per cent of holidaymakers (in both cases) travelled for more than 160 Km (100 miles). As a consequence of living closer, day trippers visited the area more often than holidaymakers in both case-studies. Yet, day trippers and holidaymakers in the D were more frequent visitors than their counterparts in the PG case. Thus, 82 per cent of day trippers in the D paid more than one visit a year (with 20 per cent exceeding 14 annual visits) whilst only 52 per cent of day trippers in the PG exceeded one annual visit (17 per cent exceeding 3 annual visits). Only 45 per cent of holidaymakers in the D and 23 per cent in the PG visited the area more than once a year.

Day trippers were probably more familiar with the area than holidaymakers, as suggested by the fact that, e.g. in the D, only 4 per cent of day trippers were visiting the area for the first time, whereas 19 per cent of holidaymakers were doing the same. A similar difference occurs in the PG case, but at lower levels of familiarity: 14 per cent of day trippers and 35 per cent of holidaymakers were visiting the area for the first time.

In the D case, frequently reported outdoor recreation activities were (starting by the most frequent): walking more than 2 miles; visiting historic sites or buildings; other activities (comprising car driving and sightseeing, visiting village pubs and shops, visiting relatives...); walking less than 2 miles; camping; looking at wildlife; and photography. In the PG case, these activities were (also by decreasing order): looking at nature in general; car driving and sightseeing; photography; bathing in rivers and reservoirs; walking less than 3 Km; walking more than 3 Km; camping; visiting traditional villages; and visiting historic sites. Comparing these rankings we note that visitors to the D engaged more often than visitors to the PG in activities implying a high degree of involvement with the landscape, such as long walks. Thus, while 56 per cent of the former engaged in walks for more than 2 miles, only 17 per cent of the latter did so. Likewise, about a third of visitors to the PG were visiting the park for bathing in streams and reservoirs, a recreational activity that depends more on the water element than on agricultural landscapes.

Socio-Economic Description of Visitors

A similar occupational structure in the two visitor samples indicates that, in both cases, most visitors were members of the urban middle class and employed in the service sector. Hence, employers represented only 7 and 8 per cent of those economically active respectively in the D and PG samples. Professional or skilled non-manual occupations represented, respectively, 45 and 42 per cent of the economically active. On the other hand, manual occupations represented only 17 and 23 per cent of the economically active. Retired people represented 19 per cent of all visitors in the D sample, but only 4 per cent in the PG sample, which is due to the much younger age structure in the latter.

This urban-middle-class character of most visitors explains the fact of the average household income of visitors to each area being larger than the corresponding national average. In fact, average household incomes in the two samples, although different (£26,030 in the D sample and £17,920 in the PG sample[6]), represent 1.75 and 2.58 of the average wage rate for the corresponding country[7] (the UK and Portugal respectively). This difference in income levels between visitors and the general population of each country should be considered when assessing the distributional effects of policy schemes for landscape conservation. In fact, it is the wealthier visitor who enjoys most of the landscape benefits generated by these schemes but it is the poorer general taxpayer who pays for them.

With respect to differences between the two case-studies, the figures just quoted show that visitors to the D area had a considerably higher average household income than those to the PG area. Yet, in both cases, a clear-cut difference exists between day trippers and holidaymakers, with the latter being considerably wealthier than the former. This can be explained based on two causes. The first is the difference in income levels between the two original populations from which these two types of visitor were drawn. (This would be particularly important in the PG case, with the wealthier Lisbon conurbation being more represented among holidaymakers). The other cause, possibly the most important one, is the fact that both travel and staying costs are, in average, higher for holidaymakers than day trippers, which causes the former to be a rather income-select group.

Differences between the case-studies and (within each case) between day trippers and holidaymakers with respect to formal education, occupation and levels of car ownership parallel the pattern of differences that was described for income. Hence, visitors to the D area (as well as holidaymakers when compared to day trippers to the same area) were better educated, employed in occupations enjoying a higher social status and owned more cars.

One of the most striking socio-economic differences between visitors to the D and PG areas refers to the age structure of these visitors. Visitors to the PG were much younger than visitors to the D: 56 per cent of the former were less than 34 years old and only 7 per cent older than 55, whilst the corresponding figures for the D were 17 and 28 per cent. This is probably explained by a recent generational shift in holiday destination, in Portugal, away from beach and towards upland areas. On the other hand, visiting the uplands was already a well-established tourist pursuit in the UK at least since Victorian days.

Day trippers are also significantly older than holidaymakers in both case-studies.

The fact that the majority of the Portuguese are still living in rural areas, coupled with existing differences between rural and urban people as regards their perceptions of the countryside, justifies that we describe here in some detail the urban/rural character of visitors to the PG area. In fact, in this case, the urban/rural variable was a very significant predictor of WTP for landscape conservation (see chapter 10). Because the vast majority of visitors to the D were urban the variable urban/rural was not so interesting for characterising the D sample.

Portuguese society experienced a strong population movement from rural to urban areas over the last three to four decades, but the urbanisation process is rather unfinished in this country: in fact, 56 per cent of the Portuguese population still lived in rural settlements in 1981 (Baptista 1993). Although along the urbanisation process the occupational and cultural frames of rural areas have been approaching those of urban areas (Baptista 1993), it could be expected that rural people in Portugal still had different cultural attitudes towards nature and had, therefore, a different perception of the countryside. Rural people would relate to the countryside according to what Cosgrove (1984) described as the insider condition. Insiders in a sociological sense do not separate the appearance of the countryside from its productive roles and, especially, from a sense of place based on a thick fabric of local social relationships (Lowenthal 1978). Only urban people, as outsiders, can view the external aspect of countryside as independent from the very social processes underlying it, i.e.: as a landscape. Hence, the urban (outsider) position would be a prerequisite for the emergence of the countryside as landscape. Thus, the fact that the UK suffered a very early urbanisation process probably explains why landscape preservation played such an important role in the history of the conservation movement in this country (Winter 1996).

Because urbanisation is quite recent in Portugal, when classifying each respondent we considered not only the current parish of residence but also the parish of childhood. Hence visitors were classified according to three categories, i.e.: those who lived in urban, semi-urban and rural settlements.[8] The first category was still sub-divided according to the parish of residence before the respondent was 16 years old. As a result of this classification, it is possible to note that 73 per cent of the visitors to the PG (as opposed to less than half of the Portuguese) were urban. This result shows that the rural population is much less represented among visitors to the NP than in the Portuguese population as a whole, which means the national park selectively attracts urban people.

It is also possible to note that, within the PG sample, a higher percentage of day trippers (than holidaymakers) were rural or had a rural origin.

It is not clear whether this selective attraction of urban people is due to income/travel cost reasons (average income of urban people is higher) or differences between urban and rural people as regards participation in outdoor recreation in general. Nevertheless, these latter differences seem to have some weight. The fact of more day trippers than holidaymakers being rural is due to the more rural character of the areas surrounding the PG, where most day trippers come from.

Visitors' General Commitment to Environmental Issues

Six particular types of behaviour were taken as indicators of visitors' general commitment to environmental issues. Three of these types of behaviour were reported by a vast majority of respondents in both surveys. Thus, approximately 90 per cent or more of visitors had read or watched TV about the countryside, wildlife or conservation and had delivered garbage for recycling as well. Likewise, approximately 70 per cent of visitors had selected particular consumption goods on environmental grounds. Another frequent behaviour among visitors to the D but not among visitors to the PG area was donating money to environmental charities: 59 per cent of visitors to the D had engaged in this practice whereas only 18 per cent in the PG sample had done so. The subscription to a magazine concerned with the countryside, wildlife or natural resources and the active campaigning for an environmental issue were only reported by a minority of respondents. Yet, 29 and 12 per cent of the visitors to the D reported these behaviours; in the PG sample, the corresponding figures were 11 and 5 per cent.

Thus, the three types of behaviour revealing higher levels of environmental concern (donations, subscription to a specialised magazine and active campaigning) were more frequent among visitors to the D than among visitors to the PG.

Using the same indicators of attitudes towards the environment, we noted that, in both areas, holidaymakers seemed more aware of and committed to environmental issues than day trippers.

Environmental-group membership within the visitor's household is more frequent in the D sample (52 per cent of the households) than in the PG one (only 6 per cent). This also revealed a completely different level of development of the environmental movement in the two countries: respectively the UK and Portugal.[9]

Visitors' Perceptions and Preferences for the Pennine Dales and Peneda–Gerês Landscapes

Visitor's perception of an area's uniqueness should be a critical variable for their valuation of policy schemes to preserve this area's landscape, as it indicates whether (and to what extent) other areas' landscapes would act as substitutes for this particular area's landscape. As already mentioned, visitors' perception of uniqueness of the area's landscape was evaluated, in both case-studies, through the use of a 4-point scale. In both cases, most respondents (64 per cent in the D and 61 per cent in the PG) considered the area 'better than most' areas of the countryside they had visited (3 points) and a significant share (24 per cent and 30 per cent respectively) considered it 'the best' (4 points). Likewise, in both cases, a larger share of day trippers than holidaymakers scored the area's landscape as 'the best', which suggests day trippers perceive the area's landscape as more non-substitutable. This is not surprising if we consider the fact that these visitors lived closer by and visited more often the area. On the other hand, some holidaymakers lived in regions closer to other areas of the countryside that can provide substitutes for the area's landscape. (Some respondents to both surveys explicitly mentioned some of these areas, e.g. the Scottish Highlands or the Peak District NP, in the D sample, and other upland areas in North and Central Portugal, in the PG sample.)

Visitors to each area were asked to select, from a checklist of the main attributes of the area's landscape, the three they preferred and would most like to see maintained for the future. Thus, answers reveal not only preferences but also the perceived risk of loosing each particular attribute. Because different attributes are relevant for different areas, answers to this preference question are separately analysed for each area.

In the D area, dry-stone walls were definitely the most preferred landscape attribute. Walls and field barns together represented more than 100 per cent of the number of respondents; meadows and wildflowers together represented 51 per cent, and broad-leaved woods alone represented 36 per cent. Note that birds and other wildlife were preferred over woodland, heather moorland and wildflowers plus meadows, but not over dry-stone walls. Heather moorland was preferred over broad-leaved woods. This is an important observation since most heather moors in the Pennines lie on the fells, outside the ESA boundaries, and, although not targeted by the ESA scheme, are currently under threat of overgrazing by sheep.

In the PG area, mountain streams and waterfalls were the most preferred landscape attribute, with 78 per cent of respondents having selected this option. They were followed by wildlife, comprising the wolf, and traditional villages, both selected by more than half of the respondents. Oak woodland was the fourth attribute in preference (39 per cent of respondents). It was followed by steep and rocky areas (29 per cent) and pine forests (15 per cent). All the other attributes (cultivated terraces, moorland, irrigated hay meadows, and stone walls) were picked by less than 10 per cent of respondents.

These results strongly suggest that landscape attributes targeted by the Pennine Dales ESA scheme are those at the core of visitors' preferences. Yet, even in this area, visitors have also shown strong preferences for an attribute not covered by the ESA scheme: heather moorland. The case is completely different in the PG area, where the first preferences of visitors go to attributes (waterfalls, wildlife and traditional villages) not specifically targeted by the agri-environmental programme in the Peneda–Gerês NP. Although a significant percentage of respondents included oak woods among the three most preferred attributes, all the other attributes targeted by this programme (i.e.: cultivated terraces, stone walls and irrigated meadows) were only selected by less than 10 per cent of the respondents. This suggests that, *ceteris paribus*, the Pennine Dales ESA scheme should be valued higher than the agri-environmental programme in the Peneda–Gerês NP.

Let us now consider the ranking, by the respondents, of the three landscape conservation programmes included in the Dales CVM scenario. Programme 1 (walls and barns) was the preferred choice for almost half the visitors; programme 2 (hay meadows) was the preferred choice for one third of them and programme 3 (woodland) was the preferred choice for only one fifth of the respondents. Programmes 2 and 3 were the more frequent second positions and programme 3 was the most frequent third position. Thus, the prevailing ranking in the D survey was programme 1 – programme 2 – programme 3.

In the PG survey, programme 3 (oak woodland) was ranked first by 54 per cent of the respondents followed by programme 1 (traditional farming in terraces), which was ranked first by 37 per cent; only 8 per cent of the respondents ranked programme 2 (irrigated hay meadows) first. Programme 1 was the most frequent second position followed by programme 2. Programme 2 was the most frequent third position (ranked third by 58 per cent). Thus, the prevailing ranking was now programme 3 – programme 1 – programme 2.[10]

Taking into account the attribute content of each programme, the rankings of the programmes just presented are clearly consistent, in both case-studies, with the choices of preferred landscape attributes presented above. Note that the choice of preferred attributes was done before the presentation of the CVM scenarios and that the ranking of the programmes was done after this presentation. Thus, the consistency between these two results shows that the presentation of the scenarios did not change, in any marked way, previous preferences of respondents for the different landscape attributes. This can be explained, in both case-studies, by the familiarity of visitors with the area's landscape and constitutes a particularly reassuring result, given the difficulties in describing aesthetic goods in ways that do not distort previous preferences of respondents for these goods (see section 4.3).

In the PG case, both the ranking of programmes and the choice of preferred landscape attributes are also consistent with the results of the independent study of preferences presented in chapter 8, where preferences were elicited as reactions to visual stimuli alone. In fact, in this study, preference scores of open deciduous wood scenes varied between 3.9 and 4.1; those of terraced landscapes between 3.4 and 3.8; and those of different meadow scenes (presenting more or less trees) between 2.4 and 3.3. This exactly reproduces the ranking of the corresponding attributes and programmes in the main CVM survey. Given that methods to reveal preferences for attributes were completely different, this coincidence of rankings is an even stronger proof of the fact that the presentation of the CVM scenario did not significantly distort previous preferences for landscape attributes.

NOTES

1. All booklets, cards and questionnaires used in both surveys are presented in Santos (1997).
2. In the Peneda–Gerês survey, the bid set for the most complete scheme was based on a Weibull approximation to open-ended WTP data collected in the survey of landscape perceptions and preferences reported in chapter 8. In both cases (Pennine Dales and Peneda–Gerês surveys), all bid sets were tested in pilot surveys previously to their use in the main surveys. The used bid sets for three, two and one-programme schemes are presented in Santos (1997).
3. In the Dales, this period started on the 28 July and ended by the 28 August 1995. Interviewing days covered weekend and midweek days on a proportional basis and interviews were carried out between 10:00 a.m. and 5:00 p.m. at four sites (Reeth, Muker, Kettlewell and Grassington; each comprising a village and the closest car park). In the Peneda–Gerês area, interviews were carried out continuously, day after day, during two separate periods: 6–8 July (pilot) and 28 July–8 August 1996 (main survey); interviews were carried out between 9:30 a.m. and 6:00 p.m. Different interviewing sites throughout the NP had been assayed in the pilot, but only three sites in the most visited, central, area of the park (i.e.: Leonte, Pedra Bela and Caldas do Gerês village) produced an acceptable number of interviews per interviewer per day. Hence, only these sites were used for the main survey.
4. Some reasons for a 'no' answer do not mean that the respondent's valuation of the particular conservation scheme is smaller than the proposed bid amount. They solely indicate respondents are refusing the CVM scenario. These answers are considered protest 'nos' and should be deleted before estimating mean WTP (Mitchell and Carson 1989). The most frequent protest reasons in both studies were: (1) general protests against raising income tax; (2) the opinion that 'farmers already receive enough subsidies'; and (3) a preference for local collection of revenue for these schemes (e.g. through entrance fees) as opposed to a general income-tax rise.
5. A more developed presentation of summary statistics of visitors to the Pennine Dales and Peneda–Gerês areas is given in Santos (1997), where the reader can find tables with all the relevant figures.
6. The average income in the Portuguese case was converted into £s by using an exchange rate of 280 Portuguese escudos (PTE) per £.
7. In the D case, average wage rate was estimated as the ratio of the amount of wages and salaries (ONS 1996) to the total number of employees employed in the UK (ONS 1997c). In the PG case, the average wage rate only refers to the industry and commerce sectors in

Portugal (Continent) and was provided by the Ministério para a Qualificação e o Emprego (1997).

8. The criterion to separate urban from rural settlements is subject to debate among Portuguese geographers. While some advocate the traditional criterion of considering as urban only those settlements with more than 10,000 inhabitants, others argue that the 2,000-inhabitants figure best reflects a typical Portuguese form of diffuse urbanisation and industrialisation of the countryside (Medeiros 1991). Hence the urban/rural variable was defined in this study as including three categories: urban, semi-urban and rural. The urban category was equated with all the *concelhos* (administrative sectors roughly corresponding to English districts) belonging to the Lisbon and Oporto conurbations plus all heads of *concelho* with more than 10,000 inhabitants. The semi-urban category was equated with all heads of *concelho* (towns) with more than 2,000 and less than 10,000 inhabitants. The remaining settlements were considered rural.

9. Note, however, that this cannot be taken as a straight indicator of environmental concern, as National Trust (NT) membership alone accounted for 31 per cent of all households in the D sample and NT membership provides free entry in Trust properties all over the country. So, in this case, there is also an element of payment for a service.

10. The fact that the prevailing ranking of the three programmes in the D survey (i.e.: P1–P2–P3) exactly reproduced the order in which these programmes were numbered and presented to respondents raised the issue of a possible order bias. Although we have no way of directly showing the absence of such bias (the order of presentation and numbering was the same in all questionnaires), the fact of the prevailing ranking in the PG survey being completely different (i.e.: P3–P1–P2) is particularly reassuring. Furthermore, the fact of the ranking of the programmes being consistent with the relative preferences for the corresponding landscape attributes, as elicited before the presentation of the programmes, provides evidence supporting the claim that preferences for attributes were not constructed nor significantly biased during the survey.

10. Willingness-to-Pay for Landscape Conservation in the Pennine Dales and Peneda–Gerês Areas

This chapter is aimed at carrying out four main tasks. First, to estimate WTP for landscape conservation in the Pennine Dales (D) and Peneda–Gerês (PG) areas, and to assess the validity and reliability of such estimates. Second, to evaluate the empirical performance of the CVM approach to multi-attribute landscape changes that was proposed in chapters 3 and 4. Third, to check whether the theory of demand for attributes discussed in chapter 3 accounts for the observed interactions in valuation between programmes. Fourth, to aggregate per-household WTP estimates to the corresponding visitor population, so that we can secure the landscape benefit estimates to be used in chapter 12 for evaluating conservation schemes on a cost–benefit basis.

Estimation of the continuous WTP variable from discrete-choice response data followed Cameron's censored logistic regression approach (section 4.5). The censored model (i.e.: the multi-attribute valuation function itself) was estimated through maximum-likelihood estimation of a logit model including the bid amount among the independent variables, with the reparameterization in (4.20) allowing us to recover the parameters of the censored-regression model from those of the logit. The approximate variance–covariance matrix of the censored model, used for interval estimation and hypotheses testing, was secured from that of the logit using Cameron's (1991) matrix-transformation approach (section 4.5).

10.1 ASSESSING THE CVM EXERCISE WITH RESPECT TO THEORETICAL VALIDITY, SEVERAL BIASES AND RELIABILITY

A first WTP model (or valuation function) was estimated, in each case-study, for purposes of evaluating the corresponding data set and WTP estimates as regards theoretical validity, absence of particular biases and reliability. This model was built using a stepwise procedure, which selected the explanatory variables from an initial list of variables that, according to theory and the

The Case-Studies

particular circumstances of each case, were expected to be related to WTP for landscape conservation. Only those variables with a significant effect on WTP at the 10 per cent level (log-likelihood-ratio χ^2 test) were selected to enter the model or to remain in it at each step in the procedure. Non-accordance between the signs of the estimated parameters and prior expectations as regards these signs was not used as a criterion to drop any significant explanatory variable. This is a reasonable way of avoiding evidence being dropped, which is not favourable with respect to theoretical validity. This unfavourable evidence should be considered as part of the validity assessment and not simply dropped when building the WTP model. The estimated WTP models are presented in Tables 10.1 and 10.2 respectively for the D and PG cases.[1] Two indicators of overall goodness of fit are reported in the upper part of each table: (1) the χ^2 test variable for the set of all explanatory variables in the logit model; and (2) the rate of correct predictions for the observed binary (yes/no) response variable. This latter was based on the cross-tabulation of actual responses *vs.* responses as predicted by comparing fitted WTP with the offered bid (the corresponding classification tables are also presented in the upper part of each table). Also reported are the asymptotic t-Student statistics and corresponding levels of significance (one-tail test) for each parameter estimate in the censored WTP model (three levels of probability were considered: 0.10, 0.05 and 0.01; indicated by the signs *, ** and *** respectively).

Theoretical Validity

Economic theory and the circumstances of each case-study suggested that WTP for landscape conservation should be related, in some specific ways, to a number of variables characterising the visitor and the conservation scheme. Thus, we had some expectations as regards the signs and sizes of these variables' effects on WTP.[2] The theoretical validity of a CVM exercise – hence, that of the resulting WTP estimates as well – is usually assessed by checking whether these effects, once estimated, are consistent with those prior expectations (Mitchell and Carson 1989). So, let us consider the estimated coefficients for the explanatory variables in models D1 and PG1 (Tables 10.1 and 10.2).

Variables P1, P2 and P3 are dummies indicating the presence/absence of each of three conservation programmes, and thus vector (P1, P2, P3) represents the programme-mix valued in each particular observation. (Of course, each Pi means different things in different case-studies: for example, P1 refers to walls and barns, in the D case, and terraces, in the PG case.) In both case-studies, all variables Pi had a statistically very significant and

Table 10.1 WTP model D1

Dependent variable: WTP for landscape conservation in the Dales (£/year)	Prediction success (%)			
Numb. of observat.: 2290			Actual	Total
Correct predictions: 78.5%			would wouldn't	
−2log-likeli. ratio: 1033.34	Predicted	would pay	49.8 14.6	64.4
Deg. of freedom: 21		wouldn't	6.9 28.7	35.6
Level of signif.: P<0.0001	Total		56.7 43.3	100.0

Variables	Parameter estimates	t-ratios	Pr.	Labels
INTERCEPT	−47.53	−2.898	***	Intercept
P1	22.05	3.650	***	Programme 1: stone walls and field barns (0–1)
P2	13.27	2.465	***	Programme 2: flower-rich meadows (0–1)
P3	19.36	3.691	***	Programme 3: broad-leaved woodland (0–1)
P1*FIRSTP1	10.97	1.530	*	Programme 1 when first in preferences (0–1)
P2*FIRSTP2	37.85	4.769	***	Programme 2 when first in preferences (0–1)
P3*FIRSTP3	19.57	2.292	**	Programme 3 when first in preferences (0–1)
INCOME	0.00079	3.952	***	Household income before taxes (£)
DAYTRIP	14.53	2.715	***	Day trip (0–1)
ACTBIRD	−26.36	−2.980	***	Birdwatching in the Dales (0–1)
ACTOTHER	−13.00	−2.490	***	Other activities in the Dales (0–1)
LANDQUAL	10.95	2.641	***	Quality/ uniqueness of the Dales landscape (4-point scale)
ATTPROD	15.00	2.659	***	Selected environmentally friendly products (0–1)
ATTCHAR	8.95	1.794	**	Gave money to environmental or conservation charities (0–1)
MEMBNT	18.93	3.579	***	Member of National Trust (0–1)
MEMBRSPC	25.51	2.455	***	Member of RSPCA (0–1)
MEMBAC	34.05	2.441	***	Member of angling club (0–1)
MEMBOTHE	30.69	2.970	***	Member of other env. group (0–1)
CATB	−14.43	−2.251	**	Retired (0–1)
CATD	34.11	2.652	***	Employer or managerial profession (0–1)
FEMALE	13.04	2.346	***	Sex (female =1)
κ	43.86	20.476	***	Dispersion parameter of the logistic random term

positive effect on WTP (Tables 10.1 and 10.2), as expected since, for most respondents, the landscape attributes delivered by each programme were economic goods, not bads. Thus, the adding of any programme to a conservation scheme should significantly increase the value of this scheme.[3]

The following group of variables refers to interactions between the

Table 10.2 WTP model PG1

Dependent variable: WTP for conservation in the Peneda–Gerês (esc./year)	Prediction success (%)				
Numb. of observat.: 3939			Actual		Total
Correct predictions: 76.7%			would	wouldn't	
−2log-likeli. ratio: 1489.89	Predicted	would pay	38.2	13.9	52.1
Deg. of freedom: 22		wouldn't	9.4	38.5	47.9
Level of signif.: P<0.0001	Total		47.6	52.4	100.0

Variables	Parameter estimates	t-ratios	Pr.	Labels
INTERCEPT	−4665	−2.838	***	Intercept
P1	3396	5.929	***	Programme 1: traditional farming in terraces (0–1)
P2	2185	4.374	***	Programme 2: irrigated hay meadows (0–1)
P3	2640	4.184	***	Programme 3: oak woods (0–1)
P1*FIRSTP1	4018	5.307	***	Programme 1 when first in preferences (0–1)
P3*FIRSTP3	4540	6.186	***	Programme 3 when first in preferences (0–1)
LANDQUAL	762	1.747	**	Quality/ uniqueness of the Peneda–Gerês landscape (4-point scale)
DAYTRIP	2821	3.730	***	Day trip (0–1)
DAYS	85	2.708	***	Days in the NP over the last 12 months
FIRSTIME	−2119	−3.689	***	Current was the first visit ever made to the area (0–1)
WALKING	2253	3.275	***	Walking more than 3 Km (0–1)
WILDWATC	5076	4.180	***	Looking for wildlife species (0–1)
VILLAGES	1417	2.108	**	Visiting traditional villages (0–1)
OTHERACT	−2973	−1.751	**	Other recreational activities (0–1)
ENVCAMP	5189	4.209	***	Actively campaigned for the environment (0–1)
HIGHED	1402	2.471	***	Went on to higher education (0–1)
RETIRED	−6602	−4.449	***	Retired (0–1)
SELFEMP	2569	2.455	***	Self employed (0–1)
INCOME	0.00091	9.448	***	Household annual income before taxes (esc.)
RURALRES	−2624	−4.131	***	Rural residence (0–1)
RURALCHI	−3994	−4.899	***	Urban residence but rural childhood (0–1)
FOREIGN	−3536	−2.805	***	Non-Portuguese (0–1)
κ	6250	24.047	***	Dispersion parameter of the logistic random term

presence/absence of a particular programme (dummy Pi) and another dummy variable indicating whether this programme was the preferred choice for the particular respondent (FIRSTPi). According to previous expectations, all of the Pi*FIRSTPi interaction terms were revealed to have a positive effect on WTP. In fact, we would expect people for whom a particular programme is the first choice to value this programme higher than other people. All these interaction effects on WTP, except the effect of P2*FIRSTP2 in the PG case, are statistically significant at the 0.10 level (Tables 10.1 and 10.2).

These interaction effects on WTP show that the value of a particular programme, say Pi, has two separate components: (1) the average value of Pi for those for whom Pi is not the first choice, which is given by the coefficient for Pi; (2) the premium that those who ranked Pi first in preferences are prepared to pay for Pi on top of the amount referred to in (1), which is given by the coefficient for Pi*FIRSTPi. There are clear differences across programmes with respect to the relative size of these two components. For example, in the D, those having P1 (walls and barns) as their first choice were prepared to pay a premium of 50 per cent on top of other people's average valuation for P1; yet, for those ranking P2 (hay meadows) first, the corresponding premium amounted to almost 300 per cent. There is an intuitive reason for this. Walls are quite obvious in the landscape and definitely make the character of the Dales. Hence, a high valuation of walls tends to be spread among all visitors, irrespective of their relative preferences for other attributes. On the other hand, in most seasons and for most respondents, meadows are much less salient than walls, being even not easily distinguished from other land uses. Hence, preferring meadows to all other attributes tends to reveal a particular awareness of their wildlife or aesthetic relevance, a fact that should increase WTP for this attribute by a very significant amount.

In both case-studies, income was revealed to have a positive and very significant effect on WTP. Assuming landscape attributes are normal goods, this is clearly consistent with standard theory of budget-constrained choice. The income-flexibility of WTP for the most complete scheme (that including P1, P2 and P3) was estimated as 0.2 and 0.3, respectively for the D and PG cases. As we do not know the elasticity of substitution of income for this mix of landscape attributes, it is impossible to infer from these estimates whether the demand for these attributes is income-elastic or inelastic (Hanemann 1991; Flores and Carson 1995).

In both case-studies, day trippers' average WTP was significantly higher than that of holidaymakers, which is consistent with prior expectations. In fact (as seen in section 9.2), day trippers live closer to the area, visit it more often and are more familiar with it than holidaymakers. On the other hand, most holidaymakers came from far away, and hence should have easier access to substitute areas. Also according to prior expectations, but now only in the PG case, both the number of days per year spent in the area and whether the current visit was the first ever paid to the area were revealed to have significant effects (positive and negative respectively) on WTP. In fact, the longer the stay the more likely quality changes will affect the individual's utility; likewise, first-time visitors were likely to be less familiar with the landscape and less aware of the area's conservation interest.

The rating given to the area's landscape quality by each respondent is also a significant positive predictor of WTP in both case-studies. Elicited in comparison with other areas of the countryside that respondents had also visited, these quality ratings reveal perceived uniqueness of the landscape as well as perceived quality. It is fully consistent with neoclassical value theory that WTP raises with absence of adequate substitutes.

Some recreational activities were also revealed to be good predictors of WTP. In both cases, reporting 'other activities' as one of the main reasons for visiting the area significantly reduces WTP; this was expected, as 'other activities' include very general outdoor pursuits characterised by low degrees of involvement with the landscape. Also according to prior expectations, in the PG case, walking more than 3 Km, looking for particular wildlife species and visiting traditional villages significantly increases WTP. However, contrarily to prior expectations, birdwatching significantly reduced WTP for landscape conservation in the D.[4]

Three dummy variables indicating respondents' general behaviour and attitudes towards the environment significantly increased WTP, as expected. These were 'active environmental campaigning', in the PG case, and the 'selection of environmentally friendly products' and 'donations for environmental charities', in the D case. These donations are also an indicator of actual payments for similar public goods. Also according to expectations, membership of several environmental and conservation groups significantly increased WTP in the D case (which did not happen in the PG case).

A number of socio-economic or educational variables, such as sex, occupation, being a foreign citizen and so on, were also revealed to have statistically significant effects on WTP in both case-studies (Tables 10.1 and 10.2). Most of these effects are according to prior expectations, although some have not an unambiguous interpretation (Santos 1997). For example, in the PG case, currently living in a rural area or having lived in a rural area during childhood reduced WTP for landscape conservation by a rather significant amount (Table 10.2). A possible explanation has to do with the deep-rural character of the PG area: urban people would value the PG landscape higher because of a favourable contrast with the urban-low-quality landscapes they are used to. (Conservationist ideas motivating WTP for landscape conservation are also stronger among urban people.) An alternative explanation stems from the idea that rural people tend to perceive the countryside as the living place of a rural community, i.e.: as insiders in the sense explained in chapter 9. This would create a difficulty in separating the appearance of the countryside (i.e.: landscape) from the underlying local social relationships, which in turn makes it difficult for rural people to think of trade-offs of money for landscape quality. In this sense, the lower values rural people held for the PG landscape would have a 'protest' content (i.e.: rejection of the CVM scenario) and could not be interpreted in welfare terms.

The results just discussed are quite reassuring as regards the theoretical validity of both of our CVM exercises in that many variables expected to affect valuation were actually shown to have significant effects on WTP, with the signs of most effects being consistent with prior expectations. However, theoretical validity does not rule out the possibility of systematic errors or biases (generally not controlled for by the variables suggested by theory which are used in models with a theoretical validation purpose) nor ensures high reliability of interval-estimates of WTP.

Yea-Saying and Other Biases

From the many biases described in the CVM literature, only a small number can be addressed when presenting the results of a particular study.

Non-thoughtful 'yea-saying' is a potentially troublesome source of bias in any DC CVM study. 'Yea-saying' results from a trend, shared by many respondents and well known by survey methodologists, to give inconsiderate 'yes' answers, even when a 'no' would better correspond to the respondent's opinion or attitude. The potential for bias is magnified in DC CVM studies, where payments are hypothetical, namely when we ask people to decide whether cherished landscapes, such as those of the Dales or Peneda–Gerês, should be conserved. In fact, many respondents may view as anti-public-spirited or unethical to reject the conservation option, regardless of (anyway hypothetical) cost implications for themselves.

The order of magnitude of the bias introduced in our WTP estimates by non-thoughtful 'yea-saying' was assessed by comparing our WTP estimates, based on DC data, with WTP for comparable goods as elicited with open-ended (OE) formats. The DC estimates used in these comparisons were secured, for each case-study, by using models D1 and PG1 to predict the conditional mean of WTP for the most complete (3-programme) conservation scheme. These DC estimates were compared with: (1) Willis and Garrod's (1991) OE estimate of WTP to preserve the Yorkshire Dales 'today's landscape';[5] and (2) an estimate of WTP to preserve the Peneda–Gerês landscape elicited in a small OE survey carried out as part of the PG case-study for bid-design purposes. These comparisons revealed that the DC estimate for the D case (i.e.: £112 a year) exceeded its OE counterpart by 260 per cent and that the PG's DC estimate (i.e.: 14 thousand escudos a year) exceeded the comparable OE estimate by 40 per cent. (Both differences were significant at the 0.025 level; one-tail tests.)[6]

When it comes to interpreting these differences, we should acknowledge how little we actually know about the compared performance of the two CVM formats in eliciting welfare-measures. On the one hand, it has been claimed that the DC format is incentive-compatible in that it induces respondents to say 'yes' when their WTP for the good is higher than the offered bid (Arrow et al. 1993). However, since payments are hypothetical, a 'yes' answer does not always mean a truthful commitment to pay the specified bid amount. Hence, it is not ensured that respondents are induced to say 'no' when the bid amount exceeds WTP. On the other hand, OE estimates cannot be taken as the criterion for judging the validity of DC estimates, as the OE format is not incentive-compatible, i.e.: it does not push respondents to give their maximum WTP. Thus, the true WTP amount will hopefully lie somewhere in between the OE and DC estimates.

To keep to the conservative side, a procedure was used, in both case-studies, to offset (at least part of) the 'yea-saying' bias. The basic assumption was to equate 'yes' answers to bid amounts representing more than X per cent of the respondent's annual income with 'yea-saying' behaviour. All these 'yes' answers were, therefore, changed into 'nos'. For purposes of measuring the sensitivity of estimated WTP to the used X, we used two particular threshold levels for this bid/income ratio: 1.0 per cent and 0.5 per cent. In addition, in the PG case, checklists of reasons for 'yes' answers, which were better designed here than in the D case, allowed us to identify self-confessed 'yea-sayers',[7] whose answers to all valuation questions (4.4 per cent of all observations after deletion of protest 'nos') were then deleted.

In the D case, using the two mentioned threshold levels for the bid/income ratio (i.e.: 1 per cent and 0.5 per cent respectively) to correct for 'yea-saying' bias reduced estimated mean WTP by 19 per cent and 38 per cent with respect to mean WTP estimated from non-corrected data.[8] In the PG case, the corresponding reductions were 12 per cent and 22 per cent.

After the data correction using the lower bid/income ratio (the highest level of correction), estimated mean WTP in the D case was still 100 per cent above (and significantly different from) the comparable OE amount. In the PG case, it was not significantly different from the comparable OE amount.

In both case-studies, we also tested for interviewer bias, by adding an interviewer variable to models D1 and PG1. This was a categorial variable, codified through indicator coding into two dummies (three different interviewers in each case-study). Neither each dummy separately nor their joint effect had a significant impact on WTP, in either case-study (log-likelihood ratio test; 0.10 probability level), and thus we cannot reject the null hypothesis of nil interviewer bias.

As acknowledged in the last paragraph of section 4.2, in DC questionnaires with multiple valuation questions per respondent, such as the ones used in both case-studies, the bid proposed in the first question may act as a value-clue framing the answers to the following questions. This is particularly plausible in cases, such as the present one, where respondents have not very precise valuations for the goods to be valued in the survey. A test for the first-bid effect was, therefore, undertaken in the PG case by adding a new variable – the bid in the first valuation question of the corresponding questionnaire – to model PG1.[9] The first-bid amount was revealed to have a very significant effect on WTP (χ^2 = 29.076). The estimated coefficient is 0.071, meaning that a 1 escudo increase in the first bid raises WTP for schemes valued in the 2nd to 6th valuation questions by 0.071 escudos. Taking into account the range of bids offered in the first valuation question (1,500–50,000 escudos), it was estimated that, on average, the first-bid variable induced a deviation of no more than 12.3 per cent around the estimated mean of WTP (for a 3-programme scheme). Thus, although significant, the size of this effect is not large enough to make the benefit estimates completely unreliable (or arbitrary) in practice.

Another interesting result is that the effect of the first-bid amount declined with the level of data correction for 'yea-saying' (Santos 1997). This suggested that 'yea-sayers' knew their true WTP with less certainty than other respondents, which would explain why they were more sensitive to value-clues in the questionnaire such as the first bid amount.

In the PG case, we also tested for the effect of an explicit budget-constraint reminder in the valuation question. In this case, differently from pilot questionnaires (which were pooled with main-survey ones for the analysis), main-survey valuation questions always started with the words 'taking into account your current income...'. A dummy variable identifying questionnaires that included this reminder of the budget-constraint was added to model PG1. The estimated negative coefficient for this variable implies that the budget-constraint reminder reduced WTP. However, this coefficient is only significant at the 0.20 level (log-likelihood ratio test). A research by Loomis et al. (1994), undertaken to assess the practical effects of including reminders of substitutes and budget constraints, as recommended by the NOOA panel (Arrow et al. 1993), also concluded that the budget reminder had no significant effect on WTP.

Reliability and Predictability of WTP

Reliability refers to insensitivity of a measurement to irrelevant side-conditions. To the extent that valuation as a concept is independent of the elicitation format, a large difference between OE and DC measurements of WTP for the same good is a reliability problem. Likewise, the occurrence of first-bid effects in surveys with multiple valuation questions per respondent is a symptom of unreliability. Both of these examples of unreliability are associated with systematic error or bias. In this case, the measurement is arbitrary, as we can manipulate the result by varying the side-conditions. For practical purposes, as seen with respect to the first-bid bias, it is important to determine how much the measurement depends on these irrelevant side-conditions (hence, how arbitrary it is).

There are, however, several forms of unreliability in CVM that do not originate bias but only reduce the precision of WTP estimates. These forms are caused either by: (1) questionnaire effects and the interview situation, which introduce random variance at the individual level; or by (2) ordinary sampling variance. The main effect of these forms of unreliability is to reduce the predictability of WTP at the individual or the sample level. The R^2 of an OLS WTP model is a good synthetic indicator of predictability at the individual level when one is working with OE (i.e.: continuous) WTP data. In fact, high reliability implies that most of the variance of WTP should be explained by a WTP model incorporating all the explanatory variables suggested by theory (Mitchell and Carson 1989). When working with censored regression models of DC data, as is the case here, we can assess predictability at the individual level by considering the dispersion parameter κ of the random term[10] or the rate of correct predictions of the binary answers. Confidence intervals (CIs) for the mean of WTP provide us with a straightforward way of assessing predictability at the sample level.

Both of our CVM surveys produced data characterised by medium–low predictability of WTP at the individual level and high predictability at the sampling level. Thus the dispersion parameter κ was estimated as £43.86 and 6.25 thousand escudos, respectively for models D1 and PG1 (Tables 10.1 and 10.2). This implies rather large 'coefficients of variation' around the regression equation:[11] respectively 71 per cent and 80 per cent (with respect to the corresponding means of WTP for the 3-programme scheme). The rate of correct predictions of the binary answers, secured by cross-tabulation of actual (yes/no) responses against predicted responses (upper part of Tables 10.1 and 10.2), was estimated as 78.5 per cent and 76.7 per cent, respectively for models D1 and PG1. Note that, although seemingly low for binary response variables, these figures are within the range of values presented by Cameron (1988) and Bowker and Stoll (1988) for logit and probit models of DC CVM data (i.e.: 73.5 – 84.1 per cent).

The estimated models performed much better in predicting WTP means at the sample level than in predicting individual WTP amounts or individual binary responses. Thus, the 95 per cent CIs for the conditional means of WTP for the 3-programme scheme were estimated as (101.08; 123.30) with model D1 and (13.02; 15.20) with model PG1 (in pounds and thousand escudos respectively).

Estimating models D1 and PG1 from data corrected for 'yea-saying' significantly improved these models' performance in predicting individual responses, although it did not significantly improve the precision of interval-estimation of WTP (Santos 1997). Thus, 'yea-saying' was mainly creating random variation of individual observations around the censored regression equation, but was not affecting the efficiency of estimation of the parameters of the regression equation itself. This seems to indicate that 'yea-sayers' had less precise WTP for the conservation schemes under valuation than other respondents – a fact that is consistent with the observation that 'yea-sayers' were more sensitive to value-clues in the questionnaire, such as the first bid.

10.2 MULTI-ATTRIBUTE VALUATION FUNCTIONS WITH SECOND-ORDER INTERACTION TERMS

The perceived quality of many landscapes seems to either exceed or fall short of the sum of the contributions of individual landscape attributes. A 'composition premium' should, therefore, be added to (subtracted from) this sum to account for the effect of a particular combination of attributes in enhancing (degrading) landscape quality. Composition effects are due to joint consumption of landscape attributes in the same scene or in scenes experienced sequentially, e.g. as part of a single journey. The composition phenomenon suggests landscape attributes may be either complements or substitutes in utility. Complementarity in utility is particularly plausible when attributes are the typical parts of a cherished landscape, as is the case with stone walls, field barns and flower-rich meadows in the Pennine Dales (section 3.1). However, as shown by equation (3.15), it is possible that attributes behaving as complements in utility turn out to be compensated substitutes in valuation, provided the income effect is strong enough. Hoehn's (1991) thesis of the prevalence of substitution in valuation across most practical contexts is based on this possibility, plus an implicit assumption of strong income effects (section 3.3). Empirical evidence presented so far in the literature supports this thesis. Thus, for instance in the San Joaquin Valley study by Hoehn and Loomis (1993), where several environmental programmes affected resources within the same region, which created prospects for complementarity, all programmes were revealed to be compensated substitutes for each other.

One interesting question for the D and PG case-studies was, therefore, whether complementarity in utility between programmes, which was expected to occur in these cases, was sufficiently strong to offset the income effect and, thus, to cause the programmes to be compensated complements in valuation. Investigating this question in these cases provided us with an excellent opportunity to test Hoehn's thesis of the prevalence of compensated substitution under quite unfavourable conditions for substitution to occur. In fact, complementarity in utility was expected to be strong in both cases.[12]

Compensated substitution relationships between the three conservation programmes for the D and PG areas were investigated by estimating, for each area, a multi-attribute valuation function specified as in section 3.4 (equation 3.32). Models were estimated, in both cases, from data corrected for 'yea-saying' according to procedures explained in section 10.1 (used threshold for the bid/income ratio was 0.5 per cent). The estimated models for the two case-studies, i.e.: models D2 and PG2, are presented in Tables 10.3 and 10.4.

Table 10.3 WTP model D2

Dependent variable: WTP for landscape conservation in the Dales (£/year)			Prediction success (%)		
Numb. of observat.: 2295			Actual		Total
Correct predictions: 83.0%			would	wouldn't	
−2log-likeli. ratio: 1543.14	Predicted	would pay	46.4	11.2	57.6
Deg. of freedom: 13		wouldn't	5.9	36.5	42.4
Level of signif.: P<0.0001	Total		52.3	47.7	100.0

Variables	Parameter estimates	t-ratios	Pr.	Labels
P1	16.28	3.030	***	Programme 1: stone walls and field barns (0–1)
P2	17.00	3.297	***	Programme 2: flower-rich meadows (0–1)
P3	23.81	4.684	***	Programme 3: broad-leaved woodland (0–1)
P1*P2	−16.07	−3.351	***	Interaction between programmes 1 and 2 (0–1)
P1*P3	−17.23	−3.597	***	Interaction between programmes 1 and 3 (0–1)
P2*P3	−20.45	−4.280	***	Interaction between programmes 2 and 3 (0–1)
P1*INCOME	0.000774	4.624	***	Interaction between programme 1 and income (£)
P2*INCOME	0.000688	4.066	***	Interaction between programme 2 and income (£)
P3*INCOME	0.000538	3.245	***	Interaction between programme 3 and income (£)
P1*FIRSTP1	9.52	2.353	***	Programme 1 when first in preferences (0–1)
P2*FIRSTP2	17.19	3.901	***	Programme 2 when first in preferences (0–1)
P3*FIRSTP3	16.12	3.265	***	Programme 3 when first in preferences (0–1)
κ	21.51	20.499	***	Dispersion parameter of the logistic random term

Table 10.4 WTP model PG2

Dependent variable: WTP for conservation in the Peneda–Gerês (esc./year)	Prediction success (%)			
Numb. of observat.: 3782			Actual	Total
Correct predictions: 77.7%			would	wouldn't
−2log-likeli. ratio: 1688.73	Predicted	would pay	36.1	13.2	49.3
Deg. of freedom: 13		wouldn't	9.1	41.6	50.7
Level of signif.: P<0.0001	Total		45.2	54.8	100.0

Variables	Parameter estimates	t-ratios	Pr.	Labels
P1	2479	3.717	***	Programme 1: traditional farming in terraces (0–1)
P2	1481	2.261	**	Programme 2: irrigated hay meadows (0–1)
P3	1335	1.828	**	Programme 3: oak woods (0–1)
P1*P2	−1073	−1.629	*	Interaction between programmes 1 and 2 (0–1)
P1*P3	−1684	−2.542	***	Interaction between programmes 1 and 3 (0–1)
P2*P3	−2004	−3.035	***	Interaction between programmes 2 and 3 (0–1)
P1*INCOME	0.000453	4.472	***	Interaction between programme 1 and income (esc.)
P2*INCOME	0.000427	4.280	***	Interaction between programme 2 and income (esc.)
P3*INCOME	0.000600	5.782	***	Interaction between programme 3 and income (esc.)
P1*FIRSTP1	2931	4.979	***	Programme 1 when first in preferences (0–1)
P2*FIRSTP2	1469	1.600	*	Programme 2 when first in preferences (0–1)
P3*FIRSTP3	3488	6.028	***	Programme 3 when first in preferences (0–1)
κ	4545	24.355	***	Dispersion parameter of the logistic random term

It is easy to show that the parameters for the interactions between programmes correspond to the pair-wise compensated substitution effects between these programmes. In fact, these parameters (non-diagonal elements of matrix **D** in equation 3.32) represent the value assumed by the partial derivatives $\partial^2 WTP/\partial P_i \partial P_j = - \partial^2 e(.)/\partial P_i \partial P_j$ (with i≠j) on the point where the Taylor-series surface coincides with the actual valuation function; and each of these derivatives exactly corresponds to the definition of a compensated substitution relationship (section 3.1). Hence, negative signs for these parameters indicate compensated substitution, whereas positive signs indicate compensated complementarity. Checking the signs of the parameter estimates for terms Pi*Pj in models D2 and PG2 (Tables 10.3 and 10.4), we verify that all of them are negative and significant at least at the 0.10 level. So, in spite of the plausibility of strong complementarity in utility in both of our landscape cases, only compensated substitution was found, in accordance with results presented by Hoehn (1991), Hoehn and Loomis (1993) and Bishop and Welsh (1992) for other classes of environmental goods. All of these results (including the ones presented here) would, therefore, support Hoehn's thesis.

However, when both models D2 and PG2 are estimated from data non-corrected for 'yea-saying', some interaction terms are not significantly different from zero (Santos 1997). This may indicate a problem with the constraints imposed on the structure of substitution effects by using a second-order specification for this structure, which is discussed in the next section.

10.3 SPECIFICATION TESTS AND THIRD-ORDER-INTERACTION VALUATION FUNCTIONS

Models D2 and PG2 were specified using a second-order Taylor-series approximation to the multi-attribute valuation function. Differently from some alternative functional forms, the second-order Taylor-series approach allows for either complementarity or substitution effects between attributes to emerge from the analysis (Hoehn 1991). Whether two attributes are complements or substitutes is revealed through the estimated sign ($+/-$) of the coefficient of the relevant interaction term. However, the second-order nature of the approach constrains each pair-wise substitution relationship to be constant over the whole valuation sequence. This is not required by theory. On the other hand, the zero-intercept constraint imposed when estimating models D2 and PG2 is required by theory but may fit the data poorly. Whether the second-order approximation and the zero-intercept constraint fit the data well is an empirical matter to be empirically addressed in this section.

First, it was checked, using a log-likelihood ratio test, whether the zero-intercept constraint was significantly reducing goodness of fit. Allowing the intercept to vary, so as to maximise goodness of fit, actually improved the explanatory power of the model: the zero-intercept hypothesis was rejected at the 0.025 level for model D2 ($\chi^2 = 5.37$) and at the 0.005 level for model PG2 ($\chi^2 = 18.58$). Thus, it seems that the zero-intercept constraint was causing more significant problems in the PG case than in the D case.

In both case-studies, relaxing the zero intercept and keeping the second-order interaction structure led to completely inverted signs of the estimated coefficients for programme variables and pair-wise interaction terms with respect to zero-intercept models. Thus, the coefficients for the programme variables became negative and those for pair-wise interactions became positive, implying that programmes are economic bads (not goods) and complements (not substitutes) in valuation for each other. Hence, although fitting the data better, free-intercept models were not acceptable on theoretical grounds for two reasons: (1) the non-zero intercept itself, meaning individuals would be prepared to pay something for nothing; and (2) negative coefficients for programmes, meaning conservation is an economic bad.

A specification that fits the data better but is theoretically unacceptable, such as that of free-intercept models, is represented in Figure 10.1. There, dots represent the supposed true values of the unobserved (censored) WTP variable. The horizontal axis represents a particular valuation sequence (P1→P2→P3). aa' represents the kind of curve that is implied by a second-order zero-intercept model, such as D2 or PG2. Curve bb' represents a second-order free-intercept specification, fitting the data better than the zero-intercept curve aa'. The convex shape of bb' actually corresponds to the estimated signs of the coefficients for programmes and programme-interactions with free-intercept models. Figure 10.1 also points out that there is a curve, such as cc', that fits the data as well as bb' while keeping a zero intercept. Curve cc' is different from both curves aa' and bb' in that it implies a third-order (i.e.: a changing) curvature. Curves aa' and bb', which represent second-order Taylor series, can only have a second-order (i.e.: a constant) curvature. Hence, none of these two can satisfy the requirement of a zero intercept while reaching the highest possible goodness of fit (as cc' can).

Figure 10.1 suggests, therefore, how to solve our current functional-form dilemma: to add a third-order interaction term among the 3 programmes (i.e.: P1*P2*P3) to a zero-intercept specification. Note that this third-order interaction term increases the flexibility of the WTP model with respect to the second-order approximation in that it allows for each pair-wise substitution effect to change in size, and even sign, along the valuation sequence. The possibility of a sign change implies that two programmes that were initially substitutes may become complements later in the sequence, or vice versa. This more flexible specification was estimated, in both case-studies, from data corrected for 'yea-saying' at the highest level of correction (threshold for the bid/income ratio equal to 0.5 per cent). The estimated models, i.e.: models D3 and PG3, are presented in Tables 10.5 and 10.6.

The increase in explanatory power associated with including a third-order interaction term while keeping a zero-intercept is statistically significant and is exactly the same as the one associated with allowing for a free intercept while keeping a second-order interaction structure (cf. the relevant tests, above in this section).[13] The third-order-interaction zero-intercept specification allowed for more efficient estimation of the coefficients of the three programme variables and the three pair-wise interaction terms than the second-order-interaction zero-intercept specification, particularly in the PG case-study (compare models D3 and PG3 with D2 and PG2 respectively). Besides, differently from the second-order-interaction free-intercept models, the estimated coefficients for the programme variables assume now positive signs, according to theoretical expectations.

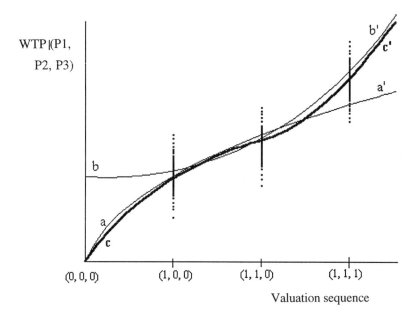

Figure 10.1 Different specifications for the multi-attribute valuation function and implied curvature

Models D3 and PG3 were used to produce point and interval estimates of: (1) conditional means of WTP for different programme-mixes; and (2) sequential values of programmes when valued at different steps of different valuation sequences, according to equations (3.33) and (3.34). These estimates are presented in Tables 10.7 and 10.8, for the D case, and Tables 10.9 and 10.10, for the PG case.

With respect to the structure of substitution effects implied by third-order-interaction models, one should consider each case-study separately. Thus, in model D3, we note that the parameter estimate for the third-order-interaction term is positive but slightly smaller in modulus than any of the three parameters for the pair-wise interactions between programmes (Table 10.5). This indicates that throughout the valuation sequence programmes behave as compensated substitutes, although the substitution effects are much reduced (almost nil) at the third step in the sequence. Hence, the sequential values of the programmes are still declining at the third step (Table 10.8), which implies the inflection point of curve cc' is beyond (or just before) the end of the valuation sequence – not significantly before, as shown in Figure 10.1.

Table 10.5 WTP model D3

Dependent variable: WTP for landscape conservation in the Dales (£/year)	Prediction success (%)			
Numb. of observat.: 2295			Actual	Total
Correct predictions: 84.0%			would wouldn't	
–2log-likeli. ratio: 1548.51	Predicted	would pay	47.5 11.4	58.9
Deg. of freedom: 14		wouldn't	4.7 36.5	41.1
Level of signif.: P<0.0001	Total		52.1 47.9	100.0

Variables	Parameter estimates	t-ratios	Pr.	Labels
P1	18.52	3.395	***	Programme 1: stone walls and field barns (0–1)
P2	19.07	3.651	***	Programme 2: flower-rich meadows (0–1)
P3	25.60	4.969	***	Programme 3: broad-leaved woodland (0–1)
P1*P2	–24.45	–4.084	***	Interaction between programmes 1 and 2 (0–1)
P1*P3	–25.70	–4.286	***	Interaction between programmes 1 and 3 (0–1)
P2*P3	–28.91	–4.819	***	Interaction between programmes 2 and 3 (0–1)
P1*P2*P3	22.59	2.322	***	Interaction among the three programmes altogether (0–1)
P1*INCOME	0.000771	4.616	***	Interaction between programme 1 and income (£)
P2*INCOME	0.000685	4.054	***	Interaction between programme 2 and income (£)
P3*INCOME	0.000535	3.235	***	Interaction between programme 3 and income (£)
P1*FIRSTP1	9.55	2.370	***	Programme 1 when first in preferences (0–1)
P2*FIRSTP2	17.31	3.936	***	Programme 2 when first in preferences (0–1)
P3*FIRSTP3	16.23	3.292	***	Programme 3 when first in preferences (0–1)
κ	21.41	20.644	***	Dispersion parameter of the logistic random term

On the other hand, in model PG3, the estimated coefficient for the third-order-interaction term is positive and larger in modulus than any of the three estimated pair-wise interaction effects (Table 10.6). This implies a different structure of substitution effects, with all three programmes behaving as compensated substitutes at the second step in the sequence, but becoming compensated complements at the third step. Thus, the sequential value of each programme declines from the first to the second step and rises again at the third step (Table 10.10) as represented in Figure 10.1.

Table 10.6 WTP model PG3

Dependent variable: WTP for conservation in the Peneda–Gerês (esc./year)	**Prediction success (%)**			
Numb. of observat.: 3782			Actual	Total
Correct predictions: 77.9%			would wouldn't	
−2log-likeli. ratio: 1707.32	Predicted would pay		36.3 13.2	49.6
Deg. of freedom: 14	wouldn't		8.8 41.6	50.4
Level of signif.: P<0.0001	Total		45.2 54.8	100.0

Variables	Parameter estimates	t-ratios	Pr.	Labels
P1	3016	4.621	***	Programme 1: traditional farming in terraces (0–1)
P2	2005	3.158	***	Programme 2: irrigated hay meadows (0–1)
P3	1890	2.659	***	Programme 3: oak woods (0–1)
P1*P2	−3173	−3.985	***	Interaction between programmes 1 and 2 (0–1)
P1*P3	−3826	−4.715	***	Interaction between programmes 1 and 3 (0–1)
P2*P3	−4118	−5.102	***	Interaction between programmes 2 and 3 (0–1)
P1*P2*P3	5617	4.324	***	Interaction among the three programmes altogether (0–1)
P1*INCOME	0.000431	4.435	***	Interaction between programme 1 and income (esc.)
P2*INCOME	0.000415	4.352	***	Interaction between programme 2 and income (esc.)
P3*INCOME	0.000583	5.846	***	Interaction between programme 3 and income (esc.)
P1*FIRSTP1	2802	4.962	***	Programme 1 when first in preferences (0–1)
P2*FIRSTP2	1408	1.601	*	Programme 2 when first in preferences (0–1)
P3*FIRSTP3	3346	6.022	***	Programme 3 when first in preferences (0–1)
κ	4348	25.204	***	Dispersion parameter of the logistic random term

To the best of the author's knowledge, these results constitute the first evidence presented in the CVM literature demonstrating that, under certain conditions, components of an environmental policy package can behave as complements in valuation. Note that it was the use of a third-order specification that made it possible to identify these complementarity effects.

They would not be identified with a second-order specification, such as those used by Hoehn (1991) and Hoehn and Loomis (1993). In fact, the second-order specification imposes fixed pair-wise substitution effects over the whole sequence and these fixed substitution effects result negative in the PG case as well. This would prevent us from identifying complementarity effects at the last step in the sequence with a second-order specification.

Table 10.7 Point and interval estimates of conditional means of WTP for different programme-mixes (using model D3)

Programme-mix	E (WTP)[a]	95 % CI[a]
(1, 0, 0)	43.01	(36.94; 49.07)
(0, 1, 0)	42.62	(36.52; 48.71)
(0, 0, 1)	42.90	(36.87; 48.93)
(1, 1, 0)	61.17	(52.75; 69.59)
(1, 0, 1)	60.20	(51.76; 68.65)
(0, 1, 1)	56.61	(48.28; 64.93)
(1, 1, 1)	72.05	(63.98; 80.12)

Note: a. values in £ per household per year.

Table 10.8 Point and interval estimates of sequential values of programmes when valued in different valuation sequences (model D3)[a]

Programme	Initial programme-mix						
	(0, 0, 0)	(1, 0, 0)	(0, 1, 0)	(0, 0, 1)	(1, 1, 0)	(1, 0, 1)	(0, 1, 1)
P1	43.01 (36.94; 49.07)	–	18.55 (8.39; 28.72)	17.31 (7.14; 27.47)	–	–	15.44 (4.12; 26.77)
P2	42.62 (36.52; 48.71)	18.16 (8.03; 28.29)	–	13.71 (3.61; 23.81)	–	11.85 (0.51; 23.18)	–
P3	42.90 (36.87; 48.93)	17.20 (7.04; 27.36)	13.99 (3.85; 24.13)	–	10.88 (–0.35; 22.11)	–	–
P1 + P2	–	–	–	29.15 (19.30; 39.00)	–	–	–
P1 + P3	–	–	29.43 (19.56; 39.30)	–	–	–	–
P2 + P3	–	29.04 (19.20; 38.89)	–	–	–	–	–

Note: a. values in £ per household per year; 95% CIs in parenthesis.

Table 10.9 Point and interval estimates of
conditional means of WTP for
different programme-mixes (using
model PG3)

Programme-mix	E (WTP)[a]	95 % CI[a]
(1, 0, 0)	6221	(5413; 7029)
(0, 1, 0)	4205	(3405; 5004)
(0, 0, 1)	6634	(5806; 7462)
(1, 1, 0)	7253	(6179; 8326)
(1, 0, 1)	9029	(7927; 10131)
(0, 1, 1)	6721	(5631; 7811)
(1, 1, 1)	11559	(10557; 12562)

Note: a. values in escudos per household per year.

Table 10.10 Point and interval estimates of sequential values of programmes
when valued in different valuation sequences (model PG3)[a]

Programme	Initial programme-mix						
	(0, 0, 0)	(1, 0, 0)	(0, 1, 0)	(0, 0, 1)	(1, 1, 0)	(1, 0, 1)	(0, 1, 1)
P1	6221 (5413; 7029)	–	3048 (1708; 4388)	2395 (1024; 3766)	–	–	4839 (3359; 6318)
P2	4205 (3405; 5004)	1032 (–310; 2373)	–	87 (–1281; 1455)	–	2530 (1054; 4007)	–
P3	6634 (5806; 7462)	2808 (1447; 4169)	2516 (1164; 3868)	–	4307 (2843; 5770)	–	–
P1 + P2	–	–	–	4926 (3637; 6215)	–	–	–
P1 + P3	–	–	7355 (6068; 8642)	–	–	–	–
P2 + P3	–	5339 (4059; 6618)	–	–	–	–	–

Note: a. values in escudos per household per year; 95% CIs in parenthesis.

The existence of a positive third-order-interaction effect combined with smaller-in-modulus negative second-order-interaction effects can be theoretically interpreted as follows. As discussed in section 3.1, compensated substitution in valuation can stem from substitution in utility or from the income adjustments that are just required to keep utility constant along the valuation sequence. These latter may lead to compensated substitution even when attributes are complements in utility, provided the effects on WTP of those income adjustments are strong enough. Complementarity in utility can arise when all attributes of a cherished conservation area like the Peneda–Gerês NP are to be conserved altogether. Lower complementarity in utility would occur when something less than the complete conservation of all attributes is considered. So, at the second step in the sequence, compensated substitution between attributes is observed, which results from independence or low complementarity in utility combined with the substitution trend induced by the effects of income adjustments. However, at the third valuation step, compensated complementarity is observed, which results from stronger complementarity in utility offsetting the effects of income adjustments. This explanation for the emergence of compensated complementarity at the last step in the sequence was already proposed in section 6.1 (in association with the issue of local non-concavity of the benefit function) along the following lines: (1) people strongly prefer complete conservation schemes as opposed to partial ones, because the former somehow preserve the 'integrity' of nature or of particularly cherished landscapes; hence, (2) they are prepared to pay a premium, over and above other components of value, for a conservation scheme that ensures complete conservation of all existing attributes.[14]

10.4 INDEPENDENT VALUATION AND SUMMATION (IVS)

Valuing every single programme included in a multiple-programme scheme as if it was the only change to occur and then summing over programmes yields the independent valuation and summation (IVS) result for this scheme. The IVS will be larger than the true value of the multiple-programme scheme (as elicited in one single step) if programmes are compensated substitutes for each other (or smaller, if they are complements; section 3.2).

All benefit estimates from the D and PG case-studies were derived using valuation functions explicitly modelling the substitution effects between programmes. In so doing, the IVS bias was avoided. Nevertheless, it would be interesting to have an estimate of the size of the bias avoided, in that this might help stressing the need for taking into account substitution effects in every study aimed at evaluating policy. Thus, independent valuations of programmes were estimated from models D3 and PG3, which were then summed over the three programmes in each case-study to compute the IVS result. The same models were also used to directly predict the valid one-step valuation of the 3-programme scheme. In the D case, the IVS result

(£128.52) overestimated the one-step value (£72.05) in 78 per cent (t = 8.50; difference significant at any usual level of probability). In the PG case, the overestimation was slightly less severe but, nevertheless, highly significant: IVS result (17,060 esc.) exceeding the one-step valuation (11,559 esc.) by 48 per cent (t = 6.28).

These results provide an illustration of the magnitude of bias that is introduced by inappropriate benefit aggregation procedures, still in use in cost–benefit policy evaluation (Hoehn and Randall 1989). Besides, note that, in principle, the larger the number of policy-components the larger the bias.

10.5 THEORY TESTS BASED ON THE RELATIONSHIP BETWEEEN THE SUBSTITUTION AND THE INCOME EFFECTS

It was shown, in section 3.1, that the substitution relationship in utility has the same sign as the uncompensated substitution effect (equation 3.7) and that the uncompensated substitution effect is secured by summing the compensated substitution effect with the income effect (equation 3.15). In addition, we expected the different attributes making up a cherished landscape type to be complements in utility (cf. sections 3.1 and 10.2). Thus, as the different programmes in each case-study were aimed at conserving precisely the most typical attributes of a particularly cherished area, the possibility of these programmes being substitutes in utility was ruled out a priori. Hence, according to the above theoretical relationships, we expected the sum of the compensated substitution effect with the income effect (i.e.: the uncompensated substitution effect) to be non-negative. This provided the null hypothesis for the theory tests to be discussed in this section.

Compensated substitution effects, income effects and the corresponding standard errors were estimated, for both case-studies, using models D3 and PG3;[15] from these results, we estimated the uncompensated substitution effects and corresponding t-ratios; the main results are presented in Tables 10.11 and 10.12 respectively for the D and PG cases.

Let us start by considering the results of these tests in the D case. The 4th column of Table 10.11 gives us the compensated substitution effects between programmes at different steps in all possible valuation sequences. All of these effects are negative, indicating programmes always behave as compensated substitutes; yet, when there is a previous programme in the sequence, the substitution effect is not significantly different from zero. Estimated income effects are very small: point estimates are two to three orders of magnitude below the corresponding substitution effects. Thus, the uncompensated substitution effects are approximately identical to the compensated ones. In no case the income effect is sufficiently strong to offset the compensated substitution effect, which implies programmes would be substitutes in utility rather than complements. Only when there is a previous programme in the sequence it is impossible to reject the hypothesis of complementarity in utility. In all other cases, substitution in utility is implied by the results with a small (less than 0.01) probability of error.

Table 10.11 Substitution and income effects, and test-variable for the sign of the uncompensated substitution relationship (model D3)

Programmes			Compensated substitution effect[a]	Income effect[a]	Uncompensated substitu. effect[a]	t-ratio	Pr. < than (2-tail tests)
Effect of	on:	Previous in sequence					
P2	P1	none	−24.45	0.07	−24.39	−4.073	0.0001
P3	P1	none	−25.70	0.07	−25.63	−4.275	0.0001
P2+P3	P1	none	−27.56	0.09	−27.47	−4.218	0.0001
P2	P1	P3	−1.86	0.02	−1.84	−0.239	0.8114
P3	P1	P2	−3.11	0.02	−3.09	−0.402	0.6885
P1	P2	none	−24.45	0.06	−24.40	−4.074	0.0001
P3	P2	none	−28.91	0.06	−28.85	−4.810	0.0001
P1+P3	P2	none	−30.77	0.08	−30.69	−4.702	0.0001
P1	P2	P3	−1.86	0.02	−1.84	−0.239	0.8117
P3	P2	P1	−6.32	0.02	−6.30	−0.821	0.4127
P1	P3	none	−25.70	0.05	−25.65	−4.278	0.0001
P2	P3	none	−28.91	0.05	−28.86	−4.812	0.0001
P1+P2	P3	none	−32.02	0.07	−31.95	−4.938	0.0001
P1	P3	P2	−3.11	0.02	−3.09	−0.402	0.6883
P2	P3	P1	−6.32	0.02	−6.30	−0.821	0.4124

Note: a. values in £ per household per year.

As regards the PG case (Table 10.12), when the compensated substitution effect is estimated with no previous programme in the sequence, all programmes are revealed to be compensated substitutes.[16] However, when the substitution effect is evaluated with a previous programme in the sequence (i.e.: at the third step in the sequence), all programmes are revealed to be compensated complements for each other, with these complementarity effects being significantly different from zero in two (out of three) cases. Again, the estimated income effects are very small as compared to substitution effects and, thus, uncompensated substitution effects are approximately identical to compensated ones. This means that our conclusions as regards substitutability in utility are exactly the same as those drawn from the study of compensated substitution relationships: programmes would, in general, be substitutes in utility at the second step and complements at the third step in the sequence.

Table 10.12 Substitution and income effects, and test-variable for the sign of the uncompensated substitution relationship (model PG3)

Programmes			Compensated substitution effect[a]	Income effect[a]	Uncompensated substitu. effect[a]	t-ratio	Pr. < than (2-tail tests)
Effect of	on:	Previous in sequence					
P2	P1	none	−3173	3.6	−3169	−3.981	0.0001
P3	P1	none	−3826	5.7	−3820	−4.709	0.0001
P2+P3	P1	none	−1382	5.8	−1376	−1.606	0.1099
P2	P1	P3	2443	0.1	2444	2.379	0.0183
P3	P1	P2	1791	2.2	1793	1.767	0.0787
P1	P2	none	−3173	5.2	−3168	−3.979	0.0001
P3	P2	none	−4118	5.5	−4112	−5.096	0.0001
P1+P3	P2	none	−1674	7.5	−1667	−1.945	0.0532
P1	P2	P3	2443	2.0	2445	2.380	0.0182
P3	P2	P1	1499	2.3	1501	1.476	0.1416
P1	P3	none	−3826	7.2	−3818	−4.707	0.0001
P2	P3	none	−4118	4.9	−4113	−5.097	0.0001
P1+P2	P3	none	−2327	8.5	−2319	−2.715	0.0072
P1	P3	P2	1791	3.6	1794	1.769	0.0784
P2	P3	P1	1499	1.2	1500	1.475	0.1418

Note: a. values in escudos per household per year.

Many of these results, namely those implying substitution in utility, are inconsistent with prior expectations. (Note that, so far, we have explained compensated substitution in valuation based on a strong income effect, which would offset the underlying complementarity in utility all over the sequence but at the third step in the PG case.) Besides, it is difficult to reject the auxiliary assumption of complementarity in utility, which is strongly intuitive here. This cast some doubts on the accuracy of equation (3.15) as a description of the way respondents' choices actually combine their budget constraint with the underlying substitution structure characterising their preferences for landscape attributes. As this equation is strictly implied by demand theory, the general theory itself becomes open to question.

As discussed in section 3.5, these theoretically inconsistent results could be interpreted as a failure of the CVM, or of the particular application of it, in producing choice behaviour conforming to theory, which would raise the issue of the theoretical validity of the CVM. However, theoretically inconsistent results are alternatively interpreted here as, simply, evidence against the theory, which led us to search for possible alternative explanations for our results.

There was still a possibility of the estimated compensated income-effect parameter being an inaccurate approximation to the uncompensated income-effect parameter in equation (3.15). These two parameters are, in general, different and the relationship between them is complex (Mitchell and Carson 1989). However, it is very unlikely that this explains the difference of 2–3 orders of magnitude that is just required to reconcile our results with demand theory. Accepting this, one should face the issue of inconsistency with theory and explore possible alternative theories. Since we are commenting the results of two case-studies, which, besides, used quite similar methods, this search for an alternative theory represents only an exploratory exercise.

A possible alternative theory, which is consistent with our results, is that people's valuations of landscape conservation are based on incomplete multi-stage budgeting. Long-term and other financial commitments may considerably reduce people's discretionary income. Hence, in the short term, which is the relevant time-scale to analyse valuation answers to a CVM survey, incomplete multi-stage budgeting would characterise the consumer's optimisation problem. Thus, there possibly are welfare-enhancing trade-offs between the amounts allocated to different classes of goods (i.e.: sub-budgets or accounts) at previous budgeting stages. However, at least in the short run, these trade-offs are not possible, as the overall re-allocation to the several accounts is bound by previous budgeting decisions. Hence, when revealing WTP for a particular environmental good, the respondent is 'taking money' from his account for say environmental conservation, which is much smaller than total income. This will cause much larger income effects along a valuation sequence than what could be expected for an individual who was 'taking money' from his total-annual-income box. As shown by Randall and Hoehn (1996), modelling incomplete multi-stage budgeting strongly increases income effects and, thus, compensated substitution as well. If incomplete multi-stage budgeting is a good explanation for people's choices, then specifying income in WTP models as average annual income and estimating the income effect from the co-variation in WTP and income across respondents will lead to specification error and biased estimates. The origin of this bias may be explained in a very simple example. Suppose an individual's income rises by £10,000. This increase will probably have a strong effect on WTP for landscape conservation, as it will mean a comparable increase in discretionary income – hence, in the individual's environmental account as well. However, this strong income effect could not be predicted from the difference in WTP between two average individuals in the sample with income differing by £10,000. Expenditure plans of these individuals are already adjusted to these different income levels, which makes the difference in discretionary income between them much smaller than £10,000. And this situation of individuals with long-term commitments adjusted to their income levels is what we have in cross-section data. Thus, incomplete multi-stage budgeting suggests that income effects at the individual level are much larger than those estimated from cross-section data (and presented in Tables 10.11 and 10.12). These much larger income effects might, in turn, imply positive uncompensated substitution effects and, thus, complementarity in utility as initially expected.

Although possibly accounting for the observed results with respect to the size of the income effect, incomplete multi-stage budgeting, as a different theory, raises a host of difficult questions for empirical valuation research, as well as for applied welfare economics. Three examples are: (1) how to specify the theory for it to be testable in a CVM setting; (2) whether this theory explains the large income effects observed in sequential valuation experiments; and (3) whether the existence of incomplete trade-offs between classes of goods undermines the possibility of carrying out compensation tests, which provide the very theoretical foundations for cost–benefit analysis.

10.6 RELATIVE VALUES OF LANDSCAPE ATTRIBUTES: CONSISTENCY BETWEEN CVM AND THE STUDY OF LANDSCAPE PREFERENCES

This section compares CVM results with the results of the study of preferences for landscape attributes that was presented in chapter 8. The aim is to assess, ex post facto, the performance of our CVM scenarios in conveying to respondents the particular landscape changes they were intended to convey. The comparison is between the values of the different programmes, as elicited in the CVM exercise, and the average preference ratings for the corresponding landscape attributes, as elicited in the study of preferences. Note that these latter reveal immediate reactions to visual stimuli and, thus, are independent from the wording of the CVM questionnaire. Thus, finding out that the ranking of the CVM values of programmes and that of preference ratings for the corresponding attributes are the same should help showing that the particular wording of the scenarios did not distort, in any marked way, respondents' previous preferences for landscape attributes.

A complete study of preferences for landscape attributes was only done in the PG case, and hence the comparison is only possible in this case.

According to the study of preferences for landscape attributes, the average respondent ranked all of the scenes of open broad-leaved woods higher than any of the terraced landscape scenes; all terraced landscape scenes were ranked higher than all meadow scenes without significant tree cover (Table 8.2). This suggested that the average respondent to the CVM survey would value programme 3 (woods) higher than programme 1 (terraces) and programme 1 higher than programme 2 (meadows). This was actually the case. In fact, the estimated sequential values presented in Table 10.10 show us that programmes 1 and 3 are consistently valued above programme 2, provided valuations are compared for the same step in the sequence. Besides, at the first step, programme 3 is valued slightly above programme 1, showing that, when independently valued, woods seem to be preferred to terraces.

We conclude, therefore, that answers to either type of elicitation method (i.e.: asking to rank photos or asking for WTP for conservation schemes after presentation of detailed CVM scenarios) seem to derive from one same set of preferences for landscape attributes. This robustness of the preference ordering to different elicitation frames (already noticed in section 9.2) is also favourable to the idea of respondents' preferences being rather stable, which relieved previous concerns about the possibility of particular words or photos included in the CVM scenario causing considerable preference shifts. Note, however, that this evidence does not imply that the absolute amounts of the WTP estimates themselves are valid, as it solely concerns the compared validity of the WTP amounts attracted by different landscape attributes.

10.7 AGGREGATE BENEFITS OF LANDSCAPE CONSERVATION

Models presented in previous sections were used to generate estimates of conditional means of WTP for different programme-mixes and sequential values of programmes, both on a per-household basis. In this section, per-household estimates derived from models D3 and PG3 are aggregated to the whole visitor population to yield the benefit estimates used in the cost–benefit analyses presented in chapter 12.

The Pennine Dales Case

As defined in chapter 9, the survey population comprises all households that visited the Pennine Dales ESA during the year of reference (the 12 months before the end of August 1995). The most reliable estimates available about visitors to the area are the figures of the Yorkshire Dales Visitor Study (PA Cambridge Economic Consultants 1992). The fact of these figures referring to the year between April 1991 and March 1992 seems not to raise any major issue regarding their use as an estimate of the visitor population three years later. Dales Visitor Study figures allow us to disaggregate the total number of visitor days to the National Park (NP) by dales inside and outside the ESA. Hence, excluding visitor days to the areas of Ribblesdale, Malham, and Bolton Abbey (outside the ESA), the remaining 4,122,000 visitor days per year correspond approximately to the ESA dales located inside the NP.[17] Most ESA dales located outside the NP are inside the North Pennines Area of Outstanding Natural Beauty (AONB).[18] However, there are no available estimates of the number of visitors to the AONB (North Pennines AONB Steering Group 1995). It is, nevertheless, known that the AONB is much less visited than the NP. Considering that roughly half of the ESA's area is inside the AONB (North Pennines AONB Steering Group, 1995) and that the AONB includes Teesdale (a frequently visited North Pennines dale), it was assumed that the figure for the ESA dales located outside the Yorkshire Dales NP is, at least, 658,000 visitor days per year. (This was assumed on a comparative basis: it is approximately the number of visitor days to Swaledale alone and is below 1/6 the number of visitor days to the ESA dales inside the NP.) Thus, an estimated 4,780,000 visitor days per year can be assumed to represent a lower-bound estimate for the whole Pennine Dales ESA. To estimate the visitor population in household units, the average number of days per visitor per year, and the average household size were estimated from our CVM sample. These figures are, respectively, 9.96 and 2.87. It follows[19] that the number of households visiting the Pennine Dales ESA during the reference year can be estimated as 167,220. This figure was used as the basis for aggregating per-household estimates of WTP for different programme-mixes and sequential values of programmes, both secured from model D3.

Table 10.13 presents aggregate benefits for the diverse programme-mixes (schemes); point estimates are based on conditional means of WTP for these schemes and lower-bound estimates are based on lower-limits of 95 per cent CIs. Aggregated sequential benefits of each programme at different steps in different valuation sequences are presented in Table 10.14; also presented in this Table are lower-bound estimates of aggregate sequential benefits based on lower-limits of 95 per cent CIs.

The Peneda–Gerês Case

There was no previous accurate study of the number of visitors to the Peneda–Gerês NP, and hence we estimated this population based on a past car-traffic counting plus elements provided by NP staff. In 1996, an estimate was computed based on data collected from NP staff who control car traffic at the entrance of a NP Reserve in the Caldas do Gerês area. Although this estimate heavily relies on the memory of the informants, it is clearly backed, for the months of July–September, by a 1990 actual car count. Thus, it is possible to take the 82,214 passing cars as an approximate estimate of the number of households that visited the NP Reserve from September 1995 to August 1996.

Table 10.13 Aggregate benefit estimates for different programme-mixes (point and lower bound-estimates using model D3)

Programme-mix	Average[a]	Lower limit of 95% CI[a]
$(1, 0, 0)$	7,192	6,177
$(0, 1, 0)$	7,127	6,107
$(0, 0, 1)$	7,174	6,165
$(1, 1, 0)$	10,229	8,821
$(1, 0, 1)$	10,067	8,655
$(0, 1, 1)$	9,466	8,073
$(1, 1, 1)$	12,048	10,699

Note: a. values in thousands of £ per year.

Table 10.14 Aggregate sequential benefits of programmes at different steps in different sequences using model D3[a]

Programme	Initial programme-mix						
	$(0, 0, 0)$	$(1, 0, 0)$	$(0, 1, 0)$	$(0, 0, 1)$	$(1, 1, 0)$	$(1, 0, 1)$	$(0, 1, 1)$
P1	7,192 (6,177)	–	3,102 (1,403)	2,895 (1,194)	–	–	2,582 (689)
P2	7,127 (6,107)	3,037 (1,343)	–	2,293 (604)	–	1,982 (85)	–
P3	7,174 (6,165)	2,876 (1,177)	2,339 (644)	–	1,819 (0)	–	–
P1 + P2	–	–	–	4,874 (3,227)	–	–	–
P1 + P3	–	–	4,921 (3,271)	–	–	–	–
P2 + P3	–	4,856 (3,211)	–	–	–	–	–

Note: a. values in thousands of £ a year; lower limits of 95% CIs (truncated at 0) in parenthesis.

If we assume that each household visited the Reserve once per visit to the NP, then (considering the average number of annual visits per household, which is estimated as 1.83, from the CVM survey) an estimated 44,926 households visited the whole Caldas do Gerês area per year. This does not take into account visitors who visited the Reserve more than once per visit to the NP. On the other hand, there are plenty of visitors to the Caldas do Gerês area that do not visit the Reserve at all but only the reservoirs, some vantage points around the village and the village itself. Thus, this estimate is, possibly, not far from the actual number of households visiting the Caldas do Gerês area. If we assume that 75 per cent of all annual visits to the NP are concentrated in the Caldas do Gerês area, then we have an approximate estimate of the population of households that visited the NP from September 1995 to August 1996: 59,900 households. This is the figure that has been used to aggregate per-household benefit estimates to the whole visitor population.

Table 10.15 presents aggregate benefits for the diverse conservation schemes (programme-mixes); point estimates are based on per-household conditional means of WTP from model PG3; lower-bound estimates are based on lower-limits of 95 per cent CIs for these conditional means. Aggregated sequential benefits of each programme at different steps in different valuation sequences are based on per-household average estimates from model PG3 as well, and are presented in Table 10.16. Also presented in this Table are lower-bound estimates of aggregate sequential benefits based on lower-limits of 95 per cent CIs derived from the same model.

*Table 10.15 Aggregate benefit estimates for
            different programme-mixes (point
            and lower bound-estimates using
            model PG3)*

Programme-mix	Average[a]	Lower limit of 95%CI[a]
(1, 0, 0)	373	324
(0, 1, 0)	252	204
(0, 0, 1)	397	348
(1, 1, 0)	434	370
(1, 0, 1)	541	475
(0, 1, 1)	403	337
(1, 1, 1)	692	632

Note: a. values in millions of escudos per year.

Table 10.16 Aggregate sequential benefits of programmes at different steps in different sequences using model PG3[a]

Programme	Initial programme-mix						
	$(0, 0, 0)$	$(1, 0, 0)$	$(0, 1, 0)$	$(0, 0, 1)$	$(1, 1, 0)$	$(1, 0, 1)$	$(0, 1, 1)$
P1	373	–	183	143	–	–	290
	(324)		(102)	(61)			(201)
P2	252	62	–	5	–	152	–
	(204)	(0)		(0)		(63)	
P3	397	168	151	–	258	–	–
	(348)	(87)	(70)		(170)		
P1 + P2	–	–	–	295	–	–	–
				(218)			
P1 + P3	–	–	441	–	–	–	–
			(363)				
P2 + P3	–	320	–	–	–	–	–
		(243)					

Note: a. in millions of esc. a year; lower limits of 95% CIs (truncated at 0) in parenthesis.

NOTES

1. These models were estimated after deleting protest 'nos' (cf. last paragraph in section 9.1).
2. A study of the variables describing visitors and their diversity, which is reported in section 9.2, supported many of these expectations.
3. This result implies that more comprehensive schemes (in terms of programmes) are valued significantly higher than less comprehensive ones. However, this does not strongly support the hypothesis of respondents' valuations being sensitive to the scope of the scheme. The fact that each respondent has valued different schemes may have forced respondents to give consistent answers across schemes, in an effort to present themselves as rational individuals. Hence, observed scope-sensitivity is not necessarily a definitive proof of respondents being capable of arriving at significantly different values for less and more inclusive schemes. Only with split-sample experiments it is possible to test for scope-sensitivity on a more stringent basis.
4. Though not expected, this relationship may have a reasonable explanation (cf. Santos 1997).
5. Adjusted for price rises since 1990.
6. The landscape changes valued in the DC and OE exercises are not exactly the same and the OE estimate in the PG case resulted from a rather small sample. These and other limitations of these DC/OE comparisons are discussed in Santos (1997).
7. That is, all those who selected one of the following reasons for a 'yes' answer: (1) 'I am in favour of conserving nature and the environment, but I would not be prepared to pay so much every year'; (2) 'I am not saying that I would be prepared to pay that amount every year, but only that this is an area to preserve'. In the D case, the option 'I am in favour of preserving nature and the environment' was selected by 45 per cent of those with a 'yes' answer. This option does not enable us to identify 'yea-sayers', as too many people selected it to state a general opinion rather than to give a reason for their 'yes' answer. Hence, in the D case we were left without criterion to delete self-confessed 'yea-sayers'.

8. Note that for these two levels of correction for 'yea-saying', only 2.9 per cent and 7.6 per cent of the 'yes' answers, respectively, were changed from 'yes' into 'no'.

9. All observations corresponding to the first valuation question in each questionnaire were dropped when estimating this new model, because for these observations the bid and first-bid variables were the same. Nevertheless, all conclusions presented below hold, as well, when the model is estimated using all six observations in each questionnaire.

10. Note that κ is our estimated measure for the dispersion of the unobserved WTP variable around the censored regression equation.

11. The standard deviation of the logistic is given by $\pi/\sqrt{3}$. κ. Note that the coefficients of variation presented here express dispersion around the fitted equation for the conditional mean of WTP. Hence, they are, by definition, smaller than (thus, non-comparable with) ordinary coefficients of variation usually presented as a measure of the dispersion of OE WTP data around the sample mean.

12. For reasons suggested above and in the section on 'substitution in utility' in chapter 3.

13. Besides, with the third-order interaction term, it is impossible to estimate a free-intercept model, as the intercept becomes a linear combination of the variables for programmes, pairwise interactions between programmes and the third-order interaction term. Thus, there are no degrees of freedom to estimate the intercept. Another way to see this problem is to note that the zero-intercept constraint adds another point observation (i.e.: no programme; zero WTP) to the three point observations already available (schemes with one, two or three programmes). Only this added point observation makes it possible to estimate a third-order curvature (cf. Figure 10.1).

14. The validity of this explanation depends on rejecting an alternative hypothesis imputing the observed interaction structure to sequencing effects between valuation questions. According to this alternative hypothesis, the premium attracted by the most complete conservation scheme would be due to the fact this scheme was always presented as the first valuation question. However, it was noticed that a significant number of respondents who expressed a positive value for the most complete conservation scheme also answered 'no' to all valuation questions involving partial conservation schemes. These respondents sometimes explained this behaviour by saying that only a complete scheme was worthwhile, which partly validates the hypothesis of complementarity between attributes underlying the positive third-order interaction. This does not completely rule out the possibility of ordering effects, which remain as an hypothesis to be tested in further research with a different survey design.

15. Section 3.4 explains how to estimate compensated substitution effects and income effects from the estimated parameters of Taylor-series multi-attribute models (see equation 3.34 and the subsection on 'model-based theory tests'). Compensated substitution effects are linear combinations of these parameters but income effects are not. Hence, in principle, only the standard errors for the substitution effects could be analytically secured from the variance–covariance matrix of the estimated model; to estimate the standard errors of the income effects we should resort to Monte Carlo experiments based on repeated sampling from the multivariate distribution of the parameter estimates (section 4.5). However, the small size of the income effects as compared to the compensated substitution effects led us to deem a Taylor-series first-order (linear) approximation to the variance of the income effect as sufficiently precise. This allowed us to analytically derive all the required standard errors from the variance–covariance matrix of the estimated model.

16. Although the substitution effect is not statistically significant in one case (joint effect of P2 and P3 on P1) and weakly significant in another (joint effect of P1 and P3 on P2).

17. Swaledale with Arkengarthdale, Upper Wensleydale, Raydale with Mid-Wensleydale, Bishopdale, Waldendale, Coverdale, Langstrothdale, Wharfedale with Littondale, Dentdale with Deepdale, Garsdale, Grisedale and Rawthey Valley (MAFF 1992).

18. South Tyne with Nent Valley, West Allen Dale, East Allen Dale, Rookhope, Weardale, Teesdale, Baldersdale with Lunedale (MAFF 1992) are inside the North Pennines AONB, but Mallerstang and Upper Eden Valley (MAFF 1992) are mainly outside both the NP and the AONB.

19. Almost surely, not all the members of every single household have visited the Dales. The average number of days per visitor per year estimated from our survey is, as well, on the high side of the true value, as individuals in summer holidays were a considerable part of the sample. So, the use of these figures led to a conservative estimate of the population of households visiting the Dales, and thus to a conservative aggregate benefit estimate as well.

11. The Costs of Landscape Conservation in the Pennine Dales and Peneda– Gerês Areas

Conserving the landscape implies adjusting the way the land is managed, which, more often than not, leads to using up scarce resources. Hence, there usually is a resource cost associated with conservation. This chapter estimates the cost of landscape conservation in the Pennine Dales (D) and Peneda–Gerês (PG) areas, considering both the financial and the social cost concept (chapter 5). In addition, in the D case, it was also possible to estimate transaction costs, i.e.: the costs of operating the policy scheme.

Most of the estimated costs refer to resources used up in conservation, such as, e.g., increased bought-in hay allowing a less intensive use of meadows; agricultural output foregone; and labour required to keep traditional farming systems working. If resources are made available by conservation, then there will also be direct market benefits associated with conservation in addition to non-market landscape benefits. So, reducing fertiliser use to enhance botanical diversity saves an amount of fertiliser that would, otherwise, be used up. Benefits such as this were entered as negative costs. Thus, estimated costs are net costs, i.e.: they measure the quasi-rent variation associated with those adjustments in management that are required by conservation.

In both case-studies, conservation schemes represented marginal changes with respect to the economy as a whole. A partial-equilibrium perspective was, therefore, adopted: conservation costs were estimated at constant market prices. Policy effects on prices were adjusted for when estimating social costs. When market prices were not available (e.g. for wall-maintenance costs), specific payment rates of known conservation schemes (e.g. per meter of wall maintained) were used as a proxy for market-priced resource costs.

11.1 THE PENNINE DALES (D) ESA CASE

In the D case, the conservation area was defined as the productive or potentially productive agricultural land within the Pennine Dales ESA: 39,900 hectares (MAFF 1995). Our CVM scenarios implied that landscape attributes would be maintained at current levels all over this area, and hence all of it was to be considered in evaluating our policy scenarios. Yet, only the area covered by ESA management agreements (25,702 hectares; cf. MAFF 1995) should be considered in estimating the cost of the ESA scheme as it is.

Cost of Programme 1 (Walls and Barns)

The conservation of stone walls and field barns as implied by programme 1 of the CVM scenario would require that: (1) walls and barns in sound condition were maintained in that condition; and that (2) repair work was done to avoid the complete decay of those in bad condition. Only the former was ensured by ESA management agreements (Table 7.1).

The absence of data for directly estimating the resource cost of maintaining walls and barns in sound condition led us to use a proxy for this cost: the per-unit payment rates offered by the Yorkshire Dales NP under the Farm Conservation Scheme. These rates were £0.17 per meter and £0.60 per square meter respectively for stone walls and traditional buildings (Yorkshire Dales National Park 1995).[1] According to a stone wall survey carried out by the NP (Yorkshire Dales National Park 1991), there were 62.6 meters of walls in sound condition per hectare in Upper Swaledale and Arkengarthdale. This figure was assumed as an upper-bound estimate for the ESA average.[2] As regards field barns, there was a ratio of one barn to 6 hectares of land in Upper Swaledale (estimated from Yorkshire Dales National Park 1994). Since Upper Swaledale has an extraordinarily high density of barns (Waltham 1987), it was assumed for the whole ESA that there was an average ratio of one barn (with 50 square meters of floor area) to 12 hectares of land. Based on all of these assumptions as regards walls and barns, the annual cost of maintaining these traditional structures in sound condition was estimated as £13.14 per hectare, i.e.: £524,366 for the whole ESA and £337,776 for the area covered by management agreements.

Let us consider now the cost of repairing walls and barns in bad condition so as to avoid their complete decay. Note that there were circa 4.9 and 6.6 meters per hectare of walls in need of minor repairs and major repairs respectively (Yorkshire Dales National Park 1991); furthermore, it was estimated that 58 per cent of all barns required some form of repair (Yorkshire Dales National Park 1994). Based on these and other assumptions,[3] Santos (1997) estimated the annual costs of wall and barn repairing as £14.94 per hectare. This represents £596,196 for the whole ESA, which added to the cost of maintaining walls and barns in sound condition gives an estimated cost of £1,120,562 per year for programme 1 (Table 11.1). This amount should not be fully allocated to landscape conservation because walls and barns still have a productive role in farming. However, as a way to lean to the conservative side when evaluating conservation policy (and due to difficulties in apportioning cost to joint productions), this cost was entirely allocated to the production of landscape benefits.

Table 11.1 Financial and social conservation costs in the Dales[a]

	Financial cost		Social cost	
	Total	ESA agree- ments alone	Total	ESA agree- ments alone
Programme 1 (walls and barns)	1,120,562	337,776	1,120,562	337,776
Programme 2 (meadows)	761,383	761,383	503,889	503,889
Programme 3 (woodland)	87,467	–	87,467	–
Transaction costs	1,389,000	1,389,000	1,389,000	1,389,000
Farmers' policy rent	–	1,499,970	–	–
Total	3,358,412	3,988,129	3,100,918	2,230,665

Note: a. values in £ per year.

Cost of Programme 2 (Hay Meadows)

Programme 2 in our CVM scenarios was aimed at conserving current levels of flower-diversity and habitat for ground-nesting birds in hay meadows by decreasing fertiliser use and imposing some further constraints (e.g. dates of hay cutting, grazing management …). In fact, most of the ESA management constraints in Table 7.1 are aimed at achieving these policy targets. Hence, to estimate the resource cost for farmers of complying with these constraints, we looked at changes in farms bound by an ESA management agreement (agreement farms) occurring since these farms entered into such an agreement. To verify that changes observed in agreement farms were actually due to management constraints in the agreement and not to general trends in farming, these changes were compared to what occurred, over the same period, in farms on identical land but not bound by an agreement (non-agreement farms). These changes and comparisons were based on the results of a farm survey reported by Whitby et al. (1992) and Saunders (1994).[4]

Changes in farming practice in agreement farms were neither massive nor pervasive, which indicates agreement farms were already not very far from ESA guidelines when they entered the scheme (Saunders 1994). Some changes can, however, be ascribed to the ESA scheme (these changes refer to the period 1986–1990). Artificial fertiliser use was reduced in 42 per cent of agreement farms (as compared to only 4 per cent of non-agreement farms) and the total decline in fertiliser use was estimated as 31 tonnes, i.e.: 122 Kg per agreement farm (Whitby et al. 1992).[5] As a result of this and the constraints imposed on cutting dates, hay yields fell in 43 per cent of agreement farms (as compared to only 7 per cent of non-agreement farms) and the aftermath of the first cut was also reduced (Whitby et al. 1992). All this led to an increase in bought-in hay and a slight shift from more intensive cattle to more extensive sheep rearing. Thus, approximately 45 per cent of agreement farms increased bought-in hay (average increase of 7.43 tonnes per agreement farm; estimated from Whitby et al. 1992), and, on average, there was a net decline of 1.54 cows and an increase of 2.34 ewes per agreement farm. The observed changes in agreement farms that were used to estimate conservation costs are presented in Table 11.2 (3rd column).

These changes in agreement farms were valued at 1994 prices using financial information provided by Nix (1993) which is reproduced in the 4th column of Table 11.2. This yielded the net financial cost of compliance with ESA management constraints: £87.11 per hectare of meadow under agreement or £27.65 per hectare of total agreement land.[6]

Financial-cost figures are, in general, different from the true resource costs of conservation for society (chapter 5). This difference is due to policy-induced divergences between prices and marginal social values of resources (i.e.: marginal values that would only reflect preferences and scarcity conditions). It is also due to the fact of financial costs including direct subsidies foregone when farmers adopt more extensive patterns of land use, which are mere financial transfers (not resource costs) for society as a whole. To correct for these effects, resort was made to Producer Subsidy Equivalents (PSE) for the outputs at stake. (PSEs represent the share of agricultural-policy support in the output, when this is valued at domestic prices and includes direct subsidies; Saunders 1987a.) The latest estimates available for gross PSEs for beef and sheepmeat in the EC-12 (6th column in Table 11.2; MAFF 1995) were used to convert the financial value of livestock output foregone to social-value terms. The 7th column in Table 11.2 presents the net social cost of conserving current levels of flower diversity and habitat in hay meadows: £57.65 per hectare of meadow under agreement or £18.30 per hectare of total agreement land. High levels of policy support for agricultural output explain why these social conservation costs are significantly exceeded (in 51 per cent) by the financial costs estimated above.

Financial and social conservation costs were aggregated to the entire ESA using the area of meadows under agreement as the basis for aggregation. This assumes that the area of meadows without agreement was already too intensified to have any conservation interest. According to Santos (1997), this is a plausible assumption; furthermore, programme 2 in the CVM scenario was aimed at protecting existing conservation values not improving them.[7] There were approximately 6,557 hectares of meadows under ESA agreements

(MAFF 1995). To account for the increase in ESA constraints since the 1992 review of the scheme (note that our cost estimates were built using pre-1992 data), aggregated costs were multiplied by a factor of 1.333. Thus, the aggregate financial conservation cost of programme 2 was estimated as £761,383 per year, and the aggregate social cost as £503,889 (Table 11.1).

Table 11.2 Financial and social costs of conserving hay meadows in Dales agreement farms

Description of change	unit	change	price (£ per unit)	financial value (£)	PSE	Social value (£)
Net change in cattle	cow	−1.54	465.00	−716.10	0.612	−277.70
Net change in sheep	ewe	2.34	62.00	145.08	0.597	58.50
Net output change (per farm)				−571.02		−219.20
Fertiliser	Kg	−122	0.11	−13.43		−13.43
Bought-in hay	ton	7.43	65.00	482.63		482.63
Net change in costs (per farm)				469.20		469.20
Net conservation cost (per farm)				1040.22		688.40
Net conservation cost (per hectare of meadow)				87.11		57.65
Net conservation cost (per hectare of land)				27.65		18.30

Sources: Whitby et al. (1992); MAFF (1995); and Nix (1993).

Cost of Programme 3 (Broad-Leaved Woodland)

Maintaining small broad-leaved woods in the Dales is mostly a matter of implementing better wood management, with no tradition in the area, as well as excluding grazing stock from woods. Hence, the main cost-components associated with programme 3 are those related to fencing, management improvement and technical advice. These costs were approximately estimated as £87,467 a year (Santos 1997). Note that these costs, except perhaps the advice component (prescription 27 in Table 7.1), cannot be attributed to the ESA scheme as it is. Nonetheless, woodland costs and benefits were used in selecting an optimal programme-mix for the Dales.

Transaction Costs

Most conservation costs estimated so far in this chapter exclude the costs of operating conservation schemes, i.e.: signing management agreements, monitoring practices and their environmental effects, and providing technical advice. Most of these costs, such as costs with skilled labour and capital, are true resource costs, and hence are part of social conservation costs. The costs of operating the Pennine Dales ESA scheme were worked out by MAFF (1995) on a pro rata basis, which produced an estimate of £1,389,000 a year. Given the importance of taking into account transaction costs when evaluating public policy (chapter 5), we entered this estimate in our analysis, although having in mind that it is only a rough approximation. Since it refers to the ESA scheme, where the woodland component is almost absent, this transaction cost estimate refers only to programmes 1 and 2.

Costs of the ESA for Taxpayers, Farmers and Society as a Whole

In the 1994/95 financial year, MAFF's expenditure on ESA payments to farmers in the Pennine Dales was £2,599,129 (MAFF 1995).[8] In addition, MAFF's cost includes the cost of operating the scheme. Thus, the gross financial cost of the Pennine Dales ESA scheme for MAFF would be around £3,988,129 per year (Table 11.1). The ESA scheme leads, however, to some reduction of agricultural output in the Dales, which reduces public expenditure related to agricultural support (mainly headage payments) in the Dales. These economies for the UK Exchequer were approximately estimated as £257,494 per year, by taking the difference between the financial and the social value of the agricultural output foregone. Thus, for government as a whole, and for taxpayers as well, the net financial cost of the Pennine Dales ESA scheme was approximately estimated as £3,730,635 per year.[9]

Adding the cost of programme 1 (considering only wall and barn maintenance in agreement land; i.e.: £337,776) to the financial cost of programme 2 gives an estimated financial cost of £1,099,159 per year incurred by agreement farmers as a result of complying with ESA management constraints. This would represent the minimum compensation required by farmers to accept compliance with ESA prescriptions. Thus, if MAFF acted as a perfect price-discriminating monopolist, the amount of payments to farmers could be reduced by up to £1,499,970. (This amount corresponds, therefore, to the rent that is transferred, every year, from taxpayers to Dales farmers as a consequence of using uniform payment rates; cf. Table 11.1.) As reducing ESA payments by that amount would require signing an individually tailored management agreement with every single farmer, transaction costs would rise with respect to those with current standard management agreements. Hence, it is not clear whether changing the scheme in this way would lead to public-expenditure savings (cf. section 5.7).

The cost of the ESA scheme to society as a whole can be estimated by adding transaction costs to the social resource cost of compliance with ESA constraints. This latter was estimated as £841,665 by deducting the level of agricultural support (£257,494) from the financial cost of compliance with ESA constraints (£1,099,159). Adding transaction costs gives an estimated social cost of £2,230,665 per year for the ESA scheme as it is (Table 11.1).

Costs of Different Programme-Mixes and Sequential Costs of Programmes

Landscape attributes included in different programmes must be independent in production so that the agency can choose to implement any possible programme-mix (section 6.2), and thus the problem of selecting an optimal mix can have a practical meaning. Independence in production also means that the costs of different programmes can be independently estimated and then added up to compute the costs of the diverse programme-mixes. In our case, programmes 1, 2 and 3 were largely independent in production. However, the costs of operating the ESA scheme ('transaction costs' as estimated above) are not easy to separate between programmes 1 and 2 (most transaction costs associated with woodland conservation were already allocated to programme 3). In allocating 'transaction costs' to programmes 1 and 2, it was assumed that fixed and non-separable transaction costs make one third of all transaction costs and that the other two thirds were to be apportioned in identical parts to these two programmes. Hence, the first programme in the sequence would support two thirds of transaction costs and the second the remaining third. Financial and social costs were summed across programmes (using this 2/3:1/3 rule for transaction costs), which generated the cost estimates for all programme-mixes presented in Table 11.3.

Using sequential cost–benefit analysis to select an optimal programme-mix required us to estimate sequential costs for each programme. These were computed by taking differences between the costs of the two relevant programme-mixes in each case. Hence, e.g., the sequential cost of programme 1 when valued after programme 2 was estimated as the difference between the cost of mix (1,1,0) and the cost of (0,1,0). Tables 11.4 and 11.5 present the estimated sequential costs, financial and social respectively.

Table 11.3 *Financial and social costs of*
different programme-mixes (D
case)

Programme-mix	Financial cost[a]	Social cost[a]
(1, 0, 0)	2,047	2,047
(0, 1, 0)	1,687	1,430
(0, 0, 1)	87	87
(1, 1, 0)	3,271	3,013
(1, 0, 1)	2,134	2,134
(0, 1, 1)	1,775	1,517
(1, 1, 1)	3,358	3,101

Note: a. values in thousands of £ per year.

Table 11.4 *Sequential financial costs of programmes (D case)*[a]

Programme	Initial programme-mix						
	(0, 0, 0)	(1, 0, 0)	(0, 1, 0)	(0, 0, 1)	(1, 1, 0)	(1, 0, 1)	(0, 1, 1)
P1	2,047	–	1,584	2,047	–	–	1,583
P2	1,687	1,224	–	1,688	–	1,224	–
P3	87	87	87	–	87	–	–
P1 + P2	–	–	–	3,271	–	–	–
P1 + P3	–	–	1,671	–	–	–	–
P2 + P3	–	1,311	–	–	–	–	–

Note: a. values in thousands of £ per year.

Table 11.5 *Sequential social costs of programmes (D case)*[a]

Programme	Initial programme-mix						
	(0, 0, 0)	(1, 0, 0)	(0, 1, 0)	(0, 0, 1)	(1, 1, 0)	(1, 0, 1)	(0, 1, 1)
P1	2,047	–	1,583	2,047	–	–	1,584
P2	1,430	966	–	1,430	–	967	–
P3	87	87	87	–	87	–	–
P1 + P2	–	–	–	3014	–	–	–
P1 + P3	–	–	1,671	–	–	–	–
P2 + P3	–	1,054	–	–	–	–	–

Note: a. values in thousands of £ per year.

11.2 THE PENEDA–GERÊS (PG) NATIONAL PARK CASE

In the PG case, the area considered for cost-estimation purposes corresponded to all agricultural land in parishes within the Peneda–Gerês NP (5,657 hectares; INE 1989) plus the area of oak woodland included in farms (1,368 hectares; indirectly estimated from INE 1989). These were the areas used to estimate the costs of different programme-mixes and the sequential costs of programmes, as they matched well the complete conservation scenarios depicted in the CVM survey. However, for purposes of estimating the costs of the Portuguese agri-environmental scheme in operation in the NP, we considered the area covered by management agreements alone, i.e.: 3,027 hectares of agricultural land and 451 hectares of oak woodland.

Cost of Programmes 1 and 2 (Terraced and Meadow Landscapes)

In the PG case, programme 1 was supposed to ensure the conservation of terraced landscapes, which are so typical of low to medium altitude valleys in the NP. These landscapes are associated with very-small-scale irrigated farming systems based on maize and annual grasses; at the lowest altitudes, high grapevines and fruit and olive trees, planted on the borders of terraces, make the character of the landscape. Terraced landscapes correspond to 3,245 hectares of agricultural land in 1,803 farms. Programme 2 was supposed to preserve the landscape of the high plateaux in the NP, where more than half of agricultural land is permanent grassland used as hay meadow. A complex combination of green meadows, dry stone walls, broad-leaved trees and small irrigation ditches along the contours makes an attractive landscape in sharp contrast with surrounding wild rocky slopes and moorland. Meadows also have an important botanical interest. Meadow landscapes comprehend 2,412 hectares of agricultural land, 1,337 of which used as meadow, in 702 farms.

There is no visible trend for farm intensification or amalgamation in the NP. The small scale of farming and the very small size of terraced fields hinder mechanisation and land-use intensification. Meadow landscapes are associated with somewhat larger farms and fields with more possibilities for future amalgamation. Small farms in the NP are economically very marginal and do not yield a level of income covering the opportunity cost of family labour. In fact, there has been a sustained flow of emigration to coastal areas of Portugal and foreign countries (Santos 1992). Field abandonment, scrub encroachment and the decay of terraces and irrigation systems, are the major landscape changes to be managed by a landscape conservation scheme in the NP. Under these circumstances, the costs of programmes 1 and 2 arise from the need to maintain in the area an amount of labour force just sufficient to keep traditional farming systems working so as to prevent further abandonment of fields and man-made structures. These costs were estimated as the share of the opportunity cost of family labour that is not covered by current levels of farm income.

Of course, keeping all these people in farms and offering them an adequate level of income creates other social benefits, such as: keeping viable local communities and services; providing effective vigilance against forest fires; and keeping rural paths open to visitors.

There are two possible perspectives for estimating the costs of programmes 1 and 2: a financial and a social cost perspective. Financial costs refer to the compensation payments required to keep the amount of labour force just required to ensure landscape conservation, provided all other policies remain as they are. Thus, current levels of agricultural support (e.g. hill farm subsidies and general agricultural subsidies as well) should enter the calculation of net farm income. In fact, when farmers compare their income level with the opportunity cost of labour to make allocation decisions, these subsidies are taken into account as part of income. On the other hand, estimating social conservation cost implies comparing the marginal productivity of labour in the economy (social opportunity cost) with the social valuation of the net farm income (i.e.: without subsidies).

To estimate financial and social conservation costs, resort was made to farm-accounting data from a number farms in the region, which were assumed to be representative of terraced (8 farms) and meadow (10 farms) landscapes (RICA 1997; Zona Agrária do Barroso 1997; and Centro de Gestão Agrícola do Barroso 1995 and 1996). The upper part of Table 11.6 presents average statistics for terraced and meadow farms.

Note that output and farm income per hectare is much larger in terraced farms than in meadow farms. This is not associated with higher capital-intensity (compare intermediate consumption and other real costs) but with higher labour-intensity. In fact, terraced farms use an amount of labour per hectare that is more than 5-fold that used in meadow farms (Table 11.6), which is related to a smaller size of terraced fields and to the fact that, in terraced farms, two crops are sequentially cultivated in the same year on the same land.

Although the level of per hectare agricultural subsidy is almost the same in both types of farms, the share of subsidy in income is much higher in meadow farms (Table 11.6). Thus, with 88 per cent of net farm income being subsidy, these farms strongly depend on current levels of agricultural support.

To estimate the opportunity cost of family labour employed in both farming systems, use was made of the average wage rate in industry and services for the North Region of Portugal (Table 11.6; source: Ministério para a Qualificação e o Emprego 1997). This should be multiplied by the number of family work units per hectare (FWU/ha) in each type of farm: according to farm-census data (INE 1989), 1.05 FWU/ha in terraced farms and 0.49 FWU/ha in meadow farms. There were, however, two problems with these figures when estimating conservation cost: (1) not all these FWUs were transferable to the labour market, and hence not all have this opportunity cost; and (2) maintaining current levels of employment in farms is not a necessary condition to achieve the landscape conservation targets at issue.

To solve the first problem, the transferable share of the family workforce was equated with labour provided by the farmer plus half of that provided by the housewife (the remaining is mostly the labour of children and the elderly; this assumption was based on a previous study of farming in the region; cf. Santos 1992). Thus, according to census data (INE 1989), this share of the workforce represented 53.6 per cent in terraced farms and 50.3 per cent in meadow farms (Table 11.6).

To solve the second problem, we allowed for some future landscape-compatible amalgamation of farms or fields. The scope for this amalgamation was larger in meadow areas than in terraced areas, where the very-small-scale network of terraces and fields is the very essence of the landscape. It was, therefore, considered that a farming structure corresponding to today's farms with more than 5 hectares would ensure the conservation of meadow landscapes, which (based on farm-census data by area classes) would reduce labour requirements from the existing 0.49 FWU/ha to 0.21 FWU/ha. On the other hand, the area threshold used for terraced farms had to be smaller (2 hectares), which, nevertheless, led to reduce labour requirements of conservation from 1.05 FWU/ha to 0.67 FWU/ha.

All of these cost estimation assumptions as well as the resulting cost estimates are presented in Table 11.6. Note that per hectare social costs are higher than financial costs because agricultural subsidies contribute to cover part of the opportunity cost of family labour. Removing all of these subsidies would increase financial conservation cost by the exact amount of subsidies removed. This leads to questioning a commonly held thesis which argues that removing agricultural support would make conservation goals easier to get everywhere (cf. e.g. Bowers and Cheshire 1983). Although applicable when there is an intensification problem (as with meadows in the D case), this thesis does not apply to situations, as the PG and many other upland areas in Southern Europe, where farm abandonment, and not intensification, is the problem to be faced by landscape conservation policy.

Financial and social conservation costs per hectare were aggregated to the whole agricultural land in the particular area covered by each programme. These aggregate costs are also presented in Table 11.6. As these cost estimates refer to all the agricultural land in each area, a reduction on a pro rata basis was necessary to arrive at the cost corresponding solely to the area covered by management agreements under the current agri-environmental scheme (cf. Table 11.7).

Table 11.6 Financial and social costs of programmes 1 and 2 (PG case)

	Programme 1 (terraced farms)	Programme 2 (meadow farms)
Average agricultural area per farm (ha)	2.38	18.72
Family Work Units (FWU) per hectare	0.64	0.12
Number of farms with accounting data	8	10
Years with accounting data	1994	1994 + 95
Gross agricultural output (with subsidies)[a]	472	169
Agricultural subsidies[a]	69	67
Intermediate consumption[a]	53	46
Gross value added (with subsidies)[a]	419	123
Other real costs (fixed costs, interest, rents ...)[a]	71	47
Farm income (with subsidies)[a]	347	76
Farm income (without subsidies)[a]	279	9
FWU/ha in all farms (farm-census data)	1.05	0.49
FWU/ha in farms with agricultural area > 2 ha (programme 1) or > 5 ha (programme 2)	0.67	0.21
Average annual wage rate in industry and services (North Region of Portugal)[b]	1,123	1,123
Per cent transferability of family labour to the labour market	0.536	0.503
Opportunity cost of family labour per hectare[a]	405	118
Financial conservation cost per hectare[a]	58	42
Social conservation cost per hectare[a]	126	109
Total financial cost[b]	188,029	101,124
Total social cost[b]	408,689	262,728

Notes:
a. values in thousands of escudos per hectare and year.
b. values in thousands of escudos per year.

Sources: Centro de Gestão Agrícola do Barroso (1995 and 1996); INE (1989); Ministério para a Qualificação e o Emprego (1997); RICA (1997); and Zona Agrária do Barroso (1997).

Cost of Programme 3 (Oak Woodland)

Programme 3 was supposed to ensure the conservation of oak woods included in farms or located in common land around farmland areas. In the NP, oak woods are a highly valued landscape attribute and recreational attraction; they also are an important and scarce habitat for wild animals and plants. Programme 3 would comprise periodical selective cuts of the underwood and other operations aimed at fostering the natural regeneration of woods; without it, woods would become invaded by scrub and poorer in wildlife. It is not easy to determine the resource cost of these woodland management operations. However, the enthusiastic reaction of farmers to the woodland component of the agri-environmental scheme (measure 22; section 7.2) shows that the payment rate offered for 'wood with high conservation interest' (14.24 thousand escudos per hectare) probably exceeds the corresponding conservation cost. Thus, this payment rate was used as an upper-bound ballpark for wood conservation costs, which aggregated to the 1,368 hectares of oak woodland included in farms gave an estimated conservation cost of 19,480 thousand escudos a year (Table 11.7).

Table 11.7 Financial and social conservation costs in the Peneda–Gerês[a]

	Financial cost		Social cost	
	Total	agreement area alone	Total	agreement area alone
Programme 1 (terraced farms)	188,029	69,570	408,689	151,215
Programme 2 (meadows)	101,124	75,843	262,728	197,046
Programme 3 (oak woods)	19,480	6,422	19,480	6,422
Total	308,633	151,835	690,897	354,683

Note: a. values in thousands of escudos per year.

Costs of the Current Scheme for Taxpayers, Farmers and Society as a Whole

Total annual expenditure on payments to farmers within the NP with respect to the three agri-environment policy measures evaluated here (measures 6, 8 and 22; cf. section 7.2) was 73,890 thousand escudos (IEADR 1996). Agricultural-policy payments to farmers within the NP, including headage payments and other direct subsidies, were estimated, from results in Table 11.6, as approximately 382,264 thousand escudos per year. Adjusting on a pro rata basis,[10] gave an estimated 202,847 thousand escudos a year for general agricultural payments in agreement land alone. As these payments induce people to keep farming the region, they also contribute to the achievement of landscape conservation goals. Although general agricultural-support payments do not bind farmers to specifically environmental constraints, they at least induce farmers to maintain current stocking rates (note most subsidies are on a per-head basis), which creates an interest in keeping meadows, pasture and traditional man-made structures in good condition. Total expenditure of the Portuguese Ministry of Agriculture (MA) in payments to farmers contributing for landscape benefits evaluated here was, therefore, estimated as 276,737 thousand escudos a year; 27 per cent paid by the agri-environmental scheme, 73 per cent by general agricultural-support policy. Note that this amount does not include transaction costs of the policy, as it was not possible to estimate these costs in the present case-study.

For the oak woodland programme, current agri-environmental payments to farmers probably cover all compliance costs and may even generate an element of rent for farmers. However, the situation is quite the opposite as regards the conservation of terraced and meadow landscapes. As a result, in these cases, we should separately evaluate the impact of agri-environmental payments in the short and the long term.

In the short term, it was seen that eligibility conditions, management prescriptions and relative payment rates for the different policy measures (namely measures 6 and 8) do not ensure that valued landscape attributes such as meadows and terraces are given adequate protection, even in land covered by agreements (cf. section 7.2). Still in the short term, note that there are no significant costs for farmers of complying with the agri-environmental scheme: compliance basically implies continuing the use of those areas entered in a management agreement as cropland or hay meadow during the 5-year-long term of the agreement. This would probably occur anyway for those farmers who entered into an agreement, as the transfer of family labour force to the labour market is slow, and it is this that controls the whole pace of changes in farming including the pace of abandonment. Thus, although the goals of the scheme are probably achieved in the short term within the agreement area, this would have occurred anyway without payments.

On the other hand, in the long term, new jobs are created elsewhere in the economy and farmers will slowly succeed in transferring the most mobile elements of the family labour force to the labour market. In the long term, what will be decisive is, therefore, whether payments are sufficient to induce part of the farming population to remain in farms, so that an amount of labour force can be retained which is just sufficient to ensure that landscape conservation goals are achieved. This possibility can be checked for, with respect to today's agri-environmental payment rates. Considering only agricultural land covered by an agreement, the average payment rate for terraced areas is 24.7 thousand escudos per hectare; in meadow areas, the corresponding figure is 20.7 thousand escudos per hectare (cf. Table 11.8). To assess whether these rates cover the long-term opportunity cost of labour, one should compare these payment rates with the financial conservation costs estimated in Table 11.6. This comparison is made in Table 11.8. Thus, we note that, in terraced areas, current payment rates only cover 43 per cent of financial costs; in meadow areas, current payment rates cover 49 per cent of these long-term financial costs. Current payment rates are, therefore, clearly insufficient to cover the long-term opportunity cost of labour. Achieving the agri-environmental scheme's landscape targets for the NP in the long term (even if we only enter current agreement area into the equation) would imply increasing the payments by at least 77,952 thousand escudos a year. Besides, note that general agricultural support policy payments have already been included as part of farm income. If agricultural support for hill farmers is to be reduced in the future, current agri-environmental payments will become still more insufficient. In addition, a predictable increase in wages elsewhere in the economy will increase the opportunity cost of labour in the future, so making current payment rates even more inadequately low.

Table 11.8 Comparison of current payment rates with financial conservation costs (PG case)

	Programme 1	Programme 2
Current payment rates (thousand escudos per ha)	24.7	20.7
Required payment in the medium-long term (thousand escudos per ha)	57.9	41.9
Share covered by current payment rates (%)	43	49

Source: average current payment rates for the areas covered by programmes 1 and 2 were estimated from IEADR (1996).

The costs of a long-term-effective scheme for society as a whole were estimated as 354,683 thousand escudos per year (Table 11.7). These social costs correspond to the financial costs that would be incurred by an effective scheme covering the area currently under agreements if all agricultural support policies were removed.[11]

Costs of Different Programme-Mixes and Sequential Costs of Programmes

As we have no estimate for transaction costs in the PG case, different programmes have no joint costs. Hence, the estimated costs can simply be summed across programmes to produce cost estimates for different programme-mixes. For the same reason, programmes' costs are independent of the evaluation sequence, and thus they are constant and identical to those presented in Table 11.7 whatever the sequence. It was, therefore, pointless to present the counterparts of Tables 11.3, 11.4 and 11.5 for the PG case.

NOTES

1. Probably, these payment rates include an element of incentive and are not solely paying for costs. Besides, maintenance work, unlike major repairs, is usually carried out by farmers themselves using spared time (Whitby et al. 1992). The social opportunity cost of this marginal family labour can be very low and depends on the marginal value of leisure. So it is likely that costs were at least not underestimated by using these payment-rate figures.
2. A study of NP landscapes by Silsoe College (1991) based on aerial photographs from the 1980s and some arguments developed in Santos (1997) support this assumption.
3. The cost of repairing stone walls was estimated as a re-building cost for 15 per cent and 50 per cent of the length of wall, respectively for walls in need of minor and walls in need of major repairs. It was assumed that there is a volume of 1 cubic meter per linear meter of wall to re-build; a cost figure of £15 per cubic meter was taken from Nix (1993), who refers to a range of walling costs of £8–£15 per meter. The average cost of repairing a barn was estimated as £2,189, as £1,750 was the average grant awarded by the Traditional Building Grant Scheme in the Yorkshire Dales (Yorkshire Dales National Park 1994) and this only covered 80 per cent of the costs. A 6 per cent discount rate (that used by HM Treasury for public project appraisal) was used to annualise the total cost of wall and barn repairing. The depreciation period for repair work was 10 years for walls and 50 years for barns.
4. Cost estimation benefited from the analysis and insights presented in these reports, from the discussion of estimation assumptions with Caroline Saunders and from all methodological discussions in Saunders et al. (1987a), Saunders et al. (1987b) and Willis et al. (1988).
5. All these percentages and figures refer only to changes taking place on land inside ESA boundaries for both agreement and non-agreement farms.
6. In 1989, total agreement area was 9,557 hectares, and the area of meadows under agreement was 3,033 hectares (Whitby et al. 1992).
7. For the same reason, our CVM results are not used to evaluate the ESA tier 2 (Table 7.1), which would imply increasing the area and enhancing meadows.
8. This amount does not include tier-2 payments in excess of tier-1 payment rate for meadows under tier-2 management, as, for reasons explained in note 7, we are not evaluating the tier-2 component of the ESA scheme.
9. This is not exactly the case. The ESA cost for UK taxpayers is lower than this: part is actually claimed back from Brussels. A general concept of European taxpayer is, however, used here to ensure comparability between the two case-studies, because the percentage EU contribution for the agri-environmental budget in the UK is different from that in Portugal.
10. Considering uptake rates of 37 per cent and 75 per cent for areas covered with programmes 1 and 2 respectively.
11. This equation of social conservation costs with the financial costs of a scheme after removing the effects of agricultural policy is only possible because we are dealing with a policy that creates no rent for farmers. Hence, compensation payments only cover the social opportunity cost of labour.

12. Cost–Benefit Analysis of Conservation Schemes in the Pennine Dales and Peneda–Gerês Areas

The main aim of cost–benefit analysis of conservation policy is to check whether the landscape change delivered by policy is welfare-improving. Most empirical applications are based on the Kaldor criterion: a policy is deemed desirable if gainers are willing to pay for it to go ahead more than the minimum compensation required by losers (section 6.1). There probably is a broad scope for welfare-improving landscape policies, because: (1) the market does not, in general, deliver socially-optimal landscapes (landscape is a public good); and (2) other policies (e.g. agricultural policy) often reinforce this trend for non-optimal landscapes to prevail. This chapter presents different types of cost–benefit analysis of conservation schemes in operation in the Pennine Dales (D) and Peneda–Gerês (PG) areas.

12.1 EVALUATING THE CURRENT CONSERVATION SCHEME IN EACH AREA AS IT IS

This section presents an evaluation of policy schemes currently operating in the D and PG areas. When comparing costs and benefits for society as a whole, mere financial transfers between individuals (not changing society's resource endowment) do not enter the analysis. However, these transfers represent actual costs and benefits for particular individuals and groups, and thus determine the formation of interest groups; they also limit (when transfers come from the conservation agency's budget) the possibility to run other environmental programmes. So, financial transfers actually matter for policy evaluation. Therefore, we also consider in this section the financial perspective on, and the distributional effects of, conservation policy.

Pennine Dales ESA Scheme

Assuming a linear relationship between area and benefits of conservation, the social benefits of the ESA scheme were approximately estimated as

£6,585,332 (Table 12.1) by multiplying the aggregate benefit of programme-mix (1, 1, 0) by a coefficient of 0.6438 (share of eligible land covered by management agreements; MAFF 1995). Note that this benefit estimate refers to visitors' WTP alone, and hence represents a considerable underestimation of the scheme's total economic value. Assuming linear benefits also leads to underestimate benefits, at least if the actual relationship is concave.

These ESA social benefits represent £256 per hectare of agreement land (Table 12.1), which exceeds the value of agricultural output per hectare of agreement farm (£143; Whitby et al. 1992 adjusting for price changes). Thus, from the point of view of society as a whole, the landscape function of farming in the Dales is more important than its conventional productive role.

The social cost of the current ESA scheme was already estimated in chapter 11 as £2,230,665 (cf. also Table 12.1). Comparing with ESA benefit yields a social benefit/cost ratio of 2.95 (2.55, using the lower-bound benefit estimate). Thus, the ESA scheme clearly passes the Kaldor compensation test: WTP of visitors alone is almost threefold the minimum compensation that would be required by alternative users of the resources used up in conserving the landscape.

However, social-welfare improvement is not the only criterion for policy evaluation. More often than not, changes in income for groups well positioned in the policy process is more important a criterion. In these days, good value for taxpayers' money is also a decisive criterion. From the perspective of government and taxpayers,[1] the ESA scheme represents a net expenditure of £3,730,635 (Table 12.1). Hence, even considering visitors alone, the general public receives an estimated landscape benefit of £1.77 (£1.52, using the lower-bound benefit estimate) from each £ of taxpayers' money spent in the ESA. So, the ESA scheme clearly provides good value for taxpayers money. Assuming that (as part of its statutory roles under the EU agri-environment regulation) MAFF is also interested in the effect of the scheme on farmers, farmers' policy rent should also be considered on the benefit side, which would raise the benefit/cost ratio for public expenditure to 2.17. Thus, the scheme is probably still more interesting for MAFF than it would be for an agency interested in landscape benefits alone.

Another important issue is that of the distribution of the ESA net social benefit between farmers and the general public.[2] From the total annual payment to farmers (i.e.: £2,599,129), 42 per cent cover compliance costs and 58 per cent correspond to a policy-rent for farmers (Table 12.1). This policy rent represents 34 per cent of ESA net social benefits (Table 12.1), with the remaining 66 per cent being received by the general public as landscape benefits net of tax-costs (Table 12.1). Although receiving the largest share of net benefits, the general public receives small per-capita net benefits, i.e.: £17.07 per visitor (less if we consider all taxpayers), whereas agreement farmers receive, on average, £2,174 each. Thus, it is hardly surprising that farmers are the strongest supporters of ESA policy (Whitby et al. 1992). To the extent that economic agents more easily perceive changes in monetary income than non-monetary welfare changes, farmers were also expected to be stronger ESA supporters than visitors (landscape benefits are entirely non-monetary while tax-costs and policy rents are entirely monetary).

Table 12.1 Pennine Dales ESA costs and benefits for those agents with an interest in the scheme[a]

Costs (–) and benefits (+) for:	£ per year	%	%	%	%	£/ha[b]
1. society as a whole						
ESA social benefit	6,585,332	100.0				256.2
Financial cost of compliance	– 1,099,159	– 16.7	– 49.3		– 42.3	– 42.8
Saving in agric. support	257,494	3.9	11.5		9.9	10.0
Social cost of compliance	– 841,665	– 12.8	– 37.7		– 32.4	– 32.7
Transaction costs	– 1,389,000	– 21.1	– 62.3			– 54.0
ESA social cost	– 2,230,665	– 33.9	– 100.0			– 86.8
ESA net social benefit	4,354,667	66.1		100.0		169.4
2. government and taxpayers						
ESA payments[c]	– 2,599,129	– 39.5				– 101.1
ESA operation costs	– 1,389,000	– 21.1				– 54.0
Total direct policy cost	– 3,988,129	– 60.6				–155.1
Saving in agric. support	257,494	3.9				10.0
Net cost for the Budget	– 3,730,635	– 56.7				– 145.1
3. farmers						
Payments received[c]	2,599,129	39.5			100.0	101.1
Compliance costs	– 1,099,159	– 16.7			– 42.3	– 42.8
Farmers' surplus (policy rent)	1,499,970	22.8		34.4	57.7	58.3
4. landscape users/non-users						
Landscape benefits	6,585,332	100.0				256.2
Costs as taxpayers	– 3,730,635	– 56.7				– 145.1
Users/non-users' surplus	2,854,697	43.3		65.6		111.1

Notes:
a. woodland conservation costs and benefits potentially implied by ESA policy are ignored.
b. per-hectare figures refer to agreement land only, not to all agricultural area in the ESA.
c. ESA payments exclude the part of tier-2 payments exceeding tier-1 payment rates.

Agri-Environmental Scheme in the Peneda–Gerês NP

The landscape benefits of the agri-environmental scheme in the PG area was estimated by sequentially summing aggregate benefit estimates for the three conservation programmes (Table 10.16) after adjusting each of these estimates on a pro-rata basis so that it referred solely to area covered by management agreements. Coefficients for these adjustments were the uptake rates for the corresponding programme. As there are six possible aggregation sequences for the three programmes, we got six different benefit estimates, the average of which was 439,548 thousand escudos per year (range: 339,661–524,663). This represents 126 thousand escudos per hectare of agreement area, which is considerably less than gross agricultural output per hectare (343 thousand escudos with agricultural subsidies; 275 thousand escudos without them).

Comparing with total payments to farmers in the NP with respect to measures 6, 8 and 22 of the agri-environmental scheme (Table 7.2) yields an estimated benefit/cost ratio of 5.95 for public money spent in these policy measures. One may consider, however, that all payments to NP farmers under current agricultural support policy (hill farming plus other, more general, subsidies) contribute to keep farmers in the area, and thus originate landscape benefits as well. Even if all these payments were considered on the cost side of the equation, the benefit/cost ratio would still be well above 1.00 (actually, circa 1.59). As a significant share of both types of payment expenditure come from the European Union (EU) budget, the scheme offers good value for Portuguese taxpayers' money.

However, as shown in section 11.2, current payment rates offered by the agri-environmental scheme in the NP are insufficient to meet the scheme's own landscape targets in the long term, as they do not cover the opportunity cost of labour employed by traditional farming. It is, therefore, relevant to estimate the benefit/cost ratio for an agri-environmental scheme offering payment rates just sufficient to cover this opportunity cost and hence to meet the landscape targets in the long term. For this purpose, we first assume that current levels of agricultural support are to remain constant in the future. Based on this assumption, the financial benefit/cost ratio of this long-term-effective scheme was estimated as 2.89. Thus, there is a cost–benefit rationale for the Portuguese Ministry of Agriculture (MA) to increase current agri-environmental payment rates in the NP, at least if expenditure on general agricultural support (hill compensatory allowances and other subsidies) is to be ascribed to other policy goals.

One may alternatively ask whether landscape benefits are large enough to offset the cost of a long-term-effective agri-environmental scheme if all agricultural-support payments were removed. This corresponds to ascribing all payments to the achievement of landscape benefits, and hence the resulting benefit/cost ratio is the social benefit/cost ratio for this scheme; this was estimated as 1.24. Interpreting this ratio as a return rate for taxpayers' money, we conclude that, even if all agricultural support was removed, a long-term-effective scheme would still remain good value for taxpayers' money. Interpreting it as a social benefit/cost ratio, we conclude that a long-term-effective agri-environmental scheme in the NP would pass the Kaldor compensation test. Hence, it would potentially raise the level of social welfare. Whether this will remain valid in the future depends on the relative evolutions of labour productivity in the economy as a whole, farming prices, number of visitors to the NP and visitors' WTP for landscape conservation. Increases in the productivity of labour, raising the opportunity cost of labour, will erode the welfare surplus currently generated by a long-term-effective scheme, whilst increases in all the other three factors will expand this surplus.

A long-term-effective scheme, by keeping a significant population in the area, would yield not only landscape benefits but also other benefits such as a more effective control of forest fires, thriving local communities and viable local services, and, in general, an open countryside (section 11.2). Hence, even considering the dynamic uncertainties referred to above, a benefit/cost ratio of 1.24 may still be confidently taken as evidence in favour of a long-term-effective scheme in the NP on social-welfare basis.

Note, however, that getting a long-term-effective scheme depends on increasing current payment rates so that they cover the opportunity cost of the amount of labour force that is just required by conservation. Without this, the scheme will not deliver long-term conservation of the traditional landscape, even if current levels of agricultural support are maintained (section 11.2).

On the other hand, with future reductions in agricultural support, policy-makers should consider raising agri-environmental payment rates in upland areas, such as the Peneda–Gerês NP, where farm dereliction is the main problem to be faced by landscape conservation. If provision is not made for this increase in payments rates landscape degradation in these areas will be an inescapable consequence of policy reforms reducing agricultural support.

12.2 EVALUATING DIFFERENT PROGRAMME-MIXES FOR EACH AREA

Section 12.1 presented benefit/cost ratios used to evaluate current agri-environmental policy schemes in the D and PG areas. This meant considering a single programme-mix for each area and assuming that costs and benefits refer only to the area currently under management agreements. On the other hand, this section discusses cost/benefit ratios allowing us to assess different programme-mixes for each area (and always referring to all eligible land). However, these cost–benefit ratios do not allow us to compare alternative programme-mixes for the same area but only each programme-mix with the no-conservation baseline scenario.

Tables 12.2 and 12.3 present benefit/cost ratios for the seven possible programme-mixes in the D and PG areas, respectively. Benefit/cost ratios were estimated using financial and social cost estimates, and mean and lower-limits of 95% CIs for benefits. Thus, four ratios were estimated for each programme-mix.

Pennine Dales ESA Scheme

In the D case (Table 12.2), financial costs are in general higher than social costs, due to agricultural support increasing compensation required to adopt less-intensive land uses (section 11.1), and hence financial benefit/cost ratios are smaller than social ones. Nonetheless, the difference is always small. Also in the D, and considering lower-bound as well as average benefit estimates, all benefit/cost ratios exceed 2.00 with most exceeding even 3.00. Hence, all programme-mixes pass the Kaldor compensation test when evaluated against the no-conservation baseline and the sizes of potential welfare-improvements are very substantial indeed for all programme-mixes.

Table 12.2   Benefit/cost ratios for different programme-mixes in the Dales

Programme-mix	Using financial costs	Using social costs
(1, 0, 0)	3.51	3.51
	(3.02)[a]	(3.02)
(0, 1, 0)	4.22	4.98
	(3.62)	(4.27)
(0, 0, 1)	82.46	82.46
	(70.86)	(70.86)
(1, 1, 0)	3.13	3.39
	(2.70)	(2.93)
(1, 0, 1)	4.72	4.72
	(4.06)	(4.06)
(0, 1, 1)	5.33	6.24
	(4.55)	(5.32)
(1, 1, 1)	3.59	3.89
	(3.19)	(3.45)

Note: a. ratios in parenthesis were estimated using lower limits of 95% CIs for aggregate benefits.

Agri-Environmental Scheme in the Peneda–Gerês NP

In the PG case (Table 12.3), the estimated benefit/cost ratios are much more sensitive to substituting social for financial costs, but, as expected, in this case benefit/cost ratios are larger with the financial cost concept. Financial benefit/cost ratios for all programme-mixes are larger than 1.00, but many are now smaller than (or close to) 2.00. However, benefit/cost ratios for three programme-mixes (four, using lower-bound benefit estimates) drop below 1.00 if we use social costs, i.e.: if the full cost of keeping population in the area (including that share of cost already covered by general agricultural support) is entirely ascribed to landscape benefits. This stresses the importance of deciding whether to consider landscape benefits alone or a broader set of benefits including fire prevention and keeping viable local communities and an 'open' countryside for visitors.

Note that, both in the D and PG cases, the mix including the woodland programme alone (programme 3 in both cases) yields extremely large benefit/cost ratios, which is due to the comparatively low cost of the woodland programme in both cases.

Table 12.3 Benefit/cost ratios for different programme-mixes in the Peneda– Gerês

Programme-mix	Using financial costs	Using social costs
(1, 0, 0)	1.98 (1.72)[a]	0.91 (0.79)
(0, 1, 0)	2.49 (2.02)	0.96 (0.78)
(0, 0, 1)	20.40 (17.85)	20.40 (17.85)
(1, 1, 0)	1.50 (1.28)	0.65 (0.55)
(1, 0, 1)	2.61 (2.29)	1.26 (1.11)
(0, 1, 1)	3.34 (2.80)	1.43 (1.20)
(1, 1, 1)	2.24 (2.05)	1.00 (0.92)

Note: a. ratios in parenthesis were estimated using lower limits of 95% CIs for aggregate benefits.

12.3 SEQUENTIAL COST–BENEFIT ANALYSIS FOR THE SELECTION OF OPTIMAL LANDSCAPES

Sequential benefit/cost ratios presented in this section allow us to compare alternative programme-mixes with each other and not only each individual mix with the no-conservation baseline as in section 12.2. In sequential cost–benefit analysis, programmes are successively added to a previously existing programme-mix; benefits resulting from this adding are compared with the corresponding costs to judge whether the conservation of the additional attributes included in the new programme passes the Kaldor test. In principle, including at each step only programmes that pass this test will lead us to the selection of a Pareto-optimal state of landscape (section 6.2).

Pennine Dales ESA Scheme

Table 12.4 presents the estimated sequential social benefit/cost ratios for the D case. As they are only slightly different from these, financial benefit/cost ratios are not presented.[3] Anyway, these would not change the conclusions to be drawn here from social benefit/cost ratios.

Note that each programme yields a benefit/cost ratio of at least 3.00 when it is the first to be included in the mix. Further on in the sequence, social benefit/cost ratios drop to lower values. Yet, considering point benefit estimates alone, all programmes keep benefit/cost ratios larger than 1.00, at any step in the sequence, which means that the most complete programme-mix, i.e.: (1, 1, 1), is selected as optimal whatever the sequence. Hence, there is no path-dependency problem in this case.

However, if lower-limits of 95 per cent CIs for benefits are used, benefit/cost ratios smaller than 1.00 already appear at the second step in the sequence. This happens when either programme 1 or programme 2 is added to programme 3; and when programme 1 is added to programme 2. At the third step in the sequence, all benefit/cost ratios are smaller than 1. Thus, using lower-bound benefit estimates, path-dependency of the optimum is already an obvious problem. Many sequences are identified which lead to select optimal bundles not including all three programmes: namely, the programme considered for inclusion at the third step in the sequence is never included in the optimal mix. Therefore, the policy recommendation of proceeding with the most complete programme-mix is only supported by the analysis if we use point benefit estimates. Note, however, that lower-bound benefit estimates imply a probably too small probability of error (i.e.: 2.5 per cent) and that many point estimates for the benefit/cost ratios of programmes excluded using the lower-limit criterion are still well above 1.00 (Table 12.4).

This somehow restores the policy recommendation of proceeding with the most complete programme-mix.

Table 12.4 Sequential social benefit/cost ratios in the Dales

Programme	Initial programme-mix						
	$(0, 0, 0)$	$(1, 0, 0)$	$(0, 1, 0)$	$(0, 0, 1)$	$(1, 1, 0)$	$(1, 0, 1)$	$(0, 1, 1)$
P1	3.51	–	1.96	1.41	–	–	1.63
	(3.02)[a]		(0.89)	(0.58)			(0.44)
P2	4.98	3.14	–	1.60	–	2.05	–
	(4.27)	(1.39)		(0.42)		(0.09)	
P3	82.46	33.06	26.89	–	20.91	–	–
	(70.86)	(13.53)	(7.40)		(0)		
P1 + P2	–	–	–	1.62	–	–	–
				(1.07)			
P1 + P3	–	–	2.94	–	–	–	–
			(1.96)				
P2 + P3	–	4.61	–	–	–	–	–
		(3.05)					

Note: a. ratios in parenthesis were estimated using lower limits of 95% CIs (truncated at 0) for aggregate benefits.

The path-dependency problem of cost–benefit assessments is easily illustrated with an example drawn from Table 12.4. So, using lower-bound benefit estimates, the adding of programme 2 to programme 3 yields a benefit/cost ratio of 0.42, whilst the adding of programme 3 to programme 2 generates a benefit more than sevenfold the corresponding cost. Thus, bringing together the same two programmes at the same step in the sequence (the 2nd) is justified as welfare-improving with the latter sequence but not with the former. Hence, the judgement on optimal policy-mix heavily depends on the evaluating sequence, which is a major weakness of cost–benefit analysis when applied to the sequential optimisation of the policy-mix (cf. also Hoehn and Randall 1989).

Agri-Environmental Scheme in the Peneda–Gerês NP

Tables 12.5 and 12.6 present the estimated sequential benefit/cost ratios for the PG case, using respectively financial and social cost estimates. In addition to path-dependency, these results illustrate a more general problem with cost–benefit analysis, which is the possible misidentification of a local maximum as a global Pareto-optimum when the second-order conditions for a global optimum are not met (section 6.1). In fact, as discussed in section

10.3, in the PG case the sequential value of each programme drops from the first to the second step in the sequence, and then rises again from the second to the third step. This reveals that, although being compensated substitutes for each other earlier in the sequence, all landscape attributes become compensated complements as we approach the end of the sequence. This initial decline in sequential benefits followed by a later rise causes the valuation function to be non-concave in the inter-attribute space (figure 10.1), in which case we may misidentify the global optimum. However, and differently from the problem of path-dependency, the solution for this problem is simple and consists of comparing the possible candidates for a global optimum. So, take e.g. the sequence P3→P1→P2 and consider only ratios estimated from mean benefits and financial cost estimates (Table 12.5).

Table 12.5 Sequential financial benefit/cost ratios in the Peneda–Gerês

Programme	Initial programme-mix						
	$(0, 0, 0)$	$(1, 0, 0)$	$(0, 1, 0)$	$(0, 0, 1)$	$(1, 1, 0)$	$(1, 0, 1)$	$(0, 1, 1)$
P1	1.98	–	0.97	0.76	–	–	1.54
	$(1.72)^a$		(0.54)	(0.33)			(1.07)
P2	2.49	0.61	–	0.05	–	1.50	–
	(2.02)	(0)		(0)		(0.62)	
P3	20.40	8.63	7.74	–	13.24	–	–
	(17.85)	(4.45)	(3.58)		(8.74)		
P1 + P2	–	–	–	1.02	–	–	–
				(0.75)			
P1 + P3	–	–	2.12	–	–	–	–
			(1.75)				
P2 + P3	–	2.65	–	–	–	–	–
		(2.02)					

Note: a. ratios in parenthesis were estimated using lower limits of 95% CIs (truncated at 0) for aggregate benefits.

Note that, when programme 3 is evaluated at the first step, it clearly passes the compensation test (ratio: 20.40). Consider, then, that programme 1 is evaluated at the second step (after 3 is already in the bundle): it does not pass the compensation test (ratio: 0.76). As programme 1 was not selected, programme 2 must be evaluated at the second step as well (with programme 3 already in the bundle). Under these circumstances, it also does not pass the test (ratio: 0.05). Therefore, we would select programme-mix (0, 0, 1) as the optimum mix. It is easy to check that taking the sequence P3→P2→P1 would have led us exactly to the same optimal mix. However, one may ask whether compensated complementarity in valuation between programmes 1 and 2 is sufficiently strong for them to pass the compensation test when considered together at the second step. This corresponds to considering the sequence P3 → P1+P2 or, which is the same, to comparing the two candidates to a global optimum, i.e. mixes (0, 0, 1) and (1, 1, 1). For this, we must look at the sequential benefit/cost ratio for programmes 1 plus 2 with programme 3 already in the bundle. This ratio was estimated as 1.02 (Table 12.5), which means that the global optimum is actually (1, 1, 1). This need to jointly consider pairs of programmes at the second step in the sequence explains the presence of the three last lines in Tables 12.4 to 12.6.

Table 12.6 Sequential social benefit/cost ratios in the Peneda–Gerês

Programme	Initial programme-mix						
	(0, 0, 0)	(1, 0, 0)	(0, 1, 0)	(0, 0, 1)	(1, 1, 0)	(1, 0, 1)	(0, 1, 1)
P1	0.91	–	0.45	0.35	–	–	0.71
	(0.79)[a]		(0.25)	(0.15)			(0.49)
P2	0.96	0.24	–	0.02	–	0.58	–
	(0.78)	(0)		(0)		(0.24)	
P3	20.40	8.63	7.74	–	13.24	–	–
	(17.85)	(4.45)	(3.58)		(8.74)		
P1 + P2	–	–	–	0.44	–	–	–
				(0.32)			
P1 + P3	–	–	1.03	–	–	–	–
			(0.85)				
P2 + P3	–	1.13	–	–	–	–	–
		(0.86)					

Note: a. ratios in parenthesis were estimated using lower limits of 95% CIs (truncated at 0) for aggregate benefits.

In the PG case, sequential benefit/cost ratios are extremely sensitive to differences between financial and social cost estimates: substituting social for financial costs reduces the sequential benefit/cost ratios by 51 to 61 per cent (except for sequential values of programme 3). Sequential benefit/cost ratios are also very sensitive to the substitution of lower-limits of 95 per cent CIs for point benefit estimates. Thus, in this case, the estimation assumptions (financial vs. social cost; average vs. lower-bound benefits) are decisive in determining which particular programme-mix is selected as optimal. Table 12.7 presents the effect of using financial vs. social cost estimates on the particular optimum that is selected with each possible sequence.

Note that, due to the problem of non-concavity of the valuation function discussed above, only the 1st, 4th, and 7th sequences are considered adequate for the determination of the optimum. So, starting with ratios estimated from financial cost estimates, the most complete mix, i.e.: (1, 1, 1), is selected as optimal whatever the sequential path. Thus, in this case, path-dependency is not a problem. However, if social cost estimates are used, each sequence yields a different optimum: bundles (0, 1, 1), (1, 0, 1), and (0, 0, 1), for the 1st, 4th and 7th sequences respectively (Table 12.7). Thus, with social cost estimates, path-dependency hinders again the selection of a unique solution for the optimal-programme-mix problem.

Table 12.7 Optimal programme-mix for each evaluation sequence (PG case)

Evaluation sequence			Optimal mix with:	
1st	2nd	3rd	financial costs	social costs
P1	P2 + P3	–	(1, 1, 1)	(0, 1, 1)
P1	P2	P3	(1, 0, 1)	(0, 0, 1)
P1	P3	P2	(1, 1, 1)	(0, 0, 1)
P2	P1 + P3	–	(1, 1, 1)	(1, 0, 1)
P2	P1	P3	(0, 1, 1)	(0, 0, 1)
P2	P3	P1	(1, 1, 1)	(0, 0, 1)
P3	P1 + P2	–	(1, 1, 1)	(0, 0, 1)
P3	P1	P2	(0, 0, 1)	(0, 0, 1)
P3	P2	P1	(0, 0, 1)	(0, 0, 1)

Provided that interactions in valuation between programmes reflect true substitution effects and are not mere artefacts of the valuation method, the path-dependency problem cannot be imputed to a particular valuation technique (e.g. the CVM). It is a general problem with sequential cost–benefit analysis itself. On the other hand, path-dependency is due to the discrete, thus incomplete, nature of the valuation information the analyst has access to. Thus, the problem has, in principle, a solution in the estimation of continuous multi-attribute benefit and cost functions, followed by analytical determination of the optimal state of landscape, where marginal costs equal marginal benefits for every single attribute as in section 6.1. Whether this reveals to be a feasible empirical endeavour is a task left for future research.

NOTES

1. In rigour, EU taxpayers (not UK's alone), as part of expenditure is reimbursed from Brussels.
2. It is impossible, with our data, to disentangle the separate effects of ESA policy on visitors and all other taxpayers (including EU taxpayers). This would be relevant, as per-capita benefits are higher to the former but it is the latter that supports most of the tax-burden.
3. But can be easily computed dividing figures in Table 10.14 by those in Table 11.5.

13. Comparisons between Case-Studies and Policy Implications

In this chapter, we compare cost and benefit estimates between case-studies with two main aims. First, to provide a further test of the theoretical validity of our CVM estimates of WTP for landscape conservation (section 13.1). Second, to derive some general conclusions relevant for current issues on farming and landscape conservation (section 13.2).

13.1 COMPARING ESTIMATED WTP FOR LANDSCAPE CONSERVATION

The results of the two case-studies reported in previous chapters provide us with an excellent opportunity for testing, under quite controlled conditions, the theoretical validity of our two CVM applications to landscape change. In fact, both surveys used identical survey instruments and were run in approximately the same way by the same researcher; moreover, WTP estimates were secured, in both cases, from identically specified models, estimated with the same econometric techniques and data-correction procedures. The conservation schemes under valuation were also similar as regards the type of targeted landscape attributes.

There were, however, differences between cases that made the comparison interesting. These differences concerned, e.g., the relevance of agricultural elements in the landscape, with agricultural area representing a larger share of the land and being more visible a landscape attribute in the Dales (D) than in the Peneda–Gerês (PG). This stronger weight of agricultural landscape elements in the D was clearly perceived by visitors, who, in turn, had stronger preferences for agricultural elements in the D and for more 'natural' elements in the PG (section 9.2). As the conservation schemes in both areas were mainly targeted at agricultural attributes, this difference in landscapes and preferences for landscapes should lead to higher WTP for the conservation scheme in the D than in the PG.

Differences between visitors to each area also led us to expect higher WTP for the conservation scheme in the D case. In fact, visitors to the Dales had higher levels of income, environmental concern, environmental group

216

membership, familiarity with the area and frequency of visits; they also engaged more often in landscape-dependent activities such as long walks during their visits (section 9.2). All of these factors were revealed to be strong predictors of WTP for landscape conservation, not only in the models estimated for validity-testing purposes in section 10.1 but also in our review of the literature of landscape valuation studies (chapter 14).

Under such controlled comparison conditions and with such well-defined expectations, the observation of higher WTP for the conservation scheme in the PG than in the D would have been a rather strong piece of evidence against the theoretical validity of the CVM for measuring landscape benefits. However, this was not the case, as the expected ranking of the WTP estimates was observed in practice and the difference between these estimates was very significant indeed. To establish this result, WTP amounts for the most complete scheme, as estimated from models D3 and PG3, were compared.[1] These estimates were £72.05, with 95 per cent CI (£63.98; £80.12), for the D; and £41.28, with 95 per cent CI (£37.70; £44.86), for the PG. Hence, the ranking of the valuations of the two schemes is according to expectations. Furthermore, the upper limit of the CI for the lower estimate (PG) is quite apart (actually, there is a £19.12 difference) from the lower limit of the CI for the higher estimate (D), and so the difference between them is significant at any usual level of probability.[2] Given the controlled conditions and well-defined expectations for this comparison between the two WTP estimates, this result leads to a favourable judgement on the theoretical validity of our CVM estimates of landscape benefits.

13.2 COMPARING THE BENEFITS AND COSTS OF LANDSCAPE CONSERVATION

This section compares the estimated benefits and costs of landscape conservation between cases. There is a set of common features to both cases, which make the comparison possible and meaningful. Hence, both cases are characterised by upland landscapes and styles of farming; both attract large numbers of visitors and command a high status among other conservation areas in the corresponding country. On the other hand, there are well-defined differences between cases, which make the comparison interesting and suggest possible generalisations of cost–benefit results to similar situations or to cases departing from the studied ones in some particular respects. The main differences between cases concern (1) farm structure (average farm size is 47 hectares in the D and 2.3 hectares in the PG); (2) productivity of labour in farming (net farm income per work-unit is £4,950 in the D and £1,020 in the PG); and (3) scale of the landscape (smaller and more complex, hence more dependent on small-scale farming, in the PG). These differences are particularly important as regards conservation costs and illustrate in detail some typical differences between northern and southern European uplands. Differences with respect to the role of agricultural elements in the landscape and types of visitors were summarised in section 13.1 and are more associated with benefits than costs of landscape conservation.

For each case-study, two scenarios were considered for comparative purposes: the 'current scheme' and a 'complete scheme'. In the D case, the former corresponds to the MAFF's Pennine Dales ESA scheme as it was. However, in the PG case, current payment rates were clearly insufficient to cover the opportunity cost of labour employed in traditional farming; thus, it was ineffective in preventing farm dereliction and the attendant landscape degradation. Hence, in this case, the 'current scheme' scenario corresponds to a scheme covering exactly the same agreement area and targeting exactly the same landscape attributes as the current agri-environmental scheme, but with payment rates raised so that it can be considered effective in the long term. The 'complete scheme' scenario corresponds, for both case-studies, to the most complete programme-mix in each case, i.e.: the one including programmes 1, 2 and 3 altogether and covering all eligible land.

All benefit and cost information was converted into £s per hectare covered by the particular scheme so as to make the comparison possible.[3] Table 13.1 presents the estimated costs, benefits and benefit/cost ratios to be compared here. Lower limits of 95 per cent CIs for benefits and benefit/cost ratios are presented in parenthesis.[4]

Per-Capita Benefits, Numbers of Visitors and Aggregate Benefits

Average benefit estimates per visitor are higher in the D than in the PG, with respect to both 'current' and 'complete scheme' scenarios (Table 13.1). Reasons for this already became apparent in section 13.1, which suggests how to adjust per-household benefit estimates for situations departing from the studied ones in some well-defined respects. Factors we should adjust for are there clearly spelled out. It was not possible, however, to disentangle the separate effect of each of these factors on WTP from the comparison between only two case-studies. This is a task for the meta-analysis of CVM studies of landscape change in the literature presented in chapter 14.

Comparing per-household benefit estimates indicates that, in each case, the current scheme generates lower benefits than a complete scheme, as expected since the former is nested within the latter.

There is a large difference between the two cases as regards the number of visitors per hectare of conservation area: for each scenario, there are twice as

Table 13.1 Comparative cost–benefit indicators for the two case-studies[a]

	Pennine Dales ESA		Peneda–Gerês NP	
	current scheme	complete scheme (1, 1, 1)	current scheme	complete scheme (1, 1, 1)
Number of visitors (households)	167,220		59,900	
Conservation area (hectares)	25,702	39,900	3,478	7,025
Visitors (households) per hectare	6.506	4.191	17.223	8.527
Benefit per household	39.38	72.05	26.21	41.28
	(33.96)[b]	(63.98)	–	(37.70)
Aggregate benefit per hectare	256.22	301.96	451.36	352.00
	(220.95)	(268.14)	–	(321.49)
Financial cost per hectare	96.81	84.17	155.92	156.91
Social cost per hectare	86.79	77.72	364.22	351.24
Financial benefit/cost ratio	2.65	3.59	2.89	2.24
	(2.28)	(3.19)	–	(2.05)
Social benefit/cost ratio	2.95	3.89	1.24	1.00
	(2.55)	(3.45)	–	(0.92)

Notes:
a. all cost and benefit figures are in £s; amounts in escudos were converted into £s using an exchange rate of 280 escudos per £.
b. figures in parenthesis refer to lower limits of 95% CIs for benefits.

much visitors per hectare in the PG than in the D case. Hence, per-hectare benefit estimates turn out to be larger in the PG than in the D (Table 13.1), differently from what happened with per-visitor estimates. This indicates that having an accurate estimate of the visiting population may be at least as crucial as having accurate per-visitor benefit estimates. Therefore, in cases where we can get per-visitor benefit estimates transferred from studies undertaken under sufficiently similar conditions and there are tight time or budget constraints, it may be worthwhile concentrating the existing resources in accurately estimating the visitor population rather than in carrying out a new survey. For example, if per-visitor benefits are expected to be similar, per-hectare benefits can be roughly extrapolated based on relative visitor numbers. Thus, think of other designated upland areas in Northern Portugal, which, although comparable to the Peneda–Gerês NP in landscape terms, receive much fewer visitors and occupy rather extensive areas. In this case, per-hectare benefit estimates would surely be much smaller (probably below £50 per hectare) than those estimated for the PG case (£350–£450 per hectare). Thus, the range of landscape conservation benefits in our two case-studies (£250–£450 per hectare) is considered roughly representative of only those areas of the countryside with significant visitor numbers per hectare and having a high conservation status at the national level.

Conservation Costs

All of our per-hectare aggregate benefit estimates, for both case-studies, are approximately within a range of 1 to 2, considering both point and lower-limit estimates. Yet our per-hectare cost estimates are scattered over a much broader range of values, i.e.: there is ratio of 1 to more than 4 between extreme values. Hence, cost-differences are the main factor explaining the diversity of benefit/cost ratios in Table 13.1. The variation in cost estimates in Table 13.1 is due to the different situations represented by the case-studies and, within case-studies, to different cost concepts, i.e.: social and financial costs.

Let us consider first the differences between financial and social costs within each case. In the D, social costs are lower than financial costs. This is due to financial costs including the compensation paid to farmers for the reduction in agricultural support that results from reducing land-use intensity to comply with management agreements. This is not a social cost, as it refers solely to a financial transfer between different areas of governmental policy, with conservation expenditure rising and agricultural expenditure declining by the same amount.

In the PG case, social conservation costs are larger than financial costs. Differently from the D, the main landscape change to be managed in the PG is farm dereliction rather than intensification. Hence, labour required to keep traditional farming systems in operation is the main input of landscape conservation policy. As agricultural-support policy actually 'pays' for part of the opportunity cost of such labour, it also covers part of the conservation cost. Hence, as financial costs are estimated taking into account actual levels of agricultural support, they are necessarily lower than social costs.

If we subtract social costs from financial costs, we obtain the variation in conservation costs that would result from a complete withdrawal of current levels of agricultural support. As implied by the comments above, a cost reduction will arise in the D and a cost increase in the PG case. In fact, if current levels of agricultural support were withdrawn, conservation cost would decline by 8 to 10 per cent in the D and rise by 124 to 134 per cent in the PG.[5] Thus, removing agricultural support would make conservation marginally cheaper (in financial terms alone) in the D but much more expensive in the PG. This result challenges the idea that reducing current levels of agricultural support would be an overall solution for current environmental problems associated with farming. Although this idea may be valid for conservation problems typified by input-restricting and investment-restricting landscape attributes, the exact opposite of it is true for conservation problems typified by input-requiring landscape attributes (for the definitions of these attribute types, see section 5.1). With input-requiring attributes, the goal is to maintain farming uses of local resources, so as to conserve those attributes that depend on continued human use. High levels of agricultural support are usually favourable to the achievement of such goal. Failure to consider this type of conservation problems when reforming agricultural support policy, may potentially lead to the jeopardy of the landscape interest of extensive farming regions, mostly located in Southern European uplands. Until now, reductions in price support have been accompanied by added payments to compensate for the effects of price reductions in farmers' incomes. Thus, agricultural policy reform has not had such a negative impact on landscape conservation in those regions. Imagine, however, that all agricultural support policy was to be withdrawn. There would be no problem if increased funds were made available for operating effective conservation schemes in those regions. From a conservation point of view, this policy scenario would be even preferred to today's situation, as payments to farmers would be completely decoupled from farming output and coupled to the level of amenity society as whole receives from farming. This would enable us to target precisely those types of farming with the highest conservation interest. However, it is open to question whether, after the withdrawal of support policy, sufficient funds would be made available to run effective conservation policies. If this is revealed to be politically unfeasible, then withdrawing support policy will lead to: (1) only small conservation results in areas favourable to modern farming (where market forces will be sufficient to support high intensity of land use and the attendant negative externalities); and (2) widespread landscape degradation throughout extensive areas with very marginal styles of farming and mostly located in the uplands of Southern Europe.

Let us now compare conservation costs in the PG with those in the D (Table 13.1). Using the financial cost concept, conservation costs in the PG are approximately twice as much as those in the D case. Using the social cost concept, this difference is magnified with costs in the PG becoming approximately fourfold those in the D case. Note that these cost estimates are based on different policy-off scenarios: intensification in the D and farmland dereliction in the PG case. This cost-difference reveals, therefore, how much more expensive conservation is when (1) it implies maintaining labour force in traditional small-scale farms to prevent landscape dereliction (as in the PG) than when (2) it is sufficient to compensate farmers for income changes resulting from marginal adjustments in farming practice, farms are larger and farm income per work-unit not so marginal (as in the D).

Benefit/Cost Ratios

Benefit/cost ratios for both scheme scenarios and for each case-study are presented in Table 13.1. In the D, all benefit/costs ratios are well above the critical value of 1.0 and larger than the corresponding ratios for the PG case. Here, for the 'complete scheme' scenario, the social benefit/cost ratio is quite close to the critical value of 1.0 (with the lower-bound estimate being even below this threshold). As per-hectare benefits are higher in the PG, this difference in benefit/cost ratios is entirely explained by the higher conservation costs in the PG case.

It is important to note that all of the above conclusions are probably too pessimistic with respect to the cost–benefit performance of landscape conservation schemes in upland areas, as they only consider benefits accruing to visitors alone. Furthermore, for the PG, there is one further argument supporting the claim that actual benefit/cost ratios are much higher than those presented here. In fact, our cost estimates correspond to the cost of maintaining adequate levels of farming population in the area, which would bring about other benefits, such as fire prevention and keeping a thriving local community. Hence, part of the estimated cost is in fact attributable to other benefits, and thus the actual benefit/costs ratios of landscape conservation alone are higher than those presented here.[6]

NOTES

1. Note that, whatever the models used, the two WTP estimates were ranked in the same order, and that the difference between them is always statistically significant.
2. An exchange rate of 280 escudos per £ was used to convert the Portuguese WTP estimate into pounds. Yet, all of the above conclusions still hold even using such an extremely low rate as 200 escudos per £.
3. Again, an exchange rate of 280 escudos per £ was used.
4. The sequential process used to approximately estimate the benefit for the 'current scheme' scenario in the PG case did not allow us to recover the corresponding 95 per cent CI; thus, the indicators in parentheses are lacking in this case.
5. The two figures for each case concern the 'current' and the 'complete scheme' scenarios.
6. This is particularly relevant for social cost estimates and social benefit/cost ratios.

PART FOUR

Methodological Appraisal and Conclusions

14. Validity, Reliability and Transferability of CVM Landscape Benefit Estimates: a Meta-Analysis

Several chapters in Part Two of this book raise and discuss many problems with the use of CVM for valuing landscape change. Conveying complex landscape changes to respondents, avoiding undue effects of irrelevant parts of the questionnaire, creating opportunities for considered choices within short interviews and accurately estimating mean WTP from discrete-choice (DC) data are some of the most important problem areas. Since many of these problems are still waiting for a definitive solution, it is important to assess whether CVM-based landscape benefit estimates are sufficiently valid and reliable to be used in evaluating conservation policy. A related issue is the assessment of the accuracy with which benefit estimates from an original landscape study can be transferred to new situations where benefit estimates are required to evaluate different policy schemes. Indeed, it is impracticable to carry out a CVM study for every single policy scheme. Hence, the transferability of benefit estimates is an essential pre-condition for the systematic use of cost–benefit analysis in conservation-policy evaluation.

14.1 DEFINING AND ASSESSING THE VALIDITY AND RELIABILITY OF CVM ESTIMATES

Validity and reliability are different criteria used to assess measurements. Validity is a judgement on the correspondence between the concept one is trying to measure and what is actually being measured. Reliability is the extent to which a measurement is invariant with respect to characteristics of the measurement instrument or context that are supposed to have no effect on the concept under measurement (independence of irrelevant conditions).

Assessing Validity

The most straightforward validity judgements are those resulting from predictive-validity tests (Schuman 1996), which consist of comparing respondents' statements on intended behaviour with actual behaviour (e.g., vote intention in polls with actual voting, purchase intention with actual purchases and so on). Mitchell and Carson (1989) prefer a similar way of validating CVM estimates: criterion validity. This is the degree of matching between a CVM estimate and a comparable estimate delivered by a method (the criterion) which is unequivocally supposed to yield results closer to the theoretical construct under measurement. Simulated markets involving actual payments have been used as the criterion to assess CVM's validity (Bishop and Heberlein 1979 and 1986). Referenda, when they exist, are recommended by many CVM methodologists as validity criteria for non-excludable public goods, such as landscape, for which simulated markets cannot be created (Mitchell and Carson 1989; Hanemann 1994).

The approach to validity more often used by CVM practitioners in assessing survey instruments is face validity (Schuman 1996), or content validity as Mitchell and Carson (1989) prefer. This is a subjective assessment of the CVM questionnaire with respect to issues such as whether the scenario is plausible, clearly presented and covers the benefit concept to be measured. To assess face validity and improve their questionnaires, most researchers subject questionnaires to a number of previous tests, such as appraisal by survey specialists, psychologists or other economists; and field pilot tests.

Construct validity is a different approach to validity assessment based on the observed association between the measure of interest and other measures that, according to theory, should be correlated with it (Mitchell and Carson 1989). Expected correlation is due to: (1) the same theoretical construct being measured in both cases (convergent validity); or (2) a causal relationship, suggested by theory, between the variables under measurement (theoretical validity).

Theoretical validity of CVM estimates has been recently assessed through split-sample experiments trying to show that CVM-elicited WTP is affected by variables that are theoretically expected to influence it (Carson et al. 1996; Diamond et al. 1993). In addition, since the first application of the method (Davis's measurement of the recreational value of Maine woods), CVM studies have reported models that explain the variation in WTP using independent variables that, according to theory, should be related with WTP. These independent variables are characteristics of the respondents (income, preferences ...) or attributes of the good (acreage of a conservation programme, difference between policy-off and policy-on scenarios ...). Models estimated and discussed in section 10.1 for the two case-studies in this book illustrate how WTP models are often used for theoretical validation.

Convergent validity has been assessed in a CVM context by comparing CVM estimates for a particular good with estimates for the same good provided by alternative valuation methods. This is usual practice since the results from Davis's study of Maine woods were compared to travel cost estimates of the same amenity with encouraging results (Knetsch and Davis 1966 quoted by Hanemann 1994). Along the same lines, Brookshire et al. (1982) compared the CVM and the hedonic price method, in an air quality study. Carson et al.'s (1994) paper is usually quoted as the most up-to-date assessment of convergent validity of the CVM: based on more than 500 comparisons between CVM and revealed-preference estimates, it shows the existing high degree of convergence between CVM and these methods.

Assessing Reliability

There are many ways to assess reliability. The classic approach is an assay of replicating the outcome of a particular measurement operation. If a CVM questionnaire is a reliable instrument, it should produce the same result when repeatedly applied with the same individuals, assuming changes in the relevant economic context are negligible. The correlation between WTP amounts stated at two occasions can be used as an index of reliability in these test–retest experiments. Low correlation implies that individual WTP answers have a high random component, which may be due to the fact of the scenario being unclear, non-plausible or not enough significant to motivate respondents to give considered answers (Carson 1991). Throughout their whole book, Mitchell and Carson (1989) have interpreted reliability in this sense, i.e.: as absence of statistical noise in CVM estimates. Since test–retest experiments are expensive, these authors proposed to use the R squared of OLS models of WTP as a measure of reliability. In fact, if only theoretically relevant variables were included in the model and if no specification problems or systematic errors (biases) existed, the empirical model would be a good approximation to the true underlying model generating the answers. In this case, the R squared is indeed a good measure of reliability. Mitchell and Carson (1989) proposed that an R squared of 0.15 or more is taken as evidence of reliability. Note that this criterion does not check for forms of unreliability that produce systematic error (bias), such as irrelevant side-effects of the questionnaire (e.g. value clues) with a directional influence on WTP means. Because they have equated validity with absence of bias, and reliability with statistical precision of the WTP estimator, Mitchell and Carson (1989) have not considered these forms of unreliability as a 'reliability' issue. Forms of unreliability introducing a systematic error can be tested for in two ways. First, using split-sample experiments. Second, by including, in WTP models, variables that should not count for valuation but that we suspect are having an undue effect on respondents' answers; then, we should check whether these variables actually have such an effect.

The Role of Theory and Interpretation in Assessing Validity and Reliability

An important issue in reliability assessments is that they require auxiliary assumptions on what should and what should not be considered relevant for the measurement at stake. Of course, to decide whether something should count towards an outcome is a theoretical matter (Baron 1996). Every measurement of economic variables is, therefore, a theory-dependent operation. A good example of the critical role of auxiliary assumptions and theory is the controversy over the meaning of regular embedding discussed in section 3.3. Kahneman and Knetsch (1992a and b) claimed that CVM produces arbitrary results, as WTP for a good is revealed to depend on whether the good is valued on its own or as a share of the value of a more inclusive good. This seems a typical reliability issue: two elicitation procedures that could, in principle, be alternatively used to measure the same object yield astonishingly different results. On the other hand, Randall and Hoehn (1996) argue that what is valued in regular embedding tests is the same good, but in quite different contexts as regards substitute goods and available income. Hence, as rightly pointed out by Randall and Hoehn, the difference between independent valuation and embedded valuation is not irrelevant from the standpoint of economic theory. Indeed, the discussion of substitution theory in chapter 3 shows us that regular embedding should be expected if the good of interest and the other components of the more inclusive good are compensated substitutes. If this substitution relationship is held as an auxiliary assumption, the very result of embedding – evidence of unreliability for Kahneman and Knetsch – becomes evidence of theoretical validity. Thus, auxiliary assumptions and theory make all the difference.

The difficulty in interpreting the fact that the open-ended (OE) and discrete-choice (DC) CVM formats often lead to different valuations of the same good is another example of a situation where it is not clear whether we have a validity or a reliability issue. In addition, the current debate on the relative merits of the OE and DC CVM formats gives us a general flavour of issues generally involved in validity and reliability assessments.

Hence, suppose that respondents are asked for maximum WTP for a particular landscape (OE format) and that they imagine the conservation programme costs £X. Suppose as well that they base their answers on this cost guess. Then, if asked whether they would increase their bids by 20 per cent to ensure that the programme will actually go ahead, most would possibly, and honestly, agree in paying such an increase (see, e.g., Drake 1992). Hence, the initial bid and probably also the revised one are not valid measurements of the Hicksian variation measure we are interested in. First, because they measure costs as perceived by respondents, not benefits.

Second, because they do not correspond to the maximum amount that could be extracted from a respondent's income to make him as worse off as without the programme.

A DC approach to questioning would have prevented this validity problem. Hence, suppose each respondent was, instead, told that the cost of conserving the particular landscape would lead to a £Y income-tax rise for him. Then, he would be asked how he would vote in a referendum if this conservation programme was on the ballot. In this way, respondents were prevented from engaging in cost-guessing behaviour. Furthermore, now respondents would also be given an incentive to give a 'yes' answer if they are better off without £Y than without the programme; in this sense, it has been claimed by many (e.g., Hoehn and Randall 1987) that the DC format is an incentive-compatible preference elicitation mechanism.

The DC question presents to respondents a choice (whether to buy a programme at a given price) that is more familiar to most, because of past purchase decisions on ordinary commodities. The DC question is also less demanding in cognitive terms. Hanemann (1996) uses this difference in cognitive burden to explain why the OE format tends to yield lower WTP estimates. When confronted with a difficult cognitive task, respondents rely on heuristic procedures that reduce the complexity of the task while introducing bias. Anchoring is one of such heuristics: when estimating a number (like maximum WTP), people typically start from a value (the starting point) and proceed by successive adjustments, which are, very often, insufficient; hence, the final result depends on the starting point (Tversky and Kahneman 1974).

It is important to stress that these facts do not always cause validity problems. To the extent they cause responsiveness of WTP to irrelevant aspects of the questionnaire – for example, the starting point bias with the iterative-bidding (IB) format – these facts represent, instead, reliability problems.

All the above cases against the OE format motivated the NOAA Panel on Contingent Valuation (Arrow et al. 1993) to recommend the DC format as best CVM practice. However, as suggested by many (e.g., Baron 1996), the NOAA Panel's verdict did not close the debate on the best CVM format. Hence, Desvousges et al. (1996) and Bateman et al. (1993) suggested that anchoring is also present in DC surveys, as respondents take the proposed bid amount as a starting point for an incomplete adjustment process. Willis et al. (1993) pointed out the difficulty of respondents in giving negative answers to socially valued proposals, such as the maintenance of the ESA scheme in England, whatever the cost of these proposals. This is obviously related to the hypothetical nature of CVM payments. They also suggest that the mainstream judgement on incentive-compatibility of the DC format is biased because this format has no in-built mechanism to prevent respondents from giving a 'yes' answer when the proposed bid is larger than their true valuation.

Moreover, 'yea-saying' is a well-known response effect in the general literature on survey methodology. This is typically not a validity, but a reliability issue. Since the estimation of mean WTP from DC data is very sensitive to unconsidered 'yes' answers to high bid amounts, these systematic predisposition to give 'yes' answers can make all the difference. Thus, many procedures have been proposed and implemented to estimate mean WTP from data including some level of 'yea-saying' (Schuman 1996; Wang 1997). So far, none of these procedures has attracted general consensus and most procedures lead to quite different results. Given all these, equally plausible and contradictory, arguments on the debate on the best CVM format, it should be recognised that there is today no compelling case for recommending, in general, one or the other format as best CVM practice.

A Meta-Analytical Approach to Validity and Reliability Assessment

Some of the approaches to validity and reliability referred to above were applied in the case-studies presented in Part Three of this book. In this chapter, however, we undertake a systematic assessment of the literature of CVM studies of WTP for landscape conservation completed to date. This assessment is aimed at providing policy makers with a measure of the validity and reliability of those CVM landscape benefit estimates that are currently available for policy evaluation purposes.

Whereas, in individual studies, validity and reliability assessments take stock of the inter-individual variation in WTP (as in section 10.1), here we explore the inter-study variation in WTP sample means. This dimension of WTP variation is analysed through the estimation of an econometric meta-analytical model aiming at explaining the variation in mean WTP estimates across studies. Variables characterising the studies with respect to the landscape change under valuation, the surveyed population and the applied methods are used as the predictors. Depending on whether or not each of these variables should count for valuation, the analysis is gauging either theoretical validity or reliability. Briefly, if WTP estimates react to things to which they should (not) react, this is evidence of theoretical validity (unreliability).

Thus, in addition to taking stock of large differences across studies with respect to landscape changes and surveyed populations, which should count for valuation, this model also enables us to assess the weight of particular methodological options (such as the elicitation format) that vary across studies and for which we have no consensual recommendation. The R squared of such a meta-analytical model is a measure of the absence of statistical noise in the variation of WTP sample means across studies; this measure parallels, in the inter-study setting, the usual approach to the reliability of intra-study individual WTP proposed by Mitchell and Carson.

14.2 CVM STUDIES OF WTP FOR CONSERVING AGRICULTURAL LANDSCAPES

Any literature review starts by establishing the relevant literature. Since it is generally impossible to ensure complete coverage, it is recommended that the procedures used to locate the studies included in the review (i.e.: the criterion of relevance, the sources and the searching procedures) are fully reported. This will enable readers to assess how representative and complete the final list of studies is, and also ensures that this list is, at least ideally, replicable by anyone using the reported procedures (Glass et al. 1981). Given our current concern (chapter 1), we included in our review all studies providing at least one CVM estimate of WTP for a change in an agricultural landscape.

The search for relevant studies was based on the following sources: (1) past literature reviews;[1] (2) recent issues of journals of environmental and agricultural economics; (3) references in collective books on farming and countryside;[2] (4) conference papers; (5) bibliographical references included in all landscape studies that have been found; (6) some prominent practitioners, who have added some references to our previous list (namely, research reports) and who, to the extent of their knowledge, have confirmed the completeness of this list. A final list of 19 studies was arrived at, which is probably biased towards works written in English and already published; it possibly misses dissertation material, conference papers and very recent research work still waiting for publication. Nine of the studies in our final list are journal articles; two are published research reports; three are unpublished research reports; one is a conference paper and four correspond to recent research work, still unpublished. The studies have been carried out in seven different countries;[3] and include: studies commissioned by the UK's MAFF; research projects funded by the EU or by national conservation agencies; and research independently carried out at several universities.

The 19 studies are quite uneven with respect to research quality. Rough indicators of quality of survey design, sampling procedures and CVM methodology vary widely across studies. Thus, unit non-response rates were between circa 20 per cent (on-site surveys) and 75 per cent (mail surveys). Item non-response rates (protests plus non-responses) varied between less than 10 per cent (DC applications) to more than 40 per cent (mail surveys). Some surveys yielded usable samples in excess of 1,000 while others, although adopting the DC format (requiring more observations for reliable WTP estimation), used samples of less than 200. These large differences across studies probably led to different levels of sampling and non-response biases; different levels of understanding and acceptance of the scenario by respondents; and different degrees of reliability of WTP estimates.

According to recommendations by leading specialists in the field of literature reviews (e.g., Glass et al. 1981), we made no a priori exclusion of studies on quality grounds. Indeed, the study of the effects of diverse aspects of research quality on research results is an empirical matter, which should be empirically assessed as part of the literature review itself (Glass 1976), not prejudged at its very beginning.

Table 14.1 presents the studies retained for analysis. Each study presented the results of one or more surveys, which referred to different populations or used different CVM formats. A total of 37 surveys are reported in the 19 studies. If one considers that in some cases each respondent valued different landscape changes, the number of results is raised to 50. Eventually, if one takes into account also different estimators (i.e.: levels of α-trimming of OE data, truncation of DC data), then the total number of estimates is increased to 66. Most of these WTP estimates have been originally elicited on a per-year, per-household basis; only three estimates required an adjustment to this basis (Santos 1997). All WTP estimates have been converted into 1996 £, using the 1996 consumer-price index for the respective country and an appropriate exchange rate against the sterling.[4]

14.3 A META-ANALYSIS OF THE INTER-STUDY VARIATION IN WTP FOR LANDSCAPE CONSERVATION

Our study of the variation in WTP across studies followed a meta-analytical approach. So, we start by what characterises the meta-analytical perspective.

Meta-Analysis: Conventional Approach *vs* Econometric Applications to the Non-Market Valuation Literature

Meta-analysis emerged as an alternative to the classic rhetoric approach to literature review in the social sciences (Glass 1976; Glass et al. 1981; and Wolf 1986). In more exact sciences, the progression of knowledge has been typically described as cumulative and linear. Each study or couple of studies provide a satisfactory answer to a research problem, and following studies explore new questions, building on accepted answers to previous questions.

Table 14.1 The used CVM studies of landscape changes

Study	Landscape change and population	Surveys	Estimates	WTP range
Pruckner (1995)	Nationwide conservation of Austrian agricultural landscapes, valued by Summer tourists (mainly foreign people)	1	2	2.67–4.47
Drake (1992) and Drake (1993)	Nationwide preservation of Swedish agricultural landscapes from conversion into forestry, valued by national residents	1	1	77.42
Stenger and Colson (1996)	Nationwide conservation of French agricultural landscapes; enhancement of the 'bocage' landscape in the Loire-Atlantique 'departement', and in one 'canton' in it; valued by the departement's residents	1	3	4.99–77.65
Halstead (1984)	Preventing urban development of the farmland area closest to the respondent's home; valued by residents in three Massachusetts towns (USA)	1	3	45.80–233.72
Bergstrom et al. (1985); Dillman & Bergstrom (1991)	Preserving public amenity benefits of prime agricultural land from development in Greenville County (South Carolina, USA), valued by the County residents	1	1	9.32
Bateman et al. (1992 and 1993)	Preservation of the Norfolk Broads landscape from flooding by the sea; valued by visitors; local and UK residents (using both OE and DC formats)	3	7	23.98–160.08
Willis and Garrod (1991 and 1992)	Conserving the Yorkshire Dales (UK) 'today's landscape', as opposed to the 'abandoned landscape'; valued by local residents and visitors	2	2	29.12–29.74
Willis et al. (1993)	Maintaining the ESA scheme in England as a whole, and in 2 particular ESAs (South Downs, and Somerset Levels and Moors); valued by visitors; local and national residents (using both OE and DC formats)	6	17	2.18–103.97
Santos (1997)	Conserving today's agricultural landscapes in the Pennine Dales ESA (UK), and in the Peneda-Gerês NP (Portugal); valued by visitors	2	4	47.40–115.29
Willis (1982); and Willis & Whitby (1985)	Preserving Tyneside Green Belt (UK) from urban development; valued by residents in two communities surrounded by Green Belt land	2	2	43.33–79.13
Willis (1990)	Preventing detrimental landscape changes resulting from current trends in farming practice in three SSSI (Skipwith Common, Derwent Ings, and Upper Teesdale; all in the North East of England); valued by residents in one area of up to 200 Km from sites	1	3	0.95–2.02
Hanley et al. (1991)	Conservation of typical lowland heath in Avon Forest Park (Dorset, UK); valued by visitors	1	1	11.78
Hanley and Craig (1991)	Preservation of the Flow Country of Caithness and Sutherland (Northern Scotland) from afforestation; valued by Scottish residents	1	1	20.33
Campos and Riera (1996)	Conservation of the 'dehesa' landscape (traditional Iberian agro-forestry farming system, combining holm and cork oaks with grazing and cereal fields) in the Monfragüe NP (Spain); valued by NP visitors	1	1	37.20
Hanley et al. (1996a)	Breadalbane, and Machair ESA schemes (in Scotland); valued by visitors; local and national residents (using both OE and DC formats)	8	12	9.19–100.35[a]
Gourlay (1995)	Loch Lomond and Stewartry ESA schemes (in Scotland); valued by local residents	2	2	13.78–21.83
Bullock and Kay (1996)	Landscape improvement from reduced grazing pressure in the Southern Uplands ESA, Scotland; valued by visitors and national residents	2	2	70.66–84.99
Beasley et al. (1986)	Preserving remaining farmland in the Old Colony and Homestead areas of south Central Alaska (USA); valued by residents in 2 communities adjacent to existing farmland	1	2	76.64–145.21
Total		37	66	0.95–233.72[a]

Note: a. Excluding a figure of £387.07, resulting from a DC CVM estimate based on a quite small sample and exhibiting an extremely wide confidence interval (cf. Hanley et al. 1996a).

This is not the case in the social sciences. Here, many studies on the same research problem often produce different answers, with such contradictory findings typically accumulating over long periods of research practice. Different sampling procedures, several types of tests, diverse variable definitions and other differences of method create part of this divergence in findings; the other part is created by differences between studies' participants with respect to class, age, education and other socio-economic variables; the remaining part of this divergence in findings is due to sampling variation.

There is an important task for literature reviews in interpreting and integrating this type of divergent findings and in arriving at some degree of consensus on what we actually know within each area of social inquiry. In this context, leading authors often adopt an idiosyncratic, authoritarian and impressionistic approach to literature reviews. These authors take advantage of their prominence to legitimate many ad hoc review procedures, such as: (1) the screening of studies to be included on grounds of untested criteria of research quality; or (2) the subjective weighting of studies' results according to these criteria. In so doing, these authors are clearly challenging, in their work as reviewers, the very rules of clarity, explicitness and empirical soundness that, on the other hand, they prescribe as good scientific practice for individual research studies. These double standards create an awkward situation, given the crucial role of literature reviews in evaluating and summarising contradictory evidence from individual studies. It is in this context that authors such as Glass (1976), Glass et al. (1981) or Wolf (1986) propose an alternative approach to literature review: meta-analysis. Meta-analysis is based on the idea that to understand and make sense of the variety of empirical findings on the same research problem, one should take into account all factors (method, context, sampling variance) that may explain this variety. Moreover, accounting for the role of such factors across large numbers of studies is generally well beyond the capacity of the human mind. Hence, the same statistical techniques which assist analysts in extracting information from individual studies' data should also be recommended to assist the reviewer in making sense of a complex collection of studies' findings and characteristics. Thus, 'meta-analysis is nothing more than the attitude of data analysis applied to quantitative summaries of individual experiments.' (Glass et al. 1981: 21). The novelty lies not on the techniques but on their application to a collection of studies. Thus, meta-analysis is supposed to introduce in literature reviewing the same scientific attitudes that underlay individual research studies, namely the idea that only non-authoritarian, explicit, empirically-based and replicable procedures can be used to derive conclusions.

The typical aim of meta-analysis is the integration of findings from a collection of studies related to the same research question, e.g. the effect of class sizes on students' achievement. Meta-analytical procedures have been devised to: (1) aggregate the results of statistical tests from individual studies so that we arrive at an overall conclusion on the significance of the observed effect across all reviewed studies; (2) build common metrics for standardising measurements of the same effect size based on different measurement scales; and (3) appraise the effects of several methodological and context variables characterising each study. These last are often known as 'mediating effects' in that they refer to the role of third variables as mediators of the main effect under study (Wolf 1986).

Three meta-analyses of non-market valuation studies have been published to date. In a pioneer paper, Smith and Kaoru (1990) reviewed the literature of travel cost recreation studies carried out between 1970 and 1986 in the USA. Walsh et al. (1992) reviewed both travel cost and CVM studies of recreation benefits for a similar period and also for the USA. Bateman et al. (1995) reviewed the literature of CVM studies of the recreational value of UK forests. All these economic applications of meta-analysis differ from the conventional approach at least in two important respects. First, the individual studies which are reviewed are not studying the same cause-effect relationship; instead, they have quite different purposes such as testing a new methodology, assessing the size of a particular bias or estimating the benefit that is required to evaluate a particular policy. However, they have in common the fact that they provide measurements of WTP for particular recreation goods. Secondly, the purpose of the meta-analysis of these valuation studies is not to summarise their findings with respect to a common research problem (which, simply, does not exist) but to address a new research problem: that of the determinants of the variation in WTP estimates across studies. This new problem is usually dealt with by analysing the inter-study co-variation between WTP sample estimates, on the one hand, and, on the other, recreational attributes, population's characteristics and methodological options characterising each study. Hence, in meta-analyses of valuation studies, the distinction between the main effect to be studied (the common theme in conventional meta-analyses) and mediating effects is meaningless. All that matters is the partial effect of each variable in explaining the variation in WTP estimates across studies. For this purpose, econometric (i.e.: multiple regression) techniques are the natural choice.

Landscape Benefit Estimates: the Problem of Non-Use Values

The previous three meta-analyses of non-market valuation studies referred to estimates of recreation/use values (access alone). They were mainly aimed at identifying the crucial variables to adjust for when transferring benefit estimates across studies. As there are so many problems in defining, estimating and using non-use values in policy evaluation, many authors think that the transferability of estimates including non-use values is a premature endeavour (Brookshire and Neill 1992). This is probably why previous meta-analysis reviewed use-value estimates alone. Yet, all landscape benefits reviewed in this chapter include non-use values, as respondents were typically asked for WTP to conserve a landscape not to get access to it.

It should, however, be stressed that whether benefit estimates from an original study could have been accurately predicted from previous studies – which is the central issue of benefit transferability – is an empirical question that should be empirically assessed. This question is separate from that of whether the original studies deliver valid estimates of non-use values (or whether such values even exist or should be used in policy evaluation). In this book, the predictability issue was addressed, using a meta-analytical econometric WTP model, in complete separation from that of the validity of non-use value estimation. However, incidentally, the econometric approach to transferability/predictability also provides information on the significant predictors of WTP estimates. As seen above, this can also be used to theoretically validate the original estimates themselves.

Thus, the present meta-analysis of CVM landscape benefit estimates allows us to address both the predictability and the validity of WTP estimates that include significant non-use components. This represents a clear extension of the current meta-analytical literature.

The Variation in CVM Estimates of WTP for Landscape Conservation

Table 14.1 shows the wide variation in sample WTP estimates within the 19 CVM studies of agricultural landscapes (minimum of £0.95; maximum of £233.72). Variation in estimates is important not only across studies, but also across different estimates provided by the same study. From an analytical point of view, variation in WTP estimates is a desirable fact if it can be associated with variation in some independent variables. Indeed, an important condition for using regression analysis as an analytical tool is that dependent and independent variables vary.

To reduce the variation in WTP estimates, we used first a simple classification of the estimates. This allowed us to check whether the problem of explaining WTP variation could be addressed by simple procedures (such as comparison of class averages) or if more refined multivariate techniques (regression analysis) were required. The type of landscape, its scale and uniqueness and the magnitude of the qualitative change are obviously amongst the factors that should explain differences in WTP for landscape conservation (Bateman et al. 1994). Hence, in Table 14.2, the available 66 WTP estimates have been sorted according to these variables to check whether this re-arrangement produces an expected pattern of inter-class WTP differences and yields acceptably low within-class WTP variation.

Table 14.2 Summary statistics of WTP for landscape conservation by type of landscape change

Type of landscape change	Studies	Estimates	Mean	Standard deviation	Range
Preserving regional or urban-fringe farmland from housing, industrial or commercial development	4	8	92.57	70.60	9.32–233.72
Conserving agricultural landscapes within ESAs, NPs or similar areas (total)	11	49	54.20	61.08	2.18–160.08[a]
when policy-off scenario means a complete change in character (e.g. afforestation, flooding or conversion of heath into arable)	2	8	73.18	49.77	20.33–160.08
when policy-off scenario is a gradual change resulting from farm abandonment or intensification	9	41	50.50	62.90	2.18–115.29[a]
Conserving agricultural landscapes in small conservation areas or recreation sites	3	5	4.20	4.53	0.95–11.78
Conserving all national agricultural landscapes	3	4	40.55	42.71	2.67–77.65
Total	19	66	54.24	61.33	0.95–233.72[a]

Note: a. Excluding an extreme outlier average of £387.07.

Although some patterns of inter-class differences emerge from the reading of Table 14.2, most of which according to prior expectations,[5] the important result of this rearrangement was that the within-class variation in WTP was revealed to be very significant and most classes' ranges of WTP estimates do overlap. This indicated that important sources of variation in WTP were not controlled for. Indeed, considering the combined effects of all relevant factors implied the use of more refined analytical tools, such as multiple linear regression. This would have the further advantage of yielding the partial effect of every single factor on estimated WTP.

Explaining the Variation in WTP Estimates: the Independent Variables

Good modelling practice requires to report every single independent variable initially considered for inclusion in the model, even if later dropped from the final model on grounds of statistical significance. In fact, only this enables the reader to check whether a particular variable is not in the model because it was not statistically significant or, simply, because it was not considered in the first place. Thus, Table 14.3 presents and defines all variables that were considered for inclusion in our meta-analytical model. Many other variables would be relevant for the present analysis, particularly those depicting in detail the particular landscape change and the surveyed respondents. These variables were, however, not available from the individual studies and were, therefore, not considered in the analysis nor mentioned in Table 14.3.

Specification and Estimation Issues

The log transformation of the dependent variable yielded the best results both in terms of goodness-of-fit and significance of individual predictors. Hence, the semi-log (dependent) functional form was selected, except as regards the income variable, for which the log-linear form performed better. Given the selected functional form, the parameter estimates for continuous variables are interpreted as elasticity, in the case of income (log-linear) and as percent effects on WTP of marginal changes in the other continuous variables (semi-log). With respect to dummy variables (semi-log), the formula put forward by Halvorsen and Palmquist (1980) was used to calculate the percentage effect on WTP of a change from 0 to 1 in the value of each dummy.

According to Wolf (1986), explicitly weighting individual observations to take into account research quality is current practice in meta-analysis. One of the main effects of different levels of research quality in the reviewed studies was the effect of small sample sizes in leading to low precision of WTP estimates (Santos 1997). Because different studies were quite uneven in this respect, it would be advisable to weight individual observations according to sample size. However, weighted-least-squares (WLS) estimators did not prove significantly different from OLS ones and did not improve statistical significance. Hence, only the OLS results are presented here.

Three outlier observations were identified, for which the residuals were consistently larger than twice the estimated standard deviation of the random term, whatever the specification assayed. All these outliers were associated with low precision of WTP estimation. Thus, they were deleted. As no

Table 14.3 Definition and sample means of the variables used in the analysis

Name	Definition	Sample mean[a]
Dependent variable: log (WTP)	WTP is the sample mean of willingness-to-pay for the landscape change on a per-year per-household basis converted into 1996 £s by using the 1996 consumer-price index for the respective country (ONS 1997a and UN 1995) and the appropriate exchange rate against sterling (average of 1994/96 rates; ONS 1997b)	49.726[b]
Conservation status of the area (proxy for quality & scarcity)	Categorial variable comprising the following 3 categories:	
(1) Conservation or recreational site	Small sites with a recreational or scientific interest, like SSSI or nature reserves; some include quite unique assets (e.g. vegetation of Upper Teesdale SSSI), but people tend to perceive them as having many substitutes even at the regional level	0.063
(2) ESA or NP	Highly cherished regional agricultural landscapes as those included in and characterising particular ESAs and NPs; much larger scale than the former; generally perceived by the public as scarce at the regional level	0.730
(3) Ordinary or mixed landscapes	Ordinary agricultural landscapes or areas including both cherished landscapes and ordinary ones whatever the geographical scope: local, regional and national landscapes (this is the omitted category).	0.207
Unique	Dichotomous variable =1 for landscapes that are absolutely unique and have no adequate substitutes at the national level	0.127
Nationwide scope	Dichotomous variable defining the geographical scope of the change; =1 for nationwide programmes	0.175
Qualitative change	Categorial variable comprising the following 3 categories:	
(1) Gradual, continuous change	Gradual changes where general landscape character is not completely altered; some attributes decline progressively as a consequence of changing farming practice or farm abandonment (the omitted category)	0.715
(2) Considerable change in character	Abrupt changes where the landscape character is completely modified, as those resulting from: conversion of heath into arable, flooding by sea, afforestation and scattered, light housing development	0.190
(3) Moderate/heavy development	Abrupt changes resulting from moderate to heavy industrial, housing or commercial development of farmland	0.095
Substitution effects	Dichotomous variable=1 when the change was valued sequentially or as a share of a broader change; these scenarios yield sequentially or simultaneously disaggregated values, which reflect substitution effects between the changes at issue	0.238
Relationship between respondents and landscape	Categorial variable comprising the following 5 categories:	
(1) Mainly non-users	Respondents are national or regional residents who are valuing restricted areas not visited nor inhabited by most respondents; this category is known (in ESA surveys) as the 'general public'	0.286
(2) Foreign visitors	Respondents are visitors but most are foreign people	0.032
(3) Residents	National or regional residents valuing a landscape change to take place across all the country or region (omitted category)	0.063
(4) Local residents	Residents in the particular areas where a local landscape change is to take place	0.286
(5) Visitors	Visitors to the area	0.333

Table 14.3 Definition and sample means of the variables (cont.)

Name	Definition	Sample mean[a]
NIMBY (for 'not in my back yard')	Dichotomous variable =1 when preservation of farmland from development is valued by respondents who live next to the particular areas to be developed (interaction between the variables 'urban development' and 'local residents')	0.095
Log (income)	'Income' is the per-capita Gross Domestic Product at constant prices (1990 US$) for the country and the year of the survey (UN 1995, UN 1997, and ONS 1997b)	17.125[b]
DC (and IB) elicitation formats	Dichotomous variable =1 for the discrete choice (DC) and the iterative bidding (IB) CVM formats	0.302
Payment vehicle	Dichotomous variable =1 when the CVM scenario used tax payment vehicles	0.833
'Tokens' technique	Dichotomous variable =1 when the value of the change at issue was elicited as a share of the valuation of a broader change and the respondent was asked to completely apportion total value among all components	0.032
Questionnaire administration	Categorial variable comprising the following 3 categories:	
(1) On-site	On-site in-person interviews	0.365
(2) Home	Home in-person interviews	0.381
(3) Mail	Mail survey (omitted category)	0.254
Level of trimming	Continuous variable expressing the level of α used for the estimation of α-trimmed means of WTP from open-ended CVM data	0.833
Truncation	Dichotomous variable =1 when the cumulative distribution of the WTP amounts was truncated (generally at the highest bid) for estimating mean WTP from discrete-choice CVM data	0.048
Outliers	Dichotomous variable =1 when the estimation of mean WTP used a specific procedure to deal with outlier bids	0.242
UK	Dichotomous variable =1 for UK surveys	0.778
Year	Year of the survey	1992[c]

Notes:
a. means were estimated for those 63 observations (excluding 3 outliers) that were used to estimate the models.
b. sample mean of the original variable previous to the log transformation.
c. median.

satisfactory system of weights was arrived at, these individual observations would be given too much weight if included in an OLS model.[6]

It is well known that hypotheses tests based on OLS estimates are subject to bias in the presence of heteroskedasticity and autocorrelation. It is probable that several forms of heteroskedasticity are present in data sets, as this, including studies with different levels of research quality. Furthermore, the fact that several WTP estimates were drawn from each individual study gives a panel structure to our data, which creates potential for correlation among residuals of individual observations from the same study. Hence, resort was made to the technique proposed by Newey and West (1987) for robust estimation of the parameter variance–covariance matrix in the presence of many known forms of heteroskedasticity and autocorrelation. Newey–West (N–W) standard errors were used to calculate different t-ratios for the parameter estimates (as done, for the same resons, by Smith and Kaoru 1990). Table 14.4 presents both the ordinary (OLS-estimated) and N–W t-ratios (these latter in italics).

Some multicollinearity was expected, as, in a significant number of cases, different observations came from the same study, and hence share identical values for many independent variables. Yet, using the usual diagnostic procedures, no evidence was found of multicollinearity significantly degrading the model (Santos 1997).

Despite a relatively small sample size (63), 14 of the 16 variables in the most complete model in Table 14.4 (model 5) have statistically significant coefficients (one more is statistically significant if we use the N–W t-ratios). Hence, the remaining degrees of freedom clearly ensure that statistical tests have enough power to reject the null hypotheses.

There seems to be no large difference between the OLS and N–W t-ratios as regards the variables that were revealed to be statistically significant. However, there is a slight trend for the latter to yield improved levels of significance. This suggests that N–W statistics were correcting for part of the heteroskedasticity and autocorrelation due to the panel nature of data.

Some variables defined in Table 14.3 have not been retained in the final models presented in Table 14.4. These variables were revealed to have no significant effect on WTP, and most of them led to serious multicollinearity problems, by significantly inflating the variance of parameter estimates for the other variables in the model. These multicollinearity problems and the low ratio of observations to variables led us to drop these insignificant variables even at the cost of some specification bias. The fact that model (5) in Table 14.4 is quite robust to the dropping of independent variables (compare different columns in this Table) suggests that this bias is not severe.

Variables dropped to estimate the final models were: (1) 'local residents' and 'visitors' (hence the omitted category now incorporates these categories as well); (2) 'payment vehicle'; (3) the categorial variable 'questionnaire administration' as a whole; (4) the 'outliers' variable; (5) the 'UK' variable. In particular, the non-significance of (3) raises an interesting issue. In fact, it is at variance with a generally held opinion according to which sample selection would generally inflate WTP estimates based on mail surveys. The self-administered nature of mail surveys would be the reason for this (Mitchell and Carson 1989). In mail surveys, respondents can read the whole questionnaire before deciding whether to participate; hence, it is probable that only those more interested in the theme will reply; and these have higher-than-average valuations. Our result of non-significance of the 'questionnaire administration' variable accords with Hanley et al.'s (1996a) conclusions on the same issue.

The non-significance of the 'on-site' variable shows that interviewing visitors on-site, often just after they had used the site, seems not to inflate WTP, differently from what had been suggested e.g. by Harris et al. (1989).

The non-significance of the UK variable is also interesting, as it suggests that the results of the analysis are transferable across different cultural contexts. However, this conclusion should be considered with caution because most WTP estimates come from UK surveys and the test only checks for differences between the UK and the other countries altogether.

A Meta-Analytical Model of WTP for Landscape Changes

The independent variables in our most complete model (model 5 in Table 14.4) can be classified into three groups: variables describing the landscape change (or 'landscape' variables); variables describing the surveyed population and its relationship to the area (or 'population' variables); and variables describing the survey and estimation techniques used in the study (or 'study' variables). Variables in the first two groups were expected to have 'legitimate' effects on WTP. On the other hand, significant effects of 'study' variables could be interpreted as reliability problems, especially in the absence of a clear reason to prefer one of the methodological options at issue (e.g., OE vs. DC formats). Hence, we compare next the explanatory power of each of these groups of variables.

A comparison between columns (1) and (5a) in Table 14.4 enables us to conclude that adding the groups of variables 'landscape' and 'population' altogether to the 'study' variables significantly raises the explanatory power of the model (compare the adjusted R^2). Adding the 'landscape' variables alone to the other two groups (compare columns 2 and 5a) also improves the model, and the same happens when one adds the 'population' variables alone to the remaining two groups (compare columns 3 and 5a). All these increments in explanatory power are statistically significant at any of the usual levels of probability (F-test for joint significance of groups of variables). Hence, as expected from theory, the type of landscape change and the characteristics of the surveyed population do matter in explaining differences in WTP for conservation.

On the other hand, comparing the models in columns (4) and (5a) demonstrates that adding the group of 'study' variables to 'landscape' and 'population' variables also significantly improves the explanatory power of the model. This indicates the importance of different methodological options in leading to differences in WTP estimates.

Table 14.4 Regression of log (WTP) on variables describing the landscape, the population and the elicitation/estimation techniques

Independent variables	Model					
	(1)	(2)	(3)	(4)	(5a)	(5b)[c]
Constant	-7.491 (-0.121)[a] (-0.106)[b]	-226.595 (-2.962) (-1.757)	-42.307 (-0.426) (-0.452)	-242.450 (-2.106) (-3.465)	-160.757 (-2.292) (-2.891)	
• *Landscape type, landscape change and substitution effects:*						
Conservation or recreational site			-1.541 (-3.575) (-4.310)	-0.487 (-0.885) (-1.536)	-0.705 (-2.101) (-2.452)	-0.506
ESA or NP			1.128 (3.771) (3.214)	0.414 (1.094) (2.482)	0.624 (2.675) (4.598)	0.866
Unique			-0.556 (-1.178) (-1.135)	0.634 (1.231) (2.006)	0.466 (1.468) (1.976)	0.594
Nationwide scope			0.925 (3.249) (4.055)	1.185 (4.104) (6.228)	1.248 (6.713) (7.032)	2.483
Considerable change in character			1.279 (2.700) (2.556)	0.228 (0.436) (0.716)	0.324 (1.018) (1.782)	0.383
Moderate/heavy development			1.893 (2.669) (3.274)	0.483 (0.610) (1.103)	0.721 (1.510) (1.805)	1.056
Substitution effects			-0.213 (-0.812) (-0.809)	-0.915 (-3.472) (-3.719)	-0.398 (-2.325) (-2.192)	-0.328
• *Surveyed population:*						
NYMBY		1.640 (3.026) (1.997)		2.234 (3.921) (7.520)	1.441 (4.027) (3.576)	3.225
Mainly non-users		-1.002 (-4.294) (-3.287)		-0.774 (-4.071) (-3.789)	-0.693 (-5.535) (-5.138)	-0.500
Foreign visitors		-2.053 (-3.403) (-8.443)		-3.024 (-5.216) (-11.460)	-2.390 (-6.383) (-12.340)	-0.908
log(income)		0.858 (1.731) (2.682)		0.263 (0.593) (1.243)	0.565 (2.087) (6.597)	
• *Survey and estimation effects:*						
DC and IB elicitation format	1.486 (5.222) (6.905)	1.076 (4.294) (6.488)	1.115 (5.589) (7.599)		0.970 (7.321) (6.087)	1.638
Level of trimming (OE data)	-0.074 (-1.334) (-1.195)	-0.047 (-1.005) (-1.272)	-0.110 (-3.036) (-2.684)		-0.074 (-3.048) (-4.495)	
Truncation (DC data)	0.130 (0.214) (0.898)	0.946 (1.894) (2.634)	-0.468 (-1.114) (-1.734)		-0.187 (-0.691) (-0.860)	-0.171
'Tokens' technique	-2.140 (-3.050) (-11.031)	-1.432 (-2.506) (-4.915)	-2.045 (-4.442) (-12.814)		-1.272 (-4.117) (-7.404)	-0.720
• *Year*	0.005 (0.170) (0.149)	0.111 (2.918) (1.742)	0.022 (0.446) (0.474)	0.122 (2.127) (3.535)	0.079 (2.267) (2.866)	

*Table 14.4 Regression of log (WTP) on variables describing the landscape,
the population and the elicitation/estimation techniques (cont.)*

	Model					
	(1)	(2)	(3)	(4)	(5a)	(5b)[c]
Sample size	63	63	63	63	63	
R^2	0.46	0.69	0.82	0.81	0.94	
Adjusted R^2	0.41	0.64	0.78	0.76	0.92	

Notes:
a. Ordinary t-ratios computed in the usual way are presented in parenthesis.
b. Parentheses in italic represent the t-ratios estimated using the Newey–West (1987) heteroskedasticity and autocorrelation-consistent covariance matrix.
c. Column (5b) presents the interpretation of the parameter estimates for dummy variables in model 5 in terms of percent effect on WTP of a *ceteris paribus* change from 0 to 1 in each particular variable; figures in this column were calculated from regression coefficients according to a formula put forward by Halvorsen and Palmquist (1980). The parameter estimates for continuous dependent variables should be interpreted as usual, that is: (1) as an elasticity when the specification is log-linear (income, in our case); (2) as percentage effect on WTP of a small change in the independent variable when the specification is semi-log (level of trimming, year).

An extremely large R^2 characterises our most complete model (0.94 or 0.91 after adjusting for degrees of freedom). This is much larger than the R^2 obtained in previous meta-analyses of valuation studies,[7] which suggests CVM estimates of WTP for landscape conservation are even more predictable than estimates of recreation values reviewed in these previous meta-analyses. Differently from these, our meta-analysis reviewed value estimates with a significant non-use component. Hence, it does not support the idea that estimates of non-use values are intrinsically unreliable.

Predictability of CVM landscape benefits is a clear indication that our WTP sample means do not suffer from non-biasing forms of unreliability (those related with random answering and sampling variance). Yet, the fact, just referred to, of WTP estimates being sensitive to different methodological options may indicate the presence of biasing forms of unreliability.

Our best model of CVM estimates of WTP for landscape conservation is presented in columns (5a) and (5b) in Table 14.4. An interesting characteristic of this model is its negative and large-in-modulus intercept; taking into account functional form, this means WTP is close to zero at the origin of all variables. This demonstrates that independent variables are the main determinants of WTP, which rules out the existence of any cross-study trend for a quasi-constant 'average' WTP amount.[8]

A thorough assessment of the validity and reliability of CVM landscape benefit estimates requires us to undertake a closer inspection of the independent variables in our best model. Hence, let us start by considering the 'landscape' variables.

The categorial variable describing the conservation status of the area behaved as expected. In fact, WTP for conservation at small conservation or recreational sites was 51 per cent smaller than WTP for the omitted category (larger areas with either ordinary or mixed landscapes); along the same lines, WTP for conservation in ESAs or NPs was 87 per cent larger than that for the omitted category (column 5b of Table 14.4). Regional scope and substitutability of the different areas clearly seem to be the determinant factors explaining this pattern of relative values.

Also according to prior expectations, uniqueness of a landscape at the national level raised WTP for conservation (by 59 per cent; cf. column 5b).

Nationwide conservation schemes attracted WTP amounts 248 per cent higher than similar non-national schemes. This scope variable had a very significant effect on WTP. It should be noted, however, that WTP for a national scheme, as implied by these results, is only 3.5 times higher than WTP for a comparable non-national scheme. This is much smaller than the ratio of a national scheme's acreage to a non-national scheme's acreage. So, WTP for conservation schemes is clearly non-additive with respect to acreage. Substitution effects between different areas may explain this non-additivity.

Likewise, WTP for a conservation scheme is 33 per cent lower when this is valued as part of a more inclusive package or when it is sequentially valued. This is clearly consistent with Hoehn's thesis of the prevalence of substitution in valuation across most application contexts (section 3.3).

The last 'landscape' variable is the categorial variable describing the magnitude of the qualitative change under valuation. The omitted category represents gradual, generally small, changes that do not completely obliterate pre-existing landscape character. Thus, it was expected that the other two categories of change would attract higher WTP amounts; and that such amounts would increase with the magnitude of the qualitative change. This is actually observed in Table 14.4: WTP to avoid 'considerable changes in character' is 38 per cent higher than that for the omitted category and WTP to avoid 'moderate to heavy urban development' is 106 per cent higher.

As regards the 'landscape' variables, we can, therefore, conclude that the signs (and, when applicable, also the compared sizes) of the effects of these variables on WTP are in accordance with prior expectations and that all these effects are significant at least using N–W t-ratios. This provides detailed evidence on the theoretical validity of the reviewed benefit estimates.

Let us now consider the effects of the 'population' variables. The coefficient for the variable 'mainly non-users' shows us that national or regional residents value non-visited areas of the countryside at about one half of the average valuation by those who visit or live in these areas. Similarly, when non-national citizens visiting an area are the majority of the surveyed population, WTP for conservation declines by 91 per cent with respect to comparable surveys of national visitors and residents.

A particular category of respondents has a rather high WTP for landscape conservation: those who live next to farmland areas threatened by urban development. It is probably a kind of 'not-in-my-backyard' (NIMBY) syndrome that, in this case, leads local residents to value the conservation of the current landscape 323 per cent higher than average WTP for landscape conservation in other contexts.

Many socio-economic variables characterising the respondents could not be included in the model because they were not reported by the individual studies. Even the average income of respondents was not reported by many studies. Because the income variable is a crucial one in a WTP model, a proxy for the average income of respondents was devised: the per-capita GDP at constant prices for the country and year of the survey (for a definition see Table 14.3). Although this is only a rough approximation, it enables us to control, in part, for the difference in purchase power across countries and over the 16 year period covered by the reviewed studies. The coefficient for log(income) is interpreted as the income-flexibility of WTP. It is, therefore, very interesting that this flexibility estimate (0.565) falls on the middle of the range of estimates of income-flexibility of WTP from most valuation studies (Kriström and Riera 1996).

The fact that 'population' variables yielded significant coefficients, with signs according to previous expectations, is clearly reassuring with respect to the theoretical validity of CVM landscape benefit estimates.

The next group of variables is the one characterising the elicitation and estimation techniques used in the particular study: the 'study' variables. One of the crucial variables in this group is the dummy variable coding the discrete-choice (DC) plus iterative bidding (IB) formats as opposed to OE formats. In similar circumstances, DC + IB formats yielded higher WTP estimates than OE formats. In the reviewed studies, the DC + IB format had, indeed, the effect of raising WTP estimates by 164 per cent with respect to OE formats.[9] Since we have no way of deciding which format is less biased (see discussion in section 14.1) the divergence between formats is interpreted as a reliability problem. This problem seems to be magnified by the large non-use component of landscape values, as the estimated divergence is higher in our case than in the meta-analyses by Bateman et al. (1995) and Walsh et al. (1992), where most estimates include use values alone.[10]

There are two further reliability problems. One is the effect of the level of α-trimming of OE data. Model 5 indicates that, for each 1-per-cent increase in α, WTP is reduced by 7.5 per cent. Mitchell and Carson (1989) suggested the use of trimmed means as a non-arbitrary way of dealing with outliers. It is, however, obvious that the level of trimming remains an arbitrary decision with a rather large impact on the final estimate.

The other problem is whether to truncate the WTP distribution. Many authors using the logit approach have truncated this distribution at the highest bid amount before evaluating its integral. On the other hand, Hanemann's and Cameron's estimators (non-truncated) make the estimated WTP heavily dependent on the tails of the logistic distribution. None of the approaches seems more soundly justified on theoretical or empirical grounds. Hence, (though not statistically significant) the difference of 17 per cent between truncated and non-truncated WTP means represents a reliability problem.[11]

The 'tokens' elicitation technique also has an important effect on WTP estimates. This technique is used when the good is valued as a share of a more complete package, which may imply substitution between the several elements in the package. Furthermore, in some questionnaires, respondents are asked to apportion a given amount of points, or tokens (e.g. 100), corresponding to the value of the package over all component goods, including the good of interest for the survey.[12] This complete character of the apportionment reduces WTP for the particular good by 72 per cent (on top of the 33 per cent reduction due to substitution effects). Notwithstanding, this may be not a reliability issue, as the 'tokens' technique seems to be the preferred strategy to secure simultaneously disaggregated values.

The 'year' variable has a significant and positive effect on WTP. For our best model, this effect means a linear growth rate of about 8 per cent a year. Note that this estimate varies from 0.5 per cent to 12 per cent a year depending on specification (Table 14.4).[13] It is, however, probable that 8 per cent is the best estimate for the growth rate of WTP, as it is the one for which more different effects (e.g., that of increasing purchase power) are accounted for by separate variables. Thus, ignoring the possibility of omitted variables also changing during the period (cf. Smith and Kaoru 1990), the 8 per cent growth rate in landscape values is interpreted as resulting from the combined effect of changes in underlying preferences and in the scarcity of good-quality landscapes.

14.4 ASSESSING THE TRANSFERABILITY OF CVM LANDSCAPE BENEFIT ESTIMATES: A META-ANALYTICAL APPROACH

A benefit transfer is the application, with the necessary adjustments, of a WTP estimate from an original study to a new context, where such an estimate is required to evaluate a policy. This is a typical secondary use of the original study for a different purpose. The possibility of accurate benefit transfers is obviously very interesting for policy makers, in that it provides the opportunity for building appropriate benefit estimates for policy evaluation, whilst saving money and time costs associated with undertaking a new valuation study for every single policy decision. The interest of government agencies in benefit transfers has been noticed by many authors in the valuation field, and some main agencies currently commissioning valuation studies are shifting their funding policies towards research on benefit transfers.[14] Given the time and expertise requirements of original valuation studies, the possibility of accurately transferring benefits across different contexts is a pre-condition for systematically using non-market benefit estimates in the cost-benefit evaluation of conservation policy.

Despite this practical interest in benefit transfers, the few systematic assessments of benefit transferability completed to date are not very optimistic with respect to the possibility of accurate benefit transfers.[15] Prospects for accurate transfers appear as even more uncertain with respect to non-use values, for which the validity and reliability issues associated with the original estimates themselves still compound the more general transferability problems (Brookshire and Neill, 1992).

It is, however, possible that one of the reasons for so many authors viewing so negatively the prospects for benefit transferability lies in the general method that has been adopted to assess these prospects. This method may be labelled as the 'search for similar conditions': 'original studies' are looked for which represent conditions as close as possible to the conditions characterising the policy problem at hand. Moreover, the original studies are subject to validity and reliability checks before they may be used as a basis for benefit transfers. This approach is followed, e.g., by Boyle and Bersgstrom (1992) and Desvousges et al. (1992). Not surprisingly, 'original studies' matching such strict conditions usually do not exist in the relevant literature. Hence, the accuracy of benefit transfers is always open to question, because the effects on WTP estimates of differences between the 'original study' and the policy context are unknown. In this context, Boyle and Bergstrom (1992) proposed two important tasks for future assessments of transferability. The first is to compare benefit transfers with original valuation studies carried out, for this purpose, at the 'policy site'. The second is to expand the use of meta-analysis in identifying the variables with an effect on WTP estimates and measuring the magnitude of such effects.

On the other hand, Loomis (1992) argued that what should be transferred are demand or valuation functions rather than the benefit estimates themselves. If these functions were transferable, we could predict the benefit estimate to be arrived at by an original study carried out at the 'policy site' by evaluating the relevant independent variables at this site and by entering these values into a valuation function transferred from existing studies.

Loomis applied this approach to the assessment of the transferability of multi-site travel-cost models across different rivers within the same state (Oregon, USA). He used a split-sample procedure. First, he dropped the observation from a particular river (the nth river), and then estimated the multi-site model without this observation (the n-1 model). Second, the (n-1) model was used to estimate the consumer surplus for the nth river. Third, a full multi-site model was estimated, including data from all n rivers (the n model), which was then used to estimate consumer surplus for the nth river. Fourth, estimates for the nth river yielded by the (n-1) and the (n) models were compared. If they were sufficiently close, this would mean the consumer surplus for the river at issue could have been accurately predicted from a multi-site travel cost demand function estimated from the other (n-1) rivers plus additional information on the independent variables characterising the nth river. Repeating the procedure for all 10 rivers, Loomis found that, in 90 per cent of the cases, the (n-1) multi-site model enabled the analyst to predict the consumer surplus for each river with an error of less than 10 per cent. Using average consumer surplus across cases to predict the consumer surplus for an individual case yielded much less accurate predictions (error usually above 10 per cent and reaching more than 25 per cent).

The original split-sample method idealised by Loomis may be adjusted and applied to a set of CVM WTP estimates, using a meta-analytical model of these estimates. This is the approach followed in this section to assess the transferability of CVM landscape benefit estimates. This approach represents a combination of the two tasks suggested by Boyle and Bergstrom (1992). First, predictions (transfers) from the meta-analytical function can be directly compared with values from original studies, to assess the accuracy of these predictions. Second, as seen in section 14.3, the coefficients of the meta-analytical function itself allow us to identify (and measure the effects of) those variables that control for the differences across studies.

The direct use of the meta-analytical function as a predictive tool represents an approach to benefit transfer that is quite different from the 'search-for-identical-conditions' approach discussed above. In fact, whereas the latter searches for an ideally identical case, the former aims at controlling for differences, in which case it is important to include in the analysis some diversity of valuation conditions.

Previous meta-analysts of the valuation literature have shown some reluctance in using meta-analytical functions as predictive devices and have limited themselves to commenting on the effects of particular variables on WTP (an exercise similar to the one carried out in section 14.3). In particular, Smith and Kaoru (1990) were especially cautious in restricting the use of meta-analysis in benefit transfer to a consistency check of usual transfer processes. Although proposing the use of meta-analysis for predictive purposes, Walsh et al. (1992) did not engage in such predictions. Instead, they used regression coefficients arrived at in their meta-analysis to discuss the particular adjustment factors proposed by a previous literature review of recreation demand studies. This use of meta-analysis to comment on adjustment factors used in practice for benefit transfers may be a very useful exercise. For example, using our meta-analysis of CVM landscape benefit estimates, one could adjust a WTP estimate from a visitor survey to predict the estimate that would be yielded by a survey of the general public using the same CVM scenario. It would only be required to use the transformed coefficient for the 'mainly non-users' variable (in column 5b of Table 14.4) to deflate the mean WTP estimate from the visitor survey.

As noted before, the issue of whether benefit estimates from a particular study can be accurately predicted from the results of other studies is an empirical one, and should be empirically addressed. Loomis split-sample method suggests a straightforward way to carry out such empirical tests of transferability. Of course, these are not validity and reliability tests of the original estimates. Hence, they cannot ensure the validity and reliability of the transferred benefit estimates. However, this is a separate issue, which should be separately addressed. By accepting this, most of the objections to the direct use of meta-analytical functions as predictive devices, for purposes of assessing the accuracy of benefit transfers, are immediately removed.

In this section, the approach initiated by Smith and Kaoru (1990) was expanded by using the meta-analytical function to predict the very WTP estimates arrived at by the individual studies. Using a split-sample approach, the meta-analytical function was first estimated with all observations from a particular survey dropped from the data. Then, this function was used to predict the WTP estimates in these dropped observations, by entering the values of the independent variables characterising these observations. Eventually, the predicted estimates were compared with the original ones to assess the accuracy of the predictions/transfers. These steps were repeated for all 37 surveys in our 19 CVM landscape studies. Table 14.5 presents the results of this transferability study.

Column (2) of this Table presents the number of cases for which original estimates were predicted with the margin of error indicated in column (1). Seven of these cases should not be used in our transferability assessment[16] and were, therefore, excluded. Thus, we have now only the 59 predicted-observed comparisons presented in column (3). As a global assessment of the accuracy of meta-analytic-based transfers of landscape benefits, we would say that 44 per cent of the estimates could have been predicted, with an error of less than 30 per cent. If one accepts a deviation of up to 50 per cent (still within the bounds proposed by Cummings et al. 1986, and Mitchell and Carson 1989) then, about 75 per cent of the estimates could have been accurately predicted without the original survey.

These transfers are not as precise as the ones secured by Loomis (1992), which had an error of less than 10 per cent in 90 per cent of the cases. However, Loomis's study covers a set of more homogeneous goods (rivers within the same state) and used exactly the same technique and models to produce the 'original' and the predicted values, which obviously increases the consistency between these values. Hence, it is not comparable with the transferability study reported here.

In general, we can, therefore, judge the predictive performance of our meta-analytical model as good, which is reassuring as regards the transferability of landscape benefit estimates.

Table 14.5 Assessment of the transferability of landscape benefit estimates

Percentage deviation of predictions with respect to observed values	with model (5a) in Table 14.4[a]			with WTP means for the closest class of landscape change		
	N of obs.	N of obs.[b]	% [b]	N of obs.	N of obs.[b]	% [b]
(1)	(2)	(3)	(4)	(5)	(6)	(7)
within 10 %	11	11	18.6	3	3	5.1
from 10 to less than 20 %	5	5	8.5	5	5	8.5
from 20 to less than 30 %	10	10	16.9	5	5	8.5
from 30 to less than 40 %	11	11	18.6	4	4	6.8
from 40 to less than 50 %	7	7	11.9	9	9	15.3
from 50 to less than 100 %	9	8	13.6	13	12	20.3
from 100 to less than 200 %	7	6	10.2	8	7	11.9
more than 200 %	6	1	1.7	19	14	23.7
within 30%	26	26	44.1	13	13	22.0
within 50%	44	44	74.6	26	26	44.1
total	66	59	100.0	66	59	100.0

Notes:
a. The model was estimated 37 times, dropping each time all observations from a particular survey to predict WTP observations from this particular survey.
b. The figures in these columns exclude the 3 outliers already excluded from the estimation of models in Table 14.4; also excluded were 4 observations for which the full specification in column (5a) of Table 14.4 cannot be estimated.

The performance of the meta-analytical approach to benefit transfers can be compared with the performance of the 'search-for-similar-conditions' approach. Hence, we took the average of WTP estimates within each class of landscape change in Table 14.2 and used this average as a prediction for individual estimates within the same class. Each of the 59 predicted estimates was then compared with the original estimate.[17] Column (6) of Table 14.5 presents the distribution of the 59 predicted-observed comparisons, sorted by the same classes of deviation with respect to the original estimate. Hence, the 'similar conditions/average class' approach exhibits a much lower performance than the proposed meta-analytical approach. For the former, only 44 per cent (as opposed to 75 per cent, for the latter) of the transferred benefits were within a 50 per cent deviation from the original estimate. Hence, the direct use of the meta-analytical function as a predictive tool is recommended as more accurate an approach to landscape benefit transfer.[18]

The ultimate test of the accuracy of benefit transfers is the comparison between the transferred benefit estimate with the original study's estimate, with respect to the precision of these estimates. Only this comparison enables one to assess the added precision that is gained by carrying out an original study at the 'policy site', instead of relying upon a benefit transfer.

For the original studies reporting CIs (or for which CIs were possible to compute), we note that 95-per-cent CIs for WTP were within a 50-per-cent deviation from the sample means in 86 per cent of the cases. Comparing this 95-per-cent probability for original studies' CIs with the 75 per cent probability of transferred estimates being within a 50-per-cent deviation from the original study's point estimate, we conclude that, as long as precision is concerned, original studies' estimates performed only slightly better than transferred ones. Furthermore, one should notice that only 86 per cent of the original estimates yielded 95-per-cent CIs within a 50-per-cent deviation from the sample means. It is, therefore, surprising how little improvement is yielded by original studies over the level of precision already achievable with benefit transfers.

The level of accuracy obtained in transferring CVM landscape benefit estimates is remarkable, especially if one takes into account the fact that non-use values are an important component of the transferred benefit estimates. This conclusion is clearly more optimistic about the possibility of accurate benefit transfers than conclusions from previous studies, namely with respect to the transferability of non-use values. However, remember that the issue of this section is only that of predictability. Whether the existing estimates from original studies (hence also the transferred ones) are valid and reliable measurements of the benefit concept at issue is still open to question. In relation to this, the evidence on theoretical validity and reliability of CVM landscape benefit estimates in previous sections is somehow reassuring. Yet, important reliability issues remain unsolved, such as the divergence between the OE and DC formats. Again, note that this is not a transferability problem: once determined the appropriate CVM format, the meta-analytical model enables us to accurately predict the estimate that would result from an original study carried out under known circumstances and using that format.

Moreover, choosing an appropriate format is a problem also for the original study since the divergence is in the original studies' results, not in the meta-analysis.

A similar issue is that of the decision between independent, sequential or simultaneously disaggregated valuations of a landscape change. Again, a choice has to be made in designing original studies as well. However, this choice is simpler than the DC/OE one, as the policy context for the cost–benefit analysis will dictate the appropriate elicitation procedure. For example, for the case studies in this book, the selection of an optimal programme mix for a conservation scheme clearly requires sequentially disaggregated values for landscape attributes (section 6.2).

NOTES

1. Namely, Mitchell and Carson's (1989) Appendix A, Bonnieux et al. (1992), Römer and Pommerehne (1992), Mäntymaa et al. (1992), Hoevenagel et al. (1992), Navrud and Strand (1992), Johansson and Kriström (1992), Turner et al. (1992), Bennett (1992), Shechter (1992) and Bateman et al. (1994).
2. Such as Dubgaard & Nielsen (1989), Hanley (1991), and Whitby (1994a).
3. Sweden, the UK, Austria, France, Spain, Portugal and the USA.
4. Price indices for the seven countries were built from ONS (1997a) and UN (1995); average exchange rates for the years of 1994–1996 (ONS 1997b) were used, to avoid that an excessive weight was given to the increase in the value of the sterling over the last months of 1996.
5. For a more detailed discussion, see Santos (1997).
6. Note this is not ad hoc exclusion on quality grounds: a clear relationship between sample size and sampling variance was already empirically established for this set of studies (Santos 1997), and these observations corresponded to particularly low-precision estimates.
7. The previous three meta-analyses of valuation literatures presented R^2 for their best models that are on the 0.35–0.45 range (Smith and Kaoru 1990; Walsh et al. 1992) or slightly exceeds 0.60 (Bateman et al. 1995). All are clearly larger than the R^2 usually obtained in individual studies' OLS valuation functions, which should not surprise us since meta-analytical models are models of sample means of WTP, and these means are already free from inter-individual variation. In this sense, mean WTP estimates are more predictable than individual WTP answers.
8. Differently from this, in Bateman et al.'s (1995) meta-analytical model the strongest explanatory variable is the intercept. As suggested by Bateman, this weight of the intercept could be explained by the fact that respondents replied with what they perceive as a 'fair price' for the good instead of WTP for it. Besides, the use of an entrance fee as the payment vehicle in the reviewed studies could suggest clues for what such 'fair price' might be (cf. also Brookshire et al. 1976). Bateman et al. noticed that the regression intercept is actually very close to possible figures that might be acting as such clues. Hanley and Ruffell (1993) found that the parking fee is a strong WTP predictor in their study, which may have a similar explanation. In our case, the much larger explanatory weight of independent variables as compared to the intercept suggests that the income-tax payment vehicle (used in 83 per cent of the reviewed estimates) does not suggest so obvious a value clue.
9. This may be compared with results by Bateman et al. (1995) and Walsh et al. (1992). Bateman et al. (1995) estimated that non-OE formats yield WTP amounts 125 per cent higher than the OE format. In the literature reviewed by Walsh et al., if we work out the difference between DC and OE and divide by average WTP for the OE format, then we

find that the DC format increases WTP estimates by only 25 per cent. Although all these and our estimates consistently report higher WTP estimates for the DC and associated formats, there are considerable differences between the estimated size of this effect.

10. See note 9.

11. Notice that this percentage difference between truncated and non-truncated estimates is on the same order of magnitude as that found by Bateman et al. (1993) and Bowker and Stoll (1988). The former found that the estimate truncated at the maximum bid reduced average WTP by 21 per cent with respect to a non-truncated estimate (log-logistic model); the latter found that, in average (for a set of functional forms and distributions), truncation at the highest bid reduced the WTP estimate by 29 per cent with respect to a 3-times-higher truncation point.

12. The 'tokens' name was used to designate this technique by Willis and Benson in the context of a travel cost application; see Benson (1992) and Willis and Benson (1989). The 'tokens' approach has also been applied by Bergin (1993), to determine the share of landscape benefits in the whole value of the recreational experience. Willis et al. (1993) used this approach, in a general public survey, to apportion the value of the ESA scheme in England as a whole to individual ESAs.

13. The two models yielding lower estimates for this growth rate (columns 1 and 3) have in common the fact that they do not account for 'population' variables. This indicates that, over the 16-years period, surveys shifted towards populations with lower valuations, as suggested by the negative correlation between 'NIMBY' and 'year' ($r = -0.74$).

14. Cf. Desvousges et al. (1992); Brookshire and Neill (1992); Garrod and Willis (1994); and Bateman et al. (1995).

15. For reviews of these assessments, see Brookshire and Neill (1992); Garrod and Willis (1994); Willis and Garrod (1995). Boyle and Bergstrom (1992) provide an interesting formal presentation of the issue and a research agenda for future assessments of benefit transferability.

16. That is, three estimates that corresponded to the outliers already excluded from the meta-analysis on grounds of very large sampling variances; plus four other estimates. These last were not used because the meta-analytical function could not be estimated dropping these observations.

17. For the sake of comparability, the same seven observations have been excluded from the analysis.

18. Of course, the 'similar conditions' approach was not strictly applied here, because (as usual) there is no study in the whole literature matching the most stringent requirements of 'sameness' proposed by the approach in its purest form.

15. Valuation and Cost–Benefit Analysis of Multi-Attribute Change: Theoretical and Methodological Conclusions

Most landscape changes are multidimensional, which has important implications for the design and evaluation of conservation policy. Chapters 3 and 6 discuss a number of theoretical and methodological issues raised by the valuation and cost–benefit analysis of multi-attribute changes. The present chapter discusses the main conclusions of the research presented in this book as regards these theoretical and methodological issues. There is not a concern for exhaustiveness, as many conclusions were already discussed throughout the book. Instead, we focus the present dicussion on those particular conclusions of this research that seemed the most significant for the multi-attribute issue and on some unsolved problems requiring further research.

15.1 VALUING MULTI-ATTRIBUTE CHANGE

The importance of demand-interactions between goods is an old and central notion in economics. However, it was only in the 1980s that the work of Hoehn, Randall and colleagues fully introduced the idea of interactions in valuation to the non-market valuation community and proposed methods to render this idea empirically operative in this particular area of economic research. These authors clearly demonstrated that controlling for substitution effects between policy components is an absolute requirement for the valid modelling of WTP for multidimensional policies and, especially, for the valid aggregation and disaggregation of benefits of multidimensional policies over individual policy components. This section discusses our results on substitution effects with the aim of addressing four main issues, which constitute the next four sub-sections.

How Important is it to Control for Substitution Effects?

Our two case-studies demonstrate the practical importance of controlling for substitution effects in the valuation of multi-attribute landscape changes.

Ignoring these effects and aggregating independently valued attribute changes over attributes would lead, in these cases, to very biased estimates of the whole multi-attribute change's benefits: these would be overestimated by almost 80 per cent (D case) or 48 per cent (PG case). For policy-mixes including more than three programmes the independent-valuation-and-summation (IVS) bias will probably be larger (as suggested by Hoehn and Randall 1989, and Hoehn and Loomis 1993). Notwithstanding, the IVS currently is the routine approach to benefit aggregation over policy-components. The results in this book as well as Hoehn's stress, therefore, that the error so introduced in policy decision-making cannot be ignored. This is, however, a very difficult problem in practice, as we must decide how far we should go in considering other policies that are to be implemented before or simultaneously to the particular policy under evaluation, in order to account for all relevant policy interactions. It should be recognised that it is, at least, impractical to jointly consider all policies across all areas of governmental action.

Only Substitution Effects, or More Complex Structures of Valuation-Interactions between Attributes?

Based on the relationship between the substitution and the income effect derived in chapter 3, we know that landscape attributes that are complements or independent in utility can be compensated substitutes in valuation. Thus, assuming a strong income effect, substitution in valuation would be more frequent than complementarity, which provides the foundations for Hoehn's (1991) hypothesis of a generalised prevalence of substitution in valuation across all valuation contexts. Hoehn and colleagues submitted this hypothesis to the empirical test in two separate studies (Hoehn 1991 and Hoehn and Loomis 1993; cf. also chapter 3). The hypothesis was not rejected in either case. The two case-studies in this book allowed us to carry out a further test of Hoehn's hypothesis. In these cases, joint consumption of attributes belonging to the same cherished landscape (the D's or PG's) suggested that complementarity in utility between these attributes would be strong, even strong enough to offset the income effect, hence leading to compensated complementarity in valuation. This was, therefore, a 'difficult case' for Hoehn's hypothesis.

   Using models similar to Hoehn's (zero-intercept second-order-interaction models), only compensated substitution between attributes was found in both of our case-studies. However, specification tests shown that zero-intercept third-order-interaction models fitted the data better than Hoehn's-like models. This was particularly visible in the PG case-study. Differently from Hoehn's models, third-order multi-attribute valuation functions allow for each pair-wise substitution effect between programmes to vary along the valuation sequence. In both case-studies in this book, the estimated coefficient for this third-order interaction term turned out to be positive and very significant. In the D case, this coefficient was smaller in modulus than negative second-order interactions. Thus, substitution effects were observed all along the valuation sequence, although declining and becoming non-significant at the third step in the sequence. On the other hand, in the PG case, the coefficient for the third-order interaction term was larger in modulus than negative second-order interactions, and thus significant complementarity effects in valuation were observed at the third step in the sequence. This result represents, to the best of our knowledge, the first evidence on complementarity in valuation between components of a multidimensional environmental policy to be documented in the literature. It also leads us to qualify Hoehn's thesis of the prevalence of substitution in valuation across all valuation contexts.

The pattern of valuation interactions between policy components observed in both case-studies suggests that a general picture for the structure of such interactions should be more complex than that which is apparent from Hoehn's (1991) and Hoehn and Loomis's (1993) results. In fact, our general frame of this interaction structure should allow for complementarity effects at least at some steps in the sequence; thus, it should allow as well for varying substitution relationships along the sequence. The particular pattern of valuation interactions along the sequence observed in our case-studies may be explained in terms of a steep rise of complementarity in utility as the scheme's scope approaches completeness.[1] In the PG case, this rise would be sufficient to offset the income effect, hence generating compensated complementarity at the third step in the sequence. In the Dales case, this rise would not be strong enough for this. Earlier in the valuation sequence, in both cases, the income effect would be sufficiently strong to offset complementarity in utility and to cause substitution in valuation. Note that, as substitution in utility between landscape attributes was ruled out in both cases as extremely implausible, the observation of strong substitution effects at the second step implies non-trivial income effects.

Is there a Typical Aggregation Pattern for Each Class of Resource?

Randall suggested that, with future accumulation of empirical results such as Hoehn's, 'economists may start to get a feel for the magnitudes of the substitution relationships and the errors introduced by the IVS procedures in various environmental valuation contexts. If this happened, the accumulated empirical experience would provide correction factors that would enable' policy analysts to aggregate benefit estimates transferred from previous studies for deriving approximately valid benefit estimates for new composite policies (Randall 1991: 314–315).[2]

It is still too early, in terms of accumulated evidence, to know whether such empirical patterns of substitution relationships will emerge for different types of environmental resources. However, our two case-studies provided us with an excellent opportunity to comment on the prospects for such a pattern to emerge in the field of landscape change valuation, as both studies followed the same methodology, used similar CVM scenarios and were applied to somewhat similar areas. It would be, therefore, reasonable to expect that, if a common pattern is to emerge, then the comparison between our case-studies should reveal, at least partly, what such common pattern might be for this particular type of landscape change.

Although there are some common themes to both cases with respect to substitution relationships, the comparative evidence is mixed and by no means suggests the emergence of the sort of homogeneous pattern of substitution relationships that could be expected in such similar situations. As regards common themes, we observe that, in both cases, the pattern of substitution effects is characterised by a second-order substitution trend combined with a third-order complementarity trend; furthermore, IVS leads to significant over-estimations in both cases. Here the similarities end. In fact, the third-order interaction term is sufficiently strong to offset the second-order terms only in the PG; in the D, its only effect is to reduce the substitution effect from the second to the third step in the sequence. A significant quantitative difference is that IVS leads to overestimate benefits by almost 80 per cent in the D and only by less than 50 per cent in the PG.

The fact that so similar cases studied using exactly the same method do not yield closer structures of substitution effects may cast some doubts on the prospect for homogeneous patterns to emerge in the future, even for quite specific resource classes such as agricultural landscape changes in upland areas. However, the accumulation of evidence might make it possible to identify general patterns for different types of resource and policy even if these patterns happen to be less homogeneous than we initially expected. Meanwhile, uncertainty about the correct aggregation structure for each case (thus, potentially large biases in aggregating transferred benefits to construct benefit estimates for composite policies) leads to advise the (expensive) solution of carrying out a new valuation study for each policy as the only IVS-bias-free solution.

Empirical Results and Demand Theory

Chapter 3 reviews several types of tests aiming at checking whether certain 'anomalies' observed in CVM studies can be interpreted as legitimate substitution effects and proposes a different type of test for the same purpose, which is based on the theoretical relationship between the income and the substitution effect. This test proceeds by checking whether both the sign and the size of the substitution effect are compatible with demand theory plus the known facts of the situation as regards substitutability in utility and size of the income effect. As discussed in chapter 3, only a stringent type of test such as this may carry the debate on 'anomalies' vs. substitution effects in CVM forward.

An important feature common to both case-studies in this book, which made it possible to carry out the proposed tests of demand theory, is that substitution in utility between landscape attributes could be ruled out a priori as extremely implausible on intuitive grounds. If substitution in utility is ruled out, the theoretical relationship between the income and the substitution effect, and the observation of strong substitution effects at the second step in the sequence, implied a non-trivial income effect. On the other hand, this was incompatible with the size of the income parameter in the multi-attribute valuation functions estimated from the same CVM data. This inconsistency between the income effect implied by the substitution effect and the estimated income parameter of the WTP model was confirmed by our re-interpretation of Hoehn's (1991) and Hoevenagel's (1996) results (see also Santos 1997).

An actual income effect larger than the one implied by the income parameter estimated from CVM data may be due to annual household income (elicited in CVM surveys) not reflecting the true budget constraint of respondents. This might occur because there are many long and medium-term expenditure commitments reducing respondents' actual discretionary income. Hence, in the short term (the relevant time-scale to answer to a CVM survey), incomplete multi-stage budgeting would characterise the consumer's constrained optimisation problem. There possibly are welfare-enhancing trade-offs to be made between amounts allocated, in previous budgeting stages, to different classes of goods (i.e.: between sub-budgets, or accounts). However, at least in the short term, these trade-offs are not possible, as previous budgeting decisions determine the overall allocation to the several accounts. Hence, when revealing WTP for a particular environmental good, respondents think as if they were 'taking money' from their account for say environmental conservation. This would cause a much larger income effect on the valuation of subsequent environmental goods than what could be expected if the individual was conceived as 'taking money' from his total annual income. The 'environmental account' is much smaller than, and not necessarily proportional to, total income. Thus entering total income in our CVM-based WTP models would lead to significantly biased estimates of the true income effect.

Though possibly accounting for the observed results with respect to the size of the income effect, incomplete multi-stage budgeting, as a different theory, raises a host of difficult questions for empirical valuation research and for welfare economics in general. A first question is how to specify the theory for it to be testable in a CVM setting. A second is whether this alternative theory, once correctly specified to be used in empirical research, would be sufficient to explain such large income effects as the ones observed in the CVM literature. A third is that short-term WTP for landscape changes based on incomplete trade-offs between classes of goods is possibly not valid a benefit estimate to assess landscape conservation policy, which, for several reasons, imply a long-term perspective (Santos 1997).

15.2 SEQUENTIAL COST–BENEFIT ANALYSIS FOR THE SELECTION OF OPTIMAL LANDSCAPES

Provided we can estimate continuous multi-attribute benefit and cost functions, the theoretical approach presented in section 6.1 to identify Pareto-optimal states of landscape is entirely applicable. However, because of practical constraints in information gathering, policy is usually evaluated within a simpler, discrete, setting, where some specified discrete changes in some particular attributes (i.e.: some 'programmes') are the only possibility. Within this discrete setting, the agency may want to select a programme-mix that is somehow optimal. Section 6.2 proposes a simple sequential cost–benefit procedure to solve this problem. This procedure delivers the best approximation to the Pareto-optimal state of landscape that is possible within this discrete setting. Sequential cost–benefit analysis was applied in both case-studies, with different degrees of success in determining the optimal programme-mix. We refer below to some of the achievements and difficulties with the proposed approach, as well as further research that is needed to address these difficulties. Particular emphasis is put on the most important problem with this discrete approach: the path-dependency of the optimum.[3]

In the D case, the particular configuration of sequential costs and benefits allowed us to avoid the path-dependency problem both for financial and social costs. This was not the case for the PG, where it was only possible to identify a unique optimal mix using financial costs. Even these modest achievements are dependent on using point estimates for sequential benefits. Substituting lower limits of 95 per cent CIs for point benefit estimates leads to path-dependency problems appearing in both case-studies, whatever the cost concept that is used. Even if all benefits were known with certainty, there would still be situations where, due to particular configurations of sequential costs and benefits, the path-dependency problem is unavoidable (this is the case in the PG with the social-cost concept). In these situations, the only way to determine the optimal programme-mix for a conservation scheme is to adopt the continuous approach. This is much more demanding an approach in terms of data gathering. The estimation of continuous multi-attribute benefit and cost functions will be explored in future research, as a way to solve the path-dependency problem. Moreover, this approach has the additional appeal of enabling the analyst to exactly determine the Pareto-optimal state of landscape in the continuous multi-attribute space, which is impossible within the discrete approach, explored in the case-studies, where only an approximation to the optimum is possible.

NOTES

1. The validity of this explanation depends on rejecting an alternative hypothesis imputing the observed interaction structure to ordering effects between valuation questions. According to this alternative hypothesis, the premium attracted by the most complete conservation scheme would be due to the fact of this scheme having been always presented in the first valuation question (while the other schemes were presented to respondents in different orders). However, it was noticed that a significant number of respondents who expressed a positive value for the most complete conservation scheme also answered 'no' to most valuation questions involving partial conservation schemes. These respondents sometimes explained this behaviour by saying that only a complete scheme was worthwhile, which partly validates the hypothesis of complementarity between attributes underlying the positive third-order interaction. In addition, the fact that both case-studies (undertaken with the same question ordering) yielded quite different structures of substitution effects supports the conclusion that the estimated substitution structures are not a mere artefact of the questionnaire. This does not completely rule out the possibility of ordering effects. Further research will investigate whether all our conclusions are completely robust to changes in survey design.
2. These correction factors would be particularly helpful to those agencies, such as the US Forestry Service, which use 'typical unit values' for different classes of environmental resources in routine evaluations of their pluri-annual plans (Sorg and Loomis 1984, quoted by Walsh et al. 1992). These 'typical unit values' are compiled from past valuation studies. They are taken 'off the shelf' and simply summed up to construct benefit estimates for each particular new policy. Usually, the original valuation studies from which these 'typical unit values' were derived have valued a particular environmental improvement as if it was the next change to the status quo. Hence, most 'typical unit values' correspond to independently valued benefits; therefore, summing them up to construct benefit estimates for a particular policy is prone to IVS bias. Of course, if the accumulation of research on substitution effects generated the correction factors that were referred to by Randall, these agencies could use these factors to considerably improve upon their current use of 'off the shelf' estimates. However, the only current means to avoid the significant aggregation biases implied by present uses of 'typical unit values' is the expensive solution of commissioning a new valuation study for each new policy.
3. A different problem is local non-concavity of the benefit function. This problem may lead to identify several relative optima. The problem was observed in the PG case-study, where it was also shown how to solve it by comparing the several candidates to a global optimum. Thus, the local non-concavity problem (differently from the path-dependency problem) has a straightforward solution, even in this discrete setting.

References

Aldrich, J. H. and F. D. Nelson (1984). *Linear Probability, Logit and Probit Models*. Beverly Hills: Sage Publications.

Andreoni, J. (1989). Giving with Impure Altruism: Applications to Charity and Ricardian Equivalence. *Journal of Political Economy* **97** (6): 1447–1458.

Andreoni, J. (1990). Impure Altruism and Donations to Public Goods: a Theory of Warm-Glow Giving. *The Economic Journal* **100**: 464–477.

Appleton, J. (1994). Running Before We Can Walk: Are We Ready to Map 'Beauty'? *Landscape Research* **19** (3): 112–119.

Arrow, K.; R. Solow; E. Leamer; P. Portney; R. Radner, and H. Schuman (1993). Report to the NOAA Panel on Contingent Valuation. *Federal Register* **58** (10).

Baldock, D. and P. Lowe (1996). The Development of European Agri-Environment Policy. In M. Whitby (ed.) *The European Environment and CAP Reform. Policies and Prospects for Conservation*. Wallingford, UK: CAB International: 8–25.

Baptista, F. O. (1993). *Agricultura, Espaço e Sociedade Rural*. Coimbra: Fora do Texto.

Baron, J. (1996). Rationality and Invariance: Response to Schuman. In D. J. Bjornstad and J. R. Kahn (eds) *The Contingent Valuation of Environmental Resources. Methodological Issues and Research Needs*. Cheltenham: Edward Elgar: 145–163.

Barrios, J.; F. Bernaldez, and J. Ruiz (1985). Content Analysis of Landscape Preferences: the Environmental Perception of Madrid Livestock Raisers. *Landscape Research* **10** (3): 2–8.

Bateman, I.; J. Brainard and A. Lovett (1995). Modelling Woodland Recreation Demand Using Geographical Information Systems: A Benefit Transfer Study. CSERGE Working Paper GEC 95-06. Norwich: University of East Anglia.

Bateman, I.; I. Langford; K. Willis; R. Turner, and G. Garrod (1993). The Impacts of Changing Willingness to Pay Question Format in Contingent Valuation Studies: An Analysis of Open-Ended, Iterative Bidding and Dichotomous Choice Formats. CSERGE Working Paper GEC 93-05. Norwich: University of East Anglia.

Bateman, I.; A. Munro; B. Rhodes; C. Starmer and R. Sugden (1996). Does Part-Whole Bias Exist? An Experimental Investigation. Paper presented at the 7th Annual Conference of the European Association of Environmental and Resource Economists: Lisbon, June 27–29th.

Bateman, I.; K. Willis, and G. Garrod (1994). Consistency between Contingent Valuation Estimates: A Comparison of Two Studies of UK National Parks. *Regional Studies* **28** (5): 457–474.

Bateman, I.; K. Willis; G. Garrod; P. Doktor; I. Langford, and R. Turner (1992). Recreation and Environmental Preservation Value of the Norfolk Broads: A Contingent Valuation Study. CSERGE, University of East Anglia (Unpublished Research Report).

Baumol, W. and W. Oates (1988). *The Theory of Environmental Policy*. (2nd edition) Cambridge: Cambridge University Press.

Beasley, S.; W. Workman, and N. Williams (1986). Estimating Amenity Values of Urban Fringe Farmland: A Contingent Valuation Approach. *Growth and Change* **17**: 70–78.

Bennett, J. (1992). Starting to Value the Environment: The Australian Experience. In S. Navrud (ed.) *Pricing the European Environment*. Oxford: Oxford University Press: 247–257.

Benson, J. (1992). Public Values for Environmental Features in Commercial Forests. *Quarterly Journal of Forestry* **86** (1): 9–17.

Bergin, J. (1993). *Recreation and the Value of Landscape*. Unpublished MSc thesis. Bangor: University College of North Wales.

Bergson, A. (1938). A Reformulation of Certain Aspects of Welfare Economics. *Quarterly Journal of Economics* **52**: 310–334.

Bergstrom, J.; B. Dillman, and J. Stoll (1985). Public Environmental Amenity Benefits of Private Land: the Case of Prime Agricultural Land. *Southern Journal of Agricultural Economics* **17**: 139–149.

Bilsborough, S. (1994). Management Agreements: Indicators of Social Values? *Landscape Research* **19** (1): 5–6.

Bishop, R. and T. Heberlein (1979). Measuring Values of Extramarket Goods: Are Indirect Measures Biased? *American Journal of Agricultural Economics* **61**(5): 926–930.

Bishop, R. and T. Heberlein (1986). Does Contingent Valuation Work? In R. Cummings; D. Brookshire, and W. Schulze (eds) *Valuing Environmental Goods. An Assessment of the Contingent Valuation Method*. Totowa: Rowman & Allanheld: 123–147.

Bishop, R. and M. Welsh (1992). Existence Values in Benefit–Cost Analysis and Damage Assessment. *Land Economics* **68**(4): 405–17.

Bjornstad, D. J. and J. R. Kahn (1996) (eds). *The Contingent Valuation of Environmental Resources. Methodological Issues and Research Needs*. Cheltenham: Edward Elgar.

Blaug, M. (1980). *The Methodology of Economics*. Cambridge: Cambridge University Press.

Bonnieux, F.; B. Desaigues, and D. Vermersch (1992). France. In S. Navrud (ed.) *Pricing the European Environment*. Oxford: Oxford University Press: 45–64.

Bostedt, G. and L. Mattsson (1995). The Value of Forests for Tourism in Sweden. *Annals of Tourism Research* **22** (3): 671–680.

Bourassa, S. (1991). *The Aesthetics of Landscape*. London: Belhaven.

Bowers, J. K. and P. Cheshire (1983). *Agriculture, the Countryside and Land Use. An Economic Critique*. London: Methuen.

Bowker, J. and J. Stoll (1988). Use of Dichotomous Choice Nonmarket Methods to Value the Whooping Crane Resource. *American Journal of Agricultural Economics* **70**: 372–381.

Boyle, K. and J. Bergstrom (1992). Benefit Transfer Studies: Myths, Pragmatism, and Idealism. *Water Resources Research* **28** (3): 657–663.

Boyle, K., and R. Bishop (1988). Welfare Measurements Using Contingent Valuation: A Comparison of Techniques. *American Journal of Agricultural Economics* **70** (1): 20–28.

Bromley, D. and I. Hodge (1990). Private Property Rights and Presumptive Policy Entitlements: Reconsidering the Premises of Rural Policy. *European Review of Agricultural Economics* **17** (2): 197–214.

Brookshire, D.; B. Ives, and W. Schulze (1976). The Valuation of Aesthetic Preferences. *Journal of Environmental Economics and Management* **3**: 325–346.

Brookshire, D. and H. Neill (1992). Benefit Transfers: Conceptual and Empirical Issues. *Water Resources Research* **28** (3): 651–655.

Brookshire, D.; M. Thayer; W. Schulze, and R. d'Arge (1982). Valuing Public Goods: a Comparison of Survey and Hedonic Approaches. *The American Economic Review* **72** (1): 165–177.

Bullock, C. and J. Kay (1996). Preservation and Change in the Upland Agricultural Landscape – Valuing the Benefits of Changes Arising from Grazing Extensification. Aberdeen: MLURI (Internal Paper quoted by Hanley et al. 1996a).

Cameron, T. (1988). A New Paradigm for Valuing Non-market Goods Using Referendum Data: Maximum Likelihood Estimation by Censored Logistic Regression. *Journal of Environmental Economics and Management* **15**: 355–379.

Cameron, T. (1991). Interval Estimates for Non-Market Resource Values from Referendum Contingent Valuation Surveys. *Land Economics* **67** (4): 413–421.

Cameron, T. and M. James (1987). Efficient Estimation Methods for 'Closed-Ended' Contingent Valuation Surveys. *Review of Economics and Statistics* **69**: 269–276.

Campos, P. (1993). El Valor Económico Total de los Sistemas Agroforestales. Paper presented to the Seminar 'The Scientific Basis for Sustainable Multiple-Use Forestry in the EC'. EC: Brussels: June 28–29th.

Campos, P. and P. Riera (1996). Social Returns of the Forests: Analysis Applied to Iberian Dehesas and Montados. In D. Pearce (ed.) *The Measurement and Achievement of Sustainable Development*. Research Report (Project CT 94-367, DG XII Environmental Programme).

Carson, R. L. (1962). *Silent Spring*. New York: Fawcett Crest.

Carson, R. (1991). Constructed Markets. In J. Braden and C. Kolstad (eds) *Measuring the Demand for Environmental Quality*. Amsterdam: North Holland: 121–162.

Carson, R. (1993). Discussion of the Diamond et al. paper. In J. Hausman (ed.) *Contingent Valuation. A Critical Assessment*. Amsterdam: Elsevier Science Publishers BV: 87.

Carson, R.; N. Flores; K. Martin, and J. Wright (1994). Contingent Valuation and Revealed Preference Methodologies: Comparing the Estimates for Quasi-Public Goods. Working Paper. Dept. of Economics: Univ. of California, San Diego.

Carson, R.; W. Hanemann; R. Kopp; J. Krosnick; R. Mitchell; S. Presser; P. Ruud; V. Smith; with M. Conaway and K. Martin (1996). Was the NOAA Panel Correct About Contingent Valuation? Resources for the Future Discussion Paper 96-20. Washington DC: Resources for the Future.

Carson, R. and R. Mitchell (1993). The Issue of Scope in Contingent Valuation Studies. *American Journal of Agricultural Economics* **75**: 1263–1267.

Carson, R. and R. Mitchell (1995). Sequencing and Nesting in Contingent Valuation Surveys. *Journal of Environmental Economics and Management* **28**: 155–173.

Centro de Gestão Agrícola do Barroso (1995). Relatório dos Serviços de Gestão de 1994. Salto, Montalegre, Portugal (non-published).

Centro de Gestão Agrícola do Barroso (1996). Relatório dos Serviços de Gestão de 1995. Salto, Montalegre, Portugal (non-published).

Cheshire, P. (1989). Applying Economic Rationality to Problems of Rural Land Management: a European Perspective. In OECD (ed.). *Renewable Natural Resources. Economic Incentives for Improved Management*. Paris: Organisation for Economic Co-operation and Development (OECD): 136–146.

Clamp, P. (1981). The Landscape Evaluation Controversy. *Landscape Research* **6** (2):13–15.

Coase, R. (1960). The Problem of Social Cost. *Journal of Law and Economics* **3**: 1–44.

Cobham Resource Consultants (1993). Landscape Assessment Guidance. *CCP 423*. Cheltenham: Countryside Commission.

Colman, D. (1994). Comparative Evaluation of Environmental Policies: ESAs in a Policy Context. In M. Whitby (ed.) *Incentives for Countryside Management. The Case of Environmentally Sensitive Areas*. Wallingford, UK: CAB International: 219–246.

COM (1997) European Union document (non-published).

Cosgrove, D. (1984). *Social Formation and Symbolic Landscape*. Totowa, New Jersey: Barnes & Noble Books.

Countryside Commission (1990). The Cambrian Mountains Landscape. Cheltenham: Countryside Commission Paper (CCP) 293.

Countryside Commission (1993). *Paying for a Beautiful Countryside. Securing Environmental Benefits and Value for Money from Incentive Schemes*. Countryside Commission Paper 413.

Countryside Commission and English Nature (1996). The Character of England: Landscape, Wildlife and Natural Features. (Map). English Nature and Countryside Commission.

Coventry-Solihull-Warwickshire Sub-Regional Study Group (1971). *A Strategy for the Sub-Region /Supplementary Report 5 - Countryside*.

Crocker, T.; J. Shogren, and P. Turner (1996). Incomplete Beliefs and Nonmarket Valuation. Paper presented at the 7th Annual Conference of the European Association of Environmental and Resource Economists: Lisbon, June 27–29th 1996.

Cummings, R.; D. Brookshire, and W. Schulze (1986) (eds). *Valuing Environmental Goods. An Assessment of the Contingent Valuation Method*. Totowa: Rowman & Allanheld.

Dearden, P. (1980). A Statistical Technique for the Evaluation of the Visual Quality of the Landscape for Land-use Planning Purposes. *Journal of Environmental Management* 10: 51–68.

Dearden, P. (1984). Factors Influencing Landscape Preferences: an Empirical Investigation. *Landscape Planning* 11: 293–306.

Desvousges, W.; S. Hundson, and M. Ruby (1996). Evaluating CV Performance: Separating the Light from the Heat. In D. Bjornstad and J. Kahn (eds) *The Contingent Valuation of Environmental Resources. Methodological Issues and Research Needs*. Cheltenham: Edward Elgar: 117–144.

Desvousges, W.; F. Johnson; R. Dunford; S. Hudson; K. Wilson; and K. Boyle (1993). Measuring Natural Resource Damages with Contingent Valuation: Tests of Validity and Reliability. In J. Hausman (ed.) *Contingent Valuation. A Critical Assessment*. Amsterdam: Elsevier Science Publishers: 91–159.

Desvousges, W.; M. Naughton, and G. Parsons (1992). Benefit Transfer: Conceptual Problems in Estimating Water Quality Benefits Using Existing Studies. *Water Resources Research* 28 (3): 675–683.

Diamond, P. (1996). Discussion of the Conceptual Underpinnings of the Contingent Valuation Method by A. C. Fisher. In D. Bjornstad and J. Kahn (eds) *The Contingent Valuation of Environmental Resources. Methodological Issues and Research Needs*. Cheltenham: Edward Elgar: 61–71.

Diamond, P.; J. Hausman; G. Leonard, and M. Denning (1993). Does Contingent Valuation Measure Preferences? Experimental Evidence. In J. Hausman (ed.) *Contingent Valuation. A Critical Assessment*. Amsterdam: Elsevier Science Publishers: 41–85.

Dillman, B. and J. Bergstrom (1991). Measuring Environmental Amenity Benefits of Agricultural Land. In N. Hanley (ed.) *Farming and the Countryside: An Economic Analysis of External Costs and Benefits*. Wallingford, UK: CAB International: 250–271.

Drake, L. (1992). The Non-market Value of the Swedish Agricultural Landscape. *European Review of Agricultural Economics* **19**: 351–364.

Drake, L. (1993). Relations among Environmental Effects and their Implications for Efficiency of Policy Instruments – an Economic Analysis Applied to Swedish Agriculture. (Published dissertation) Upsala: Dept. of Economics: Swedish University of Agricultural Sciences.

Dubgaard, A. and A. Nielsen (1989) (eds). *Economic Aspects of Environmental Regulations in Agriculture*. Kiel: Wissenschaftsverlag Vauk.

Duckworth, J. (1993). Discussion of the Diamond et al. paper. In J. Hausman (ed.) *Contingent Valuation. A Critical Assessment*. Amsterdam: Elsevier Science Publishers BV: 88.

Fines, K. D. (1968). Landscape Evaluation: a Research Project in East Sussex. *Regional Studies* **2**: 41–55.

Fischhoff, B. and L. Furby (1988). Measuring Values: A Conceptual Framework for Interpreting Transactions with Special Reference to Contingent Valuation of Visibility. *Journal of Risk and Uncertainty* **1**: 147–184.

Fisher, A. (1996). The Conceptual Underpinnings of the Contingent Valuation Method. In D. Bjornstad and J. Kahn (eds) *The Contingent Valuation of Environmental Resources. Methodological Issues and Research Needs*. Cheltenham: Edward Elgar: 19–37.

Fisher, A. and W. Hanemann (1990). Option Value: Theory and Measurement. *European Review of Agricultural Economics* **17** (2): 167–180.

Flores, N. E. and R. T. Carson (1995). The Relationship Between the Income Elasticities of Demand and Willingness to Pay. Draft Paper. Department of Economics: University of California, San Diego.

Garrod, G. and K. G. Willis (1990). Contingent Valuation Techniques: a Review of their Unbiasedness, Efficiency and Consistency. Countryside Change Initiative Working Paper 10. Newcastle: University of Newcastle upon Tyne.

Garrod, G. and K. G. Willis (1991a). The Hedonic Price Method and the Valuation of Countryside Characteristics. Countryside Change Working Paper 14. Newcastle: University of Newcastle upon Tyne.

Garrod, G. and K. G. Willis (1991b). The Environmental Economic Impact of Woodland: a Two Stage Hedonic Price Model of the Amenity Value of Forestry in Britain. Countryside Change Working Paper 19. Newcastle: University of Newcastle upon Tyne.

Garrod, G. and K. G. Willis (1994). The Transferability of Environmental Benefits: A Review of Recent Research in Water Resources Management. Centre for Rural Economy Working Paper 12. Newcastle: University of Newcastle upon Tyne.

Glass, G. (1976). Primary, Secondary, and Meta-Analysis of Research. *Educational Researcher* **5**: 3–8.

Glass, G.; B. McGaw, and M. Smith (1981). *Meta-analysis in Social Research*. Beverly Hills, California: Sage Publications.

Gourlay, D. (1995). Personal communication to N. Hanley (Hanley et al. 1996a).

Gravelle, H. and R. Rees (1992). *Microeconomics*. (2nd edition). London: Longman.

Graves, P. (1991). Aesthetics. In J. Braden and C. Kolstad (eds) *Measuring the Demand for Environmental Quality*. Amsterdam: North Holland: 213–226.

Hair, J.; R. Anderson; R. Tatham, and W. Black (1995). *Multivariate Data Analysis.* (4th edition). Englewood Cliffs, N.J.: Prentice Hall.

Halstead, J. (1984). Measuring the Nonmarket Value of Massachusetts Agricultural Land: A Case Study. *Journal of Northeastern Agricultural Economic Council* **13**: 12–19.

Halvorsen, R. and R. Palmquist (1980). The Interpretation of Dummy Variables in Semilogarithmic Equations. *The American Economic Review* **70** (3): 474–475.

Hanemann, W. (1984a). Entropy as a Measure of Consensus in the Evaluation of Recreation Site Quality. *Journal of Environmental Management* **18**: 241–251.

Hanemann, W. (1984b). Welfare Evaluations in Contingent Valuation Experiments with Discrete Responses. *American Journal of Agricultural Economics* **66** (3): 332–341.

Hanemann, W. (1987). Welfare Evaluations in Contingent Valuation Experiments with Discrete Responses: Reply. *American Journal of Agricultural Economics* **69** (1): 185–186.

Hanemann, W. (1991). Willingness To Pay and Willingness To Accept: How Much Can They Differ? *The American Economic Review* **81**(3): 635–647.

Hanemann, W. (1994). Valuing the Environment through Contingent Valuation. *Journal of Economic Perspectives* **8** (4): 19–43.

Hanemann, W. (1996). Theory Versus Data in the Contingent Valuation Debate. In D. Bjornstad and J. Kahn (eds) *The Contingent Valuation of Environmental Resources. Methodological Issues and Research Needs.* Cheltenham: Edward Elgar: 38–60.

Hanemann, W.; J. Loomis, and B. Kanninen (1991). Statistical Efficiency of Double-Bounded Dichotomous Choice Contingent Valuation. *American Journal of Agricultural Economics* **73**: 1255–1263.

Hanley, N. (1991) (ed.). *Farming and the Countryside: An Economic Analysis of External Costs and Benefits.* Wallingford, UK: CAB International.

Hanley, N. and S. Craig (1991). Wilderness Development Decisions and the Krutilla–Fisher Model: the Case of Scotland's 'Flow Country'. *Ecological Economics* **4**: 145–164.

Hanley, N.; H. Kirkpatrick; D. Oglethorpe, and I. Simpson (1996). Principles for the Provision of Public Goods from Agriculture: Modelling Moorland Conservation in Scotland. Paper presented at the 7th Annual Conference of the European Association of Environmental and Resource Economists: Lisbon, June 27–29th.

Hanley, N.; A. Munro, and D. Jamieson (1991). Environmental Economics, Sustainable Development and Nature Conservation. Report to the Nature Conservancy Council, Peterborough, England.

Hanley, N. and R. Ruffell (1993). The Contingent Valuation of Forest Characteristics: Two Experiments. *Journal of Agricultural Economics* **44** (2): 218–229.

Hanley, N.; I. Simpson; D. Parsisson; D. Macmillan; C. Bullock, and B. Crabtree (1996a). *Valuation of the Conservation Benefits of Environmentally Sensitive Areas.* A Report for Scottish Office Agriculture, Environment & Fisheries Department. Aberdeen: Macaulay Land Use Research Institute (Economics and Policy Series no 2).

Hanley, N. and C. Spash (1993). *Cost–Benefit Analysis and the Environment.* Aldershot, Hants: Edward Elgar.

Harris, C.; B. Driver, and W. McLaughlin (1989). Improving the Contingent Valuation Method: A Psychological Perspective. *Journal of Environmental Economics and Management* **17**: 213–229.

Hausman, J. (1981). Exact Consumer's Surplus and Deadweight Loss. *The American Economic Review* **71**: 662–676.

Hausman, J. (1993) (ed.). *Contingent Valuation. A Critical Assessment*. Amsterdam: Elsevier Science Publishers.

Helliwell, D. R. (1990). *Amenity Valuation of Trees and Woodland*. Arboricultural Association, Romsey.

Herzog, T. (1984). A Cognitive Analysis of Preference for Field-and-Forest Environments. *Landscape Research* **9** (1): 10–16.

Hicks, J. (1939). The Foundation of Welfare Economics. *Economic Journal* **49**: 696–712.

Hicks, J. (1956). *A Revision of Demand Theory*. Oxford: Clarendon Press.

Hoehn, J. (1991). Valuing the Multidimensional Impacts of Environmental Policy: Theory and Methods. *American Journal of Agricultural Economics* **73**: 289–299.

Hoehn, J. and J. Loomis (1993). Substitution Effects in the Valuation of Multiple Environmental Programs. *Journal of Environmental Economics and Management* **25** (1): 56–75.

Hoehn, J. and A. Randall (1987). A Satisfactory Benefit Cost Indicator from Contingent Valuation. *Journal of Environmental Economics and Management* **14**: 226–247.

Hoehn, J. and A. Randall (1989). Too Many Proposals Pass the Benefit Cost Test. *American Economic Review* **79** (3): 544–551.

Hoen, H. and G. Winther (1991). Attitudes to and Willingness to Pay for Multiple-Use Forestry and Preservation of Coniferous Forests in Norway (mimeograph). Agricultural University of Norway: Dept. of Forestry.

Hoevenagel, R. (1996). The Validity of the Contingent Valuation Method: Perfect and Regular Embedding. *Environmental and Resource Economics* **7**: 57–78.

Hoevenagel, R.; O. Kuik, and F. Oosterhuis (1992). The Netherlands. In S. Navrud (ed.) *Pricing the European Environment*. Oxford: Oxford University Press: 100–107.

Howard, P. (1992). Weighting Landscapes, Weighting People. *Landscape Research* **17** (3): 97–98.

IEADR (1994). *Medidas Agro-ambientais: Proposta de Aplicação a Portugal para o Período 1994–98*. Lisboa: Instituto das Estruturas Agrárias e Desenvolvimento Rural (non-published).

IEADR (1996). Information provided by IEADR about current areas, number of agreement farms, and payments made to farmers under the agri-environmental scheme in the Peneda–Geres NP (non-published).

INE (1989). *Recenseamento Geral Agrícola*. Lisboa: Instituto Nacional de Estatística (non-published parish data).

Jacques, D. (1980). Landscape Appraisal: The Case for a Subjective Theory. *Journal of Environmental Management* **10**: 107–113.

Johansson, P.-O. (1987). *The Economic Theory and Measurement of Environmental Benefits*. Cambridge: Cambridge University Press.

Johansson, P.-O. (1989). Valuing Public Goods in a Risky World: an Experiment. In H. Holmer and E. van Lerland (eds) *Valuation Methods and Policy Making in Environmental Economics*. Amsterdam: Elsevier.

Johansson, P.-O. (1993). *Cost–Benefit Analysis of Environmental Change*. Cambridge: Cambridge University Press.

Johansson, P.-O., and B. Kriström (1992). Sweden. In S. Navrud (ed.) *Pricing the European Environment*. Oxford: Oxford University Press: 136–149.

Johansson, P.-O.; B. Kriström, and K.-G. Mäler (1989). Welfare Evaluations in Contingent Valuation Experiments with Discrete Response Data: Comment. *American Journal of Agricultural Economics* **71**: 1054–1056.

Johnson, R.; M. Brunson, and T. Kimura (1994). Using Image-Capture Technology to Assess Scenic Value at the Urban–Forest interface: a Case Study. *Journal of Environmental Management* **40**: 183–195.

Just, R.; D. Hueth, and A. Schmitz (1982). *Applied Welfare Economics and Public Policy*. Englewood Cliffs, N.J.: Prentice-Hall.

Kahneman, D. (1986). Comments. In R. Cummings; D. Brookshire, and W. Schulze (eds) *Valuing Environmental Goods. An Assessment of the Contingent Valuation Method*. Totowa: Rowman & Allanheld: 185–194.

Kahneman, D. and J. Knetsch (1992a). Valuing Public Goods: the Purchase of Moral Satisfaction. *Journal of Environmental Economics and Management* **22**: 57–70.

Kahneman, D. and J. Knetsch (1992b). Contingent Valuation and the Value of Public Goods: Reply. *Journal of Environmental Economics and Management* **22**: 90–94.

Kaldor, N. (1939). Welfare Propositions of Economics and Inter-personal Comparisons of Utility. *Economic Journal* **49**: 549–552.

Kaplan, S. (1975). An Informal Model for the Prediction of Preference. In E. Zube; R. Brush, and J. Fabos (eds) *Landscape Assessment: Values, Perceptions and Resources*. Stroudsburg, Pennsylvania: Dowden, Hutchinson and Ross: 92–101.

Kaplan, R. and S. Kaplan (1989). *The Experience of Nature. A Psychological Perspective*. Cambridge: Cambridge University Press.

Kemp, M. and C. Maxwell (1993). Exploring a Budget Context for Contingent Valuation Estimates. In J. Hausman (ed.) *Contingent Valuation. A Critical Assessment*. Amsterdam: Elsevier Science Publishers: 217–265.

Knetsch, J. and R. Davis (1966). Comparisons of Methods for Recreation Evaluation. In A. Kneese and S. Smith (eds) *Water Research*. Baltimore: Resources for the Future (John Hopkins Press): 125–142.

Kolstad, C. and J. Braden (1991). Environmental Demand Theory. In J. Braden and C. Kolstad (eds) *Measuring the Demand for Environmental Quality*. Amsterdam: North Holland: 17–39.

Kriström, B. and P. Riera (1996). Is the Income Elasticity of Environmental Improvements Less Than One? *Environmental and Resource Economics* **7**: 45–55.

Krutilla, J. (1967) Conservation Reconsidered. *American Economic Review* **57**(4): 777–786.

Lancaster, K. (1966). A New Approach to Consumer Theory. *Journal of Political Economy* **74**: 132–157.

Land Use Consultants (1991). *The North Pennines Landscape*. Landscape Assessment prepared by Land Use Consultants for the Countryside Commission. Countryside Commission Paper (CCP) 318. Cheltenham: Countryside Commission.

Landscape Research Group (1988). *A Review of Recent Practice and Research in Landscape Assessment*. Countryside Commission Document 25. Cheltenham: Countryside Commission.

Langford, I.; I. Bateman; A. Jones; H. Langford, and S. Georgiou (1996). Improved Estimation of Willingness to Pay in Dichotomous Choice Contingent Valuation Studies. CSERGE Working Paper GEC 96-09. Norwich: University of East Anglia.

Laxton, H. (1986). The General Structure (...and...) the Agricultural Structure of the AONB. In M. Whitby (ed.). *Agriculture in the North Pennines*. Report prepared by the Agricultural Environment Research Group for the Countryside Commission.

Agricultural Environment Research Group: University of Newcastle upon Tyne: 52–76.

Linton, D. (1968). The Assessment of Scenery as a Natural Resource. *The Scottish Geographical Magazine* **84**: 219–238.

Loomis, J. (1992). The Evolution of a More Rigorous Approach to Benefit Transfer: Benefit Function Transfer. *Water Resources Research* **28** (3): 701–705.

Loomis, J.; A. Gonzalez-Caban, and R. Gregory (1994). Do Reminders of Substitutes and Budget Constraints Influence Contingent Valuation Estimates? *Land Economics* **70** (4): 499–506.

Loomis, J.; M. Lockwood, and T. DeLacy (1993). Some Empirical Evidence on Embedding Effects in Contingent Valuation of Forest Protection. *Journal of Environmental Economics and Management* **24**: 45–55.

Lowe, P.; J. Clark, and G. Cox (1993). Reasonable Creatures: Rights and Rationalities in Valuing the Countryside. *Journal of Environmental Planning and Management* **36** (1): 101–115.

Lowenthal, D. (1978). Finding Valued Landscapes. *Progress in Human Geography* **2**(3): 373–418.

MAFF (1992). The Pennine Dales ESA. Guidelines for farmers. Ministry of Agriculture, Fisheries and Food.

MAFF (1995). Information provided by MAFF about current areas, payments and operating costs of the Pennine Dales ESA scheme.

Magnussen, K. (1992). Valuation of Reduced Water Pollution Using the Contingent Valuation Method – Testing for Mental Accounts and Amenity Misspecification. In S. Navrud (ed.) *Pricing the European Environment*. Oxford: Oxford University Press: 195–230.

Magnussen, K. (1996). Substitution or Embedding? Valuation and Aggregation of Policy Components of Environmental Goods by the Contingent Valuation Method. Paper presented at the 7th Annual Conference of the European Association of Environmental and Resource Economists: Lisbon, June 27–29th.

Majid, I.; J. Sinden, and A. Randall (1983). Benefit Evaluation of Increments to Existing Systems of Public Facilities. *Land Economics* **59** (4): 377–392.

Mäler, K.-G. (1974) *Environmental Economics: a Theoretical Inquiry.* Baltimore: John Hopkins University Press.

Mäler, K.-G. (1985). Welfare Economics and the Environment. In A. Kneese and J. Sweeney (eds) *Handbook of Natural Resource and Energy Economics* (vol. I). Amsterdam: North Holland: 3–60.

Mäntymaa, E.; V. Ovaskainen, and T. Sievänen (1992). Finland. In S. Navrud (ed.) *Pricing the European Environment*. Oxford: Oxford University Press: 84–99.

Marsden, T.; J. Murdoch; P. Lowe; R. Munton and A. Flynn (1993). *Constructing the Countryside*. London: UCL Press.

McConnell, K. (1990). Models for Referendum Data: the Structure of Discrete Choice Models for Contingent Valuation. *Journal of Environmental Economics and Management* **18**: 19–34.

McFadden, D. (1974). Conditional Logit Analysis of Qualitative Choice Behaviour. In P. Zarembka (ed.) *Frontiers in Econometrics*. New York: Academic Press: 105–142.

Medeiros, C. (1991). *Geografia de Portugal. Ambiente Natural e Ocupação Humana: uma Introdução*. (2nd edition) Lisboa: Estampa.

Meyer, H. von (1989). Towards Improved Land Management. In OECD (ed.) *Renewable Natural Resources. Economic Incentives for Improved Management.*

Paris: Organisation for Economic Co-operation and Development (OECD): 122–135.

Ministério para a Qualificação e o Emprego (1997). Information on average wage rates in Portugal from 'Quadros de Pessoal do Departamento de Estatística do Ministério para a Qualificação e o Emprego.' Lisboa: Ministério para a Qualificação e o Emprego (information requested by the author).

Mishan, E. (1968). What is Producer's Surplus?. *The American Economic Review* **58** (5): 1269–1282.

Mitchell, R. and R. Carson (1989). *Using Surveys to Value Public Goods: the Contingent Valuation Method.* Washington DC: Resources for the Future.

Moxey, A.; B. White; R. Sanderson and S. Rushton (1995). An Approach to Linking an Ecological Vegetation Model to an Agricultural Economic Model. *Journal of Agricultural Economics* **46** (3): 381–397.

Navrud, S. (1992). Willingness to Pay for Preservation of Species. An Experiment With Actual Payments. In S. Navrud (ed.) *Pricing the European Environment.* Oxford: Oxford University Press: 231–246.

Navrud, S. and J. Strand (1992). Norway. In S. Navrud (ed.) *Pricing the European Environment.* Oxford: Oxford University Press: 108–135.

Neary, J. and K. Roberts (1980). The Theory of Household Behaviour under Rationing. *European Economic Review* **13**: 25–42.

Newby, H. (1993). The Social Shaping of Agriculture: Where Do We Go From Here? *Journal of Royal Society of Arts* **154**: 9–18.

Newey, W. and K. West (1987). A Simple, Positive Semi-definite, Heteroskedasticity and Autocorrelation Consistent Covariance Matrix. *Econometrica* **55** (3): 703–708.

Nix, J. (1993). *Farm Management Pocketbook.* 1994 prices. London: Wye College-University of London.

North Pennines AONB Steering Group. (1995). The North Pennines Management Plan. North Pennines Steering Group.

ONS – Office for National Statistics (1996). United Kingdom National Accounts. London: HMSO.

ONS – Office for National Statistics (1997a). Retail Prices Index – November 1996. London: The Stationery Office.

ONS – Office for National Statistics (1997b). Financial Statistics. No. 418 (Feb. 1997). London: The Stationery Office.

ONS – Office for National Statistics (1997c). Annual Abstract of Statistics. London: The Stationery Office.

PA Cambridge Economic Consultants (1992). Yorkshire Dales Visitor Study 1991. Study carried out on behalf of Yorkshire and Humberside Tourist Board, Yorkshire Dales National Park Committee, and Craven District Council.

Penning-Rowsell, E. (1975). Constraints on the Application of Landscape Evaluations. *The Institute of British Geographers Transactions* n. 66 (Nov.): 149–155.

Penning-Rowsell, E. (1981a). Fluctuating Fortunes in Gauging Landscape Value. *Progress in Human Geography* **5**: 25–41.

Penning-Rowsell, E. (1981b). Assessing the Validity of Landscape Evaluations. *Landscape Research* **6** (2): 22–24.

Penning-Rowsell, E. (1982). A Public Preference Evaluation of Landscape Quality. *Regional Studies* **16** (2): 97–112.

Potter, C. (1996). Environmental Reform of the CAP: An Analysis of the Short and Long Range Opportunities. In Nigel Curry and Stephen Owen (eds) *Changing*

Rural Policy in Britain. Planning, Administration, Agriculture and the Environment. Cheltenham: Countryside and Community Press: 165–183.

Powe, N. A.; G. D. Garrod; C. F. Brunsdon, and K. G. Willis (1997). Using a Geographic Information System to Estimate an Hedonic Price Model of the Benefits of Woodland Access. *Forestry* **70** (2).

Powell, M. (1981). Landscape Evaluation and the Quest for Objectivity. *Landscape Research* **6** (2): 16–18.

Price, C. (1978). *Landscape Economics*. London: Macmillan.

Price, C. (1991). *Landscape Valuation and Public Decision Making*. A Report for the Countryside Commission and the Countryside Commision for Scotland.

Pruckner, G. (1995). Agricultural Landscape Cultivation in Austria: An Application of the CVM. *European Review of Agricultural Economics* **22**: 173–190.

Raistrick, A. (1968). *The Pennine Dales*. London: Eyre & Spottiswoode.

Randall, A. (1991). Total and Nonuse Values. In J. Braden and C. Kolstad (eds) *Measuring the Demand for Environmental Quality*. Amsterdam: North Holland: 303–321.

Randall, A. and J. Hoehn (1996). Embedding in Market Demand Systems. *Journal of Environmental Economics and Management* **30**: 369–380.

Randall, A.; B. Ives, and C. Eastman (1974). Bidding Games for Valuation of Aesthetic Environmental Improvements. *Journal of Environmental Economics and Management* **1**: 132–149.

RICA (1997). Information on summary statistics of farm accounts, for the 'zonas agrárias' of Vale do Lima, and Vale do Minho (year 1994). Rede de Informação de Contabilidades Agrícolas (RICA): non-published.

Robinson, D. G.; I. Laurie; J. Wager; and A. Trail (1976). *Landscape Evaluation*. Report of the Landscape Evaluation Research Project to the Countryside Commission. Manchester: University of Manchester.

Römer, A and W. Pommerehne (1992). Germany and Switzerland. In S. Navrud (ed.) *Pricing the European Environment*. Oxford: Oxford University Press: 65–83.

Ruddell, E.; J. Gramann; V. Rudis, and J. Westphal (1989). The Psychological Utility of Visual Penetration in Near-View Forest Scenic-Beauty Models. *Environment and Behavior* **21** (4): 393–412.

Santos, J. M. (1992). *Mercado, Economias e Ecossistemas no Alto Barroso. Um Estudo de Sistemas de Aproveitamento de Recursos Naturais*. Montalegre, Portugal: Câmara Municipal.

Santos, J. M. (1997). *Valuation and Cost–Benefit Analysis of Multi-Attribute Environmental Changes. Upland Agricultural Landscapes in England and Portugal*. PhD thesis. Newcastle: University of Newcastle upon Tyne.

Santos J. M. and C. Aguiar (1994). Private Hay Meadows and Common Pastures: Integrated Management of Two Ecosystems. Paper presented at the European Association of Agricultural Economists Seminar on "Environmental and Land Use Issues in the Mediterranean Basin" (CIHEAM, Zaragoza, Spain, February 1994). Later published in: L. Albisu and C. Romero (1995) (eds) *Environmental and Land Use Issues: an Economic Perspective*. Kiel: Wissenschaftsverlag Vauk.

Saunders, C. (1994). Single-Tier System with Many Farms Partly Outside the ESA. The Case of the Pennine Dales. In M. Whitby (ed.) *Incentives for Countryside Management. The Case of Environmentally Sensitive Areas*. Wallingford, UK: CAB International: 41–59.

Saunders, C.; J. F. Benson, and K. G. Willis (1987a). Social costs and benefits of agricultural intensification at three Sites of Special Scientific Interest. Dept. of Town and Country Planning, University of Newcastle upon Tyne.

Saunders, C.; K. G. Willis, and J. F. Benson (1987b). Resource cost of agricultural intensification and wildlife conservation. Theoretical analysis of the social benefit/cost of agricultural output from marginal areas of land. Dept. of Town and Country Planning, University of Newcastle upon Tyne.

Sellar, C.; J.-P. Chavas, and J. Stoll (1986). Specification of the Logit Model: The Case of Valuation of Nonmarket Goods. *Journal of Environmental Economics and Management* **13**: 382–390.

Shechter, M. (1992). Israel – An Early Starter in Environmental Pricing. In S. Navrud (ed.) *Pricing the European Environment*. Oxford: Oxford University Press: 258–273.

Shoard, M. (1980). *The Theft of the Countryside*. London: Temple Smith.

Shuman, H. (1996). The Sensitivity of CV Outcomes to CV Survey Methods. In D. Bjornstad and J. Kahn (eds) *The Contingent Valuation of Environmental Resources. Methodological Issues and Research Needs*. Cheltenham: Edward Elgar: 75–96.

Shuttleworth, S. (1979). The Evaluation of Landscape Quality. *Landscape Research* **5** (1): 14–15 and 18–20.

Shuttleworth, S. (1983). Upland Landscapes and the Landscape Image. *Landscape Research* **8** (3): 7–14.

Silsoe College (1991). *Landscape Change in the National Parks*. Levenshulme, Manchester: Countryside Commission Paper 359.

Smith, V. K. (1992). Arbitrary Values, Good Causes, and Premature Verdicts. *Journal of Environmental Economics and Management* **22**: 71–89.

Smith, V. K. (1993). Nonmarket Valuation of Environmental Resources: An Interpretive Appraisal. *Land Economics* **69** (1): 1–26.

Smith, V. K. and Y. Kaoru (1990). Signals or Noise? Explaining the Variation in Recreation Benefit Estimates. *American Journal of Agricultural Economics* **72** (2): 419–433.

Sorg, C. and J. Loomis (1984). Empirical Estimates of Amenity Forest Values: a Comparative Review. General Technical Report RM-107. Rocky Mountains Forest and Ranch Experiment Station, US Forest Service, Fort Collins, Co USA.

Statutory Instruments (1986). The Environmentally Sensitive Areas (Pennine Dales) Designation Order 1986. Statutory Instruments 1986 No. 2253.

Statutory Instruments (1992a). The Environmentally Sensitive Areas (Pennine Dales) Designation Order 1992. Statutory Instruments 1992 No. 55.

Statutory Instruments (1992b). The Environmentally Sensitive Areas (Pennine Dales) Designation (Amendment) Order 1992. Statutory Instruments 1992 No. 301.

Stenger, A. and F. Colson (1996). Interpretation of an Application of the Contingent Valuation Method to Agricultural Landscapes: the Problem of Embedding Effects. Paper presented at the 7th Annual Conference of the European Association of Environmental and Resource Economists: Lisbon, June 27–29th.

Swanwick, C. (1997). Characterising the Countryside. *Ecos* **18** (1): 53–60.

Tandy, C. R. (1971). *Landscape Evaluation Technique*. Croydon: Land Use Consultants.

Turner, R., I. Bateman, and D. Pearce (1992). United Kingdom. In S. Navrud (ed.) *Pricing the European Environment*. Oxford: Oxford University Press: 150–176.

Tversky, A. and D. Kahneman (1973). Availability: a Heuristic for Judging Frequency and Probability. *Cognitive Psychology* **5**: 207–232.

Tversky, A. and D. Kahneman (1974). Judgement under Uncertainty: Heuristics and Biases. *Science* **185**: 1124–1131.

UN – United Nations (1995). *Statistical Yearbook (40th Issue)*. New York: United Nations.

UN – United Nations (1997). *Monthly Bulletin of Statistics* **51** (1: Jan.).

Varian, H. R. (1978). *Microeconomic Analysis*. New York: W. W. Norton & Company.

Vaughan, W., and C. Russell (1982). Valuing a Fishing Day: An Application of a Systematic Varying Parameter Model. *Land Economics* **58**: 450–463.

Walsh, R.; D. Johnson, and J. McKean (1992). Benefit Transfer of Outdoor Recreation Demand Studies, 1968–1988. *Water Resources Research* **28** (3): 707–713.

Walsh, R.; J. Loomis, and R. Gillman (1984). Valuing Option, Existence, and Bequest Demands for Wilderness. *Land Economics* **60** (1): 14–29.

Waltham, T. (1987). *Yorkshire Dales National Park*. Exeter: Webb & Bower.

Wang, H. (1997). Treatment of 'Don't-Know' Responses in Contingent Valuation Surveys: A Random Valuation Model. *Journal of Environmental Economics and Management* **32**: 219–232.

Weber, M.; F. Eisenfuhr; and D. Von Winterfeldt (1988). The Effects of Splitting Attributes on Weights in Multiattribute Utility Measurement. *Management Science* **34** (4): 431–445.

Weisbrod, B. (1964). Collective-Consumption Services of Individual-Consumption Goods. *Quarterly Journal of Economics* **78**: 471–477.

Whitby, M. (1994). Transaction Costs and Property Rights: The Omitted Variables? Paper presented at the European Association of Agricultural Economists Seminar on "Environmental and Land Use Issues in the Mediterranean Basin" (CIHEAM, Zaragoza, Spain, February 1994). Later published in: L. Albisu and C. Romero. (1995) (eds) *Environmental and Land Use Issues: an Economic Perspective*. Kiel: Wissenschaftsverlag Vauk.

Whitby, M. (1994a) (ed.). *Incentives for Countryside Management. The Case of Environmentally Sensitive Areas*. Wallingford, UK: CAB International.

Whitby, M. and C. Saunders (1994). *Estimating the Supply of Conservation Goods*. Centre for Rural Economy Working Paper 10. Newcastle: University of Newcastle upon Tyne.

Whitby, M.; C. Saunders and M. Walsh (1992). A Socio-Economic Evaluation of the Pennine Dales Environmentally Sensitive Area (Research Report). Dept. of Agricultural Economics and Food Marketing: University of Newcastle upon Tyne.

Whittaker, J.; P. O'Sullivan, and J. McInerney (1991). An Economic Analysis of Management Agreements. In N. Hanley (ed.) *Farming and the Countryside: An Economic Analysis of External Costs and Benefits*. Wallingford, UK: CAB International: 197–214.

Willig, R. (1976). Consumer's Surplus without Apology. *The American Economic Review* **66**: 589–597.

Willis, K. G. (1982). Green Belts: An Economic Appraisal of a Physical Planning Policy. *Planning Outlook* **25** (2): 62–69.

Willis, K. G. (1990). Valuing Non-market Wildlife Commodities: An Evaluation and Comparison of Benefits and Costs. *Applied Economics* **22**: 13–30.

Willis, K. G. and J. Benson (1989). Recreational Values of Forests. *Forestry* **62**: 93–110.

Willis, K. G.; J. Benson, and C. Saunders (1988). The Impact of Agricultural Policy on the Costs of Nature Conservation. *Land Economics* **64** (2): 147–157.

Willis, K. G. and G. Garrod (1991). Landscape Values: A Contingent Valuation Approach and Case Study of the Yorkshire Dales National Park. Countryside

Change Working Paper 21. University of Newcastle upon Tyne. Dept. of Agricultural Economics and Food Marketing.

Willis, K. G. and G. Garrod (1992). Assessing the Value of Future Landscapes. *Landscape and Urban Planning* **23**: 17–32.

Willis, K. G. and G. Garrod (1995). Transferability of Benefit Estimates. In K. Willis, and J. Corkindale (eds) *Environmental Valuation. New Perspectives.* Wallingford, Oxon.: CAB International: 191–212.

Willis, K. G.; G. Garrod, and C. Saunders (1993). *Valuation of the South Downs and Somerset Levels and Moors Environmentally Sensitive Area Landscapes by the General Public.* Research Report to the MAFF. Newcastle: Centre for Rural Economy, University of Newcastle upon Tyne.

Willis, K. G.; G. Garrod; C. Saunders, and M. Whitby (1993a). Assessing Methodologies to Value the Benefits of Environmentally Sensitive Areas. Countryside Change Initiative Working Paper 39. Department of Agricultural Economics and Food Marketing: University of Newcastle upon Tyne.

Willis, K. G. and M. Whitby (1985). The Value of Green Belt Land. *Journal of Rural Studies* **1** (2): 147–162.

Winter, M. (1996). *Rural Politics. Policies for Agriculture, Forestry and the Environment.* London: Routledge.

Wolf, F. (1986). *Meta-analysis. Quantitative Methods for Research Synthesis.* Beverly Hills: Sage Publications.

Woodcock, D. (1984). A Functionalist Approach to Landscape Preference. *Landscape Research* **9** (2): 24–27.

Yorkshire Dales National Park (1991). Barns and Walls Conservation Scheme: Dry Stone Wall Survey. (Survey report).

Yorkshire Dales National Park (1994). 1994/95 Bid and Functional Strategies.

Yorkshire Dales National Park (1995). Farm Conservation Scheme (unpublished information document).

Zona Agrária do Barroso (1997). Farm account information on two farms located inside the Peneda–Gerês National Park (years 1994 and 1995). Zona Agrária do Barroso: non-published.

Index